“We Fight for Peace”

“We Fight for Peace”

Twenty-three American Soldiers, Prisoners of War, and “Turncoats” in the Korean War

Brian D. McKnight

The Kent State University Press
Kent, Ohio

Dedicated to Lorenzo "Ren" Crowell,
1943–2014

Library of Congress Catalog Number 2013043350
ISBN 978-1-60635-207-6
Manufactured in the United States of America

Library of Congress Cataloging-in-Publication Data
McKnight, Brian Dallas.
We fight for peace : twenty-three American soldiers, prisoners of war, and "turncoats" in the Korean War / Brian D. McKnight.
pages cm
Includes bibliographical references and index.
ISBN 978-1-60635-207-6 (hardcover) ∞
1. Korean War, 1950–1953—Repatriation. 2. Korean War, 1950–1953—Prisoners and prisons. 3. Defectors—United States—Biography. 4. Defectors—China—Biography. 5. Prisoners of war—United States—Biography. 6. Prisoners of war—China—Biography. 7. Soldiers—United States—Biography. 8. Korean War, 1950–1953—Biography. 9. Americans—China—Biography. I. Title. II. Title: Twenty-three American soldiers, prisoners of war, and "turncoats" in the Korean War.
DS921.2.M35 2014
951.904'27—dc23
2013043350

18 17 16 15 14 5 4 3 2 1

Contents

Acknowledgments

When I was an undergraduate, I lived a substantial distance from school. As a result, I spent much time on campus between classes. One of the things I did to pass the time was to go to the library and read old newspapers on microfilm. I found the stories fascinating, especially those that seemed so relevant contemporarily but had been lost to history as the world changed. During one of these reading sessions, I found the story of Ed Dickenson, and from there I uncovered the stories of the rest of those American soldiers who refused repatriation at the end of the Korean Conflict.

As an historian whose primary area of research is the American Civil War, embarking on such a challenging journey as examining one of the most controversial and contentious eras of the twentieth century is a fearful prospect. Since discovering the topic and identifying its importance years ago, I have struggled with issues from laying out the story to writing a mass biography and addressing the finer intellectual nuances of the tale, while developing my own personal seminar in modern Chinese history in an attempt to better understand the era. In order to answer these and other questions, I have burdened some very good people along the way. Because they are all friends, I know my weak attempt at thanking them will be greatly appreciated.

My friend Bill Carter was perhaps my greatest advocate. He guided me through my first two books, helping me produce works that I think he would have been proud of; I began work on this one within a week of his death. It is the first book I have written without his wise counsel and it means a great deal to me as a result. As an old underdog himself, Bill always loved the topic and chastised me for putting it off. While his critiques often left me puzzled, I can now fully see his influence on my intellectual development.

Another old friend of mine and Bill's, Fred Smith, contributed mightily to the story that follows. I initially asked Fred to co-author this with me, but doctoral studies prevented his participation. However, he remained my great friend throughout the process and helped shape the narrative stylistically and analytically. Additionally, Fred spent considerable time poring over newspapers in the library at the University of Southern Mississippi and in Hartford, Connecticut, looking for information that would eventually help me tell this story.

Although old friends have cast long shadows over this book, new friends have also had an influence. Randy Mills of Oakland City University initially undertook a study of Arlie Pate, but his other projects interrupted. When approached for basic information about the group, Randy eagerly provided copies and encouragement. Throughout the process, he has remained interested in the progress of the project and has freely given his support and suggestions. Sheila Miyoshi Jager of Oberlin College provided me easy access to her copies of the court martial records of Edward Dickenson and Claude Batchelor. Ed Dickenson's granddaughter, Jennifer Dickenson, was interested in the story from its earliest days and I enjoyed meeting and corresponding with her throughout the project. Lewis Carlson, who has published much on the soldiers' experiences during the Korean War, kindly sent me an unpublished copy of Clarence Adams' memoir months before it was scheduled to appear in print. His gesture allowed me to finish parts of the manuscript well ahead of my own expectations. Jodi Foor and Rich Boylan at National Archives II, College Park, Maryland, provided important guidance and research assistance. Paul Edwards and Gregg Edwards of Graceland University's Center for the Study of the Korean War, were very gracious hosts during my brief research visit to Independence, Missouri. My friend and noted scholar of African American religion, Edward Robinson of Abilene Christian University, spent several hours with newspapers searching out elusive answers. Rachel Lewis, formerly of the University of Akron, similarly agreed to help my project by gathering some local newspaper information on two of the nonrepatriates that was otherwise unavailable to me. Ren Crowell, one of my former professors, has exhibited a steadfast interest in the project and has helped place it within the context of modern military history studies. Ron Suleski, of Harvard University's Fairbank Center, offered information about Morris Wills and put me in contact with Ezra Vogel, who supervised Wills during his time on the center's staff. Sidney Rittenberg, who spent most of his life in Mao's China, answered several important questions and gave valuable insights into the motives of many of the men. Finally, physicians and friends Allen Mullins and Melanie Skeen provided answers to medical and nutritional questions.

Partway through the construction of this story, I relocated from the University of Virginia's College at Wise, near the hometown of Ed Dickenson, to Angelo State University, in Texas, near the hometown of Claude Batchelor. At Angelo State, the late Guogiang "Joe" Zheng, an accomplished scholar of modern China, answered countless questions about the intricacies of Chinese history and culture thereby broadening my historical and philosophical interpretations. Arnoldo DeLeon, a leading scholar in Tejano history and an excellent editor, must be thanked for his assistance with several chapters. Robert Stiles served as the department's graduate assistant for the 2006–2007 academic year and helped identify and list the more than 3,300 repatriated American prisoners. Perhaps the most important research assistant on the campus of any regional university is the interlibrary loan librarian. At Angelo State, Sharon Weber works tirelessly to provide people like me with those things necessary for us to produce scholarly work.

My parents probably wonder why their son would choose to devote years of his life to studying this group of men, but they have always been supportive of my endeavors and appreciate the work I do. Similarly, my wife has aided in my development and continues to make the sacrifices that allow me to pursue my many projects. Although she has no real interest in history, Pam does understand my love for the subject and has put her fingerprints on each piece of scholarship I have produced, including coming up with the title of this book. Although I am not sure how she has contributed to this project, I must also thank my daughter, Devin. She has made me see the world in a new light, and has made me a better person along the way.

I always thank my students for their contributions to my work. They are young, curious, motivated, and impressed by those of us who stand before them on a daily basis. Of them, a handful stands out as being truly exceptional intellectually, academically, and personally. UVa-Wise students Kaylen Baker, Julie Yates, Murphy Mullins, Eric Vanover, and Matt Wright have provided me with much support and encouragement through their intellectual curiosity and attentiveness. At Angelo State, I also found an exceptional lot. They include Zach Dowdle, John Graham, Melissa Harderlie, Sterling Brown, Jesse Burnham, Charles Bowen, and Jennifer Dickens.

Finally, to the families and friends of my twenty-three subjects, most of whom are now deceased, I say with great seriousness: Do not dismiss them or be ashamed of their actions. Although they took what seems an illogical step more than fifty years ago, they did so as a result of extreme circumstances in an environment where a single compromise could easily result in a man being forced down an irreversible path.

Brian D. McKnight

Introduction

Shortly after midnight on October 21, 1953, Edward Dickenson, an American soldier in Korea, escaped from his captors. He had been a prisoner of the Chinese for nearly three years; the nature of his confinement, however, had changed dramatically during the past month. Since the onset of the prisoner exchange operation Little Switch in April and May, and Big Switch, beginning in August, thousands of prisoners of war (PsW) had been repatriated to their home nations.[1] But in September, the Chinese announced that several American prisoners of war were refusing repatriation, preferring instead to remain with their Chinese captors. Ed Dickenson was one of twenty-three Americans and one British Marine who had made this choice as a group. During the months to come, the growing domestic trend of anti-communism played out on this international stage through promises and enticements to convince those who remained to change their minds. By midnight January 24, 1954, Dickenson and Claude Batchelor had rethought their decision to stay with the Chinese and returned to United Nations lines. At that moment, the remaining twenty-one became expatriates, and the United States, which had fought so hard for the return of these men, began exacting revenge on the two who had returned.

Dickenson and Batchelor had also attempted to entice their comrades back to the United States to no avail. A beaming Dickenson had stood for photographs next to his new car and Batchelor had his wife write to the remaining twenty-one urging them to come home. These attempts to draw the remaining twenty-one men back gleaned no results and upon the passing of the United Nations imposed deadline for repatriation, Dickenson and Batchelor became scapegoats for McCarthy's America. However, while these two young men served prison terms in the United States, a peculiar thing began to happen: the other twenty-one U.S. servicemen who had eschewed their nation and its capitalistic traditions began to return home with impunity. Surely to Dickenson, in military prison at Fort Leavenworth, Kansas, and Batchelor in the disciplinary barracks at Fort Sam Houston, Texas, the irony must have been heartbreaking.

This story of the twenty-three American nonrepatriates began in the fall of 1950 when a bold U.S. Army stepped into the Korean Civil War and first met its enemy. In late October, shocked American soldiers found themselves facing more than 200,000 Chinese soldiers rather than the North Koreans they were expecting. Almost immediately, the rapid UN advances stopped, replaced by three years of stalemate. In the midst of this static struggle, hundreds of miles behind enemy lines, thousands of American servicemen, who had been captured during the initial Chinese offensive in late October and early November, suffered in prison camps.

For one of the few times in history, a combatant began systematically employing techniques of psychological warfare as a method of indoctrinating enemy prisoners. One prisoner of war described it as a uniquely Chinese form of total warfare where "the mind—the thought processes of the individual—is as much a target as the flesh."[2] For the men who languished in these prison camps, undergoing this battle for their minds, survival occupied their every thought. In many cases, the Chinese made it clear that they cared little for the health and welfare of their prisoners. In addition to the high casualty rates for American soldiers in Korea, those who were captured often suffered an even worse fate. Raymond Lech notes that of the nearly 7,200 American soldiers who became prisoners of war, most of them early in the conflict, almost half would die before being released. With a mortality rate of nearly fifty percent among American PsWs, captivity too made the war in Korea one of the United States' most sobering experiences.

Most of the men who became prisoners early in the conflict endured the infamous "Death Marches" of late 1950 and early 1951. Consisting mainly of night marches, these torturous journeys led the newly captured prisoners northward to their prison camps. It was on these three-to-four-week marches that the PW casualty rate was boosted. On the trek northward to the permanent camps, the mortality rate grew to about half (43 percent). In the case of the 600 men who marched from Bean Camp to Camp 1 on the Yalu River, fewer than 300 survived the journey. Many of those who fell into North Korean and Chinese hands were battlefield casualties whose wounds were not so dire that they could not walk with the others. In addition to the difficulties of a winter march with untreated wounds, the soldiers also suffered from disease, starvation, and frostbite. As the marches pressed on, if a man stopped walking, he was either carried by his comrades or shot by a guard. In such an environment, it is not surprising that many good soldiers came to depend solely on their survival instincts.

The American soldiers's captivity early in the war and consequent long stints in the prison camps seriously affected their ability to resist indoctrination. Having very little training regarding proper behavior while a prisoner of war, military discipline broke down and most of the men began dealing with their condition as individuals. Although many steadfastly resisted, others, having watched their captors allow prisoners to die and even kill them for minor offenses, began to see some kind of cooperation as their best hope for survival. The Chinese fomented this belief by "doing favors" for the men who did not cause trouble. If a man had dysentery, his ability to procure the medicine that would save his life largely depended on his or a friend's relationship with the Chinese. Extra rations of rice, candy, and cigarettes were also made available to the more cooperative prisoners.

Likewise, the Chinese understood that the real cooperation they received from some of the prisoners was helpful, but perceived cooperation could also be important. Within such an environment, paranoia is a great enemy. It quickly became apparent to many PsW that a certain element of their group would willingly collaborate with their captors. Despite the uneven quality and dependability of the information offered up by collaborators, the Chinese continually encouraged the practice as a way to help them win the hearts and minds of their captives. Even if a man refused to collaborate, the Chinese made the collective paranoia of the prison experience an effective tool of coercion. One commonly used tactic was to publicly announce that the commandant of the camp wanted to see an influential prisoner. The prisoner would be escorted to the commandant's antechamber where he would often sit for hours before being pitched a pack of Chinese cigarettes and sent away. Although he had not seen the commandant, or anyone else for that matter, when he emerged from the office smoking a Chinese cigarette, the minds of his comrades often ran wild despite his assurances that nothing had been said. Even if the man was innocent, the collective suspicion of other prisoners could result in his ostracism, and often, he would turn to his captors for companionship and acceptance.

Within these prison camps, there emerged three different groups to which the American captives generally belonged. Reminiscent of John Blassingame's classic slave study, which identified three dominant personalities within captivity—Nat, Jack, and Sambo—U.S. soldiers fell into the similar categories of Reactionaries, survivalists, and Progressives.[3] Like the slave Nat, Reactionaries fought their captors at every turn, often feigning ignorance or clumsiness to disguise their resistance. At the opposite end of the spectrum were the Progressives—the group from which most of the nonrepatriates came. Similar to Sambo on the plantation, Progressives, or "pros," supported and often assisted in Chinese indoctrination efforts, often to curry favor for themselves or needy comrades. Between the Reactionaries and Progressives stood the survivalists, who, like the slave Jack, vacillated between the poles in order to remain alive and as comfortable as possible. John Marks shows the stark numbers associated with collaboration. He wrote that by the time the prisoners were repatriated, 70 percent "had either made confessions or signed petitions calling for an end to the American war effort in Asia," 15 percent had "collaborated fully with the Chinese," and "only 5% [had] steadfastly resisted" all indoctrination efforts.[4] No matter how tepid their wartime resistance however, when they got home, all became Reactionaries—at least publicly.

Immediately after the infamous twenty-three refused repatriation, much attention became focused on the term "brainwashing." Coined by CIA propagandist and journalist Edward Hunter, who introduced the term in a 1950 newspaper article as a way to describe China's political indoctrination methods, it became one of the Cold War's most feared catchphrases.[5] In actuality, however, the idea of brainwashing is simply a more menacing sounding term for indoctrination, teaching, and training. But in the political climate that permeated the post–World War II era, the widespread fear of communism made the analysis of such words and their uses unpopular and semi-seditious. Despite the communist Chinese view that they could convince enemy prisoners to stay behind with their captors and therefore win a small ideological victory over capitalism and democracy, elements within the United States saw the plot as much more subversive and sought retribution from the prisoners.

Within days of twenty-one of the men getting their wish to go to China, *Newsday* book review editor Virginia Pasley was sitting with general editor Alicia Patterson. As they discussed the recent events, Patterson asked, "How would you like to go to all their home towns and see if you can find the answers?" as to why the men chose to remain behind. Undaunted, Pasley embarked on the trek that would last for three months. By the time she finished her research, she estimated that she traveled more than 15,000 miles throughout twenty-three states. The result was the book *21 Stayed.* Its individual biographical chapters provide the rare primary source materials necessary for undertaking such a project as this one.[6] Pasley's *21 Stayed,* along with scattered newspaper accounts, provide much of the material on the men prior to their emigration to China and introduced the men as "one of the most extensively studied groups in American history."[7]

In early 1955, William L. White, an accomplished author and newspaper editor from Emporia, Kansas, received a copy of a "white paper" produced by the British Army on the treatment of its PsW in Korea. Frustrated that the U.S. Army had not embarked upon such a project, White began furiously collecting information to produce his own. What resulted was *The Captives of Korea: An Unofficial White Paper on the Treatment of War Prisoners.* In *Captives,* White chronicles the experiences of both UN and communist prisoners of war in an attempt to understand the subtleties of wartime captivity. With the sources for his work still closely guarded by the government and army, White employed much political finesse to gain access to the documents and experts. White's preface suggests that the army involved itself in his study. Although his book is titled as "unofficial," he admits that military or civilian officials read parts of the text and made suggestions as to his conclusions.[8]

In 1959, Eugene Kinkead released a new, highly critical study. *In Every War But One* casts a pall over the behavior of captive Korean War–era American soldiers. What is essentially a condemnation of the perceived "soft" American youth of the 1940s and 50s, *In Every War But One* argued that the soldiers in Korea caved to communist pressure because of their pampered upbringings and the general degeneration of American society. Kinkead also argued that such ideas had permeated the army, which consciously sent poorly trained and undisciplined soldiers into the field. With the benefit of fifty years of hindsight, it is apparent that Kinkead's personal agenda was steeped in the anti-communist and McCarthyite ideologies of the early to middle 1950s. The broad populace considered Kinkead's points to be legitimate concerns in light of the threat of worldwide communism; however, every generation makes similar negative judgments about those that follow it.[9]

To answer Kinkead's polemic, Albert Biderman, an academic who had spent his professional life studying the PW experience, wrote his own assessment. Released in 1963, *March to Calumny* takes direct aim at Kinkead's conclusions in an attempt to refute what Biderman felt were gross mischaracterizations. Biderman showed that Korean War prisoners, by and large, behaved meritoriously and remarkably similarly to the PsW in America's other wars. In countering the contention that Marines held out against collaboration better than the army soldiers, Biderman made a convincing case that Kinkead had dealt with the differences between the branches of service superficially and successfully illustrated how important the time of capture was when determining what type of treatment PsW received.[10] Although Biderman did not directly say it, one of the elements that complicated Kinkead's work, and also that of White to a lesser degree, was the way the army controlled information by limiting the author's ability to interpret it. While not appearing to criticize the army, Kinkead's study was itself heavily shaped by the army. He had initially planned to coauthor the book with John Dollard, a sociologist at Yale's Institute of Human Relations, but when Kinkead met with the army on the project, officials opposed the professor's participation. For Kinkead, a journalist for *The New Yorker,* Dollard would have provided the academic legitimacy needed for such a study. Kinkead wrote, "They [army officials] said that the problem of Korean prisoner behavior was not one to be tackled from the viewpoint of psychiatry or psychology alone; and in cases in which these things were important, the army psychologists and psychiatrists were the ones to explain the study's conclusions. Therefore, Dollard, to the regret of us both, felt that he must withdraw."[11] With the army, which had initiated its own self-study in the wake of the Army-McCarthy Hearings, maintaining tight control over who worked with the documentation and what kind of conclusions were politically appropriate for the time and in its best interests, it is no surprise that Kinkead's book was polemical in nature.

On October 24, 1962, at the height of the Cuban Missile Crisis, the Korean War came alive on screen when United Artists released its newest thriller to audiences nationwide. *The Manchurian Candidate,* starring Frank Sinatra, Lawrence Harvey, Angela Lansbury, and Janet Leigh, promised "If you come in five minutes after this picture begins, you won't know what it's all about . . . when you've seen it all, you'll swear there's never been anything like it!"[12] With one of the great international showdowns taking place between Washington and Moscow, nervous Americans turned out to see this movie that centered on Korean War veterans who, while prisoners of the Chinese, were brainwashed and programmed to assassinate a leading anti-communist presidential candidate. Only a year after the release of the movie, President John Kennedy was assassinated by a former American soldier who had spent considerable time in the Soviet Union and who was an avowed communist and who had reportedly seen all of the major presidential assassination films of the era, including *The Manchurian Candidate.*[13]

When Richard Condon's novel of the same name was published in 1959, it was described by one critic as "a breathlessly up-to-date thriller." Indeed, only six years earlier, the Korean War was drawing to a close with reports filtering back home that many of the men who had endured torturous conditions in the prisoner of war camps had been brainwashed by their captors and given postwar assignments of helping to orchestrate a communist overthrow of the United States government. More recently, returning PsW had been arrested, tried, and even convicted for their collaboration while captives of the Chinese and North Koreans. Anyone who had spent any time in communist China or the Soviet Union was considered a potential suspect by the FBI. Included in this group were twenty-three former American soldiers, who had spent years each as prisoners of war of the Chinese during the Korean War. All of them had initially refused repatriation to the United States upon the halting of hostilities, with two changing their minds and returning home to long prison sentences, while the remaining twenty-one went to China to become good communists. Condon's 1959 work of fiction and John Frankenheimer's 1962 work of fantastic intrigue were in fact neither.

It would be easy to point the finger at China, or Mao Zedong, or the collaborating prisoners, or the newsmen who whipped the story into a frenzy, but in reality, blame has been assigned repeatedly over the course of the past sixty years and has done little to help us understand what happened, why the events occurred as they did, and how we might prepare for something similar in the future; it simply punishes, and often that punishment is arbitrary, uneven, and unfair. To be sure, the Korean War and its era left America with a bitter legacy of defeat, loss, paranoia, and insecurity, but these individual crises also left Americans an opportunity to forge ahead and use the lessons to strengthen the national fabric. However, very little was learned from these trials and the nation instead chose to scapegoat the outliers rather than understand them. Only a decade after the end of the difficult war in Korea, the United States was on its way into another civil war in Asia. Despite the divided sentiments of Americans about involvement in another war, the United States entered the fray in Vietnam. More than a decade later, the United States would extricate itself from this war, but this time without even a line of demarcation between democracy and autocracy like that which been left behind in Korea.

In 1968, Morris Wills, a nonrepatriate who had returned to the United States in 1965, wrote his memoir of his time in China. As one of the few accounts of life inside of Mao's China, *Turncoat* was an important contribution toward understanding China's political and military ambitions for Americans once again involved in a proxy war against communism.[14] Wills's account would remain the only detailed account by a Korean War nonrepatriate for forty years.

For veterans of Korea, Vietnam was like a recurring bad dream: a civil war, communism, big business and government running a war they did not seem to understand, no single embodiment of evil against whom to fight, and an American government either unwilling or incapable of understanding the nature of the war that the average soldier was facing on the ground. With no Hitler or Hirohito as the great representation of evil, Vietnam, like Korea, was a purely ideological conflict for Americans, many of whom had become very skeptical of business's role in government and government's highly partisan anti-communist crusade of the post–World War II era. To veterans of Korea, Vietnam looked ominously like their war and they feared for the young men who would be sent to fight it.

The men who had enlisted to fight in Korea in 1950 returned to a dramatically different nation in 1953. With the rise of Joe McCarthy and the rabid anti-communist legacy he left behind, those who had endured the privations of enemy imprisonment came home under a cloud of skepticism and suspicion. If the army would coddle and protect communists, as McCarthy accused, its soldiers were legitimate targets of inquiry. The resulting arrests and trials starkly divided the nation between those who agreed with the searching out of suspected communists and those who felt that the government had behaved overzealously. By the time of the Vietnam War, these discussions still existed—largely split along the hawks/doves line—contributed mightily to the average American's erosion of trust in the federal government. The hippies, the Left, and many moderate Americans stood side-by-side with veterans of Korea and Vietnam in their skepticism of the role and intentions of the government in international affairs. Former Korean War PsW, most of whom were by now nearly forty years old with families of their own, feared that the young man going off to Vietnam would find the same kind of imprecise war that they had, and if this new soldier were to be captured, he would be forgotten by his government, until it became convenient to persecute or prosecute him after his liberation.

On April 29 and 30, 1975, Operation Frequent Wind rescued an estimated 7,000 Americans and Vietnamese from Saigon. For most Americans who watched on television, the flickering images of rooftop helicopter rescues signaled the end of a tragic era in American history. In the years that followed, America learned to cope with outright defeat in war for the first time in its history and one of the central issues that the average American found himself drawn to was the Vietnam-era PW experience. During the next two decades, Vietnam veterans and their family members sought to understand the war through movies like *Platoon, The Deer Hunter,* and Sylvester Stallone's *Rambo* films. Unlike the Korean War veterans who returned to the United States struggling to understand their wartime experience and getting little help from those around them, the Vietnam experience had drawn a wide cross-section of the populace into a collective quest to understand.[15]

As the baby boomers aged, the Persian Gulf War finally gave the nation its first popular war against a great villain since World War II. In many ways, the American success against Iraq and Saddam Hussein in 1990 and 1991 salved the still open wounds of Vietnam. But with the shock of 9/11 and the difficult wars that followed in Iraq and Afghanistan, America returned to the anxious society that it had been fifty years before; this new ideological divide, however, replaced communism with radical Islam and terrorism in general. In the 1950s and 1960s, John Birchers, the FBI, and congressmen from both parties sniffed out commies in the hopes of purifying American political thought, but ultimately, the searchers made little headway against their ideological targets. During the early twenty-first century's wars in Iraq and Afghanistan, Americans with sympathies for the enemy again became a popular topic of conversation.

Like the twenty-three American PsW who refused repatriation after the Korean War, America's subsequent wars have found many malcontents, some of whom have been Americans whose ideological positions have driven them to eschew the American system in favor of that of the enemy. Similar to James Dresnok and Charles Jenkins, both of whom defected to North Korea while serving as American soldiers in the Demilitarized Zone in the early 1960s, John Walker Lindh, Jose Padilla, and Nidal Hasan reminded twenty-first century Americans that our own can turn into enemies. Because Americans recoil in fear when it is announced that yet another citizen, or foreign national, has been arrested on charges of terrorism, the swift punishment of the offender becomes the immediate response, when it might be more productive to invest more effort in understanding the basis of their dissatisfaction and how that might be changed in the future.

Another curious element in America's struggle to understand is how the issue of collaboration has been treated. It is understandable that people are hurt when rejected by their own, but the search for simple answers to complex questions often does the situation a great injustice. Like hundreds of Korean War prisoners who collaborated with their captors and were vilified for their activities, many American prisoners in other wars have behaved similarly and avoided criticism. During the antebellum period, slaves often compromised their positions in preference for that of the master in order to secure better treatment or increase their feeling of stability. More recently, the term Stockholm Syndrome has become linked to many instances of sympathy captives feel toward their captors. While it was easy for Americans, many of whom spent the Korean War safely at home while others suffered in PW camps, to hold these men to a strict standard, the same people would never question the behavior of Jaycee Dugard or Elizabeth Smart. In both cases, survival instincts took over in the face of hopelessness; however, in the case of these nonrepatriates, those instincts were judged to be a wrong-headed weakness.

In reality, those men who chose to remain with their captors in early 1954 offer a fascinating insight into a myriad of concerns for the modern American nation. Their refusal gave the Chinese communists a wonderful propaganda tool that the clumsy American response only reinforced. With the loyalty of these men under scrutiny, the American government was content to punish a sample for punishment's sake, rather than seeking real answers to the major questions of why these soldiers would bend to the will of their captors. In the twenty-first century, a similar situation has arisen in regard to American citizens who choose to fight in foreign countries against the interests of the United States; similarly, Americans have spent more time lambasting the individuals than considering their philosophical position.

One of the most active arguments that has arisen out of the Korean War prisoner of war studies has been over the level of collaboration within the camps. Raymond Lech suggested that most of the PsW provided aid and support to the Chinese during their imprisonment when he wrote that "[t]he majority of the captive Americans did practically everything their North Korean and Chinese captors told them to do."[16] Lewis Carlson, whose work on the Korean War PsW experience is the standard, does not find the great degree of collaboration that Lech asserted. However, for the purposes of this study, collaboration is considered to be various actions, including signing peace petitions, seditious speech, holding intercourse with the enemy, and looking out for the well-being of the individual—all things the U.S. Army and the Federal Bureau of Investigation considered to be criminally un-American in the late 1950s and 1960s. These are a few of the charges the army leveled against a handful of PsW and behaviors that the FBI spent years investigating in the hopes of finding an opportunity to prosecute.

The war in Vietnam made Americans forget about Korea and its prisoners of war. In the early twenty-first century, Carlson and Lech published books studying the Korean War prisoner of war phenomenon. Carlson's *Remembered Prisoners of a Forgotten War* paints a vivid picture of the kind of captivity these men faced through dozens of oral interviews of former prisoners, several of whom knew some of the men under examination while in prison. Surprisingly, the interviewees who were imprisoned with the nonrepatriates viewed them somewhat sympathetically, even if they had been frequent collaborators.[17] Lech's *Broken Soldiers* has appeared more recently and is a fascinating study of the PW/captor dynamic. Certainly the most thorough and critical modern treatment of the subject, it attempts to paint a complete picture of the PW experience, Chinese indoctrination, and the American response.[18]

The last decade has given modern readers a few more titles to consult. Adam Zweiback wrote an article placing the men within the context of the United States in the 1950s.[19] Gary Harold Rice's doctoral dissertation offers a lengthy and interesting treatment of the group.[20] And most importantly, Lewis Carlson collaborated with Della Adams, the daughter of Clarence Adams, to publish her late father's memoir. What Clarence left is a fascinating recollection by a largely unrepentant man. In it, Adams laid bare his feelings about both American and Chinese society, particularly in relation to race.[21]

Elizabeth Lutes Hillman studies American military justice during the Cold War era in *Defending America.* She notes that during this era, it was imperative to defend the nation not only militarily, but by "protecting American ideological superiority by spurning communist indoctrination—even under the duress and deprivation of a remote POW camp." Hillman's work thrives on a remarkable clarity that enables her to successfully argue that while many Americans considered these men to be weak-willed, the fact that they adapted to their surroundings and lived through starvation, exposure, and deprivation, speaks volumes about their strength and determination. She calls these men "the most unlikely military criminals of the twentieth century" and registers her curiosity that the U.S. Army could prosecute these men for political dissent at a time when America was engaged in its greatest ideological battle.[22]

For a military historian whose career to this point has focused on the question of loyalty, tackling such a subject is a perfect fit. The intellectual basis of these apparently disparate topics is centered on the fluid concept of loyalty and how that all-important element of military and political effectiveness can be shaped and even compromised by those whom we consider to be the least powerful of constituents. To this end, I seek to evaluate the elemental issues of warfare and public policy by employing comparative methods across time and space in the hopes of finding important elements that have, to this point, remained hidden from view.

"We Fight for Peace" illustrates to modern readers the conditions of captivity these prisoners experienced and the reasons that they chose to remain captive long after their comrades had returned. It tries to place them into a broader context as not just individuals, but men whose wartime experiences could not be sympathetically understood by a nation, and indeed a western

world, ideologically opposed to the doctrine they seemed to have embraced. While in prison, the Chinese had told them that their nation had abandoned them. After months and years of captivity, they began to believe the propaganda. And when they began filtering back home, they became fully aware that the assertion of national abandonment was not wholly false.

This book speaks to the continuum of American military history from long before the Korean War until the present day. It concludes that a government and its military have a great responsibility to those whom they send to war. It analyzes the gray area of loyalty and the mitigating circumstances that shape behavior. It contends that while men may act in illegal, unethical, or unreasonable ways, a responsible government and citizenry must ensure that even-handed justice is dispensed instead of emotional and politically driven retribution. Similarly, it preaches that a nation must act honorably in all things if it expects to earn the level of trust it seeks from its citizens, and if it does not act with the requisite honor, it must be prepared to address the suspicions of its populace. *"We Fight for Peace"* asserts that a nation, if it aspires to greatness, must educate its citizenry or suffer the consequences of popular ignorance. It requires that "with great power comes great responsibility" and that the officer corps of the military should be held to a higher standard of behavior than those they lead—a practice policies avow but actions frequently forget. It says that when an enemy wins a small propaganda victory, the nation should not help expand that victory through a reaction in direct opposition to its liberal principles. It notes the importance of human understanding and empathy when dealing with men and women who have been damaged by war and those whose behavior has been coerced by an enemy, and rejects retributive behavior as a helpful response. Finally and overarchingly, if a nation expects to stand strong and proud, it must not repeat the mistakes of past wars. To quote George Santayana, "Those who cannot remember the lessons of History, are doomed to repeat it."

ONE

Beginnings and Backgrounds

> "You know what I did this evening? When I left the post? I went out to my mother's grave and I stood there for a long time and I said 'Mom, I'm sorry. I turned out human like you wanted me, but I picked the wrong time.'"
>
> —Paul Newman in *The Rack* (1956)

When examining the soldiers who refused to return to their native land, loyalty is the primary issue and motivation the secondary. From appearances, the loyalty issue should be an easy one to address. However, by eliminating their refusal to accept repatriation from the equation, a broader picture of the men can be drawn without the overwhelming influence of enemy captivity. Surprisingly, only one of the twenty-three Americans was drafted. The remainder joined the army of their own volition, with more than one planning to pursue a commission. Twenty-one had been peacetime soldiers with initial enlistment dates preceding any serious talk of war in Korea. The remaining two joined when the conflict appeared inevitable. For men who would later come to epitomize disloyalty, their largely preemptive actions smack of patriotism. In reality, pragmatism provides the lion's share of answers regarding these twenty-three. As Clarence Adams wrote, "Most of us . . . did not even have a high school education. We had volunteered for the army because we saw no other future for ourselves."[1] Considering the backgrounds of these men, their individual decisions to join the army stemmed from self-interest rather than the high-minded idealism many have attributed to their decision-making.

Writing at the height (or depth, depending on the perspective) of the McCarthy era, Virginia Pasley found that each of the twenty-one American soldiers who went to China at the end of the Korean War possessed some trait that made him weaker than the prisoners who had accepted repatriation. In her judgment, most were intimidated by their fathers, neglected by their mothers, reared in poverty, or dim-witted. While she was correct that most of the men grew up in challenging conditions, Pasley's analysis tended

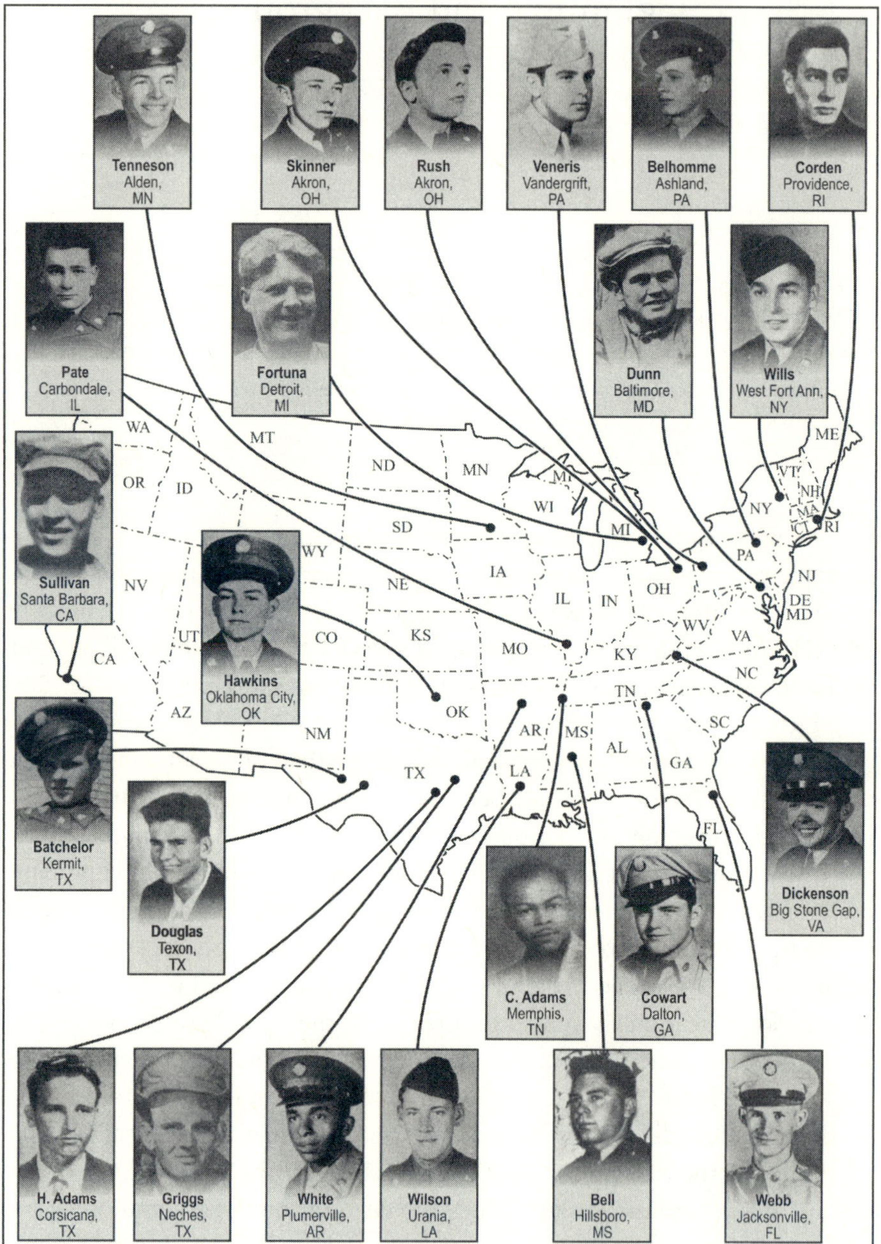

to lump the men together into a group of social and emotional defectives; however, the truth is much more complicated.[2]

The occurrence of World War II only a decade prior to the Korean Conflict ensured that many of those who fought in Korea had previous combat experience. Of the twenty-three Americans who refused repatriation, three had served in the armed forces during World War II. All had served valorously in either the European or Pacific theaters, and one had earned a Bronze Star for heroism. Even during their own fateful conflict, most of the men were considered model soldiers.

Portentous of his confusing future, Andrew Fortuna Jr. was born Raymond Craft Jr. on March 20, 1927, to an unwed Kentucky teenager who listed the boy's father as Louis Williams. When he was three years old, Raymond's mother moved him to Detroit, Michigan, where she soon met Andrew Fortuna, an Italian immigrant who worked in an automobile factory. No records confirm a marriage between Fortuna and Esther Craft, nor an adoption of the children, but that did not keep Fortuna from making little Ray his namesake. Although the relationship between Fortuna and Craft produced two children, Donald and Viola, the parents were neither responsible nor stable. Esther Craft became a transient alcoholic while her husband was arrested for various sexual crimes including bestiality, sodomy, and child molestation.[3]

As the oldest son in a severely dysfunctional family, Andrew's life was a world apart from that of the average American youth. One of his teachers remembered him as "dirty and unkempt, his clothes wrinkled and his shoes without soles" and said he sometimes "slept outdoors and often went hungry."[4] When he did attend school, he was "a sneaky child and constantly in minor trouble."[5] Many of his evenings were spent roaming from bar to bar along Michigan Avenue looking for his mother. After losing a tooth in a schoolyard fight, Fortuna's already poor attitude further soured and he quit school after the eighth grade.[6]

Andrew's brother Donald recalled that "Andy and I had a rough life . . . but he's the guy who overcame it." Donald, whose life was in turmoil as he awaited trial for "assault with the intent to rob while armed," remembered his brother as "a normal kid, well-liked, a hard worker and capable . . . He isn't like me at all." Andrew "tried to hold our family together" and was "more mature than most kids."[7]

Howard Gayle Adams's story is also interesting. A native of Corsicana, Texas, an East Texas oil boomtown, Gayle was very different from Andrew Fortuna. An extremely well-behaved youth, he fit well into the conformist paradigm of World War II–era America. Even a former teacher noted his curiously good behavior when she told Pasley, "I would have been happier if he had chucked an eraser now and then." But Gayle Adams was not an eraser thrower, he was a conformist and he had to be. Although he came from what appeared to be a complete family, his father was often away working in the oilfields; Gayle's mother shouldered the responsibility of rearing three boys while holding down a full-time job. Despite having a devoted and responsible son like Gayle who made parenting relatively easy, financial troubles and his father's frequent absences created problems. Like Fortuna, Gayle Adams sought refuge in the army. After graduating from high school, he joined up in 1942 and was sent to the South Pacific, where he served during the hottest part of that theater's battles, winning a Bronze Star for bravery in combat in the Luzon and New Guinea Campaigns. In 1945, Adams returned to Corsicana and entered Navarro Junior College. Spending 1946–1947 at Navarro studying and working part time as a laboratory assistant, Adams, who was considered to have average intelligence and a strong work ethic, nevertheless struggled academically. Although he was a marginal student at Navarro, he left college to go to work in Houston at a brewery and try to gain admission to the University of Houston. He did get into school there, but the experience proved no better than at Navarro and by the summer of 1948, he returned to the army—the only place he had enjoyed any measure of success.[8]

Of the nonrepatriate group, James Veneris was the oldest. Born on March 27, 1922, Jimmie grew up in the steel town of Vandergrift, Pennsylvania. Highly intelligent and hardworking, Veneris made good grades throughout school and graduated from Vandergrift High School in 1940 with a low "B" average, yet all was not as well as it appeared. Although his parents expressed their love for him and never visibly mistreated him, their Greek language and his American English made all but the most basic verbal communication difficult. With little to discuss, Jimmie spent much of his time with his nose in a book and looking for an opportunity to excel. In August 1940, only two months after receiving his diploma, Veneris joined the army. The next five years would take him to the South Pacific, where he participated in the campaign for New Guinea. He left the army at the end of the war and returned home to Vandergrift, where he hoped his intelligence, high school diploma, and military record would lead him to economic and social success. He was wrong. Going to work at U.S. Steel, he started at the bottom and within months, an economic slowdown led to his being laid off. When his family moved to Hawthorne, California, in 1948, Jimmie remained in Vandergrift doing small jobs waiting for his opportunity. It never came, at least not as he expected, and in September 1950, he reenlisted in the army knowing full well of the recent fighting in Korea and his likelihood of being sent into a war zone.[9]

Along with those men who saw action in Europe and the Pacific during World War II, the majority of the others joined the military during the post-war years in hopes of escaping their individually difficult situations. From their respective West Texas oilfield experiences, Appalachian hillside roots, and childhoods growing up in the shadow of profound affluence, they all found a possibility of success in the peacetime army. In combining their individual motives and America's growing sense of national security, these men could make their Americanism pay.

A country boy from the mountains of far southwestern Virginia, Edward Dickenson grew up in a family whose poverty was multiplied by its size. With six brothers and six sisters whose birth years ranged from 1907 to 1937, the clan lived off what the patriarch could grow on his small, hillside farm and earn as a local carpenter. When he was ten years old, Ed started school, but quit after the sixth grade, at the age of seventeen, to find a job that would help ease the pressure on his family. He spent the summer of 1947 at home near Big Stone Gap, but by August, he was in Richmond, Virginia. On August 12, he went to Fort Lee, a few miles south of the city, and enlisted in the army. After basic training, the army assigned him to Fort Ord, near Monterey, California. However, after only two months, the army gave Dickenson a general discharge for "fraudulent enlistment" because he failed to report his rheumatic cardiovascular disease. He returned to Richmond, where he worked for a paper company as a weaver, and later, as a packer for a biscuit company. On March 31, 1950, knowing that war in Korea was likely coming, Ed signed up for the army a second time, failing to note his disease and previous enlistment. The army assigned Ed to Fort Knox, Kentucky, where he underwent basic training and training in the 83rd Recon Battalion. After a ten-day furlough, he was sent to Seattle, Washington, en route to Korea. Boarding ship on September 1, it took three weeks to get to Camp Drake, Japan.[10]

Throughout history, men seeking to leave their pasts behind have become soldiers. Richard Corden was one of these men. Born in Pawtucket, Rhode Island, on September 27, 1928, Richard seemed destined to have a pleasant upbringing thanks to a doting mother and a father who worked for the railroad. However, his father was perpetually ill and spent much of the boy's earliest years in hospitals. When the senior Corden was home, an aunt remembered, "he seemed to resent the boy" and he "would beat him unmercifully with the buckle end of a belt." When Richard was seven years old, his mother died of pneumonia and his father passed away three months later. Suddenly an orphan, he lived with his aunt for a year before joining his baby sister with his paternal grandmother in East Providence.[11]

Living with his grandmother, Richard was remembered as very quiet and naturally intelligent. "Maybe he didn't get to go to college but he had as good an education as those boys up on the Hill (Brown University). Why, when they had a spelling bee down here at the theater—they had it on the radio—we listened and he could out-spell all of them. He read a lot of books, big books, books for grownups." His step-grandfather remembered that Richard would look out the front window and watch the neighborhood boys play. When he wanted to play with them, he would go downstairs and stand around until asked to join the games. He was also remembered as being very agreeable, and willing to do whatever was asked of him by authority figures without argument.[12]

Richard's placid nature hid an enduring restlessness. He regularly ran away from his grandmother's house and returned to his aunt in Pawtucket. His frequent truancy belied his academic talent. Although he did not want to attend school, he generally did well when he went. Often in trouble, he was arrested in February 1942 for breaking and entering and truancy, in June 1942 for truancy and probation violation, and in January 1944 for breaking and entering and larceny, with each arrest ending in a brief sentence at Sockanosset Training School for Boys. In May 1944, he was sent to a foster home and in October, he was back at Sockanosset for stealing a car. In 1945, the seventeen-year-old ran away from the institute and went to work as a welder at a shipyard. Although the school tracked him to the factory, he was left to work on his own. Shortly afterward, however, he was laid off because of repeated absenteeism. It is quite possible that most of Corden's problems were due to poor mental health. A psychiatric report in late 1942 suggested that he may have been schizophrenic or a "full-blown psychotic." It also warned that he "could possibly become a clever criminal if not properly supervised."[13]

After World War II ended, many workers lost their jobs. Richard was one of them and sought military service as an answer to his prayers. Initially turned down by the navy, he enlisted in the army in March 1946, despite his poor eyesight. For most of the next four years, he served with the Army of Occupation in Europe, except for a brief time in 1947 when he went AWOL. As a high school student, Richard had taken an IQ test and scored 134, making him the brightest of all the prisoners. With such a high level of intelligence, the army offered him an opportunity to become an officer, but his background as a petty criminal doomed him.[14]

Rufus Elbert Douglas was also an army veteran seeking to lose his past. His father died within months of his birth and his mother sought stability by marrying, but she fought with her new husband constantly. By the time Elbert was eleven, she had died, leaving him with an aunt and uncle in the West Texas oil boomtown of Texon. The death of his mother devastated Elbert, who grew into a very timid young man. While his aunt remembered him as no trouble at all, classmates confessed to Pasley that they "picked on him . . . made fun of him . . . made life miserable for him." When he got to high school, the torment grew worse. He had to go to the consolidated school in nearby Big Lake, where those who grew up in town often looked down on the oilfield children. One teacher recalled him as "hard to like," with a consistently sloppy appearance and passive aggressive patterns of behavior. In the spring of 1945, at nearly eighteen years old, but still only a sophomore in high school, Elbert quit school and joined the army. In December 1946, a discharged Douglas returned to Reagan County, Texas, where his military experience allowed him to get his high school diploma quickly. Soon, he was enrolled at Sul Ross State College, where he only lasted a single semester, before turning back to the only things he knew. First, he took a job as an oil field worker near Odessa, but shortly thereafter reenlisted in the army. That was in March 1949.[15]

Like Elbert Douglas's family, the Batchelors came to the West Texas oilfields in the hopes of securing financial stability. Born in Goldthwaite, Texas, in 1931, Claude was the family's second child. When his father lost the family's ranch in 1933, the family moved west to Ballinger, where the patriarch invested in a grocery store and tourist cabins, then to the oilfields around Royalty in 1935, and finally settled in Kermit by 1940. From the time the family moved to Royalty, they endured hard times. The Great Depression was bad enough, but for a family transitioning from ranching and business into the manual labor associated with oil, the change was crippling. Not long after arriving in Kermit, the senior Batchelor went to Las Vegas, Nevada, to work in a magnesium plant, but in 1942 he was severely injured in a car accident and hospitalized for six months. During this time, Claude's mother took full-time work on an army base and Claude sold newspapers. Claude's father recovered, returned to Kermit, and resumed working in the oilfields, where the family stabilized.[16]

As a student, Claude compiled an unimpressive record. Although he enjoyed school and made many friends, he lived two miles away and was unable to participate in many extracurricular activities. After running with an older crowd during his early teen years, he became inseparable from one friend. At sixteen, they took off hitchhiking to California, but separated to make catching rides easier. They planned to meet at his friend's relative's house, but were unable to do so and after only one night, Claude started hitching back to Kermit, now flat broke. After he returned home, Claude went to work for Standard Oil, but quit shortly afterward and got a job traveling throughout Texas and Oklahoma. However, this job did not last long and in July 1948, the seventeen-year-old enlisted in the army.[17]

Albert Belhomme had a much broader understanding of political cultures than his fellow prisoners. Born in Antwerp, Belgium, on November 7, 1928, he suffered from severe asthma that required him to live in a sanitarium from the ages of two to four. When the Nazis invaded Belgium in May 1940, Albert and his family were separated. He was sent alone to France, but made his way back to his family in Antwerp, where he learned that his mother had been taken to Berlin as a forced factory laborer. During the Nazi occupation, he lived in Antwerp with his father and great-grandmother, but in 1943 joined his mother in Berlin. Only fifteen years old, he stayed in the camp with her and worked alongside her at the Kallmayer medical equipment factory until the American liberators arrived. One of the Americans was a soldier named Theodore Seifert, who fell for Albert's mother and essentially adopted the boy as his own. Married in Germany after the war ended, the couple relocated to Seifert's hometown of Ashland, Pennsylvania, and Albert began the process of becoming an American. All who knew him described him as exceedingly bright. He had a particular gift for languages and, apart from the various tongues of his native Belgium, he spoke impeccable German, good French, and became an excellent English-speaker within weeks of his arrival in the United States in 1946. Whereas many of his fellow nonrepatriates either had absent fathers or difficult father-son relationships, Albert and his stepfather got along well. The young man was a good worker and apparently sought out a military career as a way to expedite the citizenship process. In early 1948, he sought entry into the U.S. Navy, but was refused because of his flat feet. Later that year, he joined the army and started on the path toward officer training, but his lack of U.S. citizenship derailed him. After a brief three months in Germany, Belhomme was transferred to Seattle, where he would wait until being shipped off to Korea as part of the Second Division.[18]

Perhaps the defining moment of Otho Bell's life occurred at birth with the death of his mother.[19] Throughout the years, he carried with him a tremendous sense of guilt because he "killed his mother" on her twenty-third birthday; he even came to believe that he too would die on his twenty-third birthday. Despite his prediction, Otho Bell did not die on January 22, 1954, but by an unfortunate coincidence, that was the last day he was a prisoner of war. At midnight that night, the guards left and he chose China. Elbert Bell, a hardscrabble Mississippi farmer, remembered his son Otho as shy and agreeable, and told Pasley that "I could always scare him into anything and if I had the chance I could have scared him into coming back home." At seventeen, and in the eighth grade, Otho enlisted in the army, and although he did not like the lifestyle, he extended his enlistment the next year. Between high telephone bills and repeatedly being punished for going AWOL, Bell's military career was going nowhere. However, when he was stationed in Seattle, Washington, he met a sixteen-year-old girl with whom he fell in love and married. Only three months after his wedding, Otho was ordered to Korea, leaving his pregnant wife behind.[20]

Like so many of the conflict's PsW who fell for the communist line, Arlie Pate had grown up poor. His sister Goldie recalled their childhood in East Carondelet, Illinois, as one spent on relief and wearing threadbare clothes. Although she "didn't mind too much," Arlie did and internalized his frustrations. When schoolchildren picked on Arlie and Goldie, Arlie responded by returning home "straight from school to get away from it."[21]

Seeking to escape his poverty, Arlie took odd jobs. The recollections of one of his employers illustrates several important points about young Arlie Pate. Recalling the boy's timidity, his boss said, "If I raised my voice it was like hitting him with a whip" and if "I went looking for him I would have to be careful or I would scare him." Shy, nervous, and the butt of jokes, Arlie suffered from extremely low self-esteem. Although he possessed an intelligence quotient in the average range and finished the ninth grade, his coworkers could not trust him to remember the details of his work. When he went on errands, each stop had to be written down to ensure he made them all. At the end of the week, Arlie made $25, half of which he gave to his mother, and the other he spent on himself. With part of his pay one week, he bought a pair of pants. During gym class, his pants, along with two dollars, were stolen from his locker. He never got his money back and found his slacks in a drain, ruined. Fed up, Arlie quit school that very day.[22]

Always in conflict with his father, Arlie moved out and spent a few months living with his grandmother on her farm. Living there, he made a little money as a day laborer, but not enough to survive on. He then moved to East St. Louis, Illinois, where he worked as a truck driver, but again, found the going difficult. In January 1949, he joined the army. Not suspecting another conflict might break out so close on the heels of World War II, Pate felt comfortable with his role as a peacetime soldier. By April 1950, he returned home on leave, proudly showing off his uniform and announcing that he would probably be sent to Japan soon, as "That's where most of the guys are going." Within months, he was being mobilized for an invasion of Korea.[23]

Of the group, Lewie Griggs continually stood out. Even back home in Neches, Texas, he was an outcast, albeit apparently a self-imposed one. The product of very strict parents, Lewie seldom left home for any purpose other than church or school, and therefore did not develop strong social skills. When Pasley visited the Griggs's hometown, she found memories of a boy who "stood aloof" and "Didn't speak if he didn't care to." One neighbor said that in a town like his, "everyone knows everyone else. Speaks to everyone else," but Griggs would "just go along with his head in the air. Wouldn't speak. Wouldn't even look at you."[24] In reality, Griggs was more shy and introverted than arrogant. A teacher in Palestine, Texas, recalled Lewie as "a quiet timid child who did his work well but as he grew older he developed a complex and tried to avoid people."[25]

Despite his physical maturity and intellectual adequacy, Griggs continued to fail. By the time he was sixteen, he stood six-feet, two-inches tall and had earned a letter playing football; however, his extracurricular success did not translate to the classroom. He was a consistently poor student, who treated school as if it were a useless chore. One teacher confirmed his disinterest: "He was just there. He didn't do his work. He just came and that's all." Griggs left school after being picked on by his fellow students on a school bus and then spent six weeks attending a nearby military school. Having failed at school, Lewis needed a change of scenery. Two days after he turned seventeen, on August 4, 1949, he joined the army. Less than a year later, the strapping Griggs found himself in Korea serving as a stretcher-bearer.[26]

William Cowart grew up in the textile town of Dalton, Georgia. Growing into an industrial center with the help of rural electrification, the town saw an influx of country families seeking a better life. William's mother and father came for that reason and spent their weekdays working in the factories. Despite their relative success by southern Appalachian standards, all was not well at home. The couple had its problems and by the time William was six years old, they split. From that point forward, William lived with his doting mother, but when she married a man twenty years her junior, her son had difficulty adjusting to the new life. At fourteen, he ran away from home, finally turning up in Ohio, the state to which his father had moved, although he did not even know which town he lived in. Although his running to Ohio suggests that William hoped to see his father, he likely had no clue as to what to do if he actually located him. When his father visited Dalton, William "ducked his head down . . . and ran out of the house and didn't come back until his father had left."[27]

At school, William struggled both academically and socially. His grades were low and he failed some classes, but his behavior drew the most stares. Despite his quiet nature, Cowart craved attention. A teacher recalled that he would dress ridiculously and be tardy intentionally to stand out, but that backfired and made him an even greater outcast. Finally, Cowart, not quite sixteen, left school and joined the army with his mother's permission. That was January 1949, and a year and a half later, he went to Korea.[28]

Born the third of five children, Lowell Skinner lived the first few years of his life on a farm in central Ohio. As he neared school age, the family moved to Akron, where they lived a simple life. Over the years in Akron, the Skinners moved several times before they settled into a routine on the city outskirts. Virginia Pasley described the Skinner family home as "an unprepossessing tarpaper shack," but noted that they "resented newspaper and magazine references to their home as substandard." Neighbors defended the Skinners by offering that they had spent their money on "medical bills instead of home beautification."[29]

Remembered as a generally good youngster who might have been a bit hardheaded, Lowell had his high and low points growing up. While visiting an uncle in Wyoming one summer, he drew the attention of the local sheriff when he shot a deer out of season, but one man remembered that the incident was the only time he ever got into any significant trouble. Teachers recalled that Lowell never really stood out. Possessing average intelligence and a poor work ethic, Skinner struggled in school. His teachers recalled a student who did what was asked of him, but nothing more. At fifteen, Lowell started high school, but left after only a few months and began taking various jobs. Whereas school did not suit Skinner, work apparently did. Throughout the next few years, he worked and became a moderately self-sufficient teenager. At eighteen, Lowell joined the army.[30]

The second Ohioan to renounce the United States also grew up in Akron. Scott Rush, better known as Leonard, left few clues about his early life. He was only five-feet, two-inches by the time he joined the army. Physically, he was fit, but his education had been confined almost entirely to the Miller Occupational School, a school for special needs students where he had also been identified as needing treatment for emotional problems.[31] Although he had attended Miller, his Army General Classification Test (AGCT) score was an acceptable 96, placing him well within the average of all the men who refused to return home after Korea.[32]

When Rush was a teenager, his parents moved to Marietta, Ohio, about 130 miles south of Akron, leaving him and his brother Richard behind. Richard was enrolled in a boarding school while Leonard fended for himself and lived in a rented basement room. During the day, he attended school, and in the evenings, he worked at the Mayflower Hotel as a dishwasher. In June 1949, he graduated from Miller and moved in with his parents in Marietta. Two months later, he joined the army as a photographer.[33]

Harold Webb's path toward Korea began with his birth in Jacksonville, Florida. When his mother's marriage broke up in the late 1930s, she moved with Harold and his sister Katherine to the Pop-o-Lee estate in West Palm Beach, Florida, where her stepparents acted as caretakers. Harold's early life in this lush and attractive environment belied the reality of the situation. His mother died, and soon afterward, so did her stepmother. With no one remaining within the close family circle, Katherine was sent to live with an aunt and Harold went with his father, who provided a less than stable environment. By the time he turned sixteen, Harold had wasted enough time in school and went to work full time. For two years, he moved throughout Florida until joining the army just before he turned eighteen.[34]

David Hawkins grew up in a very unstable Oklahoma City family. His mother was a Holiness preacher who forced her strict code on a young boy who fought back for his own type of enjoyment. As a young boy, he sought solace in things like comic books and movies, both of which his mother disapproved of, while he watched her divorce his father, remarry, then divorce again. David and his mother moved constantly, living most of the time in rooming houses all over Oklahoma City. Virginia Pasley wrote that he attended three different schools in a single year. He spent much time with his grandmother and lived in her house on several occasions. As a teenager, he went to California and visited his aunt and uncle for a summer and apparently found a stable family there. At the insistence of his cousins, he stayed with them for two years before returning to Oklahoma City. His uncle, whom he would credit as his father on occasion, was an active army officer. Wishing to continue that level of stability, Hawkins went back home, where he gathered documents that falsely stated his age as seventeen, convinced his mother to certify that fact, and enlisted in the army, despite the fact that he was only sixteen. His seventeenth birthday found him a prisoner of war in Korea.[35]

While economic and social success appears to have eluded most of the nonrepatriates, it was far more problematic for William White, Clarence Adams, and LaRance Sullivan. As the only three black men among the group who refused repatriation, White, Adams, and Sullivan represented an important niche the Chinese hoped to exploit; however, the inherent ethnocentrism within Chinese culture undermined most of those efforts.

William White was emblematic of black existence in the American South. The native of Plumerville, Arkansas, was born on May 9, 1930, and grew up poor, rural, and compliant within a segregated society. Like Ralph Ellison's Invisible Man or Richard Wright's Bigger Thomas, William was hardly noticed by the society that surrounded him. A classmate recalled that White spent a lot of time by himself and was generally "kind of indifferent." He "never made no fuss about it." William "just wanted to be by himself." His teachers never felt as if they knew him, and Pasley wrote, "At high school he is not even remembered." The loner had to acquiesce to the white society in which he lived and earned a good reputation as a laborer. One white man for whom he worked described him as a "good worker . . . not one of those rowdy niggers. You couldn't find a nicer boy." William's training had begun at home. His mother and father divorced while he was still an infant and his mother soon began a new life by remarrying, having more children, and sending William to live with his grandmother just down the road. To a small child, the short distance between his mother's new life and his existence probably seemed insurmountable. When he was five, he returned to his mother's house, where he lived until he was a senior in high school. He then moved in with an aunt in Kansas City, Missouri, where he went to school for one semester before joining the army in March 1948.[36]

Clarence Adams also grew up in segregation. A native of Memphis, Tennessee, his urban experience was vastly different from that of William White's rural one. Adams's youth was spent in a small house that was part of Coward Place, a Civil War–era mansion.[37] Although he played with white children in the evenings and on weekends, he lived a different existence at school. In such a situation, getting along was very important. Neighbors remembered Clarence, or "Skippy," as most called him, as "a wonderful kid . . . Everybody liked him. He was amenable as can be, never any trouble to anyone." A good student, but one who had to work for his marks, Clarence was likely affected by his four younger half sisters, whom one teacher called "brilliant" students. Hoping to compensate for his lagging behind the formidable competition of his sisters, Clarence worked very hard and demanded excellence of himself. According to his mother, by the time he reached high school, he had become withdrawn and impatient. He asked his mother to allow him to enlist in the army and she relented, hoping that he would mature and return home a renewed man. Adams remembered his path to the military differently: he was running from the Memphis police who wanted to question him for his role in a fight and saw the army as a sure getaway.[38]

LaRance Sullivan came from a severely unstable family in Santa Barbara, California, and grew up in a house that "was not safe due to drunken brawls." Born to a mother who "never cared much for staying home," the young boy spent much of his time with his grandmother, whose recollections of his good behavior and excellent personality were confirmed by many others. However, his outgoing nature betrayed a turbulent lifestyle. When he was not with his grandmother, he was left to fend for himself. One acquaintance remembered that "he ate out of garbage cans." It is therefore not surprising that LaRance, despite possessing considerable intelligence, struggled in school. While his mother made good money in a World War II industrial job, her habit of living with various men and her ongoing alcoholism left her children suffering; LaRance had to dance for pennies outside of nightspots. His teachers noticed that he was becoming gaunt and gave him a job in the school cafeteria, where he got at least one meal each weekday and began regaining weight. LaRance and his siblings were starving despite the fact that their mother made a living wage. With constant parties at home, the teenaged boy would bring his sisters to the local police department to spend the night. When his mother was finally jailed for a probation violation, the children were all parceled out to foster homes, except LaRance, who lived for several months in juvenile hall where he was free to come and go as he pleased, but was still living in a jail. In early 1948, when LaRance was not quite seventeen, his mother gave him permission to join the army after her most recent boyfriend urged her to sign the papers, "so we can be rid of him."[39]

In addressing the motives of the three black men who were members of the nonrepatriate group, America's racial climate must be discussed. Although LaRance Sullivan did not grow up in the segregated South, he surely understood the condition of second-class citizenry that his race dictated for him. For William White and Clarence Adams, their daily exposure to not only racism, but the laws that institutionalized it, was likely more formative. Both were what good blacks were supposed to be in the South: outwardly quiet, respectful, and compliant. Although none of the young men had strained relationships with the whites they encountered in their youths, the persistent stress of living in such an environment must have taken its toll, although even some blacks did not recognize the level of difficulty the three encountered. LaRance Sullivan's father dismissed racism as an important influence on his son saying, "He never knew segregation. He didn't live in the South." Similarly, Gladys Peoples, the mother of Clarence Adams, noted that her "Skippy encountered less of it [racism] than the average colored boy . . . He grew up in a white neighborhood and played with white boys as a child."[40]

While three of the twenty-three had fought in World War II, and more than a dozen others had served in the peacetime army, three more enlisted in the army after most people understood that war in Korea was inevitable. These men further illustrate the point that loyalty was not alien to these future nonrepatriates; in fact, they appear to be a very solidly pro-American group of military volunteers.

Richard Tenneson, of Alden, Minnesota, was one of the more intelligent of the nonrepatraites. Like most of the others, his youth was filled with uncertainty. He began life with his mother, but after two years, his father went to prison and Portia Howe filed for divorce. He was then given over to his grandmother, and later lived with two different aunts. Most of his moves required a change of town, or at least, of school. Devoutly religious, but insecure in her faith, his mother Portia baptized infant Richard into the Lutheran faith, then at six, as a Catholic, and at thirteen, a Baptist. In 1941, Portia found stability when she met and married Ebenezer Howe.[41]

Even though his mother's life stabilized, Richard's did not. Despite the fact that he lived for a time with Ebenezer and Portia, he did not always get along with his stepfather and apparently moved in with an aunt for a time. A teacher recalled that Richard "never really had a home or any stable environment—just an overload of sin and save the world." Always restless, he ran away from home at age fifteen after hearing that his own father had done the same. The next year, he tried to join the army, but was rejected, and then took a job with a traveling carnival and left home again. He had a brush with the law when one of his fellow carnival workers stole a car and took Richard along for the ride. Although he had nothing to do with the crime, his mother had to go to Nebraska to get him.[42]

Not long after he turned seventeen, Richard began hounding his mother to allow him to enlist in the army. In late 1950, with a year of school remaining, he argued that he was not a particularly good student, that he could go to college later under the G.I. bill, and that with the war in Korea underway, he would likely be drafted anyway. With that, Portia signed the enlistment documents and let her son go off to war. In February 1951, Richard came home on a brief leave before he started his tour in Korea.[43]

Aaron Wilson's low intelligence level should have kept him out of the army. Born in the logging town of Urania, Louisiana, he was the oldest child in his parents' ever-growing family. When he went to school, his deficiencies were overwhelming. Pasley wrote that he "spent two years in nearly every grade" and his younger sister quickly became a classmate and then passed him. When she asked about Aaron around town, Pasley repeatedly heard him described as quiet, shy, solitary, and unintelligent. Even his own family directly addressed his shortcomings when his sister said of Aaron's letters: "My brother couldn't have written those letters. . . . He was too dumb to write like that. Why, when he went in the Army he was seventeen and still in the eighth grade."[44]

Perhaps many of Aaron's problems can be credited to his medical history. Pasley uncovered that he had been so severely injured by forceps at birth that "he hovered between life and death" for two weeks. Three months later, colic with fever struck with such ferocity that his family "had to hold him in a pan of water to cool him off." After his initial difficulties, he continued to endure physical hardships. When he was not quite two years old, he had an emergency appendectomy and later, as a teenager, he ruptured himself building a barn and was forced to wear a truss.[45]

Thanks to Morris Wills's autobiography, his story is one of only two of the group that is extensively documented. Born in upstate New York to a farming family, Morris's childhood was spent in poor health. An accident burst an abscess on his appendix when he was two years old and he suffered from asthma throughout his childhood. As he began to strengthen and mature, his mother's health broke. He was about twelve years old when a doctor found a tumor on her knee. Wills recalled that his doting mother suffered for six months before the doctor amputated her leg. She died from the combination of the operation and a severe case of jaundice, however, leaving Morris and his siblings alone with a father whose primary interest was working.[46]

Not long after his mother's death, Morris began working for his uncle, who lived nearby. Soon, he had begun staying there throughout the week and only coming home on Sundays. As a student, Wills barely worked, but still kept up with the class. He was far more interested in recreation. He spent much time hunting and fishing, and by the time he was fifteen, he had saved enough money to buy a car. Wandering aimlessly, Morris decided to join the army.[47]

Surprisingly, only one of the nonrepatriates was a draftee. When conscription was reintroduced in 1948, as a way to strengthen America's shrinking military forces, thousands of men were inducted and trained. After the brief buildup that resulted from the Berlin Crisis, the army's numbers again dwindled.[48] The outbreak of hostilities in Korea brought thousands of men into the army both voluntarily and forcibly. In comparison to the twenty-one other Americans under examination, the lone conscript appears to be the weak link when discussing loyalty. But his reluctance to voluntarily join the army offers no credible evidence as to the his concept of, and adherence to, national loyalty.

John Dunn's youth differed dramatically from that of many of his disaffected comrades. Born into a well-respected family in Altoona, Pennsylvania, Jack, as his friends and family called him, did not grow up in poverty or a broken home. Although his family endured the difficulties of the Great Depression, his father managed to work through much of the crisis and by the start of World War II, he moved his family to Baltimore, Maryland, where he started a new job as a personnel manager. A shy and quiet boy, Dunn had little interest in school. Although his IQ was rated as average, he had to repeat one full grade and half of another. Because of the move and his poor academic performance, he was nearly seventeen years old when he entered Baltimore City College—a high school—for his junior year. In this environment, students were given an opportunity to choose an educational path between classical and vocational studies, or a hybrid of the two intended to allow disinterested students to graduate. Jack Dunn chose the latter and rose to prominence graduating in the top third of his class of 400. He was high-minded, well dressed, and became the president of his class during his senior year, but had no serious academic interests.[49]

Outside of school, Jack Dunn's private life was one of responsibility. A churchgoer all of his life, Jack spent his spare time at the Episcopal Church of the Resurrection. There, he volunteered for any work that needed to be done, sometimes spending as many hours working for the church as most boys his age would log on their after-school jobs. During the summer, he worked setting up for summer camps and after graduation he took on a sales route for a Baltimore snack food company. Jack spent his years after graduation succeeding in his sales job and he remained a bachelor.[50]

When the Korean War began, the draft was instituted and Jack Dunn was among those called up. When he was drafted, Jack visited with his pastor and confided that he would accept the duty because "I am in a better position than some; I have no responsibilities." The only thing standing in his way was the medical exam. The persistently ill young man was passed by the doctors and accepted into the army. But on the troop transport to Japan, another physician checked him and declared, "I don't know how you got in but I can tell you you're going back as soon as we get over." For whatever reason, Dunn was allowed to stay in the army and entered combat in June 1951.[51]

When Virginia Pasley wrote her book in 1955, America was in the midst of the Cold War and the consensus history that it spawned. For her and her readers these men needed explaining, within the context of the time: only broken men would abandon their nation in favor of Godless communism. Through her travels and interviews, she found broken men originating from broken families; indeed, only Dunn came from a stable, middle-class family. While it was easy for Pasley to dismiss these men as defective, broken, or irregular, modern scholarship has revealed that most of their peers were not much different. Americans in the 1930s and 1940s experienced professional disappointment, familial failure, criminal behavior, poor health, and humble education.

When twenty-three American soldiers choose to join the enemy rather than return to duty with their own nation's army, their loyalty has certainly been compromised on some level. Whatever their motivations for making the decision not to repatriate might have been, the results appear clear and final. In order to do these men justice and to understand the phenomenon they represented for future conflicts, this cursory glance must be turned into a full-scale examination. Twenty-two volunteers, out of twenty-three nonrepatriates, more than one of them eligible to wear decorations for bravery in battle, warrant a deeper analysis.

TWO

The Short Careers of Soldiers

> "Everyone was just trying to exist—to survive. No one was able to take charge. Every value you ever had, every standard, is slowly crushed. Money is completely useless. I've seen men burn it up, use it for toilet paper. Tobacco, salt, something to eat, that's the only thing that has value. A grain of tobacco becomes more precious than a five-dollar gold piece. Men would fight over a quarter-of-an-inch cigarette butt. They would fight over a spoonful of rice. You became an animal."
>
> —Morris Wills

Of the twenty-three men whose stories are told within these pages, none of them saw more than a few months of combat in Korea. Most were captured within weeks of their arrival in the country; fourteen of the men were taken prisoner in the month following the U.S. Army's first military encounter with the Chinese People's Volunteer Army (CPV). Of the group, the military experiences of only a handful of the men are known.

Lowell Skinner's Story

When the Korean War broke out in the summer of 1950, Lowell Skinner was stationed in Japan. Having spent the previous year at Fort Knox, Kentucky, he arrived in Japan without papers and with a misdiagnosed case of tuberculosis. For the next few weeks, he waited while his orders were recut and his diagnosis changed. By the time the red tape was unraveled, Skinner's original unit had already been deployed to Korea and he was reassigned to a new regiment. He finally made it to Korea in July.

In one battle, his lieutenant "became panicky" and nervously ordered his men to fire on a group of men in their front without verifying their identity. Skinner recalled that he and his comrades wounded about seventy-five fellow Americans that day. When the men realized what had happened, Skinner and others went forward and retrieved the wounded men. Skinner himself helped "bring back two men he had shot," one suffering from a chest wound. Years later he confessed to a psychiatrist that he "still remembers this man lying there trying to drink coffee while he tried to tell him he had shot him." Lowell "wanted to be beaten up for that."[1]

On November 1, 1950, the CPV launched their first major offensive of the war and completely overran many U.S. Army units, Skinner's included. The fact that the Chinese Army was even on the Korean peninsula surprised many within the American high command and Skinner remembered, "The officers wouldn't believe the Chinese were facing them." His unit was unprotected and "they were attacked from three sides, and over-run."[2]

Ed Dickenson's Story

On September 22, 1950, Ed Dickenson arrived at Camp Drake, Japan. Within days, he was assigned to the 8th Cavalry Regiment, First Cavalry Division, Company K, and was soon sent on his way to the fighting. He made it to Korea shortly after the Inchon Landings, the maneuver that effectively cut the Korean peninsula in half, leaving most of the North Korean Army in a vise between the Inchon and Pusan. The rout had begun.[3]

During the coming weeks, the North Korean resistance evaporated in the face of thousands of fresh United Nations troops. By late October, Dickenson's unit was near Unsan, well north of the 38th Parallel, on its way to the Yalu River. Although Ed Dickenson fought in Korea for only slightly more than a month, he stood out as an excellent soldier. During his initial two-month enlistment, he had failed to make an impression on his superiors and was classified as a "satisfactory" soldier; however, when he joined the second time, his hard work and dedication helped turn him into one of the best men in his unit. While in training at Fort Knox, he was graded as "excellent" and his performance in the field prior to his capture was classified as the same.[4] Years later, just weeks after Dickenson's voluntary repatriation, his former squad leader, Earl J. Milliken, remembered him to newspapermen as "one of the best soldiers we had, a kid who really loved America."[5]

On Halloween night of that year, a full moon illuminated a shocking sight. In front of Dickenson's squad were countless Chinese soldiers. Due to lapses in American intelligence and skillful maneuvering by their army, the Chinese had rushed nearly 200,000 soldiers into North Korea to meet what they interpreted as a threat from the United Nations forces moving northward toward the Manchurian border. That night, the Chinese surrounded the entire Eighth Regiment. For the next three days, nearly 800 encircled Americans attempted to fight their way out, but failed. Knowing little more than the fact that his company had been shredded by enemy attacks, Dickenson, like many others, searched for his own way out of the dilemma. Dickenson's squad leader recalled that harrowing experience. Having been wounded on the first day of the fighting, Milliken heard spotty reports of the happenings at the front. By November 5, "all of K Company except seven men were killed or captured. Dickenson was one of those captured."[6] That day, Chinese soldiers found him hiding in brush. For the next three years, he would be a prisoner of war. Later, Dickenson illustrated the apparent hopelessness of facing so many of the enemy. "At the time of my capture, it seemed that the Chinese soldiers outnumbered the United Nations soldiers about seven or eight to one." A poor, uneducated, country boy, Edward Dickenson's estimate of comparative enemy strength was close.[7]

Upon his capture, Dickenson joined a van of hundreds of soldiers being marched northward. He recalled marching for seventeen days before the column finally stopped. They were at a temporary camp that the prisoners would aptly name Death Valley. There, the men encountered the worst conditions they would face. With about three thousand men living in the deep, shaded valley, in unheated huts, during the depth of the Korean winter, all the while on starvation rations, it is surprising that any of them survived the ordeal. Some of the men who survived that winter in Death Valley recalled that the temperatures often dipped to thirty degrees below zero and that about fifty of the men had worn their army uniforms out during the march and were now half naked. During the four to six weeks the men stayed in the old Japanese mining camp, an estimated one-sixth of their number died from disease and starvation.[8]

Claude Batchelor's Story

Claude Batchelor arrived at Yokohama, Japan, on December 1, 1948. After a couple of weeks awaiting orders at Camp Zama, he was formally assigned to the 1 Cavalry Division Band at Camp Drake as a trumpeter.[9] For the next year and a half, Batchelor played his trumpet and lived as other soldiers did while on their Pacific assignments. In January 1949, Batchelor met Kyoko

Araki and the two began to see each other regularly. In July, Batchelor and Kyoko married in a Shinto ceremony.[10]

On July 13, 1950, Batchelor was reassigned to the 8th Cavalry Regiment and notified that he would be departing for Korea within days. Two days later, Batchelor and the rest of the Regiment boarded ships and left for Korea. After three days at sea, they made landfall on the peninsula. Over the course of the four months that followed Batchelor's arrival, Company E fought its way northward, pushing the North Korean army farther back within its original borders day after day. By October 31, the 8th Cavalry stood a full sixty miles north of Pyongyang, where it had set up its defenses.[11]

Batchelor remembered that on the evening of November 1, he and about fourteen other men from Company E, were sent from their company's main position to a distant outpost. When they were about halfway there, they heard and saw the flashes of explosions from the direction of their former position. Radioing back to headquarters, they failed to get a response, and at around midnight, they ran across another small group who confirmed that the Chinese had overrun their company. There was a lieutenant with the new group, so he took command and ordered the men to bed down for the night. The next morning, they began trying to move south, hoping to get back to their lines. Traveling along the crests of mountain ridges, the squad came upon a road where they met the enemy for the first time. Batchelor remembered that the Americans and the Chinese saw each other at about the same time and before diving for cover, he saw the squad leader shoot one of the enemy. Knowing that they were behind enemy lines, the lieutenant ordered the men to retreat in the direction from which they had come. They spent that night in a small valley and woke the following morning with the same plan of moving south, but after only traveling about a mile, they encountered the enemy. Fortunately for the squad, the Chinese had not seen them so the Americans retreated into a small, wooded hollow close enough to hear enemy voices on the other side of the ridge. After an uneasy night of standing watch, the men discovered the Chinese had gone and after spotting an enemy patrol, retreated into the same small valley where they had spent the night two days earlier and settled in for another uneasy night.[12]

When they awoke on the morning of November 6, the men had not eaten anything substantial in nearly five days. With their stomachs now pressing the issue, the squad took off in search of sustenance. They soon came upon three men, whom they thought to be enemy soldiers. Rushing the trio, the Americans killed two Chinese soldiers and freed the third man, who was a

South Korean prisoner of war. Instead of thanking his liberators, the Korean told Batchelor, who was translating for the group thanks to his exposure to Japanese, that the enemy surrounded them and there was no hope of escaping. The Korean soldier told the Americans that a small village stood across the valley and they might find food there. Now desperate, the squad crossed the valley and entered the village, hoping to find it unoccupied. Almost immediately, they saw Chinese soldiers standing about fifty yards away in front of a house, but kept walking through the village. The lieutenant passed the word that no one should fire their weapons as they were certainly outnumbered. Curiously, the Chinese saw them, too, but made no movement. The Americans continued straight through the town, stopping briefly to ask for, and be denied, food at each house. As they nervously exited the far end of the village, the Chinese began scrambling for cover. The squad spread out and fired into the town before trying to flee across rice fields. With a machine gun firing on them from a distance and poorly aimed mortars dropping behind them, the Americans crossed a river and entered the wooded hills beyond. They spent that night on top of a small hill, completely starved. Many of their number were unable to continue, while the pursuing Chinese surrounded them. Watching flashlights in the distance moving around them all night, the Americans knew the next day would be one of decision. At daybreak, Batchelor heard someone scream, "here they come," and he immediately saw a Chinese soldier near him. As a group, they retreated to a small hill below their position and found more enemy soldiers. Taking their stand at that point, the Americans regrouped and fought it out with the Chinese for nearly two hours. With many of their number wounded and two men killed, the American lieutenant gathered the men and told them that it might be in their best interest to surrender. Batchelor remembered that the lieutenant's suggestion "t[h]rew the men into a chaos. Some of them were waving yellow scarves shouting surrender and some kept on firing yelling no we don't." After a frenzied few minutes, the American squad decided to give up.[13]

The Americans threw down their guns and tried to prepare themselves for the unknown. After being searched and having their weapons and ammunition confiscated, the men were lined up near a ditch as a Chinese soldier with a British machine gun approached them. Standing on the right end of the line, Batchelor expected to be shot on the spot and began planning to go down with the first shots and hope to pass for dead, but the gunfire never came. Looking down the line of men on his left, he was surprised to see a Chinese officer going from man to man, taking their hands off their heads and shaking hands with each of the men. Soon, the Americans were led to a small house where they were given food and cigarettes. Later that day, several of the men were detached to carry the confiscated weapons to a central location where they met several other captured Americans.[14]

With a sizable van of prisoners, the Chinese formed the men into columns of two and began marching them deeper into North Korea. Claude Batchelor did not remember how many days they marched, but he did recall that the Chinese halted for about four days midway through the trek to allow the men to rest. During the break, the Chinese asked their captives about their prior civilian occupations and their jobs in the army. With this information in hand, the captors broke the men into small squads, appointed squad leaders, and assigned each squad to a building. Batchelor's squad leader was a private first class who had driven a truck in civilian life, but did not want to head the group. Unbeknownst to the Chinese, Batchelor's squad elected a master sergeant as its real leader with the private first class acting as a figurehead. The morning after the election, a few of Batchelor's squad tried to build a fire in the house's kitchen, but it got out of hand and set the whole building ablaze. With their house in ashes, the Chinese sent Batchelor's squad into a cave. Later that morning, soldiers came and ordered the private first class squad leader to go with them and Batchelor confessed that he never expected to see the young man alive again; however, after about three hours, he returned and reported to the group. He told the men that the Chinese had "given him a long lecture on burning down the people's property and made him write a s[e]lf-criticism of himself. They told him that we would have to pay for the house our [*sic*] of our rations." After a few days, the Chinese turned the prisoners over to North Korean soldiers, although a few of the Chinese remained with the group, and the northward march resumed.[15]

It took another week, but the American prisoners finally made it to Pyoktong, on the Yalu River. Within days, however, the prisoners were moved a few miles away when American aircraft attacked the city. During December 1950, they lived in a collection of houses in a small valley with Batchelor's squad somewhat separated from the rest of the American prisoners. Charging the American cooks with selling much of their food on the black market, Batchelor complained that he and the others were nearly starving while a handful of prisoners profited. Although North Koreans were officially in charge of the Americans, the Chinese cast a long shadow. With no indoctrination plan yet established, the men only had to endure hearing occasional statements about the "lenient treatment policy" and the soldiers being "duped by the big business magnates of wall street." The only formal change came in the enforcement of the rule that prisoners call each other "comrade."[16]

In the middle of January, the prisoners were moved back to Pyoktong, where conditions improved somewhat. Once in their new quarters, the men were allowed to cook by squad. This meant that the rations were delivered to each squad's cook and that he was responsible for feeding his men. However, the house that Batchelor's squad inhabited did not have a kitchen so the men had to have their food cooked by the squad next door and the cheating continued. Soon, the squad received their own pot and started cooking for themselves. Through March 1951, the random lectures continued while many of the prisoners died.[17]

Clarence Adams's Story

In September 1947, Clarence Adams was eating breakfast in his mother's kitchen in Memphis, Tennessee, when he heard the police knock on the door and ask for him. Within the past few days, he had gotten in a fight with a white hobo and had fought and stabbed a black thug from his neighborhood. Adams did not know which crime the police were interested in, but he vowed not to stick around to find out. He sneaked out the back door and went straight to the army recruiting station and enlisted. Later that day, he boarded a troop train to Biloxi, Mississippi.[18]

From Biloxi, Adams went to Fort Dix, New Jersey, for basic training and by December, he had finished his training course and was sent to Korea. Decades later, Adams confessed that he was not the best soldier while in Korea. He fell asleep on guard duty and, despite not knowing how to drive, took a sergeant's order to back a truck out of a garage and drove it through the wall. The next December, Adams left Korea and was stationed at Gifu, Japan, for about a year and a half. In the summer of 1950, the Korea question was coming to a head, but Adams felt confident that he would not be involved in whatever happened. He was reassigned to Fort Lewis, Washington, and only had a few months remaining on his enlistment when President Harry Truman announced the outbreak of hostilities and involuntarily extended him and countless others for an additional year.[19]

Landing at Pusan in August 1950, Clarence Adams found himself "right smack in the middle of a shooting war" on his second day in the country. The next month, Douglas MacArthur's landing at Inchon cut off the North Korean supply lines and sent the Korean communists into a frantic retreat northward.

In November, Adams and the rest of the UN forces rested in Pyongyang before resuming the offensive that would put them in Kunu-ri by Thanksgiving Day, November 24. There, Adams and his comrades enjoyed Thanksgiving dinner without realizing that "It would be three long years before [they] got another decent meal."[20]

The day after Thanksgiving, the Chinese attacked and the UN forces began a slow withdrawal. Adams remembered that "[f]or the next several days we got no sleep" and "did not even have time to eat." Adams's artillery unit set up its big guns, fired them, then loaded them back on trucks, and withdrew to another firing position. On the morning of November 29, their retreat was in full swing. Adams's artillery unit lay down covering fire to aid other units in their escapes, but by the time they were relieved, the Chinese had closed around them and it was getting dark. When a mortar hit both the head and tail of the convoy, the Americans were trapped. Adams crawled underneath a truck with a machine gun, but Chinese gunners zeroed in on him quickly and another Chinese soldier set up a machine gun at the head of the column to watch the rice paddy that spread out along one side of the road. Adams watched as small groups of men took off across the paddy and were mowed down by the machine gunner. He knew that he had to get out so when another group started across the paddy, he too ran, but at an angle away from the others and alone. Somehow, he made it across.[21]

Although Clarence Adams had escaped immediate danger, he was far from safe. All throughout the moonless night, he ran, hoping that he was going south, but not really knowing his direction. At one point, he rounded a curve in the path and nearly ran into another soldier coming the other way. With only a glance, Adams knew the man was Chinese because of the Russian Burp Gun that he was carrying. Both men wheeled toward each other and fired, but none of the bullets found their mark. Then, Adams was shocked to see the Chinese soldier turn and continue running. He realized that the other man was just as scared as he. That night, he kept running until he collapsed in the snow from exhaustion.[22]

When he awoke the next morning, he was nearly frozen. His feet were frostbitten and in very bad shape. He looked around and saw dead bodies scattered and decided to crawl amongst them hoping to avoid capture by the Chinese and that more Americans would wander nearby. Not long after, he heard American voices and joined a small group searching for a way out. These fifteen or so men began moving in the direction they thought to be southerly, but the last man in line reported that he thought they were being followed. The small column turned a curve and went into the brush for an ambush of whomever was following, but no one appeared. Thinking that whoever was following them was allowing them to keep walking in the wrong direction, the men emerged from the bushes with the intention of backtracking, but at their first steps, they were attacked. Men scattered in every direction; Adams and another man ran and jumped into a ditch. When they hit the ditch, they looked up to see a lone Chinese soldier standing over them. Not wishing to take a chance, both American soldiers threw down their guns and became prisoners of the Chinese.[23]

Like the reports from countless other soldiers, when the Chinese approached the American soldiers to disarm them, the Americans were surprised with handshakes and hugs. Adams himself recalled that one of his captors hugged both him and the other man and then sat down with a handful of grain. That was the first food Adams had eaten in days.[24]

In the meantime, since the Chinese did not release all of the names of those men captured in late 1950, the army told Clarence Adams's mother that her son had been killed in action. Along with that terrible news came a military life insurance check for $10,000, but a year later, when Adams's name appeared on a prisoner of war list, the military demanded its money back. Fortunately for Mrs. Adams, she had put the entire amount in the bank and was able to withdraw it and return it to the government without much difficulty.[25] After a couple of days of waiting, Adams joined a large group of captured Americans on their way to the permanent prisoner of war camp. For the march, the North Koreans took charge of the men and began pushing them northward. Although the march only lasted ten days, Adams struggled because of his frostbitten toes and, try as he might, he could not keep up. He knew if he fell out of line, he might be shot, but nevertheless he began to falter. Finally, he was alone just walking on the road in the direction that the column had traveled. Although he lagged behind every day, sometime late at night he would catch up with his column, get a few hours of sleep, eat a rice ball, and resume the march. On December 10, 1950, Clarence Adams arrived at Camp Five with about five hundred other captured Americans.[26]

Richard Corden's Story

When the war in Korea began, Richard Corden was stationed at Fort Lewis, Washington. He remembered, "we were immediately alerted. . . . Then came out something about the police action and it would be very short, at the most two months, maybe one month and the thing would be over." For Corden, "It wasn't an actual war at all, and we would soon be coming home. When I went to Korea that's how I felt."[27]

Looking back on his first days in Korea, Corden was struck by the fact that "just about everybody was in the war." He remembered a young Korean boy who was caught digging through a pit where old administrative papers were thrown. The kid was stuffing these papers into his clothing, possibly to hand over to North Korean military officials, but when caught, the "sergeant in charge just gave him a kick in the pants, and sent him on his way." Sometimes they found "old men up in their sixties, with radio receivers and so forth under their loose fitting pants."[28]

In late November 1950, Corden's unit was advancing toward the Chosin Reservoir. His element "had reached the second objective of our five objective plan, when the Chinese counter-attacked." Quickly, his division realized that the surrounding divisions had retreated and "that we were sticking out," but the Chinese moved to cut the Americans off. Over the coming days, the Chinese methodically tightened the noose by "closing this perimeter and cutting us up into smaller and smaller groups." Corden remembered that he surrendered with between 200 and 300 men. After an initial march to the vicinity of Pyoktong on the Yalu River, Corden and the others settled into the difficult life of being a PW.[29]

Albert Belhomme's Story

Albert Belhomme joined the army in order to ease the process of becoming a citizen. As a Belgian-born survivor of the Nazi occupation, Belhomme came to America seeking the new start that the nation had given countless other immigrants. He recalled that once settled in Ashland, Pennsylvania, he tried to get various jobs, but was always restricted by his lack of U.S. citizenship. He heard that joining the army could streamline the process and signed up. Once a soldier, Belhomme took the requisite tests and qualified to attend Officer's Candidate School, but again, his citizenship stopped him from advancing. He later lamented, "I could have been useful. I spoke several languages fluently, but I was not a citizen." He also remembered that because he had spent three months in Germany as a child, he had to go through a battery of loyalty tests and was cleared, but only for duty in a "zone of interior." Because of the contingencies of war, the army ignored the interior classification and sent him to Korea to fight. A few months later, on November

30, Belhomme and eleven other men from an artillery battalion were taken prisoner by the Chinese.[30]

Morris Wills's Story

Morris Wills arrived in Korea in January 1951, while Ed Dickenson and Claude Batchelor were starving before being moved into Camp Five at Pyoktong. Wills was assigned to the Second Division's 38th Regiment, Company E, as a replacement and was immediately thrown into action as an ammunition carrier in a machine gun squad. About five days after his arrival, Company E was ordered out of its foxholes, moved about ten miles up a snowy mountain, and dug in. The next day, they moved on, but this time they dug in on a low mountain overlooked by a communist-held ridge. Within hours, the outgunned and out-positioned Americans withdrew. In what the lowly private saw as a poorly conceived and executed battle, Morris Wills saw his first action.[31]

From late February into early March, the Eighth Army pressed Operation Killer, a counteroffensive led by General Matthew Ridgeway in response to China's November 1950 offensive. By the time Operation Killer got underway, the Chinese had begun their own withdrawal, thereby making Ridgeway's advance an overwhelming and fairly easy success, aside from the terrible weather. As a frontline soldier, Wills saw it differently. He told the story of his unit finding two Chinese prisoners, both badly wounded. Wishing to remain unburdened by prisoners, the sergeant asked for volunteers to shoot the two. Wills slunk away while two other young soldiers shot the prisoners. A few days later, on March 11, Wills's squad engaged in its first major fight. By late morning, the casualties had mounted and the ammunition carrier had become a machine gunner. He stepped in and performed well by drawing the fire of a hidden machine gun for his fellow Americans, who climbed the hill and killed the gunner with bayonets. However, Morris Wills's day would get worse. When a mortar round fell into the middle of his moving squad, half of the men were either killed or seriously wounded. The other half continued to move forward and when night fell, the men sat down where they were and remained there all night. The next morning, they were parched from having had no food or water the previous day, and descended the hill toward a stream. As he started to lean his machine gun against a bush, one of the others yelled, "Wills, look out!" and he recoiled. However, the damage was done and the trip-wired charge went off. The blast caught Wills in the left thigh and knee while it hit a few of the other men in their faces.[32]

In that brief second, Morris Wills thought he had been delivered from Korea; however, he would be disappointed. When medics arrived, they ripped Morris' pants leg up to the knee where they found a very serious wound. Having had a shot of morphine, he settled in for what would have otherwise been a painful stretcher ride out. The litter bearers delivered him to a Jeep driver who cautioned Wills that the road ahead was mined. His wound required surgery and the army evacuated him south, where he expected to be flown to Japan. By the time the train arrived, however, his leg was infected and doctors ordered him to a Swedish hospital, while the others went on to Japan. After surgery to remove the shrapnel, Wills remained with the Swedish unit recovering for more than a month. When the doctors cleared him to return to action, he was temporarily assigned to a replacement depot for several days awaiting transfer. While there, he ran into an old friend who was a guard at the depot. After talking for a while, Wills learned that there was a shortage of guards and he could ask to be assigned there instead of returning to the front lines. After inquiring about the transfer, he found himself in a first sergeant's antechamber waiting for the NCO to finish his telephone call, but destiny intervened; the NCO's attitude offended Wills, so he left and never went back.[33] On May 3, 1951, with only two months remaining before he would rotate out of Korea, Wills returned to a unit that looked far different from the one he had left. Over the next two weeks, he regained his machine-gunning skills in a couple of small battles, and on May 18, his company went into battle again, this time at Hill 755. It was late afternoon by the time Wills's company got dug in. His foxhole was just below the crest of the hill overlooking a little ridge. Across the ridge stood a small, but dense forest. Just as Wills was getting settled into his foxhole, a call went out that the Chinese were attacking and he grabbed his gun and went into action. Later, he remembered that the enemy charged his company's position five times throughout the night. In the middle of the night, the two machine gunners on top of the hill burned out their barrels and Wills was ordered to bring his gun up. However, by the time he started up, the Chinese had already moved onto the high ground and began firing down on him. Seemingly trapped between the hammer and the anvil, Wills's company was ordered to withdraw. The companies on each side had already fled the area and when the order was announced to the men of Company E, a free-for-all ensued. Wills grabbed his machine gun with one hand and pulled out a .45 pistol with the other to aid in his escape, but halfway down the hill, he ran into a small group of Chinese soldiers crossing the path in front of him. With no more than twelve feet separating them, Wills and the Chinese had what he described as "a fire fight . . . like one of those old western movies." He shot three or four of the enemy soldiers before they started throwing grenades at him. When one came right at him, he dove over a hill for cover, but the grenade followed, seemingly chasing him down the steep and rocky embankment. On the way down, the grenade went off behind Wills but he continued sliding and falling before finally settling in a heap at the bottom. Having lost his helmet, machine gun, and the clip out of the .45 on the way down, he began walking and quickly found his company forming a secondary line of defense. After spending an anxious night, the company set off marching and began climbing, ultimately finding themselves on top of a mountain. Wills had given his .45 away to a wounded man and picked up a rifle, but he and the others were not able to fight. They had been without sleep for three days and had neither food nor water for two days. Luckily for the Americans, an order came through withdrawing them back to the 38th parallel.[34]

Expecting to get some sleep and a hot meal, the men of Company E were disappointed. After they made it back to the road, they boarded trucks and realized they were being sent back to the line. As they motored toward the front, they passed retreating French soldiers who warned the Americans, "You're crazy going up there. You'll never get out again." Wills and the others climbed the same path that the French had retreated on and kept moving up the hill along winding paths not knowing what lay in front of them. Morris Wills recalled that along the path the advancing Americans ran into some more retreating Frenchmen and his squad leader fell in with the French and went back to the rear. By the time they reached the top of the hill, Wills was the squad leader, a position he would hold for about four hours.[35]

Once the Americans settled in, the Chinese attack came quickly. Wills recalled a horrible fight in which no one knew where anyone else was and soon he and the others found themselves surrounded on three sides. Having been told to remember the path in case a withdrawal was necessary, Morris grabbed his gear and high-tailed it down the hill as soon as a pull back was ordered. Scouting the path of retreat ahead of the litter bearers and other soldiers, he rounded a sharp curve in the dark and saw an Asian soldier standing in front of him. When the soldier extended his hand to Wills, the American relaxed expecting that the man he faced was South Korean. However, while shaking the soldier's hand, another stepped out of the bushes and took Wills' gun while a few others emerged holding Russian submachine guns. After disarming him, the Chinese led Morris Wills around the curve where a dozen other captured Americans sat.[36]

When Wills was captured, he was tired, hungry, and thirsty, and becoming a prisoner of war nearly pushed him over the edge. Sitting there with the other captives, Wills was nearly suicidal. As other soldiers held their hands above their heads, Morris just slumped not caring and ignoring the pleas of the others to keep his hands up. "I didn't care. If they want to shoot me, all right, shoot me, I don't care." Not long after, U.S. artillery began hitting their position and Wills remained sitting there wondering if death would be better than his current situation. He lived through that first night, however, and was marched by his captors back through his former regimental headquarters where the Americans had abandoned all their vehicles and other supplies. The Chinese wanted to salvage as much from the American encampment as possible so they put Wills and several other men behind the wheels of Jeeps and other vehicles to drive them north. Wills's elation at the prospect that he might be fortunate enough to drive rather than walk was short-lived as the first truck got stuck and the plan was abandoned.[37]

After the Chinese gathered all the prisoners and escorted them up the side of a mountain to spend the day, Wills remembered his intense hunger. The soldier next to him had an extra can of hamburger and was kind enough to give it to the nearly starving man. Nearly twenty years after the fact, Morris Wills remembered that can of meat: "I ate it bit by bit, spent about twenty minutes eating it." Something important happened on that hillside. Wills recalled, "We were all in a state of shock. We didn't know how much longer we were going to live. They might kill us, I thought. Or we might just die from lack of food. Or we might get killed by our own men. This was the beginning of the process by which we would lose all our standards." Later in the evening after their capture, the men were marched back down the hill and fed by the Chinese for the first time. At a small Korean house, the Chinese set up a wooden trough filled with a thick, hot, pinkish liquid. It was boiled sorghum, "like we fed cattle at home," and Wills filled his cup, getting about twenty grains along with the broth. For the next several weeks, this concoction served as the men's only food, although it sometimes included "a few weeds they had picked and cooked." After eating, the G.I.s were pushed into the small house for the rest of the evening.[38]

That night at about 10:00 P.M., the Chinese removed the men from the hut and started marching them north. By the next morning, their number had grown to about fifty men and the Chinese stopped them for the day. The men were fed more sorghum in the early dawn. They were hidden under the canopy of the trees by day and rousted out in the late evening to continue their march. Over time, the American column grew to about three hundred, with several armed Chinese guarding the men. Although marching at night partially obscured the men, they feared that the Chinese trucks that shared the road with them were likely to be targets of American planes. Whenever an air raid was called, the men dove for cover in the ditches and Wills looked for an opportunity to escape. None came, however, and he continued on toward the unknown destination.[39]

By mid-June, hunger and hopelessness were overtaking the men. Morris Wills remembered awaking every morning and finding two or three men dead. Although the Americans wanted to bury those who had died, the lack of food cost them the energy to do it. In addition to the dual enemies of starvation and exhaustion, the men had to watch as one after another of their number fell by the road and were never again seen. It was clear to Morris Wills that the Chinese had no interest in converting them to communism, just in getting them to the prisoner of war camp.[40]

In late June or early July, the group stopped for several days in an abandoned village that would become a temporary camp. Soon, they were on the road again and after many more miles they again settled temporarily. This time, they were living in an old Japanese mining camp, quite possibly the one dubbed "Death Valley" by the first groups of prisoners held there. In the mining camp, the men lived in barracks complete with wooden floors. Although the men were now sleeping in a shelter, their malnutrition persisted. As many as seven or eight were often found dead in the mornings; in retrospect, Morris Wills estimated that a full one-third of the prisoners died during the march. His own weight dropped to about 100 pounds, and that for a man who stood well over six feet tall. Wills noticed that the Americans tended to die easier than the others. Regarding the officer who led the Turkish prisoners as a "God," he noted that none of them died, to his knowledge. The British and Filipinos were also fairly well organized and died in fewer numbers.[41]

In August, the men were on the move again. This time their trek was even longer than before and Wills thought the mountains would never end. Again, they marched at night and frequently came under air attack, including one instance when the men ran into a railroad tunnel and the American planes kept attacking the openings hoping to bury the men alive. The farther north they went, the more Russian trucks they saw. When the Chinese army marched the men through the city of Sinuiju, on the Yalu River, they saw many North Koreans turned out to witness the spectacle. The prisoners finally arrived at Camp One, located in the extreme northwest corner of North Korea, near the Yalu, on October 8, 1951.[42]

Richard Tenneson's Story

At 6:00 A.M., on May 19, 1951, Richard Tenneson was taken prisoner by the Chinese People's Volunteers. On the same day that Morris Wills became a PW, Tenneson was with a group of American soldiers in full retreat south toward their lines. Anticipating that they were very close to friendly forces, or maybe even already behind the line, and with darkness enveloping them, the group settled in for the night. Early the next morning, they heard American tanks in full retreat and soon found themselves surrounded by Chinese infantrymen. As Tenneson and about fifty others were taken prisoner, they were informed that they were prisoners of the Chinese, who were their friends, and given pamphlets explaining how the American industrialists were the root cause of the war. Almost immediately, they were started on a meandering, and sometimes circular, march into Chinese-held territory that lasted nearly a month.[43]

On June 15, they arrived at a collection station called "The Pines," where they were exposed to Chinese indoctrination for the first time. They were told that South Korea had started the war and the theme of American industrialists perpetuating the conflict was continued. There, they wrote their first letters home, although the Chinese mailed very few of them. After only a week at "The Pines," the men were sent to another location, "Mining Camp," where they remained for about two and a half months. By the time they arrived at "Mining Camp," the group was malnourished, exhausted, and filthy.[44] They were perfect subjects for full-scale indoctrination.

Jack Dunn's Story

After being drafted into the army and finishing basic training, Jack Dunn found himself stationed at Fort Jackson, South Carolina. Still very close to his family, he sent cards and gifts frequently, in addition to making occasional trips home. His mother remembered that Jack would pile into a car with several of his army buddies and drive 500 miles north to Baltimore just to make a weekend visit. These trips were limited, though, as the army sent Dunn first to Seattle, and then to Japan.

Once in Japan, Dunn's unit did not have a chance to get comfortable. Within twenty-four hours, he and the others were en route to Korea. He arrived on June 1, 1951, with the 23rd Regiment, 2 Infantry Division, and was made a radioman. One of Dunn's fellow soldiers told his family that after only three weeks in Korea, "Jack was with a forward unit that was surrounded and cut off." When the lieutenant was wounded, each man began trying to escape through the closing enemy net. While the others tried to flee, Dunn remained behind with the lieutenant. Both were captured quickly and the lieutenant shot and killed. When Jack joined a group of prisoners on its march to a temporary holding camp, he found several of his friends, and witnessed one of them being shot.[45]

James Veneris's Story

After rejoining the army in September 1950, James Veneris found himself being rushed to the front as a replacement during the initial Chinese push. Arriving in the war zone in November, he spent the coming year fighting with the Second Infantry Division. The beleaguered unit had been the first to land at Pusan in the summer and by the time Veneris reported, it had already absorbed staggering punishment. Once the Chinese offensive was blunted in late November, the Second Division's position stabilized somewhat, but it remained at the forefront of the fighting for the duration of the war.

Throughout 1951, the Second remained active and engaged, and as the year progressed, it lost thousands of men to injury and capture. Significantly, the bulk of those men who joined Veneris in his refusal to return to the United States served in the Second. They included LaRance Sullivan, who was captured on November 25, 1950; Richard Corden, Otho Bell, Albert Belhomme, Aaron Wilson, Samuel Hawkins, and William White, all taken by the Chinese on November 30; Rufus Douglas, who was captured on New Year's Day 1951; Morris Wills and Richard Tenneson, both of whom became prisoners on May 18, 1951; John Dunn, taken on July 24; and Veneris, who, on December 1, was the last nonrepatriate captured. In all, more than half of the future nonrepatriates were veterans of the Second Infantry Division.

Three decades later, Veneris recalled that he was traveling north in a military convoy when the Chinese closed a trap around them. "The convoy stopped, it got dark, and then about 2 o'clock in the morning, I heard bugles blowing." At that point, the Chinese army attacked the trapped column in the darkness. Veneris and others escaped over nearby mountains and hid until hunger pushed them toward their enemy. Realizing "there was no way out and it was getting cold," he decided to surrender after watching the Chinese distribute food to their prisoners. After being temporarily housed in a hillside village, Veneris and the others were sent to permanent camps.[46]

Andrew Fortuna's Story

Of all the things that people said about Andrew Fortuna, they had to acknowledge the fact that he was an eager and effective combat soldier. Immediately after the Japanese attack on Pearl Harbor, fifteen-year-old Andrew joined the army, but was released when officials found out his real age. After waiting two and a half years, he enlisted again, this time on June 7, 1944, the day after D-Day. By the end of the year, he was in the Rhineland fighting the last phase of Operation Market Garden, and early in 1945, he participated in the campaign for central Europe. In 1946, he left the army and returned to Detroit, where he got work in an automobile factory. He worked there for six months before being laid off and then drove trucks and operated heavy equipment for a year to make ends meet. With the postwar economy tightening in 1948, he rejoined the army, and as a World War II veteran, could wear the Combat Infantry Badge, Good Conduct Medal, and World War II Victory Medal.[47]

In the summer of 1948, the army moved Fortuna from Fort Lawton, Washington, briefly to Alaska, and finally to the 5th Cavalry Regiment, then in Japan. Shortly after his arrival, he fell in love with a Japanese woman and married her. The two produced a son, but when the baby died of polio, the marriage broke up. As a peacetime soldier, Andrew ran into trouble when he misappropriated a military truck and was court martialed in November 1949. The board convicted him, ordered a forfeiture of nearly $50 a month for six months, and confined him at hard labor for the same amount of time. By the summer of 1950, he was bound for Korea.[48]

Once on the ground, Fortuna was assigned to an intelligence and reconnaissance platoon for his regiment. He and the others scouted ahead of the main force, probing to find the enemy by "going up and down every hill in Korea." In November 1951, he found himself north of the Chong-Song River, about ten miles ahead of the American position, when his group was ambushed by the Chinese. He was among eleven Americans captured.

While the preceding accounts are individual and seemingly unrelated, the larger circumstances of these men's captures merit attention. Five of the six were model soldiers up to the point of their capture and none of them exhibited cowardice in battle. Each also witnessed what he interpreted at the time, and has since been confirmed, a poorly coordinated American military effort. Coupled with a seemingly invincible enemy in the Chinese, each man entered captivity bewildered at the strength of the enemy and the apparent weakness of his own military forces.

THREE

Captivity and Compromise

> "This gentlemen, is the new duress. It isn't brainwashing, it never was. No drugs were used. No attempt was made to eradicate the mind. But every device was used to make it suffer. In Captain Hall we have a strong man whose combat record shows him capable of standing immense physical pain without giving an inch, yet the same man had no chance when forced to undergo a program of confession and mental agony. This program worked in stages. First, you create an atmosphere of terror and uncertainty, then you take away the leaders, tear down health and morale, infiltrate the ranks with informers and when you can't get informers, spread the word that you've got them anyhow, turn an army into a nightmare school and the soldiers into small boys who depend on you for childish rewards and punishments. Make them all lonely and distrustful, then pick out the loneliest and go to work on him. Make him think that you alone hold the power to forgive. Then find the personal hidden key, and once you've found it, turn it hard. Every one of us has that key."
>
> —Edmond O'Brien in *The Rack* (1956)

For the soldiers who became wards of their enemies in late 1950, the reality proved worse than a nightmare. While starvation, disease, and ill-treated wounds steadily sapped their physical strength, the wanton disregard for their condition weakened them spiritually. Within weeks, many of those who had been only a short time before the steadiest of soldiers, began a steep descent into the ultimate form of pragmatism. Each had to decide whether he would remain loyal to the principles of his military duty or save his own life. While many men withstood the pressures placed on them by their captors and the torturous conditions of their imprisonment, a sizable number, possibly more than half of those taken early in the fighting, compromised themselves in the hopes of survival.

The process of indoctrination began at the first moment of captivity. Many American soldiers reported that upon being taken prisoner, they were offered handshakes and cigarettes by the Chinese. The Americans had heard horror

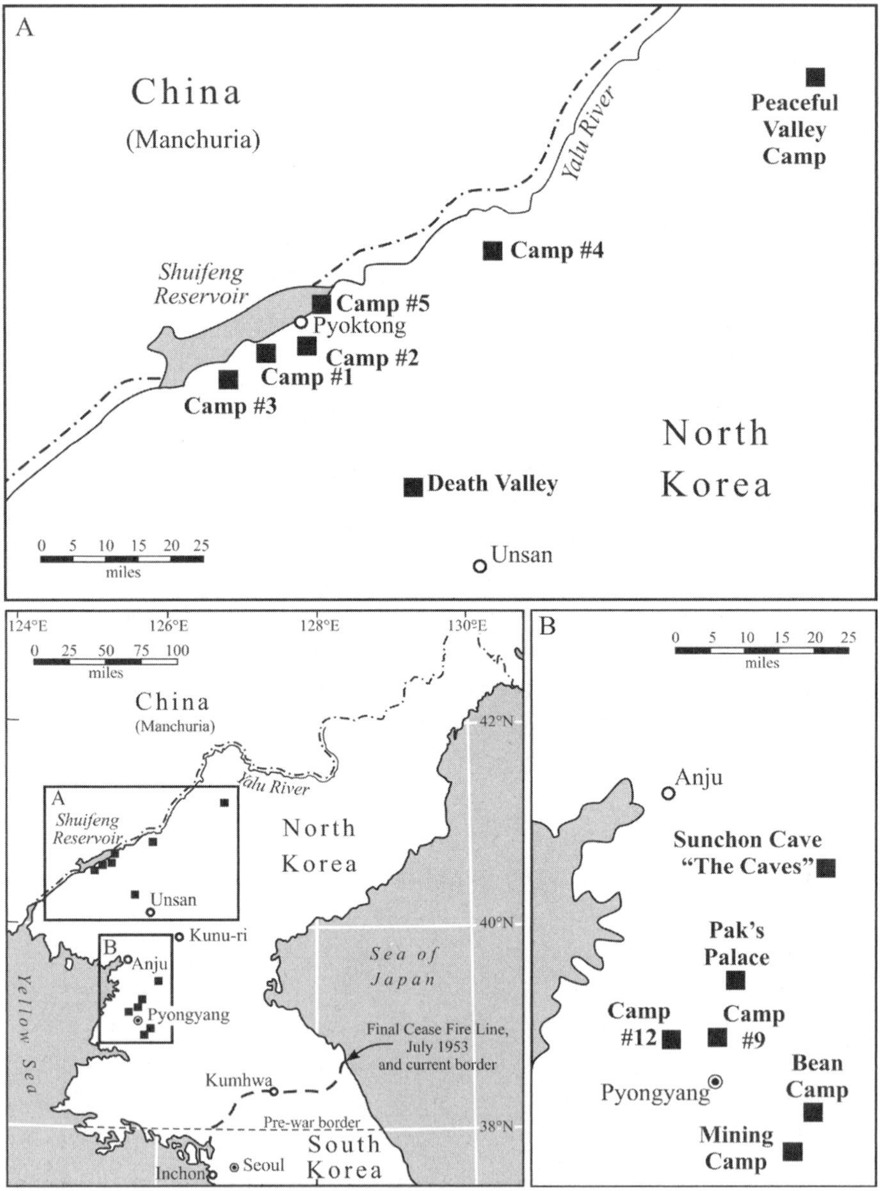

stories about indiscriminate killings by North Koreans who considered prisoners of war to be burdensome, and so they were relieved to receive such a greeting instead. Once captured, the prisoners would be asked innocuous questions with which any logical person would agree, such as "Are you for peace?" The Chinese would then begin collecting information about the men and testing their level of commitment.[1]

Suddenly having thousands of American PsW presented the Chinese army with a significant challenge in finding a place to house them. Not wishing to keep their prisoners so close to the front lines, the Chinese began hurriedly building permanent camps near the Yalu River. However, building these camps, however primitive, would take time, so the Chinese began marching their captives northward. During these death marches mortality rates skyrocketed. The first stop for those men captured in the initial Chinese onslaught in November 1950 was one of the many temporary camps set up to hold them until more permanent facilities could be prepared. Records indicate that the first temporary camps were established immediately after the first prisoners were taken near Unsan, meaning that Edward Dickenson, Lowell Skinner, and Claude Batchelor were among the initial group to be sent to a temporary camp known as the "Valley."[2]

Valley Camp was located only ten miles south of the Yalu River and primarily housed men of the First Cavalry Division who had borne the brunt of the Chinese offensive. Initially, 200–300 men who had been captured near Unsan were held there, but over the coming days and weeks, that number grew to about 1,000. Because of wounds, malnutrition, poor living conditions, and the lack of appropriate medical care, an estimated 50–70 percent of those interned at the Valley died before it was closed after only two months.[3] Easily the most dangerous of the temporary camps, Valley Camp's mortality rates were astonishing. Interestingly, the Valley, along with several other prison camps, had no real restraints other than armed guards. Instead, the prisoners were held in the valley by a combination of inhospitable terrain, terrible weather, and debilitating malnutrition.[4] Repatriated prisoners reported that the weather was so cold at Valley Camp that dead bodies were stacked in the open waiting for a thaw that would allow them to be buried.[5]

The poor conditions in Valley Camp, combined with its intentionally weak organization, allowed the Americans to become wholly self-interested and individualistic. The North Koreans initially controlled the camp, but during December, the Chinese moved in and took charge of the prisoners. Neither the North Koreans nor the Chinese organized a formal structure other than dividing the men between officers, enlisted, and wounded, with basic squads to ease management. As a result of their captivity and the absence of order, many of the men devolved into a state of savagery in which it was easier to banish a sick man to the elements than to help him survive. To augment this controlled chaos, the Chinese administrators further undermined military discipline by declaring that American military rank no longer existed. Many of the enlisted men eagerly accepted the order as a way to reject those officers they had either resented before their capture or considered ultimately responsible for their situation. Shortly after the beginning of the year, the foundation for breaking down the men and rebuilding them in accordance with the wishes of the Chinese was established and the men of Valley Camp were moved to the newly created Camp Five at Pyoktong.[6]

Most of the men who were captured from the middle to the end of November in the vicinity of Kunu-Ri were held at a new temporary camp called "Death Valley." Considerably larger than Valley Camp, Death Valley held nearly 2,000 prisoners at its height, most of whom had served with the Second Infantry Division during the Battle of the Chongchon River. The bulk of those later nonrepatriates was captured during the late November actions. Those who endured the deprivations of Death Valley included Richard Corden, Otho Bell, Scott Rush, LaRance Sullivan, Albert Belhomme, Aaron Wilson, Samuel Hawkins, William White, Harold Webb, and Clarence Adams.[7]

Death Valley was an old World War II–era Japanese mining camp located in very mountainous terrain about fifteen miles northeast of Anju-Sinanju. There, the men found exceedingly harsh conditions, which claimed an estimated 40 percent of the prisoner population; the remaining prisoners reacted similarly to those at Valley Camp. Dr. William Shadish, a prisoner of war in Death Valley, estimated, "100% of us had dysentery at one time or another; 100% were suffering from severe weight loss; 100% suffered cold injury, 15% of whom suffered tissue loss; 25 to 30 prisoners developed infectious hepatitis in February 1951, and 50% of them died; 100 to 150 contracted pneumonia and very few survived; nutritional edema began to develop during the latter part of February 1951." Conditions were so bad that of five army doctors in the camp, only Shadish and one other survived the brief, but horrifying ordeal. Although Death Valley operated for only three months during the harsh winter of 1950–51, it became the final resting place for hundreds of American soldiers.[8]

As at Valley Camp, the men at Death Valley lived in severely overcrowded conditions and were severely undernourished. Later, the men would recall being covered with lice, sleeping in such crowded quarters that the entire room had to be awakened in order for a single man to turn over, and the slow death of diarrhea caused by a diet wholly consisting of ten ounces of cracked corn each day. In bovines, cracked corn is digested through four stomachs; in humans, it largely passes through the body undigested. Although the camps had huts for the men to live in and each hut had a stove, very little firewood was available and usually each room held twenty to thirty men. The overcrowded conditions required some of the squads to sleep in shifts.[9] By the end of February, the men who had survived the ordeal of Death Valley were moved into permanent camps.

Apparently used as an experimental camp, Peaceful Valley, or Camp 10 as it was formally known, held about 300 men captured during the fighting near the Chosin Reservoir during the first week of December 1950. Moved north toward the Chinese border, the camp was in the city of Kanggye. Although no confirmation exists, Arlie Pate may have been held at Peaceful Valley.[10] The conditions the men there experienced were vastly different from those visited on their comrades in the other camps. They enjoyed very good living conditions in comparison to the men in the other camps and a relatively low mortality rate, but had to sit through indoctrination lessons in repayment. The Chinese administered the camp and the men imprisoned there noted that their captors welcomed them as "liberated 'brothers-in-arms.'" By the time Peaceful Valley was closed in late March 1951, the indoctrination efforts had gleaned considerable results as a sizable group of PsW had been willing converts and become known as "The Workers." That month, as a way to begin their indoctrination, several of them were taken south to speak with newly captured UN soldiers about the treatment they could expect from their captors. The Chinese army took nineteen of the men, eighteen of whom were Marines, to the front lines where they allowed the men to escape back to the American lines with propaganda materials.[11]

Valley Camp, Death Valley, and Peaceful Valley were the largest temporary camps, although several, smaller sites existed. Bean Camp and Mining Camp were located farther south than the others and was used until October 1951 as a way station for northbound U.N. prisoners. Together, the camps held about 1,900 men in conditions similar to those at Valley Camp and Death Valley and the mortality rate was about 25 percent.[12]

Although the men did not realize the broad implications of their condition, the Chinese had already begun their indoctrination process. As outlined by William Sargant in *Battle for the Mind,* the first phase was establishing a perpetual state of exhaustion. Taking advantage of starvation, the bitterly cold winter of 1950–51, the long laborious march to the permanent camps, and the general anxiety accompanying imprisonment at the hands of one's enemy, the Chinese very quickly broke the prisoners down into desperate individuals who saw no hope for their futures other than the charity of their captors. After the prisoners had generally given up hope, the indoctrination phase began, in which large blocks of time each day were set aside for study. Just as the first phase produced a physical weakening and exhaustion, the second phase exhausted the mind. At this point, the captors classified the men either as potential converts or hopeless resisters. The next phase was that of crisis. The potential converts found themselves under increasing pressure while those deemed reactionary were generally left alone. After several months of this treatment, those who continued to be targets of indoctrination would eventually break down. Richard Walker wrote that invariably the first man breaks and often does so "with hysteria and sobbing at night." The next day, the behavior either continues or is restarted in one of the small group meetings and often "launches a chain reaction" among other members of the group, some of whom become "babbling maniacs." In conflict with what many people considered strong American values, Walker found that those who were cynical or had good senses of humor were least likely to be affected while the very emotional and the deeply religious were often the first to break. At this point, called "tail-cutting," the person's old priorities—family, friends, spiritual beliefs, social beliefs—are replaced with new information. Suddenly, the communist jargon that had peppered the early phases of the indoctrination process became meaningful to the men and began to define their new lives in accordance with the wishes of their captors.[13]

Morris Wills's personal experiences corroborated Sargant's theoretical explanation:

> Every value and standard he had ever had was crushed. There was very little food, the place was dirty, and lice infested and no one ever took baths. The men wore their clothing until they fell off their backs. It was also apparent that the Chinese were poor and had little to give their prisoners. In the beginning there were rumors among the prisoners that they would be rescued but after a while inmates lost hope. Some just simply gave up and died. Others, like Wills, who were living in a psychological vacuum, and who felt deserted by the United States, found their frustration turning into anger and their depression turning into revolt. There was nothing to do in camp except read. Wills was young and idealistic. The steady diet of Marx, Engels, and the *Daily Worker* with which he was fed made an impression and intensified his feelings. As he said, "It all looked great on paper," and he became sympathetic.[14]

The same concepts of indoctrination that scholars like Sargant explained in their works were lived by those men who suffered through the PW experience.

In early 1951, the UN PsW began being moved into permanent camps. The first camp was at Pyoktong, where 400 to 600 men from Valley Camp arrived in January. The remainder came from Death Valley and Peaceful Valley, those from the latter likely mixed in with the general population to assist in indoctrination efforts. This would become known as Camp Five and serve as the general headquarters for the Chinese PW program. It was the largest of the Chinese prisoner of war camps, holding about 3,500 prisoners at its peak.[15]

Notably, conditions did not necessarily improve in the permanent camps. It is estimated that during the first months of 1951, Camp Five had a 50 percent mortality rate, equal to if not worse than those of Valley Camp and Death Valley. Camp Seven was opened shortly afterward and held those men not able to fit into Camp Five. Over the course of the coming months, several such permanent camps were built by the Chinese. Camp One was built in the spring of 1951 and Camp Three, a Reactionary camp where prisoners resistant to communism were held, in the fall, both serving the purpose of managing the overflow of undesirables from Camp Five. Camp Two was established in October 1951 to segregate officers. Camp Four came into being in August 1952 and segregated non-commissioned officers. Over the late spring and summer of 1951, conditions slowly began to improve.[16]

Clarence Adams was among the first men to arrive at Camp Five. When he and about five hundred others walked into a hastily organized camp on December 10, 1950, they expected warm food and comfortable buildings, as the communists had promised. However, they found entirely different conditions. Recalling that there were "no hot meals, no beds, no blankets, and no medicine," he and twenty-four other PsW were assigned to a single eight-by-ten foot hut. In such quarters, the men had to improvise their living arrangements. Since "there was not enough space for everyone to lie down, our legs would stretch over each other's chests. The air smelled so bad that when it was my [Adams's] turn to lie down, I put my nose to a small hole in the wall to get some fresh air."[17]

Once inside Camp Five, Adams began noticing the terrible condition of his comrades. During the march, starvation had been the norm, but the men expected that to change once they reached a permanent camp. However, at Camp Five, the poor conditions continued and Adams witnessed hundreds of deaths. He recalled that the first to die were the men who had been marching with untreated wounds. The weeks of malnutrition had taken a severe toll on many others, resulting in their deaths. Then, disease began carrying the already emaciated men away. With that initial purge of the weak and wounded, the remaining prisoners slipped into an existence only degrees from outright death with most of them hovering around ninety pounds. Adams recalled that all of the men were suffering from severe dysentery and the entire camp was covered in human excrement. To remedy this, some of the men had dug a slit trench and placed logs on each side to sit on. One day, a fellow fell backward into the latrine and lay there interminably as "no one had the strength to pull him out." The men "were too weak to do much of anything" and as a result, many froze to death when they collapsed in the snow or ate unclean snow trying to get water.[18] In that first winter, the daily death rate stood at between twenty and thirty men in the larger camps. In Camp Five, from January through March 1951, an estimated 1,500 men died.[19]

Overlooking Camp Five. Prisoners of war looked at China across the Yalu River every day. The cramped nature of the camp is apparent, with most of the living quarters huddled together and other facilities surrounding them. (Courtesy of the National Park Service, Andersonville National Historical Site, ANDE 3572)

Sanitation committees organized by the Chinese tried to alleviate some of the problems. Lewie Griggs was a member of such a committee with the duty of ensuring that every member of his squad killed their fair share of flies each day. One prisoner remembered that Griggs's "job consisted mainly of counting the flies that each POW killed and keeping the count on a roster."[20] In the tradition of Maoist China, the prisoners acted together to fight problems.

Although many former prisoners of war recalled starvation-level rations, evidence suggests that the food provided to the prisoners was adequate to maintain life. Eugene Kinkead's study of the Korean prisoner of war experience found that the regular army ration contained about 3,500 calories, but at its lowest level, prisoners were fed 1,200 calories per day, a ration probably exceeding that of the regular Chinese soldier. So few calories will result in dramatic weight loss, but not starvation. Complicating matters was the kind of food available. Initially, North Koreans fed the men cracked corn and millet boiled until soft enough to eat and an occasional handful of soybeans. When the Chinese took over responsibilities for the UN prisoners in late 1950 and early 1951, the Americans complained that the soybeans caused diarrhea. Once the Chinese relented and took the soybeans away, the prisoners lost much of the protein in their diet.[21] A State Department white paper written from the accounts of returned American prisoners found that while Americans considered the harsh diet given them by their captors as "unappetizing and perhaps even repugnant," it was reasonably nutritious and was likely the same type of food fed to the Chinese troops. The paper's author confessed that the meager food was "probably all the Chinese had to offer." One returned prisoner remembered that an early meal given to the men consisted of a thick soup made of fish heads and rice. Despite their hunger, many of the men refused to even taste it.[22] Kinkead wrote that the prisoners "seemed to be waiting, wistfully and unrealistically, for the arrival of American chow."[23]

As a result of the malnutrition, captive Americans suffered significant medical problems. An examination of 68 of the first Americans to be repatriated during the later stages of the war revealed that 100 percent suffered significant weight loss. The subject of one case study claimed to have weighed 140 pounds at the time of his capture and estimated that his weight fell to under 100 pounds during the first months of captivity. By the time they were released in the Spring of 1953, the group's general health had improved dramatically, yet 94.1 percent of the men remained underweight, averaging 24.6 pounds lost, probably about 20 percent of the average soldier's weight, and 81 percent suffered from infestation of intestinal parasites. The returning PsW suffered edema of the legs at a rate of 27.9 percent. This painful retention of fluid in the lower extremities resulted from a protein insufficiency. Atrophic tongue, caused by a vitamin B-12 deficiency, afflicted 48.5 percent of the returnees and resulted from a diet devoid of red meat. Normally, the lack of B-12 takes at least two years to manifest serious symptoms, but due to their long-term captivity, the men began suffering from the tongue ailment in addition to an irregular gait and memory loss. Diminished vision, including night blindness, affected 36.8 percent of the men. This was largely due to their lack of vitamin A. It can also be assumed that their sleep deficiency resulted in lowered testosterone, and some of the long-term heart problems the men suffered from, including the one that possibly killed Rufus Douglas in 1954, came from a lingering vitamin B-1 deficiency.[24]

One of the central problems Americans faced as captives of the Chinese was that they did not understand the differences between the cultures. Many prisoners considered the food they were given to be unfit for human consumption, while the Chinese felt themselves to be good hosts by providing for the prisoners so well. The open trench latrines that the Chinese people used in their daily lives were so humiliating to the Americans that some of the men called them "fiendish tortures."[25]

Interestingly, Kinkead used Turkish prisoners as his example of men who effectively withstood the Chinese torture and remained loyal to their government. He noted that one central difference between the Turks and the Americans was the willingness of the former to come together as a group for the common good, including mutual defense and the sharing of all rations equally. While this was true and played a major role in saving the Turks from the sufferings endured by the Americans, Kinkead's argument neglects the state of politics in the United States at the time. In holding up the Turks as the exemplar for survival, he is suggesting that American PsW, who, like most Americans during the 1950s, were terrified of communism and its communal lifestyle, should have embraced that which they were in Korea fighting against. For a man writing toward the end of the McCarthy era, Kinkead failed to see the irreconcilability between the philosophy and reality of captivity.[26] Major William Mayer, an army psychiatrist, felt the same way and noted the same weaknesses. Mayer said that American PsW employed an "every man for himself" attitude, but failed to see the American individualistic and capitalistic basis of such an outlook.[27]

Claude Batchelor made it to Camp Five about a month after Adams. Although still living at near starvation levels, he remembered that food became easier to get because Pyoktong was so far to the rear. When his squad settled into their hut, they found that the fireplace was dilapidated and would not hold a fire. Initially, Batchelor had his squad's food cooked in the kitchen of the squad across the street, but soon realized that his men were being shortchanged on their food. He and his men then set to work on their fireplace and flue and in short order, had their own kitchen established.[28]

Clarence Adams also remembered the food situation. Although his fellow soldiers elected the company's "spoon man," his starving comrades watched like a hawk every time he ladled out the day's grain ration. Each day, the men would get a cup of hot water and about a quarter cup of corn, beans, or sorghum. Most men ate every unpalatable grain, but a few tried to save part of their food to eat later. Adams remembered that this was not a good idea because "once it became dark, those who did not give a damn would steal anything they could get their hands on."[29] Miraculously, thousands of men lived in these conditions for more than two years.

The conditions that the captured Americans endured drove many of them into an animalistic state. Operating at near starvation levels, the men only had enough energy to care for themselves, and their moral direction adjusted to the dire circumstances. Clarence Adams propped corpses up in his hut to get additional rations of food until their condition was visibly apparent.[30] Dr. William Shadish recalled that he and his staff "would keep four or five dead bodies in the hospital as long as we could so we could get more rations."[31] Adams also observed, "We would fight viciously for any scrap of food and strip the dead of their clothing, boots, and anything else that might help the rest of us survive."[32] Ted Sprouse affirmed Adams's sentiments when he recalled hearing a struggle outside of his hut and finding a frozen man the next morning. The man was too sick and weak to go to the latrine and when he defecated on himself inside, someone threw him out into the cold.[33] These conditions desensitized the men. One repatriate remembered, "At first, when a buddy died, I'd get very upset and not talk to anyone for days. But after it happened so many times, I didn't seem to care—and I wouldn't feel anything."[34]

Further undermining traditional military authority and camp camaraderie was the rise of open homosexuality among a small, but visible element of the prisoners. Leonard "Lucky" Bell had a steady boyfriend, but was not monogamous in his relationship, and was known to perform sexual favors for a variety of the men in the camp. Bell's behavior was controversial and evoked hostility from many straight soldiers. He reportedly took "all his clothes off except his underwear and socks and paraded around the room, acting and trying to sing like a girl." A white soldier named Copeland "was really a 'Queer', as he let his hair grow and curled it like a girl."[35]

As the winter of 1950–1951 wore on, living conditions further deteriorated. Some of the wounded men were still lingering, but their existence was becoming burdensome to the others. One day a soldier became frustrated with the stench coming from the legs of a badly wounded man he slept next to and began "kicking his wounded legs." That night, Clarence Adams heard a scuffle in the darkness and when he awoke the next morning, the wounded man had died and an unknown attacker had killed the man's tormentor from the previous day.[36]

For Clarence Adams, that spring became his turning point. When the ground began to thaw, he and several others started digging for roots. After much experimentation, he found several and continued to supplement his meager rations throughout the season. However, he also began to realize that frostbite was going to take his right foot if he did not act against it. With the ends of his toes having turned black, he decided that he had to amputate them if he was to survive. Taking the metal arch out of one of his boots, he sharpened it and settled on the plan. With the improvised knife, Adams "scraped my toes to the bone. Then I counted to ten and cut two of them off at a time. Actually, I counted to ten about twenty times. I'd keep telling myself, 'Just count to ten and do it.' But when I'd get to ten, I'd start over again. Finally, I put the knife where I figured the joint was, counted to ten one last time, looked away, and cut the toes off at the joint."[37] After the trauma of amputating his own toes, the weather moderated and the food improved. Within months, Clarence Adams began to think he might survive his ordeal.

Edward Dickenson also broke under the strain of captivity and starvation. John A. Davis remembered meeting Dickenson in February 1951. At the time, Dickenson was serving as a cook and, as Davis claimed, shortchanging the men on their food and trading what he held back for cigarettes and candy. Although Dickenson did cook for his squad, Davis's allegations are questionable. Identifying Dickenson as a cook is correct, but placing him as the cook in Camp Five's sick compound is dubious since the entire camp, at that time, was essentially a sick bay covered with human excrement. Also, alleging that Dickenson would withhold food is logical, but to claim that he would trade the food for candy is curious considering Dickenson, whose weight dropped to under 100 pounds during this part of his captivity, desperately needed the very food he was allegedly trading. Since starvation was rampant at that time, Davis's story would have been much more convincing if he had accused Dickenson of eating the food himself.[38]

A second, even more damning, allegation involved Dickenson violently attacking a sick man, ultimately causing his death. Davis stated that he witnessed Dickenson refuse a sick man food, which resulted in a heated argument. "Dickenson thereupon slapped this man and shoved him backwards out the door, causing him to fall down two or three stair steps, to the ground." Other prisoners picked the man up and took him to his room, "but he was unable to move his legs due to the fall." Davis later learned that the man was recovering from the fall, but was taken to the sick ward where he died.[39] Davis's story is problematic. Of the 3,500 men in Camp Five, no other prisoners made a single allegation of violence against Dickenson nor did any man corroborate the story, which, as Davis told it, was a very public incident. Additionally, Steve Glowacki, who worked in the kitchen at the same time as Dickenson and testified against him at his court martial, failed to mention anything suggestive of such an event taking place.[40]

Harvey Mitchell remembered a similar story about LaRance Sullivan. He said that while at Death Valley, Sullivan was in charge of dispensing food to his squad. Mitchell recalled that Sullivan would deliver the food, but then take some that he had held back and sell it to men in other squads. He also reported that Sullivan and another man had beaten a sick prisoner. The man was left lying on the floor and reportedly died two days later. Apart from Mitchell, no one else recalled the story.[41] Overall, such accusations, while possibly truthful, were very difficult to verify and ultimately prove.

In spring, once the weather and rations had improved, the Chinese began redefining the nature of captivity. Emboldened by their successful indoctrination of the PsW at Peaceful Valley, the Chinese began organizing captivity around ideological conversion, with Camp Five serving as the central station. The men had been interrogated while they were still in the temporary camps, but these interrogations had been irregular and somewhat amateurish. However, once the men moved into the permanent camps, the sessions became much more organized and ideologically structured. William Shadish remembered the Chinese approach as "If you do not do what we ask, we will not feed you, and you will die here."[42] Robert J. Lifton, a former U.S. Air Force psychiatrist, identified the Korean War PW experience as having a first phase of physical deprivation and a second of emotional abuse. At the point that prisoners passed through the first phase and were well into the second, the process of "brainwashing," or indoctrination, could begin by isolating the prisoner, limiting his independence of thought, and reprogramming him politically.[43]

Indoctrination efforts began at Camp Five in early February 1951. Lectures focused on the leniency of the Chinese captors and on hygiene. Claude Batchelor recalled how Lin, an instructor who would earn the moniker "Screaming

Skull," conducted the first session: he got up on a mound of dirt and began chastising the men because the ground was covered in feces. Many of the men were stricken with diarrhea and dysentery and could not make it to the latrines, so the camp quickly became a morass of human excrement. Lin also encouraged the men to get out and exercise as many only left the barracks to use the latrine. Within days, the Chinese instituted a policy requiring morning exercise formations and established patrols to make the men clean up their own misplaced waste.[44]

The Chinese also began selecting a few men to circulate peace petitions among the prisoner population. The first was dated February 1, 1951, and condemned the United Nations for inflicting suffering on the innocent civilian population of Korea. The four hundred petitioners ran the gamut from later Reactionaries to Progressives and included three future nonrepatriates: Belhomme, Fortuna, and Veneris. The list also included Bohus Janda, who would later agree to testify against Batchelor. The second petition was dated February 11, 1951, and was signed by 279 prisoners. It called for an immediate end to the war and the public acknowledgment of Western complicity in starting it. At the time both petitions were being circulated, those men who signed were most certainly teetering on the edge of starvation and were living among scores of dead and dying men. In scanning the list of the signatures, one notes that only one nonrepatriate, the Scotsman, Andrew Condron, signed his name, as did the famous news photographer Frank Noel, who would later befriend Claude Batchelor; and Franklin Barrett, who would later testify against Edward Dickenson.[45]

The willingness of nearly seven hundred prisoners to sign such petitions may be viewed with skepticism by modern readers, but such behavior must be considered alongside the difficult circumstances the men endured. Claude Batchelor remembered that from January through May 1951, "the maral [morale] of the men was extraordinarily low." In addition to those who refused to leave the huts, others began to sell food and cigarettes. He noted that Harold Webb was one of the offenders who could get ten dollars for a bowl of food and one or two dollars for a pack of cigarettes. Batchelor, having been elected squad leader, lamented the fact that the men had become malingerers who would rather feign sickness than help bury the bodies of their dead compatriots. "As a result much of the work was piled on the shoulders of comparatively few men" forcing a handful of willful men to "sweep, cut wood, do details, etc."[46]

Postwar studies threw more light on the extent of collaboration. J. A. C. Brown found that 13 percent of PsW were "frank collaborators" while the same percentage occupied the opposite end of the scale as Reactionaries.[47] Julius Segal's research on army repatriates found that 70 percent "made at least one contribution to the enemy's propaganda effort." Of this group, 39 percent signed petitions, 22 percent made propaganda recordings, 16 percent held full time jobs as propagandists, 11 percent wrote newspaper articles, 5 percent drafted the petitions, and 5 percent circulated the petitions.[48]

On April 1, 1951, all of Camp Five's prisoners were gathered together for their introduction to the newly filled prison camp. After the prisoners filed in, a dozen or more Chinese administrators entered, including several who would become the camp's main interrogators. One stepped forward and began speaking to the group. Wong was bright, spoke perfect English, and had a penchant for pornography, which earned him the nickname "Dirty Pictures" once the prisoners found out. As Wong spoke, the prisoners paid little attention, preferring instead to talk among themselves and shower Wong with catcalls. Wong erupted:

> You are the aggressors and if you don't accept the lenient policy and change your views, we have dug a hole which we are going to throw you in. You capitalist warmongers do stink. We are quite right in burying you. A person who does not accept our doctrine is not a human being because he is not for the masses and a man that is not for the masses does not deserve treatment any better than you give an animal. As an animal, we have a right to eliminate you. You will learn the truth and we don't care if it takes one year, two years, ten years, twenty years; we don't care if you die here because we will bury you and bury you deep so you won't stink.

Wong's point was well taken, particularly in light of the amount of death they had witnessed in the preceding months, and a pall fell over the crowd. From that point on, the men understood the seriousness of their plight. Not only would they have to survive, their captors would attempt to make their minds the price to be paid.[49]

Within days, the lectures began and the Chinese started allowing marginally more food. Claude Batchelor considered the food improved, "but still insufficient as far as nourishment was concerned."[50] It is estimated that the initial rate of 1,200 calories per day doubled at this point; a level that would remain steady for the remainder of their captivity.[51] However, as the food increased, the Chinese expected more from the men. "We had to go to the lectures unless too sick and the Chinese knew that several men were playing sick and if a fellow didn't lo[o]k sick to the instructor he went regardless."

Although Batchelor would be condemned for being a Progressive who was open to the communist message rather than joining the Reactionary group, in his mind, those who malingered and resisted made life rough on legitimately ill men who were forced to attend lectures by Chinese officials who had grown paranoid of prisoner motives.[52]

During the initial indoctrination sessions, conversion was difficult. The message continued to focus on the lenient treatment policy of the Chinese and accusations that the U.S. armed forces had maligned the peaceful Chinese people during their military training. However, few men actually paid attention to the lectures, mainly because of their poor physical condition. Early on, "there were only two people . . . that cooperated with the Chinese and claimed to believe their policy." Batchelor identified the men as John Moore, who would later testify against him, and Allen Robertson. Both men were assistant platoon leaders and Batchelor remembered that "[o]ne of them did a lot of blackmarketing."[53]

Otho Bell also traded on the black market. In addition to receiving better clothing and medical treatment than the other prisoners, Bell dealt some of his surpluses to the highest bidder. Donald Lever recalled that Bell "sold a G.I. [a] spoonful of sugar . . . for $25.00 and on another occasion sold a pack of cigarettes for $50.00 to another prisoner." Bell would also apparently take advantage of suffering prisoners. Lever remembered that Bell "once sold a bowl of pork to a prisoner named Miller," who was deceased by the time of Lever's recollection. Lever claimed that "Miller reportedly paid Bell $1,000.00 for this bowl of pork," which may or may not have been true considering the large amount of money claimed.[54] Charles Durrah witnessed Bell's food thefts during the direst days of captivity: "Between January 1951 and March 1951, during a pneumonia epidemic, I saw Bell on several occasions steal food from sick POW's in the hospital . . . where I was working." He told investigators, "On one occasion during this time . . . I saw Bell sell some of the food he had stolen from the sick POW's to a fellow POW, David Woods of St. Louis, Missouri." While enhancing his own comfort, Bell's behavior had ramifications for the others. Durrah said that to make up for the seeming food shortage, the first squad saw their rations cut in half for three weeks. During this time, "POW's Oliver Stoney and John Perry, of my squad, died. I do not think they would have died if the food ration was not reduced."[55]

Early in the process, the Chinese began to further formalize their technique. Interpreters came around to the squads asking everyone about their education level, military service, and jobs they had, both military and civilian.

A few days later, the Chinese came back and named squad leaders and monitors. Batchelor was chosen monitor, although no reason was given, and began a three-day indoctrination session for his new job. As monitor, he attended lectures like everyone else, took notes, and then returned to his squad where he would lead discussions based on the day's material. Every day, he had to report to headquarters where he would discuss the progress of the lesson with the platoon instructor. One of the fringe benefits of his position came in the form of tobacco. At headquarters, tobacco was given away freely and Batchelor and the other monitors would "take it back to our squads where everyone [*sic*] of our 11 men would get a couple of drags on each cigarette."[56]

As monitor, Batchelor trod a fine line between following the orders of the Chinese and maintaining his loyalty to the squad. In regard to the discussions he was forced to lead, he explained how he and the others half-heartedly fulfilled the requirements of the Chinese. During these discussions, the men would criticize themselves for stealing some small article in the past or even having thoughts of theft. Batchelor took notes and the discussions faded until an authority figure appeared, at which point the men could rely on the notes to affirm that they had been faithfully discussing their past weaknesses. "This always seemed to impress him and he would give a short talk on the evils of stealing and escaping and then let us alone." Shrewdly, Batchelor, as well as others, often used the preconceptions held by the communists against them. When a platoon instructor asked why the men did not discuss politics, "We told him we didn't understand politics and didn't know [what] to say concerning it." The platoon leader responded, "this was the capitalist way of thinking and the capitalists used this to take advantage of our, The working class's, ignorance to deceive us."[57]

Shortly after the formal lectures began, Batchelor's squad got into trouble for picking lice rather than studying the lesson at hand. The Chinese brought the men to a vacant lot where they ordered the men to study. After three hours, the instructor returned and asked if they had discussed the information. Now frustrated, the men "were getting pretty well fed [up] at having to listen [to] all this stuff about our Govt. . . . we were fed [up] with the treatment we were getting so we decided to tell this Chinese just how we thought about this entire business." Batchelor threatened to quit as monitor and the group collectively vented on the instructor. After dismissing the men, the Chinese instructor kept Batchelor behind, along with Clyde Smith, another disgruntled monitor, and asked them to give him their complaints and he would try to have them addressed.

> We told him that he knew that there was blackmarketing going on and that he should put a stop to it. We told [him] that we needed more chow, better medical facilities, tobacco and not so many lectures. He then ask[ed] us how to improve the lectures. We told [him] that this chief gets up there and says things we don't know anything about, that he does nothing but slander the American govt. and we knew that all of it couldn't be true. Our stomachs hurt, we craved tobacco, etc. We told him that if he improved our food, medical supplies and gave us tobacco they would get more cooperation from the men and they would listen to the studies better.

Before the instructor left, he asked Batchelor to keep his monitor's job a little longer and sent the monitors back to their squads. When he returned to the hut, Batchelor told the men about his conversation "and we all agreed that this was a good time to press matters but at the same time to cooperate a little bit more so they would think we were more sincere."[58] Whatever the reason, things continued to slowly improve for the PsW.

Years later, while on trial for collaborating with his captors, Claude Batchelor alleged that what the army called collaboration was actually humanitarian leadership. By ingratiating himself to the Chinese, he could use his influence to help his fellow prisoners. Although this claim was met with skepticism, some of Batchelor's fellow PsW affirmed this theory when they testified that Batchelor had used his position for the benefit of sick and injured soldiers.[59]

Clarence Adams told a similar story: "I sensed that if conditions were to improve we were going to have to cooperate with the Chinese. They kept telling us that we ought to cooperate . . . after thinking about it for some time, I took it upon myself to cooperate." When his questioner asked if he benefitted personally from his cooperation with the Chinese, Adams shot back, "it was not a matter of personal gain. The Chinese didn't have a damn thing to give you." He contended that he "cooperated with them for the good of everybody" and insisted that he never "ratted or squealed on any of my fellow soldiers."[60] Years later, Michael Cornwell remembered that Richard Corden, his squad leader, used his position similarly. Describing Corden as "a super-intelligent person . . . an absolute intellectual," he noted, "Corden could get more out [of] the Chinese than any of us because he could be so diplomatic."[61] Ted Sprouse remembered Corden as an ultimate idealist who was "well liked by everyone."[62] Seeking answers to the lingering questions from his lonely childhood, Corden found that communism offered explanations. Cornwall concurred, "the Chinese gave him something he never had."[63]

Sprouse remembered that while Corden studied communist literature and was friendly with camp officials, he "was principled in misguided ways." He would not allow a fellow prisoner to be mistreated and if he thought a man's complaint was a legitimate one, he would carry it to headquarters and register it with camp officials. "Although I didn't agree with Corden, I had to admit he was a decent guy."[64] Similarly, Bob Price told CIC interrogators that Albert Belhomme "acted as speaker for the men when they thought they needed something bad enough."[65] Roosevelt Powell Jr. remembered that "[i]n the winter of 1952 or early part of 1953 [Larance] Sullivan helped Charles Smith . . . get admitted to the hospital for treatment of his lungs."[66] One Reactionary confessed on board ship heading home that "I don't like those people [Progressives], running down our government and all that, but they did improve the chow when they took over our camp."[67]

An unidentified ex-PW, under questioning by the FBI in reference to the activities of Lowell Skinner, also supported this line of reasoning and claimed that "concerning Skinner and the other nonrepatriates that he believed they were all primarily interested in the welfare of the other prisoners of war and themselves and that what they did they did in an effort to improve conditions in the camp." Claiming "all POW's had to cooperate with the communists in order to exist," the men who collaborated were doing so as humanitarians. This man contended that because of the large number of men who cooperated with the communists, Camp Five had a better staffed and supplied hospital than many of the other camps and that those who resisted suffered terribly. Arguing that "some of these "heroes" [those who resisted]," died and were buried at the camps, while "others who cooperated not only returned but were instrumental in saving the lives and improving the conditions for other POW's," the man stood steadfastly by his feeling that collaboration was the responsible thing to do. He added that the Chinese were such effective keepers that many men "were chosen by the communists to cooperate with them and that the individual had no other choice but to cooperate." To close the file, the investigating agent wrote of his witness that, "he would make a better witness for the defense than for the prosecution."[68]

There is also evidence that Jack Dunn worked to aid his fellow prisoners. He started his captivity in Camp Three, built for Reactionaries, and was not known to be a collaborator. Marine corporal Alfred Graham called Dunn's parents in 1953 and told them that when he was near death, their son gave him his only blanket. He described Dunn as remaining by his side and nursing him back to health over an extended period of time. As Graham slowly recovered from his wounds and illnesses, he never forgot what Dunn had sacrificed for him. "I wouldn't be alive today if it wasn't for Jack Dunn."[69] Another man, recovering from tuberculosis, remembered Jack as being "the one who brought over his blanket. He gave me big shares of his rations. . . . He kind of nursed me and a couple other guys." Dunn did this even though he "had malaria and bad stomach trouble." He confessed, "I didn't get to know Jack too well but as far as I was concerned, he was a good guy and I think the others who were with me would say the same thing."[70]

Recalling his friendship with William Cowart, Irv Langell explained the innocence with which Cowart approached prison life and how a man could slip from representing the group's interest to only representing his own. He described Cowart as, "a good-looking young man, a woman-killer you might say, at least he thought of himself that way," but confessed that Cowart was young, ignorant and "very easily led." Although "He thought he was trying to protect himself in order to survive," Langell would catch him compromising himself with the Chinese and ask, "Bill, what the hell is wrong with you?" Cowart saw nothing serious in his actions and responded, "I'm not doing anything wrong. I'm just getting some food." Because of his overt collaboration with the communists, "At the end, everybody was on his ass. They told him they were going to kill him for collaborating."[71]

Lieutenant Wadie Rountree was one of those on Cowart's ass. Rountree described him more harshly than Langell, "as a perpetual sorehead with a bad attitude." He affirmed that Cowart had been threatened and thought "he stayed behind because he feared reprisals from other prisoners as well as from the U.S. government." Like Langell, Rountree did not see Cowart as a true believer in communism, just an opportunist.[72] Cowart's poor personal hygiene, combined with his cooperation with the Chinese, resulted in his ostracism from PW life. His fellow PsW later reported that Cowart had little regard for cleanliness and that "his body odors were so offensive that his prison mates made him sleep outdoors even in cold weather." Several years later, Major George S. Prugh, an influential army lawyer gathering evidence for possible prosecution of the men, agreed with Langell and Rountree's assessment of Cowart calling him "young, stupid, frightened, ostracized by fellow PsW."[73]

It is unknown why Otho Bell relented to communist pressure, but it is certain that he was collaborating with the Chinese as early as June 1951. That month, Bell visited Kenneth Spingola, a friend within the prison camp. To convince Spingola to let him have some boots, Bell told him that he had it on good authority that the Chinese were going to raid the camp and confiscate all non–Chinese-issue goods. Believing Bell, Spingola lent him the boots. Later, Spingola learned that Bell needed the boots for his role in a Chinese-produced movie "depicting the American forces as the aggressors in Korea and illustrating mistreatment of Korean civilians by United States Army personnel."[74] Robert Brooks recounted how "the Chinese took approximately fifty men from Camp Number 5, Bell included" and outfitted them with uniforms and Second Division patches to be worn in the making of the movie.[75] The group was gone for more than a week making this movie, which depicted, among other things, American soldiers running down Korean civilians in Jeeps and gunning them down in cold blood, along with future nonrepatriate William White raping a Korean girl.[76]

While Batchelor was apparently being a pragmatist and Cowart and Bell were opportunists, Lowell Skinner was a true believer in the communist message. Fellow prisoners remembered him spending the bulk of his "time talking to various prisoners, trying to convince them that Communism was right in every respect and that the United States was in the wrong."[77] "On at least three or four occasions in [classified] SKINNER attempted to persuade [classified] to accept communism pointing out the advantages he would have in the camp and stating communism was the better form of government."[78]

When Batchelor and Smith lodged complaints about the insulting nature of the prescribed message, the Chinese forced the squads to combine their kitchens. By bringing the messes together, larger groups were formed, allowing for the sharpening of the focus on the communist message. The new lectures were critical of Chaing Kai-shek and "left out charges against our govt. and started telling about New China and Old China . . . How the landlords had exploited and mis treated [*sic*] the peasants, etc." Batchelor recalled that these lectures were more palatable because he had heard similar lectures given by the army and directed at Chinese society while stationed with the First Cavalry band in Japan before the war. After subjecting the men to these types of lectures throughout May and June, the Chinese began refocusing their indoctrination efforts on the Korean question and American interference.[79]

Batchelor identified the ideological lectures of May and June 1951 as being the turning point for many PsW. He noted that "[f]ood had picked up considerably, Ther [*sic*] weren't many people at all who were dying and the men as a whole started cooperating more with them [the Chinese] and many of them [the men] began to give the Chinese point of view in the discussions." The Chinese divided the larger group they had only recently created into three smaller groups. About forty of the most accepting men made up group A, while group C had about a dozen of those hostile to the Chinese message. Group B had the largest number: those who were middle of the road. The three groups were lectured individually and then combined for a mass discussion. Batchelor astutely observed, "The principle that the communists were going by was that a certain number of men became more advanced than others and were good to be leaders of the masses. The masses in this case was B group. The advanced elements of society were always fighting against the Reactionary or backward elements of society to gain the leader ship [*sic*] of the general masses. In this case the Reactionary or backward elements were C group—the smallest." After a period of lectures, the Chinese brought the groups together in a field and allowed groups A and C to compete for members of the B group. By the end of the session, most members of the B group had joined the A group, not necessarily for ideological reasons, but because they would enjoy the protection of the Chinese if they did so.[80]

Beginning in June, the lectures focused on the concept of peace. Most of the prisoners saw little harm in discussing such a sentiment, but the Chinese returned to the tactic of criticizing the United States in conjunction with the peace lessons. With many men, including Claude Batchelor by this time, becoming impressed with the Chinese communist message, the camp administrators began allowing the men to elect representatives to a handful of sanctioned clubs and organizations. Batchelor received the third highest vote total in his platoon and became the secretary of the Daily Life Club. Within weeks, it died and was replaced with a more specific cause. American soldiers were unhappy with their Chinese cooks and the Chinese army could use them to feed their own rather than enemy prisoners, so American PsW began electing cooks from their own ranks. At the time, food was improving in quality and quantity and the health of the men improved.[81]

The peace focus of the summer's lectures quickly presented the PsW with a problem that would come back to haunt many of them. In June, a Chinese instructor told Batchelor's group:

> that another group had thought about writing up a peace petion [petition] for everyone who wanted to sign. When the instructor left our group we talked it over. We decided that we could draw up a sort of letter without incriminating us in any way and it would satisfy the Chinese and would maybe help out our living conditions there a bit more. Evidently all the groups had come to the same conclusion. For next the Chinese decided to get each group to draw up a letter to see which one would be sent. This took some time and during the course of it the Chinese came to us and told us that the officers had decided to elect a peace committee to go out of the PoW camps and tell the world of the pow's [*sic*] desires for peace. The Chinese ask us what we thought of it and asked us to discuss the matter. We discussed for about two days on this

> matter and the Chinese would come around to see how things were going and would also voice their own opion [opinion] on the thing. They said this peace committee would be able to go to Europe and tell the world that pow's [*sic*] desires for peace and would also be able to cary [*sic*] the names and addresses of the pow's [*sic*] so that they could inform their folks that they were in good health and not to worry—that they would be home as soon as the war was over. We in our group decided that this might [be] a good chance to get some one [*sic*] out of there to let the world know that we were still alive at any rate.

With that, the men gathered on a parade field and took nominations. Claude Batchelor was run by some of the men of his group and about twenty of them stood to tell the others why he was the right man to hold the position. They credited him with doing his share of work on details, cutting wood, and his help with sick men. After the final vote, Batchelor was among the twelve elected to the committee. Preston Ritchie had received more than 1,200 votes and became Chairman while Lt. Jeff Erwin, Capt. Kashko, Sgt. John Porter, Edward Spencer, and Leroy Carter Jr. were picked to go to Pyongyang to "fight for peace."[82]

In the meantime, the Chinese administrators began forming peace committees at the company level. Andrew Condron was one of Batchelor's company's five representatives. Despite the Chinese motivations for establishing the peace committees, the prisoners used them to air complaints about the food, medical care, and recreation. Again, the complaints were heard and soon the companies began to see slight progress with the arrival of more medical supplies and a few basketballs.[83]

In July 1951, the Chinese announced to the men that peace talks were starting. At the urging of the Chinese, the peace committees crafted petitions imploring their readers to support efforts to bring the war to an end. Hundreds if not thousands of American soldiers signed these petitions driven not by Chinese influence, but by their difficult experiences as prisoners. Although the men did not know if their petitions made it back home to the United States, Claude Batchelor did see some of the letters printed in the *Shanghai News*.[84]

In the wake of the start of the peace talks, two things began to happen within the camps. First, conditions rapidly improved, particularly the amount and quality of food. This was likely due to the possibility that a prisoner exchange could conceivably take place quickly and the poor condition of American prisoners would be an embarrassment to the Chinese People's Volunteers (CPV). The increase in food can also be attributed to the season. By July, many crops were in and diverted away from the starving Chinese countryside to the front in Korea, even if some of those fed were the enemy. The second result was a sudden increase in the length and intensity of the indoctrination lessons. Batchelor remembered that "[t]hey began to have lectures from the time we got up till the time we went to bed at night" and "[t]hey even cut down on our chow period so we could have more time to discuss." He explained that the content bordered on what one would find in an advanced college classroom and focused on the development of civilizations and the economic, social, and cultural transitions made throughout the stages of development.[85]

By the summer of 1951, the Chinese communists had held thousands of American soldiers for more than seven months. During that time, the Americans had experienced a viciously high mortality rate as a result of untreated wounds, starvation, and disease. After the initial shock of captivity and a few months of intense deprivation, the Chinese opened an indoctrination program designed to drive wedges among the prisoners. Now, the Chinese captors would begin to see success.

FOUR

Winning Captive Hearts

> "You're in a prison camp; nobody breaks. Months and months of cold and torture and starvation and nobody breaks. Then one day a man does break and his own men kill him for it. And the commander of the camp is furious because he's been robbed of the one victory he's been able to achieve. So he calls in the ranking officer and he says to him 'I have reached the limit of my patience, either you cooperate or I kill all sixteen men.'"
>
> —Richard Basehart in *Time Limit* (1957)

When American soldiers became prisoners of the Chinese, they expected physical torture, starvation, and disease, but not psychological warfare. However, in the mind of Mao Zedong, the American soldiers were a fertile ground for recruitment. Most soldiers came from the poorer segments of American society and had been insulated from any significant knowledge about communism by politicians fearing a possible rise in its popularity. Furthermore, captivity insulated these men from any information other than that which the Chinese supplied and made them dependent on their captors for everything necessary for their existence. The results of this volatile experiment shook the United States to its core.

The basic formula used by the Chinese to bring vulnerable soldiers around was very simple. First, the "mind-conditioning" phase, as army psychiatrists later named it, sought to instill a negative opinion of the United States in the minds of the prisoners. One frequent argument alleged that Wall Street had conspired with the United States and South Korea to start a war and improve the struggling postwar economy. Although there is no irrefutable evidence to support such an assertion, one cannot ignore the obvious link to the military-industrial complex outgoing President Dwight Eisenhower had warned the nation about in his 1961 farewell address. The second part of the Chinese system, "suction," presented the prisoners with life in a communist utopia as compared to that in the capitalistic United States. By this time, many of the emotionally vulnerable and physically weak Americans began to agree with the ideological tenets of their captors.[1] So severe was this system of ideological pressure that a Catholic priest subjected to these same stresses in 1936 began doubting that he was actually a priest.[2]

It is important to note that by the military's definition of torture, very few of the men endured such an experience. Kinkead noted that the army considered torture to consist of "the application of pain so extreme that it causes a man to faint or lose control of his will." When pressed by Kinkead, a G-2 colonel noted, "The Army does not consider prisoners being made to stand in water, being improperly clad, being kicked, slapped, or kept in cramped quarters as torture." The colonel compared the stress derived from such circumstances "of the same general order as a combat soldier undergoes."[3] On a very basic level, the colonel was correct; however, the stresses of combat and captivity cannot be compared, just as the factor of being in the hands of one's enemy cannot be quantitatively measured.

After several weeks of intensive study, the tactics began to work and the men started to wear down. Batchelor recalled that the men were initially cooperative and fairly open with their opinions since the subject at hand was simply world history, but as they tired, their patience wore thin and many lashed out. Called into Lin's office one evening, Batchelor was asked to survey a list of names and offer comments on those he knew. He spoke on behalf of several men and Lin responded that those on the list were sabotaging the lectures. The next day a formation was held during which the men on the list were called to step forward. Informed that they were being moved to another camp because of a housing shortage, those men were gone by the end of the day. Batchelor thought they had been sent off to a labor camp, but he later realized that Camp Three was their destination.[4]

Whether or not Batchelor knew it, the Chinese had identified him as an elite Progressive camp leader. By August, his captors approached him with a plan to set up a special squad with Batchelor as its leader. He balked, fearing that this would place him even closer to the administrators, of whom he had begun to grow more cautious. They assured him that the squad was not a Progressive squad, but would serve as an exemplar of behavior and cooperation to the rest of the camp. Despite his reservations, the Chinese announced the new squad's formation the next day and installed Batchelor as its head over his protests. He claimed, "We never accepted any favoritism and did not get any resentment from the company." Batchelor sometimes surprised his captors by refusing small favors, like an occasional pack of cigarettes, preferring instead to talk about sending sick men to the hospital for treatment.[5]

Beginning in August or September, the Chinese decided that they could combine their message of communist indoctrination with recreation for the men. A theater group was organized, which would exclusively put on plays that sent the proper message to the men. Batchelor, who volunteered to play the lead in *The Russian Question,* remembered that it "didn't carry any epithets against the American Govt. nor was it anti-American but it was definitely propaganda in favour of the Soviet Union." With the success of the play in Camp Five, the Chinese decided to send the troupe to some of the other camps to perform. Leaving on September 30, 1951, the actors traveled with a basketball team to Camp One. Upon his arrival, Batchelor found that the prisoners were electing members to their peace committee.[6] The fact that this event was taking place at Camp One a full three months after the elections at Camp Five indicates that Camp Five, by now known to Progressives as Pyoktong University, was a test case and had fulfilled Chinese expectations.[7]

By November, Batchelor and the rest of the troupe were back at Camp Five. One day, the Chinese called him to headquarters, where they informed him he was being transferred but did not offer any details. Batchelor returned to his squad, packed his things, and was escorted to the building that housed the recreation office. There, the Chinese had set up a primitive printing press where the camp newspaper, *Toward Truth and Peace,* was published. Robert Hickox wrote most of the articles but Batchelor "did not have much to do at all" and as a result, he spent his days reading the literature lying around the shop. For a bored PW, even pro-communist tracts such as *High Treason, The Great Conspiracy,* and *The Twilight of World Capitalism* became interesting reading. By this time, hearing the one-sided message of his Chinese captors was gleaning results in the case of Claude Batchelor: "I had already started leaning in their general direction and it didn't take too long for these books portraying what was supposed to be American public [opinion] to complete the process. I began to believe a lot of it. I and [Robert] Hickox talked several aspects of the situation over and we came to the same conclusion."[8]

Shortly after Batchelor relocated to the recreation building, the Chinese established a new company. Named Fifth Company, but informally known to the camp as the Progressive company, it was made up of those prisoners who were "either believing their propaganda or leaning that way." Once formed, it provided these men with special study to help foster their loyalty and bring them closer to their captors. For two months, these men lived together and learned the nuances of the communist message, then, as the New Year neared, the Chinese sent them back to their squads further armed for indoctrination.[9]

On January 1, 1952, Batchelor and Hickox were moved back to a squad where they roomed with known Progressive Harry Copeland and future nonrepatriate Rufus Douglas. Batchelor claimed that the Chinese sent them into the squad and billeted them together in order to provide a communist-friendly environment among the men. At the same time, the lectures had ceased, allowing the Chinese to see if the program could maintain momentum on its own. Apparently moving too slowly, the men were called to headquarters, where it was suggested they begin to draw up and circulate another peace petition. Batchelor remembered that Paul Schnur, Lowell Skinner, and Robert Hickox gathered the signatures. Schnur was perfect for the Chinese cause as both his mother and father were longtime leftists back home in San Francisco where the elder Schnur served prominently in the Congress of Industrial Organization.[10] After acquiring about sixty signatures, they sent the petition to Schnur's mother: "Later we heard that she had circulated it all over the United States and she wrote Schnur that she had made 10,000 copies of it and [it] was printed in several magazines and newspapers."[11]

With the success of that single petition, the Chinese were emboldened and pushed throughout the summer of 1952 to expand the petition drive. Supplying the Progressives with favorable newsprint, the Chinese painted a picture of a nation seething in dissatisfaction over the state of the conflict in Korea. Claude Batchelor remembered that "news bulletins concerning a few organizations in the states who [were] getting peace petitions circulated and they were getting a wide response." Encouraging the men to discuss the possibility of expanding their petition project, the Chinese handpicked speakers who encouraged the others to join them in their fight to end the war.[12] In the end, only one man refused to sign. Those who signed were not intimidated or tortured into adding their names, but agreed to do so because of the selective information presented by the camp administrators.

After getting the leading Progressives on board for the petition drive, they then had to figure out a way to get the men in camp to sign. As the Chinese had turned up the heat by intensifying the frequency of lectures, a good number of men had committed. However, these apparent defections also had the reverse effect of pushing many men away from the communist cause and into the Reactionary camp. With some men making inroads with the camp administrators, they became personae-non-grata within the prison's general population and targets of the growing resistance groups that operated under the general umbrella of the term "Reactionary."

Many soldiers began to join together into groups primarily for mutual protection. Loosely divided between the Progressives, who supported their Chinese captors and sometimes helped with indoctrination efforts, and Reactionaries, who sought to maintain military discipline and resist Chinese overtures, these groupings came about for a variety of reasons. The Progressives were organized by the Chinese, who essentially controlled their activities through bribery and coercion; one small organization in Camp Five, however, was called the Red Dean Squad. Consisting solely of a squad of men who were loyal Progressives, the Red Dean Squad also had its unofficial hangers on. Among these was Lowell Skinner, who helped the squad circulate petitions and "spent much of his time in company with many members of the group."[13]

The camps proved fertile ground for the development of many Reactionary organizations. One such group was the Ku Klux Klan, which grew to reach all of the camps except possibly Camp Two. An unidentified author called its establishment in spring 1952 "natural," considering the KKK's anti-Progressive doctrine. Additionally, members of the KKK would have been fighting against the overarching idea of equality as preached by the Chinese communists. Although little is known of the KKK's operations within the prison camps, race does not appear to be as great an operational influence as general opposition to communist indoctrination. Members' main foci seemed to be on disrupting indoctrination efforts, upsetting camp life and harassing the authorities, and trying to prevent UN PW cooperation through anonymous threats and warnings sent to suspected Progressives.[14]

Since Camp Five was the largest and most devoted of the camps to the indoctrination program, it stands to reason that it would also have the best-developed Reactionary sentiment. Exceeding the KKK in popularity, the Circle was formed in March 1952 by fifteen members of Lloyd Pate's squad. Although Pate said he did not know "What in the hell was the "Circle?" he certainly led one of the most effective PW opposition organizations.[15] The Circle operated democratically, encouraging and assisting in escape attempts, warning fellow PsW against becoming Progressives, and generally resisting the Chinese. In *Reactionary,* Pate explained the group's tactics: "There was one particular individual in the company who enjoyed himself by getting up at formations and reading some communist lectures. We straightened him out real quick by telling him if he didn't stop it he'd find himself floating facedown in the river some morning. He became one of the biggest Reactionaries in the company. The Chinese would tell him to do something and instead of jumping to it like he did before, he'd tell them to go to hell."[16] Fearing that Progressive informants would infiltrate their group, the squad petitioned the Chinese guards to allow them to move to an isolated part of the camp. The Chinese saw the benefit of separating the Circle from the rest of the camp and surprisingly granted permission. By August 1952, the Chinese had had enough of the Circle and broke up the organization by reassigning many of the men to different companies and jailing some of the leaders.[17] Apart from the KKK and the Circle, other, similar organizations such as the Non–Benedict Arnold Club, Un-American Activities Committee, and Informant Net provided a refuge for men who sought to join an organized resistance.[18]

To combat these elements of opposition, the Progressives began offering some minimal level of anonymity to those who would support them. Batchelor and the rest of the petitioners agreed that threats from the Reactionaries intimidated many men who might otherwise sign their petitions, so they began having the Chinese call selected men to meetings in certain buildings where they could hear the Progressive message safely away from the prying ears of the Reactionaries.[19]

This tactic had several important results. As the men were called to the appropriate buildings and presented with the communist message, their fears shifted from a retributive Reactionary element that would punish them for cooperating with the Chinese to a frustrated camp administration that could, without required justification, inflict any measure of punishment on the men it considered to be resisters to their "lenient treatment policy." Additionally, the Chinese understood that the main enemy of a captive population was its own paranoia. Years later, soldiers would testify with complete certainty in court using such noncommittal phrases as "he had the reputation," "it could have been," and identifying the accused as "looking nervous and afraid."[20] One of the prosecuting witnesses attributed his testimony as to the untrustworthiness of Edward Dickenson to this vague sense: "You know, inside you, you know. You just feel it; you get the feeling."[21] The influence of paranoia upon the behavior of a captive people cannot be underestimated. Cecil Inman remembered that Chinese instructors would take certain prisoners for private walks just to breed suspicion among the others. Some men would be jealous because another was getting special treatment, while others would ostracize the PW in question because they now suspected him of being a collaborator.[22] James Thompson recalled in his Korean War memoir, that the Chinese would call black soldiers for an interrogation, but then have cooks bring sumptuous dishes into the building in full view of whites. After the interrogation session, the blacks might be taken off details for several days.[23] Whites saw blacks being treated exceptionally well and wondered what they had told their interrogators to warrant such fare. In reality, the food was often dangled in front of the famished men as a torture tactic to pull information out of them. Dr. Philip Bloemsma, who had spent five years as a prisoner of the Japanese during World War II, was an expert on captivity's effect on one's sanity. He noted that rumors were a common, almost necessary part of camp life.[24]

Within such a rumor-driven society, the Chinese could control the great majority of their prisoners through their control of information. In addition to frequently planting rumors within the camp, the camp administrators publicized selected pieces of legitimate news if it served their purpose. As the prisoners were deciding whether or not to formulate another peace petition, newspaper articles about growing disenchantment with the war at home were enough to convince even the most skeptical.[25] Additionally, an individual's own memory could be used as a weapon against him. As most of the men had been captured and imprisoned by the Chinese and North Koreans within a span of weeks early in the war and their last free memory was of a quarter million Chinese soldiers, it was easy for them to surmise that the UN forces would be soundly defeated. Most American soldiers underestimated the Chinese anyway, and as the weeks turned to months and then to years, the hopelessness bred by their captivity was often attributed to a weak or beaten American military force. Furthermore, the weakness of the capitalist ethic, the ultimate indoctrination lesson, could be illustrated by the apparent unconcern of the U.S. Army for its captive soldiers. All of these beliefs, whether true or false, could be easily shaped into a way to open even the most skeptical minds.

The Chinese interrogators did not have to work very hard for Richard Tenneson. A product of a very unstable home environment, Tenneson came to Korea deeply frustrated by his childhood. A fellow PW remembered that Tenneson "talked a good deal about his family and how his family cared very little for him." Shortly after being moved into Camp One, Tenneson became sick and was hospitalized for four months. The combination of tuberculosis and his difficult background made him an easy target for the Chinese. A member of his squad remembered that when Tenneson was released from the hospital, "he had turned 'Progressive.'"[26]

Otho Bell's movement into the Progressive camp came at a great price, at least temporarily. Bell was a very troubled man, particularly in regard to his use and abuse of alcohol. He had been allowed to write letters home to his wife and daughter in Washington state and his father and other family in

Mississippi. Unfortunately, Bell's letters which were filled with communist propaganda or they would not have been released by the Chinese, offended his father with dramatic results.[27] After receiving one of these letters, Bell's stepmother apparently had had enough of her stepson's anti-American sentiments and in the spring of 1952 wrote him back disowning him. Donald Stewart saw the letter and remembered that Bell's stepmother "wrote that she had heard that Bell was siding with the enemy, and . . . wondered what kind of a son she had. She stated in the letter that she didn't want him to come home and that if he did she would disown him." Since his wife had recently had a baby, she also questioned "what kind of a father the baby would have."[28] When Otho read the letter, he lost his mind. Fellow prisoners remembered that he had a very public nervous breakdown for three days where he "He would stare into space for long periods of time and he would talk to himself."[29] A group of fellow prisoners were ordered to grab him and take him to the camp infirmary, where he remained for seven to ten days. Wayne Martin was one of the men who carried Bell to the hospital and he remembered that Bell, "was talking incoherently . . . of some one being after him who desired to kill him."[30] After a few days in the hospital, Bell returned to his squad seemingly well.

Bell's mental health would not remain stable, however. Throughout his imprisonment, he struggled with his sanity. John Beers's friend, a Marine Lieutenant Henry, reported that "he had seen Bell in the hospital at Pyoktong and . . . Bell appeared to be completely insane."[31] Aryanari Mizoguchi put it simply: "Bell is a mental case."[32] Tadao Niato corroborated the other stories, telling CIC agents that "Bell is mentally unbalanced and has been treated by the Chinese medical authorities because of a nervous disorder."[33] Another former PW stated, "Bell appeared to be mentally unbalanced."[34] By the time of the repatriation controversy, Bell's mental state had improved considerably. Pedro Rivera-Perez saw Bell on his last day at Pyoktong and noted that he appeared mentally fit.[35]

Whereas Bell's family rejected his pro-communist overtures, Richard Tenneson's mother proved helpful. Portia Howe had spent her life seeking the same kind of perfect world the communist instructors were promising Richard. During his time as a PW, Richard confided his Marxist conversion to his mother and she apparently helped him and his cause when she could. Hoping to help her son, she organized the sending of Christmas cards to the PsW in Korea, which pleased Richard, but, in Richard's words, "you could have done a lot more for us POW [*sic*] as well as man kind as a whole if you would of [have] had all of those people write to the president telling him to stop the war."[36] Howe apparently agreed to assist her son in questionable ways. While still a PW, Richard wrote her, "You have probably had visitors, you didn't know, with a strange request, I hope that you carried out my wishes."[37] In another letter, he echoed similar statements, "If a person from the D.W. comes to see you comply with his wishes."[38]

Edward Dickenson's path toward collaboration started about the same time. In the early summer of 1952, Dickenson and Virgil "Okie" Rutherford approached Fred Obroff about escaping from the camp.[39] As the three began hoarding food and the other supplies necessary for their attempt, they allowed Martin Christensen to join at the last minute. Very late on July 25, 1952, the four men ran out of the camp under cover of a driving rainstorm. They walked throughout the night, finally arriving at a ridge about four miles from camp intending to rest for the day. However, at about 9:00 A.M., Chinese guards ended the brief odyssey when they walked up the ridge and recaptured them.[40]

When they were taken back to camp, the Chinese administrators were ready for them. The escapees were taken directly to the camp headquarters, where they were interrogated individually. Obroff contended that the Chinese found a compass on Christensen, and Dickenson took the Chinese back to the ridge and showed them where the group's signal flag was hidden.[41]

In serious trouble, each of the men gave up parts of the plan to the Chinese. By the time Obroff was taken in for questioning, the paranoia of prison life took over. Fred Obroff had a homemade compass and when the Chinese asked him about it, "Right then I felt that Dickenson had squealed." In reality, he did not know which of the other three had given up his compass, but his negative predisposition toward Dickenson marked him as the primary suspect. An additional weakness in Obroff's story involves Dickenson's involvement in the plan in the first place. Obroff claimed that he knew Dickenson had been a strong Progressive, but when approached by him and Rutherford, he eagerly agreed to join in the escape plan.[42] One must wonder why a man sympathetic with his captors would wish to escape and why other men, knowing the weakness of his character, would agree to go with him.

Once the Chinese were satisfied with their interrogation of the men, they confined them to jail. Christensen was given the longest sentence, thirty days in solitary confinement, while Dickenson got twenty-five days, and Obroff twenty-one days, while Rutherford only spent about two weeks locked away. Although Obroff remained convinced that Dickenson had informed on the group, it seems curious that the Chinese would sentence Dickenson to the second-longest term in payment for his information. Obroff never wavered in his condemnation of Dickenson and claimed that after about ten days in jail, Dickenson was transferred into the same cell with Obroff and Rutherford, where he admitted that he had given the Chinese information: "The Chinese put a gun in my face and threatened to kill me so I told them everything." Dickenson had squealed, but it seems unlikely that he was the only one the Chinese could intimidate into providing information. Obroff further damned Dickenson because he was interrogated six or seven times during his imprisonment while Obroff and Rutherford were only questioned two or three times. Furthermore, Obroff considered Rutherford and Christensen to be more reliable because they "were beaten with clubs, rifle butts and struck by Chinese fists," while "Dickenson never mentioned that he had been beaten."[43]

Further complicating the story was Christensen's recollection of the events. First, he contended that the men were at liberty in the Korean countryside for eighteen hours, drastically different from the ten hours claimed by Obroff. Additional inconsistencies include Christensen's memories of his time in jail. Like Obroff, Christensen placed Rutherford as the first to be released and noted that Dickenson and Obroff served roughly the same time, twenty-two days, while Christensen pinpointed his time in jail at thirty-six days. Christensen claimed that when Tong interrogated him, he asked about a .45 caliber pistol the Chinese accused him of having.[44] When he denied it, the Chinese administrator showed him a paper mentioning the gun with Dickenson's signature and thumbprint in red ink. Christensen further stated that "[a]ll of the prisoners of war, except the Progressives with whom Dickenson always associated, hated Dickenson." He closed his statement about Dickenson with extensive testimony about the rumors he heard in camp, but with no primary evidence to support his conclusions.[45] Although Obroff was convinced that Dickenson was a rat and had informed on their plan, he offered nothing more than hearsay as evidence.

On July 30, 1952, another escape attempt was undertaken. Three PsW met at a latrine and changed out of their prison uniforms. As they were putting on military fatigues, Richard Tenneson walked up. The men knew that Tenneson was a Progressive and that he knew what they were doing, so they told him to serve as lookout while they sneaked out of the compound. After crawling through a millet field, the three swam a river and hid in the mountains on the other side, but were soon captured by Korean soldiers. Later told by fellow prisoners that Tenneson had gone directly to Chinese headquarters with information about the escape, the three men spent a month in small cages hating Tenneson.[46]

Andrew Fortuna's course was altered by a controversy in which he played no part. In June 1952, an armed Chinese guard went into a PW squad room where he was attacked. Those standing nearby remembered hearing a commotion before seeing the guard flying out of the door of the building followed quickly by his rifle. When other Chinese guards came to the rescue, they arrested Harold Addington, claiming that he had incited the others to attack the guard. The Chinese took him away and beat him mercilessly within sight of the other prisoners. At some point, Addington broke away from the Chinese and ran. He made it several hundred yards to a PW compound. When the Chinese caught up to him, they grabbed him by the feet and dragged him all the way back on his face and continued to beat and kick him. Addington spent the next two nights and one day hanging off the ground by his thumbs and was then taken down, tied with his arms behind his back and put in the "hole" for forty-eight days.[47]

Roy Lee Jenkins was standing with Fortuna watching Addington's beating when the prisoner broke away. Addington ran into the compound with Fortuna and Jenkins and begged them to help him. While they watched the beating, Jenkins remembered hearing an uncharacteristically serious Fortuna say, "I will never buck them again. From now on I will do anything they say." From that point forward, Fortuna cooperated with his captors and over time, in the estimate of Jenkins, "came to believe the Chinese propaganda."[48]

It did not take long for Fortuna to establish himself as an effective propagandist. Although he was uneducated, he wrote articles for the camp newspaper, likely with significant polishing from his fellow Progressives and camp authorities. Most important, however, was his friendship with Anthony Brunelo Jr., a talented cartoonist. A Progressive, Brunelo used his talent to draw propaganda cartoons for the camp newspaper and various bulletin boards, including images of "a large Chinese soldier stepping on an American flag while chasing American troops who had thrown their weapons away and were running," and a heart with a knife through it, symbolizing the heart of "American imperialists" and the knife as "peace." Although Brunelo hoped to protect his friend and did not divulge much information to the FBI agents who visited him after he returned home, it is clear that in several cases he allowed Andrew Fortuna to sign his pictures as the artist, and likely shared in the benefits of Fortuna's being in the good graces of the Chinese.[49]

Studies indicate that the vast majority of prisoners became ultimate pragmatists once they were captured, but a minority became radicalized and doctrinaire as either Reactionaries or Progressive informers.[50] Lloyd Pate was the ultimate opponent to his Chinese captors. He despised Progressives and spent about half of his nearly three years as a PW in solitary confinement. However, as he aged, he mellowed and recalled his experience with one of the nonrepatriates: "We had Progressives who would never rat on another American, but they did go along with the Communist line. One of them was Jim Veneris. We called him the Greek, and I had a lot of conversations with him in Camp Three. As far as I know, he never ratted on a fellow prisoner. I think he was the only one of the twenty-one who really did believe in Communism."[51] In his memoir, Pate elaborated on his relationships with some of the Progressives. Of Veneris, he wrote, "He admitted to me he believed in communism. To the best of my knowledge he never ratted on me, and I never had a report from Bill that Veneris was a rat. Give the devil his due."[52] Pate was less gracious toward Scott Rush, whom he did not trust. Pate "didn't think any secret was safe with him." Pate said that Rush "didn't believe in communism, and hadn't done anything in camp except ratting and writing some articles for the Chinese." Pate supposed that "[h]e wouldn't have got in any trouble if he had come back, because he wasn't as bad as some other men. He was scared and weak."[53]

Harold Whorton also hated Progressives and the Chinese, dealing with them using outright violence. A native of Alabama, with the nickname "Jeff Davis" and generally considered to be mentally unbalanced even by his friends, Whorton stood out among PsW as a man to be avoided. Illustrative of this point, in the summer of 1952, he dragged a Chinese supervisor into a squad room and began beating him. Larance Sullivan was there at the time and ran to headquarters to report the incident. Surprisingly, Whorton only received a fifteen-day sentence for the assault. When he was released, Sullivan sought to exact revenge for the assault on his Chinese comrade and punched Whorton in the mouth.[54] Sullivan could be brave while under the watchful eye of the Chinese, but he feared retribution from Whorton. The night after he had struck him, Sullivan decided to sleep with another squad. When Walter Chambers asked him why he was spending the night away from his own squad, Sullivan replied that he was afraid that "Jeff" would get him during the night. Sullivan considered the Alabamian "crazy and he was afraid Whorton would kill him." A few days later, Whorton was again arrested by the Chinese officials, beaten, and jailed, presumably on information provided by Sullivan.[55]

Of all the nonrepatriates, Sullivan had one of the worst reputations as a collaborator and informer. Returned PsW, while liberal in general with their accusations, singled Sullivan out as one of the worst offenders. Ellis Jackson called him "the most hated prisoner in Camp #5" because of his penchant for open collaboration and his obvious malleability in Chinese hands. Sullivan carried with him such a stigma that the men distrusted anyone who was seen conversing with him.[56]

All of these concerns came together in Claude Batchelor's mind in the summer of 1952. Having passed much of his imprisonment reading the available Marxist books, magazines, and newspapers, his mind was growing ever more friendly to the communist philosophy. However, as the tensions steadily increased between Progressives and Reactionaries, and his own position became more solidly Progressive, he began to take stock of his situation. After reading some communist literature, which planted the seed of skepticism in his mind, and comparing the quality of life the communist claimed to have against information derived from the books, "[a]ll these instances got me to thinking pretty seriously." He thought about his age and level of education "and became afraid that what I was doing might be a dangerous thing" and that "the idea that the peace fight could easily be another way the communists had for swinging people over to communism." He decided that the best thing to do would be to stop cooperating with the Chinese. That was easier said than done, however.[57]

The process by which a collaborator was created is illustrated in an unidentified PW's statement to the FBI:

> The Chinese made it amply plain that good students got rewarded—poor students did not. There was always the threat of getting even less food, no medicine, and no mail, etc., for the men who were not good students. I myself succumbed to this pressure and wrote two articles at the Chinese suggestion in the first two weeks. They continually hounded us to write down our opinions no matter what they were and all POW's did so. If a man seemed to agree with them, they stepped up the campaign and concentrated on him until he seemed to really reject them. If a man rejected them too hard, he got tougher living conditions. I would say there was no escape from them once you seemed to let yourself go along with them. I know as a fellow POW that CLARENCE ADAMS was coerced to the above extent.[58]

Similar to Edmond O'Brien's soliloquy in *The Rack*, this anonymous statement reinforces the power that the Chinese held over their captives.

When Batchelor began second-guessing his cooperation with the Chinese, he tried to distance himself from the group he had helped form. Hoping to have a break from "nothing but politics all the time," he "learned how to play chess" and "got one of the fellows who could speak French to help me learn that." He noticed that despite these diversions, the stress of his situation shortened his attention span. Hoping to diminish the stress he was feeling, he began smoking marijuana.[59] Although McCarthy-era propaganda would suggest the Chinese drugged their captives to make them accept communism, they, in fact, strictly forbade the smoking of marijuana and being caught with it assured fast and hard punishment. Raymond Lech reported that marijuana grew wild beside the road at Camp One and an estimated 80 percent of prisoners there smoked it as a diversion. A former PW affirmed Lech's comments about the availability of marijuana and put the percentage of smokers at 95.[60] One prisoner contended that his "company consisted of approximately one hundred men. Of this number, all except five, smoked marijuana almost daily." He affirmed that "[t]he Chinese gave lectures on the evils of using this drug and tried to discourage its use, but it was available growing wild and work parties would bring in supplies of it for camp use."[61] At Camp Five, many of the men cultivated it in their own sparse gardens, hiding it from guards by mixing it in with other tall plants.[62] Several of the men who refused repatriation smoked marijuana while imprisoned, including Otho Bell, who was described as "a constant user" and an addict; Morris Wills, who was reportedly a heavy user; and Lewie Griggs, who "would smoke it any time of day that he had it."[63] Apart from marijuana, Bell sought any way to escape the conditions of his captivity, no matter how brief. A heavy and dangerous drinker throughout his life, he also knew of other drugs that could be had in prison camp, including chewing gum that could be impregnated with a narcotic, probably from the infirmary.[64]

One of the best stories about marijuana use among PsW in the camps involved Richard Tenneson. Fearing he would be caught with his substantial store of pot, he stripped off the good leaves and kept them in one bag while depositing the stems and other trash pieces in another. He took the bag filled with stems and broken pieces to the commandant and meekly apologized for using the drug. The commandant took the bag away from him and Tenneson turned and left, keeping the good parts for himself. For the next several months, Tenneson was held up to the other PsW as a positive example of a man's repentance for his actions all the while using marijuana and remaining above suspicion. Every time someone would accuse Tenneson of using pot, the Chinese interpreter would stand up for him and say, "I know he quit. He gave me his bag."[65]

Like many of the other prisoners, Claude Batchelor was afraid of Lin, not because of his ferocity, of which he was certainly capable, hence his nickname "Screaming Skull," but because of his sensitivity. Batchelor did not want to meet with him personally, "because I was afraid he would be able to talk me into starting in again. He had a way of approaching a man from his own personal viewpoint and gaining his confidence. I know of some men that cried when they talked to him of their past lives."[66]

Getting away from Lin would not be easy. In August 1952, Batchelor gave one of the men his resignation from his propaganda activities and asked him to deliver it. Soon, someone came to tell Batchelor that the commander wanted to see him, but the Texan did not go. He spent the remainder of the day away from the company hoping to avoid being seen by the Chinese administrators. Having fought insomnia for months, Batchelor sat up alone until 1:00 A.M. when Rufus Douglas rose to bake the day's bread. Helping Douglas until daybreak, he returned to the squad and lay down. Again, a guard arrived ordering him to headquarters, but Batchelor complained of sickness and the guard left. Knowing that Lin would not be put off indefinitely, Batchelor went to the latrine and planned to pass more time, but was caught and personally escorted to headquarters. Refusing to speak, Batchelor listened as the silver-tongued Lin began to work his magic. Finally, he told Lin that he would not speak about his feelings, but he would write them down. Lin brought him pencil and paper and left him alone in a room. An emotionally crippled Batchelor was impressed with Lin's compassion when he "noticed that the Chief [Lin] didn't go to eat. He sat outside and [waited for] me. As for myself I had to struggle to keep from crying."[67]

Insisting that if he were just left alone for a while, he would feel much better, Batchelor was allowed to move into a room by himself. The prisoner remembered that after he explained his feelings to Lin, "a fellow from my squad [came] up with my bedding." That night, "[t]hey moved me into a room all by myself and brought me a couple of books to read. Then they left me alone." Batchelor found this situation to be more harsh and isolating than peaceful. "I never got to see anybody or anything, I was left completely alone for about a week and a half. Then my mental condition got even worse. I thought I would lose my mind. I couldn't sleep or eat." By September, his mental health was deteriorating to a dangerous degree and he asked to be moved back to his squad.[68]

Still resolved to stay out of the indoctrination effort, Batchelor volunteered for details and spent time with the squad, but "refused to do anything in relation to study. I refused to go to the meetings and refused to go see the instructor." Lin sent some Progressives to talk sense to him, but Batchelor remained committed to his change and told them "I was not doing any thing any more. I went out and worked with my squad on our section of the playground. And did absolutely nothing more." The Chinese persisted and had him come to headquarters, where several different captors would talk with him. Frustrated, Batchelor began to stand up for himself in the hopes that the Chinese would finally get the message that he was through with them. Captors, however, are seldom intimidated by their captives and the Chinese quickly put him in his place. Batchelor went to headquarters when called and "the camp education director asked me to go in his room and wait. I did so and he and his interpreter came in and sat down. They started thumbing through a couple of magazines which made me mad." When Batchelor took out his tobacco and began rolling a cigarette, they offered him a ready rolled one, but he refused it. The situation deteriorated from there, Batchelor insisting he be jailed for his impertinence and the Chinese threatening to do just that. The education director ordered him back to his squad and told him to pack his things, that he was being transferred: "The next morning they took me to GHQ [general headquarters]. The political director saw me up there and told me he wanted me to work with the others up there on the camp newspaper. I told him I was not going to do any thing." The Chinese moved him into a room with an interpreter and spent more than a month taking turns trying to change his mind. After weeks of meetings with Chinese officials, but no contact with any Americans, Batchelor finally agreed to "write out a long criticism of myself and then he would think about [allowing Batchelor to return to his squad]. I wrote up about 25 pages saying just about any thing I could think of."[69]

Although he did not recognize it at the time, Batchelor's criticism was his breaking point. His interpreter roommate suggested that Lin might look favorably on an open letter from Batchelor congratulating Lt. John Quinn on his recent germ warfare confession. Quinn, along with Lt. Kenneth Enoch, both B-26 crewmen, had been broadcast on Radio Pyongyang admitting that they had dropped germ bombs. Batchelor wrote the letter and the next day he was taken to meet Quinn. In Quinn, he found a kindred soul. Both men had been isolated and placed under an incredible amount of strain because of their past compromises and unknown futures. Batchelor and Quinn dined together with several of the Chinese instructors and Quinn revealed that he was kept in solitary confinement. Later, he noted that his first year in captivity was spent partially in a cold cave with one other PW followed by eight months alone, except for a single interrogator, who spent several months asking him the same questions over and over and recording discrepancies in his answers. When he and Batchelor went to the latrine together, he confided in the Texan that he had not spoken to other Americans in several months and was incredibly lonely. The next day, Batchelor introduced Quinn to his company and then "Quinn [*sic*] gave a long speech on how he dropped germ bombs."

That night, Batchelor attended a study meeting during which time he read his criticism to the group. "I called myself despicable, but headed [*sic*] and a coward. The men all applauded me for it and made a lot of comments on how thoroughly I had criticized my self. (I didn't mean a word of it.)" Having done what the Chinese wished, Batchelor was allowed to move back in with his company.[70] From that point forward, Claude Batchelor fully understood who was in charge within the prison camp.

The summer of 1952 also challenged other Progressives, especially those at Camp One. Arlie Pate had begun working closely with the Chinese in July, and in August, he and ten other "pros" were moved into special quarters for their own protection. However, after a few weeks, "some 50 or 60 prisoners of war from all the various companies broke into this building and assaulted and beat up the Progressives." One of the attackers recalled for the FBI that "[o]ne night we all went into the place where they met, and fought them hand to hand." He did not remember if anyone had been seriously hurt or who was involved in the fight, but the Chinese later announced that one man had been killed, the same day that one of the men "was taken before a court . . . and sentenced to 2½ years in jail for what they called illegal activities."[71] Having failed in their efforts to protect the men collectively, the Chinese returned them to their former squads.[72]

Arlie Pate's shift to collaborator was surprising in its completeness. A member of his squad recalled that "[f]or the first 6 months or so of our association Pate was just another prisoner sharing our dislike of the Chinese and our attitudes toward them and enjoying no special favors from them," but by the summer of 1951 that began to change.[73] By mid-1952, Pate's captivity had changed him. One former prisoner said, "Several times PATE struck some of the wounded prisoners including myself during arguments over his refusal to attempt to aid the other prisoners."[74] Another former PW remembered that a soldier named Donald Cobb was suffering from dysentery and the effects of a bullet wound in his leg. A very weak Cobb confided in his friend that "PATE was stealing his rations of food." Cobb's friend stood up to Pate and challenged him, but that only made matters worse. Pate began pointing out Cobb's absences at morning formation and the Chinese predictably ordered him brought out and sent to work. Within days, Cobb's condition degenerated to the point that he required constant care from his fellow prisoners. Pate apparently lobbied the Chinese to place Cobb in the camp hospital, called the Death House by prisoners, and two weeks later, Cobb died.[75]

Lewie Griggs also earned enemies through his mistreatment of other PsW. In October 1951, a shoeless and ill prisoner named Joe Busbey refused to go out on a wood gathering detail. When the Chinese caught wind of his absence, they locked Busbey in a turnip cellar, intending to keep him there all day. When the detail returned to camp and learned of Busbey's fate, they went to headquarters and lobbied the commandant to release their friend on account of his illness. Moved by their request, the commander ordered Busbey's release from confinement in front of a small group of Progressive PsW present at the time. The Progressives spoke up and insisted that Busbey be returned to the cellar the next morning until he had finished his punishment. Busbey was therefore released at night, but spent several of the coming days in his turnip cellar. The group of Progressive PsW who insisted on Busbey's continued punishment included Lewie Griggs. It was suggested that the reason these Progressives wanted Busbey to be returned to the cellar was because he was a Reactionary. One of his fellow prisoners remembered that Busbey "spoke 'stars and stripes' all the time and he commented that he didn't have the education but he had the common sense to know better." Busbey, "rubbed it in, more or less."[76]

Otho Bell could be cruel, too. In February 1951, one of the men in Bell's squad was too sick to work and when Bell tried to force him to go out on a burial detail, he could not comply. Joseph Robinson remembered that Bell, who was better fed and cared for than most of the others because of his position, "grabbed 'Luke' by the arms and dragged him outside and put him on the ground." Robinson noted that "Luke" remained on the frozen ground for more than two hours before Bell left the room, giving the men a chance to bring "Luke" back in. "He died sometime the next day."[77] Cecil Gable filled in a few of the story's holes. As he was returning from a detail, Gable saw a man known to him as Shee lying outside in the cold. He dragged Shee back into the squad building. Although he did not know the circumstances surrounding Shee's being out in the cold, he did confirm that his bringing the man back into the warmth did not forestall his death.[78]

Robinson remembered another incident regarding Bell's treatment of his fellow prisoners. In February 1951, Bell ordered the men out to cut firewood. One of the men was in no shape to work that day and returned to the squad room shortly: "Bell tried to force this man to return and an argument arose, whereupon Bell beat this man with his fists." Again trying to go out and help cut wood, the man returned to the squad room for a second time. Not wishing to see Bell beat the man again, Joseph Robinson volunteered to cut the man's share of the wood that day, which apparently pleased Bell.[79]

Otho Bell was also an accomplished informant. When a PW known as Sandy told a friend about food and clothes that he had stolen from headquarters in preparation for an escape attempt, Harold McKibben saw Otho Bell hurry to headquarters. About five minutes later, Chinese officials came for the offending man.[80] Roy McClain, Charles Jefferson, and Billy Brown stole some firewood from behind the Chinese headquarters in early 1952. Spotted by Bell, the three men knew they were in trouble when he immediately went into the building to report the transgression. They were made to stand in the cold for hours without their coats.[81] Harrison West visited with Bell one day in early 1952 and the two talked about informants. West asked Bell if he had ever squealed on anyone; Bell at first denied it, but then relented. He confessed that in March or April 1951 there had been a theft of food from one of the company kitchens. When the Chinese authorities accused Bell of being the thief, he "blurted out the name of the POW of Spanish descent." Shortly, Chinese guards arrested the man and a terrible beating ensued. Bell admitted that after the man was beaten, he was thrown into the "hole" for a week.[82] Bell also spied on Reactionary PWs by hiding in the attic above the room where they frequently met. He would then go to Tong,[83] Provost Marshall at Camp Five, and tell him what he had heard. Ed Dickenson personally learned how cold-hearted Bell could be. Upon their refusal to be repatriated in the late summer of 1953, Bell confessed that he had informed on one of Dickenson's escape plots in the fall of 1951. After Dickenson had come to him asking for a pair of shoes, Bell had gone straight to the camp's commander and Dickenson was back in custody within thirty minutes.[84]

Clarence Adams was also identified by numerous returnees as an accomplished informant. The most damning of accusations against Adams was that in April 1951 he ordered a sick prisoner, Oliver Stoney, out to gather wood. Because of his weakened condition, Stoney stole the firewood instead and was caught by the Chinese. Whether or not Adams informed on Stoney or refused to stand by him once caught, returning prisoners pinned Stoney's punishment on Adams, as squad leader. Stoney was made to stand barefoot and lightly dressed, at attention, in the snow. Ten days later, Stoney died of pneumonia.[85]

In fall 1952, John Ekenbarger was a monitor and periodically reported the results of lecture discussions. In response to one discussion on racial discrimination, Ekenbarger disagreed with the group and stood by his own belief that the United States was not discriminatory. Otho Bell left the discussion at that point and did not return. Later that day, however, Clarence Adams came to Ekenbarger's hut and "asked me if I didn't like Negroes or just didn't like him." Expecting a fight, the other prisoners led Ekenbarger and Adams outside, where they found that Adams had brought about a dozen of his friends. Quickly calculating the odds, Ekenbarger refused to fight Adams and told him to send his friends back to their quarters. After the others left, Adams asked the same question again, to which Ekenbarger responded that he "didn't like guys who were Un-American like Adams and Bell." The two argued some more and as Adams and Bell left, Ekenbarger warned them, "You had better watch your step." Within minutes, Chinese guards came for Ekenbarger and Virgil Rutherford, who had witnessed the incident, for questioning. By the end of the day, Ekenbarger was serving fifteen days in solitary confinement.[86]

Self-criticism was an important part of the process of softening the prisoners and making them more receptive to the communist message. The Chinese often punished small offenses by forcing prisoners to write out their life stories. Once the autobiographies were written, the Chinese would examine them and often return them to the prisoners to add more contrition. If they refused, they would be punished in a variety of ways, including isolation, torture, or reduced rations. While the Chinese expected that the men would come clean with all of the details of their lives and wartime transgressions, the prisoners understood that the subtleties of the English language could be used to oppose the purposes of their captors. Albert Biderman provided several examples of how prisoners could use language to manipulate the self-criticism: "I promise never again to call Wong, that no-good, dirty, son of a bitch" and "I promise I will never again be caught stealing the property of the People's Volunteers" were two favorites.[87]

In November 1952, the Chinese put together the largest propaganda show of the war. From November 13–26, athletes representing several PW camps along the Yalu River competed in the inter-camp Olympics. That summer, the Games of the XV Olympiad had been held in Helsinki. Although neither North Korea nor China fielded a team in Finland, the administrators of the Chinese indoctrination program thought it would be an excellent propaganda opportunity to create competitive games for the PsW. To prepare for the games, Camp Five built a temporary stadium to welcome the 500 PsW drawn from the nearby camps. For nearly two weeks, inter-camp athletic competition was mixed with propaganda operations to paint a rosy picture of conditions within the prison camps. The opportunity did not disappoint, as the men enjoyed themselves while giving the Chinese plenty to photograph and record in their news reports.[88]

The inter-camp Olympics illustrate several important changes in the PW experience. Apart from the blatant propaganda element of the games, the PsW were clearly healthier than they had been just a year before, when starvation was rampant in all of the camps. When John L. Thomas won the 100-meter race with a time of 10.6 seconds, he was only .4 of a second off McDonald

Bailey's world record set the year before and .2 of a second off the gold medal time of Lindy Remigino of the United States in the 1952 Helsinki games.[89] Less impressive, but still worth noting because of the amateur and untrained status of the PsW, Tony Eagles, an Englishman, won the 400-meter race with a time of 1:1.2, fifteen seconds off the standing world record of 45.8.[90]

Soon after the games, the Chinese resumed their indoctrination efforts and elevated Batchelor to a position of power. Robert Hickox had been the favorite since early in their captivity. He had been trusted to monitor radio broadcasts out of Tokyo and make news announcements to the camp, but after confidential informants began reporting suspicious activity to the Chinese, Hickox lost his access to the radio and was ordered to begin taking all of his news from magazines and newspapers. The Chinese then offered the job to Batchelor, who had become one of Hickox's closest friends. When Claude Batchelor broke the news to his buddy, Hickox encouraged him to take it in the hopes that Batchelor could get them access to the radio.[91]

Batchelor's elevation to the main news spot in Camp Five coincided with a visit by Alan Winnington. As a correspondent for the *Daily Worker,* Winnington came to Korea in 1950 to report on the war and became a frequent visitor to the Chinese prison camps where he provided a sterling example of a Westerner committed to communism. As Winnington was preparing to leave, the Chinese allowed several prisoners, including Batchelor, to go into Pyoktong, where the visitor was housed. At a farewell dinner at which only Westerners were present, Batchelor complained about the heavy-handedness of the Chinese in regard to indoctrination efforts and about the lack of news out of Tokyo. Winnington agreed that allowing the men to see only one side was shortsighted and promised to take the issue up with the Chinese before he left. The next morning, Winnington stopped in and told Batchelor that he had the promised conversation and thought the Chinese would come around shortly. However, after several days, nothing came of Winnington's prediction and Batchelor raised the issue again with his superiors. Frustrated by the Chinese refusal to open the airways, Batchelor threatened to quit, but the Chinese pacified him by allowing only sports broadcasts. For the remainder of his captivity, Batchelor argued for access to Western news reports, but the Chinese refused, preferring instead to write the news announcements themselves to be read by PsW over the camp's public address system.[92]

In October 1952, at the Nineteenth Party Congress, Georgy Malenkov presented a report that caught the attention of the Progressive PsW. Offered in conjunction with Stalin's *Economic Problems of Socialism,* Malenkov's report clearly agreed with Stalin's recent announcement that a new purge of the

Communist party in the Soviet Union was necessary. Within months, however, Stalin was dead and Malenkov found himself propelled into the tyrant's seat. Seemingly understanding the incredible tension that Stalin had caused, Malenkov began touting a world in which the Soviet Union and the United States could live in "peaceful coexistence." With olive branch diplomacy being sanctioned by the Soviets, Mao fell into line and Malenkov's report became standard reading. Claude Batchelor recalled that "It seems as if they [the Chinese] thought Malenkov's Report was the most important thing to happen during our entire period of captivity." One prisoner remembered that Clarence Adams had given a speech in early 1953 on peaceful coexistence, although he considered the lecture to be communist propaganda "because it advocated peace on the enemy's terms."[93] The Chinese strongly urged study of the report and Batchelor and the other high-level Progressives obliged. However, the report was important enough to the Chinese that they wanted virtually all of this group's discussion to center around it and the men quickly tired of the subject. Additionally, the Chinese wanted some of these discussions to be held in their presence, further testing the men's commitment. Frustrated by this, Batchelor and several of the others refused to continue their discussions of the Malenkov report and by late winter 1952–53, the report had run its course—at least for the purpose of prisoner indoctrination.[94]

In late 1952 and early 1953, the Chinese at Camp One instituted Operation Detect. Headed by Bobby DeGraw and a camp intelligence officer, this was a program of collecting information on Reactionary prisoners. Arlie Pate and Richard Tenneson represented their individual companies and wrote out reports on the men they considered to be resistant to the efforts of the communists. For two months, the informers would gather and turn in signed statements about their fellow PsW.[95] Through their efforts, the Chinese learned much about the suspected collaborators within the camp.

When the Reactionaries learned of this operation, they made a daring move. With one prisoner standing watch outside of Camp Headquarters, another broke into the building and ransacked the commandant's desk. Over the coming days, while the Progressives were working with camp officials to find the culprit, dozens of documents were being circulated through the compound. It seems that the purpose of the clandestine raid had been to gain access to reports written by confidential informers. The man who initiated the break-in had planned an escape attempt, but the Chinese had found out about the scheme and punished him. He had always suspected that Arlie Pate was the informer. That night he found the evidence he sought, along with about twenty-five other damning reports, and took it all with the intention of revealing the identities of the camp informers. Back at the squad, the men read the documents, buried them in the ground, and slid them into hidden spaces in the walls and floors, but did not specifically acknowledge that they had seen anything. It was clear to the informers that they had, though, and once the camp began seeing evidence of these men's duplicity, much of it in their own handwriting, the lives of fellows like Arlie Pate and Richard Tenneson suddenly became much more difficult.[96]

By the spring of 1953, Claude Batchelor was at his breaking point. The depression he had suffered from for over a year had not eased and he was slowly being pushed to desperation. In February, Batchelor met Frank "Pappy" Noel, an Associated Press photographer who had worked for the AP since 1930. Although neither his fellow PsW nor his captors knew it for quite some time, Noel was a famous man. In 1943, he had won the second-ever Pulitzer Prize for photography with his shot, "Water," which showed the survivor of a torpedo attack in the Pacific begging for water while in a lifeboat. A veteran of combat photography, Noel had been sent to Korea in 1950 to follow the tense situation there. Captured along with about 120 other men on November 9, that same year, Noel was treated as a military prisoner until late 1951 when his true identity became known.[97]

Once the Chinese verified that "Pappy" Noel was a celebrated photographer, they began using him for propaganda purposes. Beginning with an effort by some newsmen to get a gift of food, cigarettes, and whiskey to Noel in time for Christmas, 1951, the small plan grew larger when one of the men suggested, "As long as we're dreaming, how about a camera?" In what became known as "Operation 'Father Christmas,'" journalists on both sides of the ideological divide were able to get Noel a camera and use his photography as a way to draw the two nations closer to the truce table. With the permission of Chinese authorities, who censored Noel's work before its release, the Associated Press began receiving his shots by the end of January 1952. "Operation 'Father Christmas'" had been a success. For the remainder of the war, Noel would supply the Associated Press with hundreds of photographs taken from behind the barbed wire curtain.[98]

Batchelor and Noel became close friends during the last months of the war and began planning an escape together. Although most prisoners fantasized about escape as a way of passing time, Noel actually did something about it. During his more than three years in captivity, Noel planned four escapes and actually carried one out with some brief success. As early as February 1953, reports had filtered through the ranks that an exchange of sick and wounded PsW was imminent, but Noel had heard similar talk before. He

Frank "Pappy" Noel sits between two men shortly after his release in August 1953. Noel, an Associated Press photographer, had been captured along with hundreds of American soldiers early in the war and held captive by the North Koreans and Chinese. In 1943, Noel had won the second-ever Pulitzer Prize for Photography. (Still Pictures Division, NARA II)

recalled that "we had gone through this process of building up our hopes and breaking them down when negotiations would start and stop. I wanted to go again." Noel did not know Batchelor well so "I dropped a couple of items there that I thought if it leaked out, that I would know about it." However, Noel heard nothing and began to realize that Batchelor was trustworthy. In April, he confided his plan to Batchelor and told him he needed a map. When Batchelor saw him a few days later, he gave Noel a map and Noel knew he had a partner.[99]

While Batchelor procured, Noel planned. In addition to the map, Batchelor began hoarding food and secreting it to Noel, who could store it in his hut. Fortunately, real-world situations began to unravel the plan. After Operation Little Switch became a reality in April 1953, hopes were high among the PsW. Over the coming months, the Chinese "fattened up" the malnourished prisoners and rumors of their impending release grew more convincing. Noel and Batchelor, although hopeful, were not convinced. They planned their escape for August 1, the heart of the rainy season, because "the only time you could escape out of that country up in there is when the monsoons started, and that was in August, because you need the protection of the rain." The plan never came to fruition because on August 1, "Big Switch started. If it didn't start, we were going to take out then."[100]

In the midst of Batchelor's and Noel's planning, truce talks began to make progress for the first time in nearly two years. On April 29, 1953, Operation Little Switch began. Small, but significant, Little Switch provided for the exchange of sick and wounded PsW. Over the course of the coming days, 149 Americans, 64 other UN troops, and nearly 500 from the Republic of Korea were released south, while more than 6,600 North Korean, Chinese, and civilian prisoners were sent north. American soldiers and civilians alike celebrated this new progress.[101]

Edward Dickenson saw Little Switch as his opportunity to gain freedom. With a long-standing heart ailment that had gotten him discharged from his initial enlistment in the army several years earlier, Dickenson exaggerated his condition in the days preceding Little Switch. Apparently feigning attacks, men "would have to carry him on a stretcher to sick call." William Hansen and another prisoner tired of the work and doubted Dickenson's story, making him walk to see the doctor. Ultimately, Dickenson's attempt to escape Camp Five failed.[102]

With the coming of Operation Little Switch, quiet hope trumped outright elation within the prison camps. Because the Chinese administrators selected the men to be repatriated and classified them as "sick and wounded," they stocked Little Switch with many Progressives who were either no longer useful to them or who might be effective operatives within the United States. Interestingly, Batchelor remembered that when he voiced his opposition to sending Progressives back during Little Switch, the camp administrators countered that "these POWs could get back and help their propaganda." By sending Progressives back and keeping Reactionaries in camp, the Chinese captors hoped to prevent the returnees from being used for pro-American propaganda purposes. Paul Schnur, Robert Hickox, and William Hinkle were the three most prominent on the list of repatriates, although several of the men evinced interest.[103]

On the evening before Little Switch, the Chinese threw a party for those who were homebound. Frank Noel attended, capturing several images with his camera. As the night wore on, Batchelor and Noel said goodbye to many of the men they had befriended over the previous years. Batchelor remembered that the departing prisoners encouraged him to "keep up doing the Progressive work I was doing" and that a drunk Robert Hickox told him to "go back to the company to help the other Progressives there." The next day, the prisoners, along with the photographer Noel, proceeded with the formal exchange.[104]

Richard Tenneson wrote his mother about the celebration. He complained that he had "just got over a hangover" after a night of parties to mark the coming release of sick prisoners in Little Switch. He confessed that he "went under the table the first party," but "it wasn't a good feeling to shake hands with the guys to leave knowing that they are going home and not knowing when or if you are going home." He bragged that since he was vice chairman of the company club, he was invited, and dined on "pork, chicken, beef, fish, eggs, fruit and wine and brandy," but made no mention of whether any of these delicacies were made available to the prisoners not considered Progressives.[105]

Whether it can be credited to the conditions of their captivity or their level of indoctrination, the Chinese and North Korean prisoners cut a dramatically different figure from their UN comrades. John Toland wrote that the communist prisoners left their imprisonment defiantly, with many of them refusing anything from their captors upon their departure. On the other hand, the southbound prisoners were quiet and compliant. When asked about their experiences, few spoke candidly, preferring to refuse comment or talk only about those men left behind in the Chinese camps. The Associated Press reported that "American soldiers returning from the Communist prison camps told a story today of generally good treatment," surprising readers back home. Claiming to have left a caring and compassionate enemy captor, some of the American soldiers made such positive comments about their PW experience that the army began to consider psychological evaluations for the newly returned men.[106]

Upon the return of these Americans who remembered "generally good treatment," the army responded by sending several of them for psychiatric evaluation. Of the 149 sick and wounded released in late April, most of them came home where they reconnected with family and friends while periodically visiting military hospitals for ongoing treatment for physical ailments. However, what a spokesman for the army called a "small group" was flown to Valley Forge Army Hospital for other purposes.

On May 1, the Associated Press reported that twenty-two former prisoners of war identified as "victims of Communist propaganda" had landed at Travis Air Force Base, where one of their number, Paul Schnur Jr., of nearby San Francisco, was dropped off and sent to Letterman Army Hospital. Schnur's impromptu transfer caused rumblings about whether his influential father had anything to do with the Department of the Army singling him out. Continuing on to Andrews AFB, Maryland, in a hospital plane with barred windows "used for transporting 'psychos,'" the men thought their long journey was over until they saw two more planes waiting for them. From Maryland, they took a short flight to Willow Grove, Pennsylvania, and then a drive to Valley Forge Hospital in Phoenixville. On the bus ride to the hospital, the men began to liven up with the realization that they were indeed home, even if under suspicion.[107]

Although the army claimed to have intentions of keeping the details surrounding these men a secret, it released a statement to gauge public sentiment. To explain the secrecy surrounding the group, the army explained, "these men may have been misled under conditions of duress and hardship during the period of their captivity. It is our position that they are victims of Communist propaganda."[108] Unfortunately, the story was poorly coordinated on a variety of levels and brought considerable embarrassment to several agencies, including the White House.

Once the group arrived at Valley Forge, they settled into comfortable surroundings. Counting the men who had flown from Travis and a few others who arrived separately, twenty-three men reported to the hospital late in the evening of May 1st. The group was treated to a steak dinner, which one of the men turned down in preference for "a good old U.S. ham sandwich and a glass of milk." One officer noted that the men "ate and ate and ate," and several of them drank "seven or eight cartons of milk." With their stomachs full, the exhausted men had all fallen into bed by 4:00 A.M. Despite having the liberty to sleep as long as they wished, old habits died hard and many of the men awoke after only four hours to eat again. With private rooms, plenty to eat, and all the comforts of home, the men gathered around the telephones to talk to their anxious families. At the same time, the hospital administrators began trying to explain some of the information that the army had released. The hospital's information officer notified a clamoring press corps that none of the names of the men would be released in the near future and added that some of the soldiers "may be under the influence of communism" after their experience as prisoners of war.[109] By the next day, the repatriated men had read the newspapers and found out about the army's statements that suggested their collaboration with the enemy. The hospital spokesman said that the men felt "burned" by media coverage and asked the reporters, "How would you feel if you fought for your country and were captured and wounded and then flew 10,000 miles to a hospital to find you were being labeled a possible Communist? . . . Well, that's how these boys feel."[110]

On May 3rd, several of the patients insisted on speaking with reporters at the hospital in the hope that they could clear their names. Using phrases like "depressed," "insulted," and "bitter beyond expression," ten of the men met newsmen while four were too ill to attend and another four were "too bitter" to speak. As the men stood and spoke, two of them recounted hearing Lt. John Quinn's germ warfare confession, with one noting that "a majority in his compound might have believed the charges . . . at that time." Several admitted that they had signed petitions and other documents while prisoners of war, but noted that coercion was an important tool of the Chinese. Another revealed that he signed a "confession" while under the effects of pain medication after having his arm amputated.[111] Of the ten who spoke that day, the names William Hinkle, James Ball, Robert Hickox, and Richard Morrison appear in various records as likely collaborators.[112]

In the coming days, the collection of doctors and government agents who made up the ward's staff began delving into the men's minds. The three men under the most suspicion were Hickox, Hinkle, and James Pinkston, in addition to Schnur, who remained in California. Hickox came from a good, steady family, but was "emotionally immature" and had a long history of delinquency, including excessive drinking. At Valley Forge, he claimed to be "merely a pro-Communist, writing approximately six items for them," but evidence suggested that he was much more serious in his support and evaluating personnel suggested that the FBI place him under surveillance. Like Hickox, Hinkle drank heavily and openly avowed communism, and he admitted that while in prison, he was "two-faced" and either wrote or signed several pro-communist tracts in exchange for small luxuries like cigarettes and candy. Pinkston was exceedingly bright, steady, and comfortable within himself. Openly confessing his atheism and his own personal preference for communism, he appeared an eager participant in the Chinese indoctrination program. At Valley Forge, he even attempted to have what hospital personnel considered "Communist propaganda printed in *Life* magazine."[113]

With Hickox, Hinkle, Pinkston, and Schnur under suspicion, the other repatriates settled into a comparatively relaxed existence, although many remained on the army's radar. Walter McCollum, a thirty-four-year-old master sergeant, expressed his desire to remain in the army and continue what had been a nearly twelve-year career at that point. Although he had signed peace petitions and had served as a study monitor, he claimed to have done so under duress by the Chinese and was considered by the examiners at Valley Forge to have been minimally indoctrinated. Carl Kirchhausen was a German Jew who fled Hitler's rise in 1938. After migrating to England, he came to the United States. When drafted into the army, he declared that "[h]e was unwilling to serve and attempted to evade the draft on the basis of being a non-citizen." While a prisoner, Kirchhausen was apparently a willing collaborator and serious student of communism. Even while at Valley Forge, he espoused the belief that "the U.S. participated in bacteriological warfare and that Communist prisoners were tortured on Koje." Kenyon Wagner described himself as "pink" and declared that the United States "is militaristic and [the] aggressor in Korea." John Porter signed a few propaganda leaflets, but apparently was untouched by the communist philosophy. When he met one of the physicians at Valley Forge, he announced, "Sir, I have heard we is to get some rehabileration [*sic*], all the rehabileration [*sic*] I need is to get into a double bed with my wife." After only a few days at Valley Forge, most of the men, including those under the most suspicion, were granted thirty days' leave.[114] It is assumed that John Porter was "rehabilerated" at some point upon returning home.

The Valley Forge project became fodder for the Chinese and Soviet presses. The Chinese took note that the United States was now participating in brainwashing activities and forcing these men who had learned class theory from their prison experiences "to abandon their Progressive beliefs." Several months later, as China and the United Nations were sparring over the required explanation sessions for nonrepatriate prisoners, the Chinese were still bringing up the "evil arts Americans would use to make North Korean and Chinese prisoners refuse repatriation."[115]

Medically, the observation at Valley Forge gleaned important results. Physicians noted that the men initially appeared dull and apathetic after they were released. Their brains seemed to have been shut down and they "discussed emotionally charged material with bland indifference." The men also had "an appreciable lack of sense of time" and "little concern for the future." When asked about the future, their plans "were poorly conceived, of a short-term nature and highly unrealistic." It did not take long, however, for the repatriates to begin mentally transitioning back to the United States. They began asking for hair tonic and aftershave lotion. The mental health community had found that soldiers returning from World War II had suffered from the "hero for a day" syndrome in which a returned soldier was revered briefly, but once that attention faded society was left with "dependent demanding individuals." Of the 149 Americans returned in Operation Little Switch, 27 (19 percent) were found to have a significant psychiatric disability. Most prevalent were five cases of Schizoid Personality, three cases of Anxiety Reaction, two cases of Transient Personality Disorder; and two instances of Schizophrenia.[116]

Between Little Switch and the finalizing of the truce, Claude Batchelor was called out by his Chinese captors to go on long walks. He recalled that the Chinese were very cautious regarding him and they seemed to be trying to return to his good graces. By May, Batchelor had agreed to move back into his company of Progressives and was slowly being brought back into the pro-communist fold. He reprised his role in the play *Golden Boy* and started attending club meetings and study sessions. Despite what Batchelor said about his slow return to camp life, the Chinese were quick to ask him to begin giving lectures on communist political economy. He refused, as did another American, but Andrew Condron taught lessons to his fellow Brits at Camp Five.[117]

In early June, Batchelor was called to headquarters and asked about his state of mind. By this time, he had returned to his friends and was expecting the war to come to a close, so he agreed to participate in a Progressive conference among all of the prison camps. Condron and Batchelor represented Camp Five; Bobby DeGraw and an Englishman, Thomas Davies, were from Camp One; and Veneris and Bohus Janda from Camp Three. Over the course of the coming days, Batchelor tried to gauge his colleagues' levels of commitment. The Chinese had asked him to organize a Progressive movement within the United States and to evaluate what the men thought their futures might hold in the United States. After talking with Veneris, Batchelor was convinced that the man feared political retribution. He spoke to Janda and DeGraw, who both agreed with Veneris's assumption. As a result, Batchelor and the others continued to discuss the benefits of a Progressive organization back in the states that might be able to influence whatever punitive action lay in store. During the coming months, their ranks thinned considerably, and ultimately only served to convince a couple of dozen UN soldiers to remain with the Chinese.[118]

FIVE

Politicians and Their Careers

> "People who voice an opinion for peace in the United States are persecuted and their voices suppressed. There is not a democratic government in the United States as long as McCarthyism and McCarranism are allowed to exist."
>
> —Morris Wills

In addition to the story thus far, there exists a corollary tale that must be considered alongside that of the men who were beginning their ordeal as prisoners of war. Instead of taking place in the icy North Korean winter, it was set in the warm and secure halls of the United States Capitol where the nation's politicians began conveniently forgetting about the thousands of American soldiers who were facing injury and death half a world away. Rather than deal with the cause at hand, politicians in Washington, D.C., were busily redirecting the attention of their constituents away from the fighting men and toward a more politically useful end. Using fear as their central tactic, a number of senators and congressmen alike spent 1950 and 1951 resurrecting the Red Scare of the 1920s and whipping up anti-communist sentiment. At the head of this movement was a mixture of newcomers and old hats whose words would promise to cripple communism, but whose activities served the Chinese propaganda machine very well.

If ever a man was born to be a politician, it was Joe McCarthy. He combined his humble background and tireless energy with an innate ability to glad-hand and ingratiate himself with his constituents. The result was a candidate who fostered fierce loyalty among his constituents because he knew them and they knew him. However, these are the tactics used by most politicians and Joe McCarthy had an ace in the hole. In addition to the glad-handing and collecting of friends, the complex nature of his mind allowed him to approach issues in ways never considered by some of his colleagues. David Oshinsky described him as a man "who had little respect for community values," and one who might periodically show respect for tradition, but was willing to play the "lawless, unsocialized fellow who elbows his way to the center by overwhelming his rule-bound neighbors." One of McCarthy's fellow attorneys recalled, "Joe lived in a different moral universe," one driven wholly by the questions of "What do I want and how do I get it." He added, "Once he got rolling, you had to step aside. It was every man for himself, sort of what anarchy must be like." Another story dealt with his tactics in seeking a judgeship. Although he had privately pledged his support to a dear friend, mentor, and law partner who was planning to enter the race, McCarthy wanted the job for himself and rather than challenge his friend, he beat the man to the punch and announced his candidacy first, thereby making his associate's personal friendship and political candidacy untenable.[1]

Joe McCarthy's take-no-prisoners approach to politics promised results, but he also understood the importance of a strong public persona. Although adept at handshaking and kissing babies, McCarthy saw the importance of capitalizing on America's involvement in World War II if he expected his political ascendance to continue. In the early months of 1942, he acted on his impulse and joined the Marine Corps after a friend advised, "Look, if you've got to be a hero to be a politician, join the Marines." Within weeks, First Lieutenant McCarthy took his oath and by summer, he was in the Pacific theater serving as an intelligence officer. Fearing that the people of Wisconsin would forget the circuit court judge who had abandoned his bench for the war in the Pacific, McCarthy began sending back reports of his wartime experiences to local newspapers. Despite his valuable service in intelligence, in his mind, it was not enough to carry his political aspirations throughout the war. When his unit was ordered to Guadalcanal, the circumstances were perfect for the expansion of his service record. With little going on near the island by that time in the war, the pilots passed the time by "breaking records." Their most frequent target was the nearly abandoned Japanese air base at Rabaul where they would fly the most missions, drop the most bombs, or fire the most ammunition. Seeing his opportunity, McCarthy tagged along on one of these missions where he was "allowed to blast away at the coconut trees." Upon his return to base, a publicity officer verified the story, wrote a press release, and "Tail-Gunner" Joe McCarthy was born.[2]

Within months of "Tail-Gunner" Joe's public relations windfall, he started his run for the United States Senate from the South Pacific. Throwing himself into the race for the Republican nomination in 1944, he depended on direct mail to get his name out to the voters. Although he lost the race, he did finish a very respectable second in a crowded field. With his hopes for elective office brightened, McCarthy resigned his commission in early 1945 and returned to Wisconsin, where he began campaigning for Robert M. LaFollette Jr's senate seat. In a hotly contested Republican primary, "Little Bob," who had succeeded his famous father and held the seat for twenty-two years, lost to McCarthy by fewer than 5,000 votes. In the general election, he found himself pitted against Howard McMurray, who apparently ran as a Democrat to help defeat LaFollette. McMurray reportedly said, "I won't get elected, but I'll see that Bob doesn't either." That was true. With McMurray's help, Bob lost his job and Joe McCarthy took it. Running on a platform that would later become predictable, "Tail-Gunner" Joe stepped in line with GOP leadership and adhered to the maxim that in 1946 "the choice . . . is between Communism and Republicanism"—which was particularly convenient after Howard McMurray received the unwanted endorsement of the Wisconsin Communist Party. In November, McCarthy scored an overwhelming victory at the polls. However, the intersection of "Little Bob" and "Tail-Gunner Joe" did not end there. More than six years later, in February 1953, a combination of clinical depression and the fear that the now powerful Senator McCarthy would call him before his Subcommittee on Investigations drove "Little Bob" to put a pistol in his mouth and pull the trigger.[3]

Patrick Anthony McCarran was already a force in Washington, D.C., when Joe McCarthy arrived. Fifty-six years old when he was first elected as a senator from Nevada in 1932, McCarran stood out as a freshman. Like many other Democrats of that era, McCarran rode the Great Depression to the nation's capitol, but his coming career would depend on the communist threat for its impetus.

Pat McCarran's political career had been disappointing. He had sought national office several times and failed in each attempt. Finally, when he did win election, it was to the State Supreme Court, a position that specifically forbade the pursuit of another office while still a sitting member. It seemed that he would never reach Washington, D.C. With the economic difficulties of Herbert Hoover's administration, many Democrats saw renewed political opportunities, and McCarran was one of them. In 1932, the man who had often alienated those influential within his own party received the Democratic nomination for the United States Senate. By the end of the year, he had scored a narrow victory over former governor and two-term incumbent senator, Tasker Oddie.[4]

For the next three terms, Pat McCarran firmly entrenched himself as one of Congress's most committed and effective senators on a variety of issues, but communism grew to become his calling card. Having developed into one of the most avowedly anti-communist members of the Senate, McCarran was heartened when President Harry Truman sought to strengthen espionage laws in the summer of 1950. Truman, understanding the political advantages that might be exploited by congressmen hungry for a stronger anti-communist stance by the administration, reached out to McCarran requesting the change, but warning that it should be done in such a way that it would not restrict constitutional liberties. With Truman's broaching of the subject, a Pandora's box had been opened. The Korean War was only weeks old and if the President wanted a bill strengthening national security, Pat McCarran would eagerly provide it.[5]

Richard Nixon carved out his early niche as a member of the House Un-American Activities Committee (HUAC). The committee had been created in 1938 and operated during World War II, when its twisted logic supported the internment of Japanese-Americans, while refusing to speak out against the activities of the Ku Klux Klan because it was "an old American institution." Immediately after the war ended, it achieved its greatest level of influence, and before the end of 1945, its status changed from a select to a permanent committee.[6]

Like McCarthy, Nixon arrived in Washington thanks to the congressional elections of 1946. After looking for but failing to find an opportunity to run for the California State Assembly, the thirty-three-year-old attorney threw his hat into the ring for Jerry Voorhis's seat in the United States House of Representatives. Challenging Voorhis was certainly a political risk as the congressman had held the seat since 1937 and had made a noticeable splash in 1943 when he revealed serious irregularities in wartime petroleum contracts. A devoutly religious man whose pre-congressional life was spent on humanitarian projects, Voorhis was unprepared for the buzz saw he ran into with Richard Nixon.[7]

When Nixon became the Republican nominee for the 12th Congressional District, he attacked the campaign with a measure of vigor unseen in previous races for the seat. First, and most prominently, Nixon struck at Voorhis's endorsement by a political action committee (PAC). Through political mercenary Murray Chotiner, Nixon's campaign supplied regional newspapers with releases attacking their opponent's endorsement by the Congress of Industrial Organization's PAC (CIO-PAC). During the transition years of the Depression and World War II, the CIO grew into a haven for hyper-leftists. Barely receiving the CIO-PAC endorsement in 1944, the moderate Voorhis was the only major California Democrat left off the support list in 1946, with the board voting specifically to deny him any aid whatsoever. To the incumbent, this was no big insult, as he served on HUAC as a moderating voice and fully understood that some of the anti-communist fears surrounding labor unions were legitimate. In fact, within days of the CIO singling him out as the lone non-recipient of their support, he wrote, "I frankly hoped I wouldn't get it. . . . I believe the communists are in substantial control of CIO. . . . I think that is why I didn't get the endorsement." Voorhis did, however receive the official support of the National Citizens Political Action Committee (NCPAC), a moderate, nonunion, sub-element of the CIO, which promoted the expansion of democracy through civil rights, social welfare, and the gentle prodding of the Soviet Union. Although some of the NCPAC's membership reflected the communist sympathies present in the CIO, anti-communist liberals like Ronald Reagan were also members. For thinking men, the differences between the CIO-PAC and the NCPAC were stark; for Murray Chotiner and the newspapers of southern California, those differences did not matter. Before Voorhis realized that the coming race would be difficult, Chotiner was able to confuse the PACs for the public and effectively cast the humanitarian who had founded and run a Boys' Home as an enemy of the downtrodden. One newspaper even asked, "shall it be the people represented by Nixon, or the PAC by Voorhis?"[8]

Since the Bolshevik Revolution in Russia, the United States had grown very suspicious of the expansion of communism. With Franklin Roosevelt's election in 1933 and the advent of the New Deal shortly thereafter, the outcry against an international communist conspiracy, which had faded during the late 1920s, began anew. World War II's uneasy partnership between the United States and the Soviet Union seemed to signal better times ahead, but with Harry Truman's ascendancy at the close of the war and the overt territorial greed exhibited by the Russians, postwar optimism quickly dissolved. With the world situation crumbling around them and the American public growing fearful in the nuclear age, politicians in Washington, D.C., exploited the red menace for their own political gain.

The fundamentally democratic nature of the House of Representatives meant that Americans' concerns about communism would first be addressed in that body. Of all the congressmen to try to make a name on the back of the communist menace, Richard Nixon was one of the most successful. He came to Washington having successfully exploited communism in his race against Jerry Voorhis and quickly made a name for himself as a strict party man with leadership potential. Nixon's work ethic helped him cruise through his first term with fair assurance that he would be reelected without much of a fight, but in August 1948 a gift for himself and the Republican Party fell into his lap.

Whittaker Chambers, while working himself into position as one of America's most talented writers, had also become a Soviet spy. Beginning in 1932, he led the Ware Group, a collection of Soviet sympathizers working within the federal government. However, in 1937, Chambers broke with communism and left the espionage business with a few rolls of withheld microfilm that he hoped would keep the Soviets from killing him. Throughout the late 1930s and well into the 1940s, he carved out for himself a very respectable career with *Time* magazine as a senior editor.

On August 3, 1948, Chambers took a seat in front of HUAC and testified about his involvement with the Communist Party. The testimony was largely a recounting of his previous accounts until he began naming names. For the first time, HUAC had found a witness not only willing to confess his own role but to implicate several others, all of it orchestrated by Richard Nixon's dogged research and planning. Overnight, America was introduced to Chambers, Alger Hiss, and the man who brought them to justice, Richard Nixon.[9] In the end, Chambers, the confessed spy, was never charged with any crime and continued his life, working at various times for *Life, Newsweek,* and, for a time, William F. Buckley Jr.'s *National Review;* Nixon became Vice President, and later, President; and Hiss served forty-four months at Lewisburg Federal Penitentiary for perjury.[10]

More immediately, however, Chambers's HUAC testimony put President Harry Truman's reelection bid in jeopardy. Having already been painted as an appeaser of communism, the revelation that the federal government was employing more than a dozen sympathizers shook the administration just three months before election day. In Truman's defense, he had initiated an extensive program of loyalty checks on existing government employees in March 1947. By July 1949, more than 2.5 million men and women were evaluated; just over 10,000 were identified as warranting further investigation. With hearings forthcoming for many of this number, 785 resigned before their hearing, leaving nearly 5,500 to face judgment. Only 332 of those who were ordered to withstand a hearing were found to be of questionable loyalty and 102 were dismissed because of the findings.[11] Through resignation and dismissal, Truman's program removed more subversive threats from the federal government than Nixon's, McCarran's, and McCarthy's work combined, and often with similar, albeit much more subtle, tactics.

As a freshman senator, McCarthy seemed to do everything within his power to alienate himself from his colleagues. He misrepresented facts, spoke out of one side of his mouth while voting with the other, took senior senators to task publicly, and generally bullied his way through debates. With such a reputation growing within the chamber, his prospects looked bleak . . . particularly after having not been given a major committee assignment in 1949.[12] Seemingly weaseled out of any opportunity to distinguish himself by his senatorial colleagues, McCarthy took the job of shaping his career into his own hands.

In April 1949, Joe McCarthy began his enduring assault on the U.S. Army. The massacre of at least seventy-two American soldiers by SS men at Malmedy, in Belgium, in late 1944, proved to be an event ripe for exploitation. By the end of the war, the army was screening German soldiers to determine which ones had participated in war crimes, including the Malmedy Massacre. Very quickly, the U.S. Army identified the unit and the men who had done the killing at Malmedy and started the process of building cases against them. Seventy-three of the SS were found worthy of standing trial for the killings. Starting in the late spring of 1946 and lasting into the summer, the trials took place at Dachau, the infamous Nazi death camp. On June 16, all seventy-three SS were convicted of actively participating in the slaughter; forty-three were sentenced to death, twenty-two received life imprisonment, and the others garnered more lenient punishments.[13]

On the surface, it seemed that the Malmedy Massacre had been avenged with the court's decision to punish the perpetrators; however, later investigations found that American investigators had coerced the numerous confessions. Watching his already limited influence in the Senate dwindling, McCarthy began doing the unthinkable: defending "the clearly innocent GI Joes of the German army." Considering the intensely patriotic rhetoric McCarthy would adopt in the early 1950s, his choice to defend former Nazi soldiers is surprising. His advocacy for the Malmedy Nazis helped him in Wisconsin's German communities, however, and introduced the United States to his personal and irrational suspicion of the army. Ted Morgan called it "the first Army-McCarthy hearing."[14]

McCarthy failed in his argument that the Special Investigation Subcommittee of the Committee on Expenditures, on which he served, was the proper venue for the examination of army techniques. Falling to the Armed

Services Committee, the case was essentially removed from McCarthy's grasp, although the committee invited McCarthy to attend the hearings and question witnesses. He got off to a fiery start when he announced on the opening day of the hearings that he wished to evaluate "how confessions were obtained . . . [m]ock trials . . . physical force . . . Was this 'American Justice'?"[15] In another exchange, he passionately declared, "an innocent man will scream about as loudly as a guilty man if you are kicking him in the testicles, and an innocent man will perhaps sign the same confession that a guilty man will if you kick him long enough and hard enough."[16] In the end, McCarthy's attempts to defend the Nazi soldiers against what he viewed as a Pentagon whitewash failed, but barely five years later, some of the twenty-three American nonrepatriates would argue the same points with McCarthy and the culture he had helped create.

After several months of fearing that his political career might end with the election of 1952, McCarthy stumbled on the issue he could ride to victory. In early February 1950, the GOP sent him out on a brief speaking tour. With speeches scheduled in Las Vegas and Reno—centers of support for his intraparty nemesis and senatorial powerhouse Pat McCarran—and Huron, South Dakota, Joe certainly had not drawn the best lot. However, on February 9, in Wheeling, West Virginia, he spoke on the topic of communist infiltration of the government. He announced that "I have in my hand a list of 205" communists who were working in the Department of State. Over the course of the coming weeks, the numbers changed several times, the list never materialized, and the politicians in Washington began to squirm. All the while, the American people, terrified by the possibility that communists had infiltrated the center of government, hung on every word of the unremarkable senator from Wisconsin and the newspapers, which were mesmerized by his accusations.[17]

Joe McCarthy spent 1950 fighting for his political life. With his unimpressive legislative record behind him, it seemed that the 1952 election would be an easy one for Democrats . . . or even another Republican . . . to win. In an attempt to rescue his senatorial tenure, McCarthy rode the only horse that had given any indication of viability—subversion within the United States government. That horse threatened to throw him in early 1950 when a majority of his senatorial colleagues voted to examine his claims about disloyalty within the State Department. The resulting investigation became famous as the Tydings Committee named for its chairman, Maryland Democrat Millard Tydings. If McCarthy wanted a public hearing, Tydings was ready to give it to him, promising, "you are going to get one of the most complete investigations in the history of the Republic." However, after receiving the names of 112 purported communists, Tydings only called nine individuals, several of whom were questionable enough to give McCarthy cause to declare himself vindicated.[18] In the end, the Tydings Committee approached the issue of loyalty too narrowly. It sought to discredit McCarthy and accomplished its purpose on a party vote.[19]

McCarthy certainly had enemies outside of his party, but Republicans were themselves divided on his pursuit of the loyalty issue. Much of McCarthy's strength came from the support he received from one of the deans of Republican politics. Senator Robert Taft of Ohio privately encouraged McCarthy's ideological jousting, but the Wisconsin senator had influential critics within his own party. On June 1, 1950, Senator Margaret Chase Smith stood in the chamber and read her "Declaration of Conscience," in which she and several other moderate Republicans spoke out against McCarthy's "selfish exploitation of fear, bigotry, ignorance, and intolerance."[20] McCarthy spent the year of 1950 growing his cause, and at times it seemed that he would fail, but by the end of the year, Joe McCarthy was the name most frequently associated with rooting subversive elements out of the government.[21]

As hostilities began in Korea in the summer of 1950, McCarthy saw support for his cause grow significantly. North Korea was a small and relatively insignificant nation compared to China, which the United States had courted with democracy for more than a decade; however, Korea became the great communist bogeyman of the early 1950s. Moreover, as firmly as the United States was supporting South Korean interests, the North Korean army was continually compressing the democratic nation into a very small corner of the peninsula. Such a poor showing by freedom and democracy, particularly one backed by a superpower, in the face of communism and totalitarianism, frustrated and angered the American people. Briefly emboldened by Douglas MacArthur's landing at Inchon in mid-September, those Americans susceptible to McCarthy's message of fear were again terrified by the Chinese entry into the war in November and Truman's firing of MacArthur the following spring. To many, Truman had dismissed the only military leader who really cared about stopping the communist menace.[22]

While hundreds of thousands of young Americans were a world away in Korea and Japan, a perfect storm was brewing in the United States. The anticommunist sentiments that had been slowly simmering since the end of World War II had been whipped into a frenzy by ambitious politicians. However powerful the Nixons, McCarthys, and McCarrans could be through their elective offices and committees, enlisting America's premier law enforcement agency lent added strength to their cause. J. Edgar Hoover had allegedly helped save America from the communist menace in the 1920s; now he returned in the 1950s to exploit American paranoia.[23]

J. Edgar Hoover had always avoided the appearance of being politically involved, mainly because he had to appear independent, if for no other reason than to secure his blank-check budget from an ever-changing Congress. This philosophy especially pertained to HUAC, primarily because of the negative press the committee conjured. After World War II, however, that began to change. Beginning in 1947, Hoover gave periodic assistance to the committee and even aided Richard Nixon's investigation of Alger Hiss the next year. As the war in Korea raged and Joe McCarthy rose to prominence, Hoover's role grew more political as he became one of the senator's most important allies by supplying him with whatever information he had in an effort to corroborate McCarthy's claims.[24]

By 1952, Hoover and McCarthy were working closely together but that would not last. Hoover saw his cooperation with McCarthy as a way to continue the anti-communist fight, even if he had to partner with the controversial senator. Despite McCarthy's inherent carelessness with the facts and figures, Hoover did consider the senator to be a kindred spirit fighting the good fight. McCarthy needed Hoover even more. Perpetually walking a dangerous political tightrope, McCarthy needed the certainty that the steadfast Hoover could provide. With McCarthy giving voice to the evidence gathered by Hoover, the anti-communism fight could proceed with confidence.[25] Although the Hoover-McCarthy team appeared to be one of great strength, a calculating man like Hoover could not work long with the impetuous McCarthy.

Although Hoover had to give up one important, but fragile, connection in McCarthy, he had already begun cultivating another. In the Spring of 1951, Hoover started to cooperate with the Senate Internal Security Subcommittee (SISS) and its chair, Pat McCarran. Hoover had helped HUAC in the past and tried to feed information to McCarthy, who had always disappointed him with his inability to keep the facts straight or his ambition in control. In McCarran, however, Hoover found a kindred spirit with some measure of professional reserve. Within weeks, the committee was using the FBI as its investigative arm and Hoover was reveling in his secret role in bringing public humiliation to the disloyal.[26]

In reality, McCarran's committee was the most effective and legitimate of all the anti-communist efforts, largely due to the cooperation J. Edgar Hoover provided. Hoover did not trust either Nixon or McCarthy, so when McCarran, a man whom the FBI director considered responsible, took up the fight, he vowed to use his bureau to help the Nevadan fight the good fight.[27]

The Korean conflict would give anti-communist politicians their great rattling saber. Railing against the Soviets, fellow travelers, and subversives had found some significant appeal in the prewar United States, but a full-blown war promised to make some of these saber rattlers national heroes.

SIX

The Shocking Refusal

July 27–October 20, 1953

> "A man can be a hero all his life, but if in the last month of it, the last week, or even the last minute, the pressure becomes too great and he breaks, then he's branded for life. You can't ask a man to be a hero forever; there ought to be a time limit."
>
> —Richard Basehart in *Time Limit* (1957)

At 10:00 A.M. on July 27, 1953, Gen. William Harrison of the U.S. Army and the North Korean People's Army's General Nam Il sat together silently signing the papers that would effectively end the Korean conflict. Twelve hours later, the shooting stopped and both sides settled into an uneasy peace.[1] Although that day ended the shooting war, over the preceding weeks both sides had come to the realization that the end of the war was near and begun considering the coming peace.

One of the central cessation issues was the exchange of the thousands of prisoners of war held by each army. Ideological competition remained fierce, and both sides understood that much could be gained politically if enemy prisoners refused repatriation. In this arena, the United States felt that it had a decided advantage. Facing a more difficult task, the Chinese, who held most of the UN prisoners, began trying to convince a core of foreign soldiers to remain behind as converted communists. They achieved moderate success in this endeavor when twenty-six Americans, and several Brits, Turks, and Belgians—apart from several hundred South Koreans—agreed to forego repatriation.[2] For the first time in American history, United States soldiers had to be enticed back home after a war ended.

Among the masses readying themselves for departure from Chinese prison camps in July 1953 was Ed Dickenson; but the hand of fate interceded and changed his life forever. Sometime around July 20, Dickenson's Chinese commander summoned him to the camp's central office for a lecture on the merits of voluntarily remaining with the Chinese. Despite promises that "any POW who wanted to remain and go to China would receive an automobile, a home, a job, a cow and a woman," Dickenson remained adamant in his hope of returning home to the mountains of Virginia and dismissed the commandant's overtures. With the soft touch having failed, Lin, another of the Chinese prison administrators, approached Dickenson about the same matter two days later. When asked if he would refuse repatriation to the United States, Dickenson repeated his wish to return home and Lin "became angry and told me that if I did not consider staying with the Communists, he would send all of the articles and recordings I had written and made, to the United States Government." Lin warned Dickenson that the U.S. government would frown on his activities while a prisoner and assured the detainee that it "would prosecute me for collaborating with an enemy." Lin's ploy worked. Having become dependent on the Chinese for every aspect of his existence during his imprisonment, Dickenson believed his captors' story and agreed to stay with the Chinese.[3]

Pleased with Dickenson's decision, Lin handed the soldier a sheet of paper and told him to write out an application for non-repatriation and to include the following:

> I have been disturbed for weeks. I could not sleep at nights. This strange disposition was noted by my buddies, and they often asked me what was wrong with me. I told them that I was trying to make up my mind on a very, very important matter. I told them that I was trying to make up my mind about Communism and non-repatriation. I told them that the decision was the greatest I have had to make. In making this great decision, I had to think of my home, my family, my religion, and everything that I have held dear in my past life. Becoming a Communist and a revolutionist means giving up my religion, because religion and Communism do not mix. I have to give up my family ties, because Communism comes first, and in order to be a good Communist, one must put it before everything else. Also, to be a good revolutionist, one has to give up family. I have thought of all these things, and have now made up my mind to refuse repatriation, and go to China.

The next day, Dickenson submitted the handwritten letter to Lin who then asked him to complete a questionnaire. Dickenson recalled that most of the questions regarded whether other PsW might refuse repatriation and rethink the wisdom of their returning to the States. On July 24, he submitted the completed survey, but spent that night regretting his choice. The next day, he found Lin, told him that he had reconsidered, and would return to the United States. Lin responded that it was too late, that Dickenson's application to remain with the Chinese had already been forwarded to the United Nations. Having lived for three years in an environment that did not tolerate complaints and punished minor infractions swiftly and harshly, Dickenson accepted Lin's word on the matter and tried to "make myself satisfied."[4]

Fear also worked on Arlie Pate. While he never broached his motivations, several of his fellow prisoners offered their guesses at his reasons for not returning to the United States. One man noted that Pate "was afraid to return for fear of what might happen to him for his conduct while a POW." Another man, interviewed by the FBI two years after being repatriated, told the agent that the men who chose to remain with their Chinese captors "were afraid to be repatriated because of their fear of reprisals."[5] Fellow nonrepatriate Edward Dickenson elaborated on Pate's motivations by explaining that he feared that he would be held accountable for the death of an imprisoned officer. Pate claimed to have killed "an American lieutenant in the winter of 1951–52 over a black market deal that involved food." He noted that the victim was "Lieutenant Jackson and . . . that he had choked him to death."[6] When the FBI read Dickenson's report on the death of Lieutenant Jackson, an investigation was started culminating in a report refuting Pate's contention. There was a Lieutenant Jackson who died as a prisoner of war, but his date of death did not correspond with Dickenson's stated date, nor did he have any known ties to the black market.[7] Like much of the information floating around prison camps, the issue of Lieutenant Jackson may have been elaborated to the point that it lost fundamental elements of truth. A returned PW remembered that Clarence Adams had pressured "a boy by the name of Jackson, from Texas, to write letters . . . saying Camp 5 was being bombed" by American planes. Jackson refused to cooperate and several other prisoners came to his defense. "Some of the prisoners threatened to beat Adams up, and somebody threatened to hit him with a piece of firewood we had hidden in the hut." Adams marched to the Chinese headquarters and before long, Lu visited the men and made Jackson and several others stand at attention in the freezing cold. Jackson collapsed and died as a result.[8] In such a rumor-driven environment, the name Jackson and the story that a Progressive helped cause his death remained in the minds of men for years after they had either witnessed or heard about the event, despite the looseness of the details.

Similarly, Richard Corden's activities while a PW marked him as a target of violence. One day, Corden came into the squad and found a note on his bunk. The anonymous author promised to kill him if he did not stop collaborating with the Chinese. Corden took the note to headquarters and was moved out of the squad that very day.[9] Ted Sprouse, although not a Progressive, was friendly with Corden. He urged Corden to reconsider his decision to remain with his captors arguing that Corden could examine communism from within a free society and did not have to go to China in order to learn more about the concept. He felt that Corden's interest in communism was sincere, but that a fear of retribution from fellow PsW contributed to his decision not to repatriate.

Andrew Fortuna had also made enemies while a prisoner of war. In addition to his active participation in Chinese indoctrination activities and rumors that he had informed on escape attempts, other PsW accused him of taking "food away from other prisoners of war by physical force." Henry Valencia claimed that Fortuna caused the starvation death of a fellow prisoner in the winter of 1951. He also alleged that Fortuna heaped duties upon another prisoner who was suffering from dysentery, which led to his death.[10]

Claude Batchelor first met William Cowart during Big Switch. Originally at Camp One, Cowart had been sent to Camp Five in June and was living alone separate from the other prisoners. His room, although private, was under constant guard and he was not allowed to mix with his fellow prisoners because of the possibility of violence toward him by reactionaries. Cowart told Batchelor that he had tried on numerous occasions to escape from Camp One to avoid fellow Americans rather than the Chinese. There had been several threats hurled his way and Cowart claimed that there had even been "a few attempts . . . made on his life."[11] Virginia Pasley confirmed Cowart's situation when he said in an interview, "Cowart had been an informer, he said he had, he told me why, and he was afraid to go home, once they trapped him."[12]

Similarly, Richard Tenneson feared for his life because of his reputation for informing on others. Jack Chapman, who had participated in a riotous protest against Chinese propaganda efforts blamed being found out on Tenneson. After the Chinese punished the reactionaries, Tenneson was placed under guard at headquarters in an attempt to protect him from retributive action. When he was released from protective custody and returned to the regular camp, a group of reactionaries beat him up badly. From that point forward, it was rumored throughout the camp that Chinese officials had given Tenneson a knife for his protection and the assaults stopped.[13]

Clarence Adams also made his decision to remain behind with the Chinese out of fear. In July, after the armistice was signed, he had to make a decision, but it would be a difficult one. Although Clarence wanted to return home, he would have to do so amid threats from his fellow prisoners. As an openly Progressive, outspoken, black man inside Camp Five, he had heard many threats over the previous three years, but now, as a potentially free man, several of the other prisoners were promising punishment. One man even threatened to throw him overboard on their trip home. In addition to the direct, personal threats, Adams expected that once he returned, the army would throw the book at him for his collaboration. When Adams approached one of the Chinese instructors with his concerns, he was told that he could choose to go to a neutral country instead of returning to the United States. Adams, however, asked if he could go to China and the next day he received news that the Chinese would allow it. Adams knew that some of the Americans were planning to stay behind and worried that he would be the only black man to refuse repatriation. Friendly with William White, Adams approached him and asked if he would be interested in remaining with the Chinese. Indeed interested, White then recruited Larance Sullivan to join the group. Rumors swirled through the camp about some of the men refusing repatriation, but no names were announced.[14] Larance Sullivan also received threats if he returned home. An unidentified former PW told the FBI that Sullivan had been warned, "[i]f you go back to the States we will get you there, or if you are on the boat with us, we'll throw you overboard."[15] Otho Bell, William Brown remembered, "always acted as though he was afraid and did not associate with other prisoners."[16] Indeed, he may have had good reason to fear a return trip home. Tom Hollis, an Australian soldier, swore that if Bell did not stop espousing communism to the other soldiers, Hollis would find Bell after repatriation.[17] John Ekenbarger, the man who had nearly fought Clarence Adams in a racial dispute, swore he would kill Otho Bell for informing on his fellow PsW.[18]

Fear was the most significant reason that men refused to repatriate. Informants reported back to the U.S. Army that the men had been turned into "a bunch of scared kids" because of their PW experience and that the communists had convinced them that if they returned to the United States, the FBI would question them until they had no more information to give and then kill them.[19] Virginia Pasley stated that Otho Bell's primary reason for refusing repatriation was because he was told by the Chinese that the U.S. Supreme Court had sentenced him to death in absentia for crimes he committed as a PW.[20]

A few of the men may have also resisted repatriation out of protest against the state of affairs within the United States at the time. In the early 1950s, Joe McCarthy and Pat McCarran loomed large through their anti-communist crusade. Richard Tenneson, a native of Minnesota, had known of McCarthy's regional reputation before the war. Several years later, as a guest on William F. Buckley's *Firing Line,* Tenneson recalled, "McCarthy was a word in our household before I left home. Something my parents were afraid of." In addition to other reasons for remaining behind, McCarthy's intrawar rise to prominence "was an extra thing for me personally."[21]

More pragmatic reasons may have also been in play. Otho Bell, who had a wife and infant daughter back in Spokane, Washington, was reported to have been sexually involved with some of his fellow prisoners. One returning PW told Counterintelligence Corps (CIC) agents that Bell had become a homosexual in the early months of 1953.[22] Richard Godlewski stated that Bell had told him that he was having an affair with a soldier named Taylor and that "during one night in May or June 1953, made the rounds of Second Platoon Area of Company #3 and had abnormal sexual relations with practically all members of the platoon."[23] Charles Taylor recalled that Bell "engaged in sodomy with PsW and with one Chinese named Mao (who was an instructor in 1st Company)."[24] Leroy Lam reported that he "saw him in the act with a Pvt Thomas R. JACKSON."[25] John Dixon's CIC interview revealed even more information about Bell's activities while a PW. Dixon acknowledged, "I even slept with [Bell] for eighteen months. Sleeping with BELL was not like sleeping with a woman but it was better than nothing."[26] In addition to Bell, three others within the nonrepatriate group carried the stigma around camp. When John Spivey interviewed with the CIC, he stated that he had caught Larance Sullivan and William White, both of whom refused repatriation, in a homosexual act.[27] One of the men volunteered that a pressing reason for Richard Corden's decision to stay was the fact that he was homosexual and had gained some acceptance while a prisoner of war.[28] Later FBI interviews confirmed these suspicions among Corden's fellow PsW. One interviewee "observed him on a number of occasions holding hands with Chinese officials."[29] Another reported, "Corden was generally regarded by all the prisoners in our group as a sexual pervert" because of the stories told by an unidentified prisoner [FBI classified] "who slept in the bunk next to Corden." This former PW alleged that "Corden had tried to induce [him] several times to engage in acts of sodomy."[30] One of the members of Corden's squad volunteered, "I have heard him engage in both rectal and oral sodomy . . . at night during the period we were in Camp #5."[31] By the end of the year, more stories were surfacing. In an article appearing in the *Washington Post,* the subject of homosexuality was brought up and it was alleged that several Western journalists had seen at least two of the men with their hair growing long and wearing women's clothing.[32]

Unlike many of the others, Jack Dunn appears an unlikely candidate to remain behind. Not identified as a collaborator or even a notable Progressive, Dunn may have been scared that he had participated enough to draw legal attention once he returned or felt unsafe among certain other prisoners, but as late as April 23, 1953, he wrote his family, optimistic about an impending return home. In that letter, he told his mother, "I'm still patiently waiting to go home . . . it looks good."[33]

While fear and pragmatism had convinced some of his compatriots to remain, others saw a great opportunity in going to China and were sincere in their wishes to do so. West Texan Claude Batchelor, a leading Progressive figure in Camp Five, recalled that when Commander Chang called him in to discuss the possibility of defection, he considered the idea mainly because of his own dependence on the Chinese for news, particularly about the United States. Complimenting Batchelor on his ability to lead men and preach the merits of communism, Chang further promised Batchelor that if he consented to the Chinese offer, he would lead the group, travel extensively, live a successful life, and enjoy some measure of fame. Batchelor and Lowell Skinner consulted with Samuel Hawkins and Howard Adams about staying. Batchelor and Howard Adams asked fellow Texan Rufus Douglas if he would "go by our homes and explain to our folks why we stayed," but Douglas surprised the two by telling them that he, too, was refusing repatriation. Batchelor remembered that "more Americans wanted to remain behind than the Chinese cared to have . . . and [the Chinese] refused to permit some to remain." The Chinese forced three men, among them Wilburn "Clue" Watson, to repatriate. Watson's return would come back to haunt Dickenson and Batchelor.[34]

In Camp One, the Chinese made Morris Wills the same offer. Throughout late July and early August, he had watched the men from Camp Five roll through Camp One, which had not yet been liberated, on their way back home. Recalling that he was angry that he "had been left there to rot" by the United States, Wills spent several days making his decision, finally agreeing to the proposition, whereupon he was whisked away to join the others at Camp Five. The Chinese had been selective in their recruitment and had kept secret their plans to take some Americans back to China after the war. Wills wrote that he did not even know that Richard Tenneson, also a resident of Camp One, had agreed to stay until the two met at the headquarters that last day. In Wills's estimation, if the opportunity to go to China had been announced publicly, "[c]ertainly from our company there would have been four or five more and as many as twenty-five from the five companies in Camp One alone."[35]

Other Camp One personnel elected to remain with the Chinese for what now appear to be completely outlandish reasons. Wesley Biers, one of the camp's leading Progressives, contended that he, Bobby DeGraw, and Wilburn

Watson planned to cooperate with the Chinese in order to ingratiate themselves to the point that they could spring a trap on the communists. Having applied for and received permission from the Chinese to stay behind, Biers said, "my real purpose was to sabotage the Chinese plan to get prisoners to remain in China after the armistice." He contended that he and Bobby DeGraw came up with the plan to infiltrate the nonrepatriate group by remaining "behind and try to convince them to change their minds" about refusing to return home.[36]

In reality, Biers and DeGraw, and possibly Watson, were considered leading Progressives by their fellow PsW. In questioning former PsW about the prison camp activities of Lewie Griggs, DeGraw's name came up repeatedly. Apparently close friends, Griggs and DeGraw were remembered as going to Chinese headquarters, where they would spend several hours, then return to their quarters nearly drunk.[37] Another returnee recalled that Griggs and DeGraw were members of various communist committees and DeGraw was described as "a bigger Progressive than Griggs" and the "big shot" among Progressives in the camp.[38]

Later investigations by the FBI gleaned more detailed information about how the Chinese went about identifying potential nonrepatriates. One former Progressive who had been permitted to stay with the Chinese remembered, "The Chinese passed out forms to be filled in by those prisoners who did not want to return home. A prisoner who filled out this form was required to put down his complete personal history along with his reasons why he wished to remain behind." He also recalled that while he was still at Camp One, "I was notified by the Chinese that I was accepted as one of the non-repatriates." A couple of days later, the Chinese threw the Camp One nonrepatriates a going-away party complete with plenty of alcohol, food, cigarettes, and even a few female Chinese soldiers.[39] Lowell Skinner recalled, "it was an easy choice . . . to live in China." As a young, idealistic man who had been constantly exposed to pro-communist ideology, "he honestly believed that in China there existed a way of life that gave everyone an equal opportunity to get ahead, based only on the person's abilities."[40] When one of Richard Corden's fellow prisoners inquired about the armistice, Corden responded, "Well I guess you boys will be going home before long." The man asked what he meant, Cordon said, "I think I should stay here because it is the right thing to do" and asked the other prisoner if he would consider staying.[41]

Wills, Tenneson, Wilburn Watson, Bobby DeGraw, and Wesley Biers were transferred to Camp Five by truck. When the small group arrived on August 6, they met the men from the other camps who had bought the communist line. For the next three months, the Chinese put the men through a regimen of "criticism and self-criticism" in an effort to verify the degree of loyalty of each man to test his decision. The contingent chose Batchelor as their leader and Richard Corden as the assistant.[42]

On August 23, a ship arrived at Camp Five to transport the prisoners to the repatriation centers. Clarence Adams remembered that while the others lined up to get on board, those who refused to return climbed into a truck and were driven to the top of a high hill nearby: "There we stood in silence and watched as the others boarded the ship and left the harbor. Only then did it really hit me that I had reached the point of no return."[43] Lt. William Funchess was one of the last men out of the camps and saw the entire group of nonrepatriates in their new "special camp." He recalled that on his way to his own repatriation, the truck in which he was riding stopped at a small compound where "[a]bout 20 young POWs approached the truck and told me they were going to refuse repatriation." Funchess was surprised when one of the fellows "suggested that I get off the truck and join them." The lieutenant loudly refused.[44]

During the three months that followed their fateful decision, the men were subjected to a strong program of political indoctrination. Each day, they would meet to critique themselves and the others. An unidentified nonrepatriate[45] recalled that after a Chinese official commended them for doing "a wise, proper and good thing; he said that we were no longer prisoners of war and . . . from now on, we were 'comrades'."[46] Wills remembered that one of the major issues the group singled him out for was his farmer father's entrepreneurship. Writing years later, he recalled that his family's 175-acre farm in upstate New York was modest by American standards, but it was a vast amount of land for a typical Chinese. The group thus considered Wills the son of a "rich peasant," though not a "landlord," since he did not employ any outside help.[47] In addition to basic political indoctrination, much of their time was spent being "briefed on how to answer questions and how to conduct ourselves when it came our turn to enter the Neutral Zone at Freedom Village and to inform the Neutral Inspection Teams that we did not desire to be repatriated."[48] The indoctrination sessions were highly stressful and the students apparently became very committed to their purpose.

When they were not undergoing political indoctrination, the defectors rehearsed for the challenges of the coming months. Having been nominated by China and North Korea to supervise all soldiers refusing to be repatriated to their nations of origin, India sent a military force to the armistice line and began preparing to take charge of their controversial prisoners. Part of their duty was to lead sessions in which explainers would try to undo the psychological work accomplished during captivity. The UN explainers were given unsupervised time with the men in small groups to discuss the merits of voluntary repatriation or the finality of refusal. Accordingly, the men had to be prepared to argue their views and the Chinese needed to be able to trust that their recruits would not crack under the pressure of explanation and the ambience of the small, friendly meetings. To combat this possibility, the men went through a seemingly unending series of practice interviews. Morris Wills remembered that in these meetings, the Chinese encouraged them to "sing, make noise, turn your back—anything to keep from listening to what [the explainer] had to say."[49] Dickenson recalled that LaRance Sullivan proposed they "answer questions in a slow, southern accent, as though we were too lazy to talk," and that the men, "with a blank face," should "act dumb and stupid." More direct means might also be employed. The men could spit at the interviewers or follow the example of James Veneris, who planned to chew garlic and "spray [it] in the faces of the explainers."[50] One of the most feared tactics never materialized. Several of the nonrepatriates worried that when they entered the explaining room, they would find themselves face-to-face with family members.[51] Through these and other tactics, the Chinese hoped to convince the explainers of the group's seriousness and devotion to the idea of communism and voluntary migration to China.

While the men at Camp Five prepared to meet their UN explainers, thousands of other former prisoners of war made their way home. This latter group included dozens of committed Progressives whom the Chinese had successfully convinced to work for peace back in the United States through political subversion. Like real Manchurian candidates, this nucleus of men was to "keep in touch with each and every other Progressive" and to "organize in their immediate communities." The Chinese hoped the men would maintain in the civilian world the belief systems they had learned in prison, with the strong ones watching over the less committed. Dickenson even went as far as noting that the nucleus group was "scheduled to have a convention in Chicago on an undetermined date," and that members were to communicate by telegram.[52] The so-called "Ex-Prisoners of War Welfare Association" would govern these activities and serve as a cover for the American pro-communist movement.[53] Dickenson explained that the Chinese believed that the United States would be ripe for revolution within a few years following the end of the Korean War. During the intervening time, the nonrepatriates would be educated at a communist school in Beijing and be prepared for their return to the States as agitators and propagandists. The Chinese theorized that the revolution would begin within American labor organizations during an economic depression and that the freedoms ensured by the U.S. Constitution would allow the subversive movement to thrive right under the nose of the federal government. Ultimately, the United States political system would collapse and the nonrepatriates would be poised to take over and lead the nation. Dickenson remembered that "[w]e were told that as Americans, we would be the Government leaders, from President down to the lowest office holder."[54] With the future political direction of the United States seemingly laid out, the contingent had further business to transact before moving to the Neutral Zone, where the nonrepatriates would be turned over to the Indian delegation.

When the nonrepatriates from all of the camps came together at Camp Five in early August, the group contained Wilburn Watson, Bobby DeGraw, and Wesley Biers; three men who would later be weeded out.[55] Batchelor remembered that although Watson had professed his intention to go to China, the Chinese, along with his comrades at Camp Five, never trusted him.[56] Watson claimed that when he was initially captured, he had been carrying documents identifying him as a deputy sheriff in Tishomingo County, Mississippi. According to Watson, the Chinese believed he was a secret agent sent to disrupt camp life and beat him until he signed a document confessing the same.[57]

In his own statement, Batchelor remembered Watson differently. While confirming that the Chinese distrusted Watson's intentions, Batchelor observed that Watson held sway over DeGraw, Biers, and fellow Mississippian Otho Bell, and was gaining influence over Albert Belhomme and Ed Dickenson. After asking questions of the latter two, Batchelor reported to the Chinese that while Watson's behavior was somewhat suspicious, he did not pose a serious threat to the group. But the Chinese countered with charges that cast doubt on Watson's commitment to communism: marijuana use by Watson, DeGraw, Biers, Bell, and Belhomme; suspicious meetings among Watson, DeGraw, Biers, Bell, and sometimes Dickenson; Otho Bell's recent revelation that he wished to go to Czechoslovakia rather than China; Watson's uncanny ability to separate the personal nature of his defection from the political aspect of his action; and Watson's own frequent suggestion that good negotiators could extract favors from the United States in return for changing their minds.[58] Whatever Watson's motives, his behavior bred suspicion.

During the middle of August, the Chinese approached Watson and members of his circle hoping to extract confessions of any subversive plans they might be entertaining. Vigorous questioning of Watson, DeGraw, Biers, and Bell gleaned results. Batchelor recalled seeing Bell bawling like a child and confessing to his Chinese interrogators that the men had made a deal for marijuana, sake, and a woman. After the scene played out, Batchelor sat down with Bell, who shocked him by admitting that while all of the events had occurred, his behavior was a performance. According to Bell's confession, the Chinese wanted a reason to expel Watson, DeGraw, and Biers from the program, and had approached Bell threatening to send him home if he did not corroborate the story against the other three. While Bell had shared in the marijuana and sake and was privy to the deal for the girl, he did not know the true nature of the men's intentions. Bell convinced Batchelor that these weak-willed individuals had been directed by the Americans to infiltrate and destroy the Chinese experiment, and with this knowledge, the nonrepatriate group forced the three transgressors to renounce their intentions to go to China and apply for voluntary repatriation. The three were then released to the Americans. For effect, "someone suggested that we sing the international [Internationale] while he was leaving. We did so and that was the last we saw of Clew Watson."[59]

The issue of Watson, DeGraw, and Biers is difficult to evaluate. It is possible that at least DeGraw and Biers may have elected to stay behind for reasons other than a sincere wish to become international "peace fighters." They may have felt that as Progressives they would not survive a slow Pacific crossing among those men whom they considered enemies. They may have agreed to refuse repatriation and voluntarily join the others in an attempt to dissuade the nonrepatriates in the hopes that last-minute meritorious behavior would save them from later chastisement. Conventional wisdom, however, suggests that these three were little different from the other twenty-three with whom they voluntarily entered Chinese custody.

While a prisoner at Fort Leavenworth, Kansas, in 1956, Ed Dickenson revealed his recollection of Watson in an FBI interview. Dickenson said that in conversations between himself and Watson, the latter suggested that when the group got to China, their freedom would be further limited by "tail gunners." Not knowing the meaning of the term, Dickenson asked Watson, who elaborated, saying that there would be "spies or persons following us around" and that they would "still be a prisoner but with some freedom." Dickenson confessed that "the accusations leading up to this trial were based mostly on the conversations" between himself and Watson.[60] Later, this resulted in Watson's, Biers's, and DeGraw's expulsion and explains Watson's eagerness to testify against Dickenson at his court martial.

Months later, both Batchelor and Dickenson would wish that their encounter with Watson, Biers, and DeGraw had been their last. In both courts martial, Watson appeared prominently as a prosecution witness telling a drastically different story about the events of late August 1953. Watson remembered that one evening, while sitting and talking with some of the other men, the Chinese called him to company headquarters. He was immediately marched off to jail, but brought back to camp the following morning. Rather than being released to his quarters, he was taken to an unfamiliar building, where he found his fellow nonrepatriates assembled to try him on the charge of spying for the United States. The commander announced to the assembly, "we are gathered here to decide the fate of Watson." Having already confessed to being an American spy in order to win release from six months of solitary confinement several months earlier, there was ample evidence against him. The commander presented Watson's confessions and his implication of two other, unnamed men, to the group and then asked for their opinions. A surprised Watson remembered that "they felt there should be something done with me . . . they felt like I should be killed." However, Andrew Condron, the Scotsman, stood up and spoke: 'Well . . . due to the fact that you people have watched Watson all the time, he couldn't have learned anything that could help anyone, and, I feel like that since he has been kept in solitary confinement, since he has been placed in the hard labor camp, since he couldn't have possibly done anything detrimental to the Chinese, I think he should be allowed to return home." With that statement, the Chinese officers in attendance conferred and ordered Watson, and his implicated co-conspirators Biers and DeGraw, to request repatriation.[61]

As dramatic as both stories are, the memories of Watson and Batchelor must be carefully dissected. Watson's contention that his peers had essentially ordered his execution before the eloquent Scot saved his life, played well after the war, but his version of the events bears scrutiny. Although none of the men in question can be believed without reservation, Watson's tale appears contrived within the context of McCarthy's America. With his return to the United States, he underwent rigorous questioning by agents of the Counterintelligence Corps. Understanding that he would have to offer testimony against his former compatriots, army lawyers may have taken the initiative to help him shape his story; after all, in comparison with those remaining with the Chinese, he was inconsequential. By placing Watson in the only honorable position within the group, the others were implicated en masse. Furthermore, it is also curious that the Chinese apparently accepted Condron's argument immediately, while dismissing the collective wishes of all the others, many of them the handpicked leaders of the prisoner group. At the same time, both Dickenson and Batchelor, while obviously foolish to confess to such a hideous charge, made no mention of any serious conflict with Watson, though in their statements they admitted to various other potentially damaging events. Batchelor noted the marijuana, sake, and woman issue and Dickenson mentioned Watson approaching several of the nonrepatriates to convince them to go home. In his testimony against Batchelor more than a year later, Watson attempted to explain the reason for his presence in the nonrepatriate camp, alleging that the Chinese had forced him to sign a request to remain behind after his stint in solitary confinement.[62] While his explanation was plausible, the Chinese who ran the prison camps had effected the deaths of hundreds of other prisoners for lesser reasons than Watson's. If indeed his jailers were as afraid of him as he attempted to make the court believe, the fact that he survived captivity and eventually returned home is quite intriguing. In reality, it appears that Watson, DeGraw, and Biers at least temporarily agreed to remain behind; however, after their misbehavior and banishment, they all took the most convenient route for themselves and the U.S. Army by turning into critics of their former comrades.[63]

With the business of Watson, DeGraw, and Biers now finished, those remaining spent the night of September 1 enjoying Chinese hospitality. They had learned how to handle themselves in front of the explainers as their political indoctrination had been very effective. After a long night of food and drink, the men left the next morning on their two-day truck ride south to the city of Kaesong, where Indian troops held them in a neutral zone near the 38th Parallel for the three-month explanation period. There, they would meet with representatives from the U.S. Army who would attempt to counter the procommunist line to which the men had been exposed for nearly three years.[64]

Upon their arrival in Kaesong, the group remained in Chinese custody before being transferred to the neutral camp. After setting up their tents and getting themselves organized, the men were ordered by their Chinese handlers into a meeting with Wilfred Burchette, a journalist for *Ce Soir,* a Paris newspaper sympathetic to the Chinese.[65] Burchette sought to instill in the men the belief that their decision to stay with the Chinese was irreversible and that they were not to show any weakness in the face of the explainers. A delicate task by its very nature, Burchette received valuable help from a recent event that illustrated the high level of mistrust prevalent among the American public and the willingness of the U.S. Army to sacrifice even the most respected soldier.

On May 1, the United States Army had flown twenty suspected Progressives, who had been liberated during "Operation Little Switch," back to the States. One of that number was a twenty-four-year-old San Franciscan named Paul Schnur Jr., the son of an influential leader of the Congress of Industrial

Organization. As the son of a man who sympathized with Julius and Ethel Rosenberg and was described in newsprint as a "retired Leftist," the younger Schnur knew skepticism, but thought himself safe from anti-American suspicion after the army, upon his repatriation, awarded him the Bronze Star for valor. During the two months that followed, the army put Schnur through several psychiatric evaluations at Letterman Army Hospital in California. Deciding that Schnur held some communistic beliefs, the army gave him an "undesirable discharge" for being "disloyal or subversive" only weeks it had recognized him for his bravery and selflessness. When asked about this sudden turn of events, Schnur responded, "I can't understand it all, and I can't understand what I did to get such a discharge." "All I can remember is making two records while I was a prisoner, one telling my family I was okay after my capture . . . around Christmas 1950 and the other . . . on the same order, made in April of 1951."[66]

Burchette took some creative license with Schnur's story in order to convince the men that they would certainly be prosecuted if they returned to the

Paul Schnur receives the Bronze Star medal upon his release during Operation Little Switch. A few moments later in the same ceremony, Robert Hickox, a leading Progressive, was given a Purple Heart. Within weeks, Schnur would be tarred a collaborator in spite of his battlefield performance. (Still Pictures Division, NARA II)

United States, and told the gathering that many former Progressives had been jailed as communist agents, some of them being held at Camp Drake, Japan, where they might be shot for their actions while prisoners. Encouraging them to make every use of publicity to highlight the poor treatment they could expect from America if they changed their minds about remaining with the Chinese, Burchette left feeling confident that he had accomplished his purpose.[67]

After three or four days of living in tents at Kaesong, the men moved into a barracks. Chinese administrators expected this time to help the men gel into a cohesive group able to withstand the challenges and questions presented by the explainers, but instead it was a period of contention and dissatisfaction within the group. The proverbial straw came in the form of an irrational demand from William Cowart. The group had gathered to discuss which uniform they would wear while in the Neutral Zone, and Cowart stubbornly refused to don a hat. Since his voice offered the only dissent, the remaining men expected Cowart to conform to their wishes, but Cowart only offered a compromise that would make hats optional, apparently testing his standing within the group. Cowart eventually conceded to group pressure, but not without some lasting significance. Claude Batchelor remembered the hat issue as a turning point for the group, as their former unity disintegrated into individualism. As for Cowart, he became even more contrary as time passed and was gradually ostracized from the group.[68]

Attempting to repair the damage caused by the hat furor, Commander Chang asked each man to vote by secret ballot for those among them about whom they felt they knew the least. The selected men would then stand before the group, analyze themselves, and undergo a critique from their peers. Again, problems surfaced. Three of the most committed nonrepatriates were selected, but not wishing to have his handpicked leaders questioned, Chang opted to ignore the vote of the group and chose a different set of less influential men. Batchelor bragged that he was the only person not to receive a vote, but he also understood that the group was rife with mistrust.[69] At a time when the twenty-four needed to exhibit complete and unwavering loyalty to each other and their mutual cause, a serious case of distrust had surfaced.

To bring stability to the cohort, Commander Chang ordered an election to decide upon seven leaders to head the group while in the Neutral Zone. According to the results, Batchelor was to be the acknowledged leader, Andrew Condron was to act as a conduit between the American and Korean prisoners, Richard Corden would represent the Americans to the Indian delegation, James Veneris was responsible for ensuring the men were fed, Larance Sullivan was to assume charge of outdoor recreation while Clarence Adams took care of indoor recreation, and Albert Belhomme would guide their study sessions. In this manner, the Chinese established a system through which they could control the remaining men. Batchelor remembered that "[a]fter these men were elected Commander Chang called myself and Condron in and told us that he was going to break the group down into 7 so each representative would have a group." After that, Chang assigned each of the seven representatives two or three men to supervise to ensure that their resolve would not weaken.[70]

Shortly before the group departed for the Neutral Zone, Chang called Batchelor, Veneris, Condron, and Corden into his office and asked them if any of the men were either uncommitted to their decision to go to China or unsure of the wisdom of their choice. Batchelor singled out William Cowart, the instigator of the recent hat furor, and Aaron Wilson, who was seventeen and in the eighth grade when he joined the army.[71] Condron and Corden offered the names of Arlie Pate and Harold Webb. Batchelor and Corden talked with Cowart and tried to convince him to go home, but to no avail. Finally, Batchelor explained that the entire group distrusted him and that returning to the United States would be the best thing for him. Cowart got mad and acquiesced; however, without explanation, Chang called Cowart into his office and convinced him to reconsider. Chang told Batchelor that he did not want Cowart harboring resentful feelings as his demeanor would likely help American propagandists. In reality, Chang was likely tightening the group's reigns to draw them together as the explanation period drew near. Batchelor's talk with Wilson proved even more frustrating, as the latter flatly rejected leaving, identifying fear as his central reason for staying behind.[72]

Condron and Veneris then spoke with Harold Webb whom they judged to be sincere in his intentions and dedicated to the cause. However, their talk with Arlie Pate turned out differently. Pate steadfastly stood his ground and Condron and Veneris referred his case to Commander Chang. Following Chang's talk with Pate, he reported to the leadership group that Pate would definitely stay for personal reasons. The Chinese officer reported that Pate had confessed to killing another American prisoner, an officer with supposed black market ties. Pate admitted to having hit the officer, who fell and hit his head on an exposed rock and died. Reasoning that Pate might be prosecuted for murder if he returned to the United States, Chang thought the humanitarian thing would be to allow him to remain with the others.[73] Again, it seems that Chang had set up a straw man for the group to attack and for Chang to rescue. With all of their talk of "peace" and "unity" during captivity, verifying Chang's story through Pate might have smacked of disrespect for both men.

With Chang's position further reinforced and the group theoretically drawn closer together, the Chinese commandant ended the process of examination, self-analysis, and interviews with a speech asserting the need for the men to be sincere in their intentions. Immediately following the speech, Chang was surprised to see Richard Tenneson approach him and ask if they could speak privately. Stepping away from the others, Tenneson told Chang that homesickness had persuaded him to return home, but promised to work for peace inside the United States. Drawing the nucleus of the group together once more, Chang asked their opinion on the Tenneson issue. To a man, they agreed that he should be returned home because his dissatisfaction would weaken his resolve to be a good revolutionary. Again Chang broke with the group. Arguing that Tenneson should remain behind, he moved the homesick American into the headquarters building for a week. At the end of that period, Tenneson decided to stay.[74]

Hoping to avoid further complications, Chang organized a system of indirect supervision. He called Batchelor, Veneris, Belhomme, Clarence Adams, Sullivan, Corden, and Condron together and appointed them to lead seven small groups, mainly with the purpose of exerting influence over subordinates and maintaining cohesion. Batchelor remembered that Chang had worked very hard putting the groups together based on common likes, dislikes, and levels of mutual respect.[75] Even this new move could not settle the restless bunch. A serious fissure developed when Corden established his own secret group, which included Belhomme, Veneris, and a couple of others. Since their main purpose for remaining behind was to work for the benefit of those the war had touched so intimately, the five men's sincerity and conviction might have been applauded. However, Chang's purpose was political and he very quickly quashed Corden's plans. An embarrassed and timid Corden skulked back into line.[76]

Wilfred Burchette then reappeared, intending to brighten the face of the anti-repatriation movement. Revisiting stories about the U.S. government holding Progressives as spies and suggesting that execution would be their lot, he also told the PsW that Progressives had been billeted with anti-communist reactionaries on the troop ships bound for home. During their return journey, Progressives were reportedly beaten and intimidated into making damning statements to the Counterintelligence Corps interviewers about their own behavior while imprisoned and about the actions of others. To protect themselves, Burchette suggested the nonrepatriates write detailed explanations of their reasons for remaining behind so he could publish them for the world to read. All the men complied and Burchette took their individual statements and wrote a single proclamation for them all to sign. Batchelor reviewed the document and generally agreed with the language. He did note that the men expressed fears of facing arrest and possible execution as Burchette had reported. Batchelor later confided, "Burchett had not mentioned it [reports of mistreatment] in this statements and I wondered why. However, I thought he must know his business so I did not say any thing."[77]

On September 25, the group left Kaesong for the Custodial Camp in the Neutral Zone. Since it was shaped like a crescent, the men soon began calling it Banana Camp. There, an Indian delegation, whose supervision had been accepted by all sides, was to hold the men, with minimal contact with the outside world. Having enjoyed total control over their former charges, the Chinese organized elaborate schemes to maintain contact with and influence over the men while they marked time in the neutral camp. The men adopted a dog, whom they dubbed "Nonrepat," and attempted to train it to carry messages between themselves and the Chinese delegation. Nonrepat, however, was either not interested in politics or an anti-communist at heart because the scheme failed to work.[78] They then turned to more stable and traditional means. Claude Batchelor remembered that several days before the planned relocation, Chang called Condron and himself into the commandant's office. There, he acquainted the pair with a map of the new facility, identifying various buildings, among them their barracks and the hospital, both of which, he assured Batchelor and Condron, would be fully staffed by Chinese. Using a secret code derived from two military serial numbers, a book, and a typewriter keyboard, members of the group's nucleus could send messages to Chang through staff intermediaries at the hospital.[79] Morris Wills expanded upon the details of this clever plot, writing that Commander Chang even planned to shave his head and work in the hospital. Although Chang never went that far, Wills remembered looking up from a dentist's chair and seeing the commander "telling me not to let the cat out of the bag."[80]

Once settled into the custodial camp, the twenty-four men began their four-month wait. Effectively on their own for the first time in years, the group maintained itself through the elaborate organization previously crafted by the Chinese. After a couple of days, Claude Batchelor felt it necessary to send a coded message to Chang, letting him know that all was well, but Chang's long reply caused unanticipated problems. Expecting that decoding the message would take a good bit of time, Batchelor and Condron retired to a distant building planning to work on it well into the night. Not long after they spread out the various decoders, Corden and Belhomme walked in, curious about what Batchelor and Condron were doing. They covered the papers and curtly explained that they were working on something very secretive, causing the two visitors, who were unaware of the code, to become concerned that the proceedings involved them. Although Corden relaxed, Belhomme remained tense and Batchelor promised to discuss the matter come morning. At dawn, the tension remained and despite a frank discussion, Batchelor and Corden's relationship suffered permanent damage. Ironically, Chang's decoded message reminded the men of unity; yet petty jealousy and suspicion had begun to take a toll on the men.[81]

Of major concern to Chang was the possibility that the explainers would bring the soldiers' family members to the sessions as an enticement to return. Although this did not happen, the Chinese knew that if family members plucked at the heartstrings of the nonrepatriates, they stood a good chance of losing some, if not all of the men. Instructing them on how to deal with the situation if it indeed arose, Chang sent word that they should tell their loved ones to seek political asylum and join their husbands and sons in China.[82]

Quiet since his refusal to wear a hat, William Cowart began drawing renewed attention from the Chinese, who were effectively connected to the goings on within the camp. It seems that Cowart was "going around getting the names of all the Koreans and their former addresses." The Chinese considered any deviation from the prisoners' initial plan as potentially subversive so they asked Corden, Condron, and Batchelor to investigate Cowart's behavior. Batchelor never believed that Cowart was seditious, "because he did not have the intelligence," but it was a legitimate concern. After looking through Cowart's diary, Batchelor determined that nothing of concern was transpiring. In an effort to be thorough, however, the nucleus group agreed to question Cowart, Aaron Wilson, and William White. Suspecting White to be involved in some sort of subversive plan and knowing that Wilson was Cowart's only friend within the camp, they met with the men separately and came away convinced that nothing was awry. The root of the problem was apparently the impending cold weather. Having to rely on body heat, the three men planned to move in with the Korean nonrepatriates once the season turned cold. As for Cowart, his interest in taking the Koreans' addresses was prompted by his desire to send them complimentary copies of his planned book. Batchelor concluded that such questionable behavior "did not help Cowarts position in the group any." His presence became so uncomfortable that after he sprained his ankle, Cowart was admitted to the hospital, where he would remain until repatriation in January 1954.[83]

The first weeks with the custodial troops had been very difficult for Batchelor. In the eyes of the Chinese, Richard Corden had slowly been eclipsing

Batchelor as group leader and the rivalry led to feelings of animosity that would not fade. Moreover, Batchelor, whose early commitment to the Chinese was unwavering, saw through Corden's polished façade. Batchelor later wrote that he and Condron had both become suspicious of Corden for a variety of reasons. First, "[h]e was spendin[g] all of his time with the Koreans and none of it with the group" and "Belhomme was doing the same." Second, Corden also was apparently reconsidering his ultimate destination, which they considered an insult of sorts considering the level of Chinese investment in their indoctrination. He told Batchelor of his plans and said that others in the group were of like mind. Corden refused to name anyone except Dickenson, and Batchelor immediately responded by calling on Dickenson for verification. Meeting outside the barracks, Dickenson told Batchelor that he was uncertain of his destination and then he apparently went inside to sleep. Batchelor remained outside talking with Veneris about Dickenson and Corden, oblivious to the fact that Dickenson had already decided that the United States would be his unstated destination.[84] Batchelor later wrote, "Dickenson never came in that night. We learned the next morning from the Indians that he was repatriated."[85]

While the men adjusted to their lives as nonrepatriates, their families back home were forced to do the same. On September 23, Beijing radio announced the names of the soldiers who had embraced communism and wished to remain with the Chinese. As one might imagine, the news shocked the folks back home. In Big Stone Gap, Virginia, Ed Dickenson's mother Bessie told the local newspaper that she had received more than thirty letters from her son and all of them spoke of his wish to come home. Bessie Dickenson assured reporters, "I will not believe this is true about my son until it is proven." Only a few days earlier her family had been visited by Elmer Powers, a man who had been in Camp Five with Dickenson, who assured her that he had seen her son on August 5 and that he was still alive and in good health, but that he had been put on a truck and taken away.[86] Clarence Adams's mother, Gladys Peoples of Memphis, Tennessee, echoed similar sentiments of disbelief. "I don't believe it—it's just another Communist trick." She assured herself and others that if Adams had indeed "cast his lot with the Reds, it's because they forced him to do it." Ms. Peoples was completely unprepared for the news as her son had never given any indication in his letters of staying behind. She said that "[h]e very seldom mentioned his prison life and never discussed communism."[87] The shock was greater for Arlie Pate's father. Having been told on the morning of September 24 that his son's name had been announced as a member of the group of the last returning PsW, Daniel Pate nearly broke down when a reporter informed him otherwise. Theorizing that Arlie was being forced to stay, the Pate family, like all the others, remained steadfast in their support of their son.[88] Howard Gayle Adams's father felt confident that his son was "just kidding the Reds" and that "he's trying to outsmart them."[89] Frank "Pappy" Noel, the Associated Press photographer, had been captured and then spent thirty-two months imprisoned with Batchelor at Camp Five. He never believed Batchelor to be staying behind voluntarily. The two men had plotted an escape and Noel remembered that although Batchelor was moved into the Chinese headquarters, he "wished he could get out from under their hands."[90]

Despite the initial shock, the families of the nonrepatriates had to act in the hopes of being able to bring home their loved ones. To supplement hometown letters, Veterans of Foreign Wars chapters sponsored the recording of phonograph albums carrying messages to the prisoners. Hoping to have a member of each man's family record a message, the VFW had hurriedly put together the project in the expectation that the records could make an early flight to Japan. In the case of the Pate family in Illinois, the parents and children were driven to Springfield at seventy miles per hour with a police escort for their 1:00 A.M. recording session. Ed Dickenson's parents traveled one hundred and fifty miles to Knoxville, Tennessee, to tape their plea.[91]

Predictably, these recordings were touching. Arlie Pate's mother was so broken up that it took "more than a half-hour to record three minutes of coherent speech."[92] Rufus Douglas's aunt mixed the news of the deaths of his uncle and half sister with her hopeful plea for his return.[93] When it came time for Daniel Pate, Arlie's father, to record his message, the rough old farmer asked, "What's wrong with you, boy? Why don't you come on home like you ought to?"[94] Despite the effort and emotion spent producing and delivering these messages, all of the nonrepatriates refused to listen to them.

Harry Myers, an influential member of the Los Angeles County Council of the American Legion, suggested to his organization that it fly the prisoners' mothers to meet with their sons personally, and many citizens wrote directly to President Eisenhower at the White House suggesting the same course. While those within the federal government debated the proposal, it gained a groundswell of support, even from Senator James Eastland of Mississippi, who wrote the President on behalf of Otho Bell's family.[95] Portia Howe, Richard Tenneson's mother, had already inquired about journeying to Korea and several other mothers volunteered to go see their sons if they would not come to their mothers. Although none of the family members were ever allowed to visit, Ms. Howe's neighbors helped raise money for her trip and she eventually made it as far as Tokyo, Japan, before being turned back.[96]

While the families of the men agonized over the fates of their brothers, sons, and husbands, many saw dirty looks and heard threats from their neighbors. Claude Batchelor's father, on the occasion of his son's repatriation, told reporters, "I've almost had two or three fights over this thing—you know guys poppin' off."[97]

By October 1953, the United States stood as a nation in shock. After fighting Korea's terrible war for more than three years, a second battle raged. The spectacle that twenty-three Americans and one Brit would willingly remain with the Chinese was a slap in the face of democracy and capitalism at a time when the United States was completely immersed in the Cold War.

While the nonrepatriates were relatively unified in their ultimate purpose of going to China, their motives and commitment levels differed greatly. Within weeks, one would depart and begin telling the world the story of life with the Chinese. Two months later, a second would leave, both to face personal crises at home. Soon after, the remaining nonrepatriates traveled to China.

SEVEN

The Returns . . .

Ed Dickenson—October 20–December 31, 1953

> "Your son was a hero, I give you my word, hundreds of days, he was a hero, and only one day did he break. But in the name of God aren't all those other days worth something? Does he lose his standing in the human race because he broke on that one last day?"
>
> —Richard Basehart in *Time Limit* (1957)

From the time the first prisoners began leaving the camps in August through the first three weeks of October, the American dissenters had shown the world a unified front against the temptations of the West. Behind closed doors, however, the story differed. Suspicion and paranoia led to infighting, with only a few of the men being above doubt and some testing their positions within the group. As long as those difficulties stayed contained and remained out of the public eye, all could run smoothly, but on the night of October 20, 1953, Ed Dickenson walked out and requested repatriation. Dickenson's departure confirmed to the U.S. Army that the group had its fissures and his counterintelligence interview later revealed the depth of those differences. For the next three months, Ed Dickenson became the army's willing assistant in its efforts to entice the rest of his comrades home.

The evening of October 20, 1953, had been a distressing one for Dickenson. That day, the Chinese had found out that he, along with a few others, planned to remain in North Korea rather than relocating to China. Such a departure from the wishes of the Chinese could not be tolerated, and so Claude Batchelor, the group's leader, called Dickenson outside the barracks that night and asked for an explanation as to why he was considering North Korea over China. After being noncomittal to Batchelor, Dickenson returned to his quarters. His conversation with Dickenson over, Batchelor remained behind and discussed the problem with James Veneris. At around 10:00 P.M. Dickenson sat up in his bed and whispered to Howard Adams, who slept in the next bed, then to Morris Wills, on his other side. Neither man answered. He tried again, this time louder: "I'm going to get some medicine for my tooth ache." Again there was no response from among the men's breathing and snores. Having verified that his roommates were asleep and knowing that Batchelor and Veneris were still talking outside, he sneaked out of the building and walked toward the stockade gate. Taking his toothache ruse to the gate, Dickenson told an Indian guard of his malady and asked to go to the UN hospital.[1] There, an on-duty NCO asked, "What is wrong with you?" and Dickenson replied, "Nothing's wrong with me, I want to be repatriated."[2] With the American's intentions clearly stated, the Indian soldier took him to headquarters, where Dickenson repeated his intentions to the officer in charge. That night, he stayed in the Indian headquarters, a guest of the neutral custodial force.[3]

The next morning, a smiling and relaxed Ed Dickenson proudly stepped out of a Jeep at the entrance to the UN compound and strode up a path toward a simple table upon which lay the documents that would set him free. Saluting sharply en route to his destination, Dickenson took a cigarette from a pack given to him along the way. Lighting the American tobacco, he "angrily crumpled a pack of Chinese cigarettes and threw them aside." As he stood in front of the small table and answered the requisite questions asked of him by the officers there, the young soldier made a convincing show of his repatriation proceedings. With his repatriation complete, he agreed to take a couple of questions from the small assembly of reporters, but said very little, only that some of his former compatriots would follow his lead and that he was grateful to be "back in the hands of the Americans."[4] Whether sincere or calculated, the survival skills learned during his nearly three years of captivity served Dickenson well.

Thousands of miles away, in Virginia, Ed Dickenson's parents were fast asleep when news arrived of his conversion. Listening to the radio on Tuesday night, October 20, Van Buren (Dave) Dickenson had heard a vague report that an unidentified member of the dissenting group had changed his mind. Ed's mother, Bessie, "knew it was Ed" and "started shouting." Feeling confident that their boy had come to his senses and would be home shortly, the couple "went to bed at 8:00 P.M. and went right to sleep." At 10:45 P.M., George and Thelma Marrs, who lived at the mouth of the hollow where the Dickensons lived, were awakened by a ringing telephone carrying news of Ed's repatria-

Edward Dickenson takes the short walk to freedom. The previous night he had faked a toothache in order to visit the dentist. Once there, he requested repatriation to the United States after having initially refused it during Operation Big Switch. The coming days, weeks, and months would bring Dickenson much celebrity along with frustration and disappointment. (Still Pictures Division, NARA II)

tion. Hopping in their car, the Marrs drove nearly a mile up to the Dickenson place, by then very dark and quiet. When they roused the family and delivered the news, the silence was broken for the rest of the night.[5]

Although the political climate of the early to mid-1950s would erode popular support for men like Ed Dickenson, the community's initial reaction to his return had been supportive and even his earlier decision to remain with the Chinese had been met with sympathy for the suffering of his family. Local and regional newspaper coverage spouted their support and encouragement not only to Dickenson, but to all the men. James Kiser, of nearby Big Stone Gap, had flown numerous combat missions over Korea and had spent twenty-five months as a prisoner of war. When asked to speak on Dickenson's return, he answered, "Of course, I'm very happy to hear that he has changed his mind and is coming home." When asked about Dickenson's previous public espousal of communism, Kiser responded, "its easy, and hard, too, to understand how a captured man could get his thinking confused." Noting that "Dickenson was captured early in the war, in prison much longer than I was, and I'm sure he went through more torture—starvation, beatings, threats," Kiser surmised, "It is all enough to drive a man nuts in a much shorter period of time than 34 months."[6] The *Bristol* (VA) *Herald-Courier*, a newspaper that would later turn on Dickenson, suggested that all of the PsW deserved the chance to reconsider their decision without punishment, given the psychological warfare practiced by the Chinese.[7] The American Legion post in Big Stone Gap publicly offered Dickenson membership and even sent a delegation to his parents' home to deliver the invitation.[8] Even President Dwight Eisenhower praised the young soldier's decision to return to the United States. Eisenhower, a man who knew the military maxims of duty, honor, and country as well as anyone, told reporters that "American prisoners in Korea were subjected to so much Communist propaganda he sometimes wonders [why] more of them didn't fall for it." Having just shared an hour-long breakfast with former PW, Maj. Gen. William F. Dean, Eisenhower was fresh on the subject and well-versed in the Chinese techniques. He was sure that Dickenson "would never regret his decision to return home."[9]

It would have been nice if Eisenhower had been able to believe his own words. In the months that preceded Dickenson's return, Wisconsin Republican Senator Joseph McCarthy and Secretary of the Army Robert Stevens became embroiled in a feud over what became known as the Monmouth Hearings, investigating lax security and possible large-scale espionage at the research center for the Army Signal Corps.[10] From that point forward, McCarthy came after the army, while Stevens fought against the senator's campaign. The conflict between the two boiled over in early 1954, just as Dickenson was arrested and charged by the army. When Joe McCarthy began investigating how the army dealt with communists within its ranks, he found terribly uneven treatment. With the army clearly lacking an overarching policy on the subject, McCarthy took advantage of the abundance of select cases that would prove his point that the army was soft on communism. He chose Dr. Irving Peress as his target. In Peress, McCarthy found a representative case of army carelessness regarding the communist threat.[11]

The case, which David Oshinsky described as centering around "a pink dentist who managed to parlay some unanswered loyalty forms into a nice promotion and an honorable discharge from the Army," started McCarthyism on the path toward its demise. Seeking a way to lay bare the army's coddling of confirmed communists, McCarthy took Peress; Gen. Ralph Zwicker, commander of Camp Kilmer, New Jersey; and ultimately, Secretary of the Army Robert Stevens, to task as to how the army dealt with communists within its ranks. By the time McCarthy finished sparring with Zwicker, he had made a lifelong enemy of Stevens. Interestingly, this fight spurred Stevens to show McCarthy and the nation how tough the army could be on communism and those soldiers sympathetic to it.[12] In order to do this, the army needed a communist to sacrifice and Ed Dickenson unknowingly sat in waiting.

Local newspaperman Carl Knight stood by Dickenson throughout his ordeal. Knight remembered Dickenson as having "a typical background. . . . Why he hardly knew what communism was all about, much less enough to become a Communist." Recalling that "[h]e was the kind of boy who, if you were kind to him, would lean on you. You see how the Communists got him. They won him with kindness when he was in a difficult spot."[13] Another neighbor echoed that opinion declaring, "[h]e's a boy who would cling to you if you were good to him."[14]

Dickenson being prepared for one of his early interviews at Tokyo Army Hospital. The Army's initial support faded rather quickly and within only a couple of months it became clear that Dickenson, along with Claude Batchelor, would be scapegoated for the behavior of an entire segment of the PW population. (Still Pictures Division, NARA II)

Dickenson was apparently happy with his decision to repatriate and his community, state, and nation overjoyed knowing that he would soon be home. But no one could have been more pleased with his change of mind than American military officials. After signing the papers that returned him to U.S. custody, Dickenson hopped aboard an aircraft destined for Tokyo. For the next three weeks, he spent his nights at Tokyo Army Hospital recouping his health and his days at the Dai Iti Hotel recalling his captivity. Each day, army officials picked Dickenson up at 9:30 A.M. for delivery to the Dai Iti. There, he would recount his experiences of the previous three years for Counterintelligence Corps officers Capt. Bert Cumby and Lt. Richard Cole. Raymond Lech wrote of the two, "Cumby and Cole were smooth as silk. They both wore civilian clothes, and Dickenson never knew they were CIC agents or army officers. Everything was done on a casual, first-name basis."[15] No doubt, Dickenson's interrogators were "smooth," but the young soldier did know they were military officers and likely understood that their interest in him was not mere curiosity. He had lived for three years in an environment that bred paranoia and fear, and surely did not lose his suspicion of people's motives immediately upon repatriation. When he read and signed his official statement on November 6, it clearly noted Cumby's rank as Captain and Cole's as First Lieutenant.[16]

At the Dai Iti, Ed Dickenson spent his days answering a never-ending stream of questions about his experiences while in captivity and the inner workings of the group of men who remained. Although he could not answer some queries regarding the more subtle aspects of the group, he could provide American authorities a list of the men who acted as leaders and those who belonged to the rank and file. Jogging Dickenson's memory for any nugget of information that might suggest that some of his former comrades were wavering in their commitment to go to China, the interrogators hoped that the men in Panmunjom could devise a method to reach those with weaker loyalties to the Chinese. Although uncredited by name to Cumby or Cole, one of the two officers optimistically told a newsman, "If we can crack the leader, some of the rest should follow him in requesting repatriation."[17]

While Cumby and Cole gathered information they thought might lead to a breakthrough in the PW crisis, the prisoners themselves faced challenges back in their camp. Although Commander Chang preached stability, he subtly undermined it in order to maintain his position of primacy even though he had limited contact with the group. Probably souring on Batchelor's leadership in the wake of Dickenson's defection, Chang began slowly supplanting him with Richard Corden. The resulting rivalry between the two Americans would drive the erstwhile leader to the fringes while elevating the new man to the top position. Within weeks of Batchelor's demotion, the fallen man's high-mindedness had been replaced with the same basic emotional concerns of the other men.

By late October, the relationship between Batchelor and Corden was deteriorating. One of the sternest tests of the men's commitment came when the group received mail for the first time since their announcement that they planned to stay behind. Upon that announcement, mail began pouring into Korea for the men from friends, families, and strangers. The custodial force simply handed the mail over to the prisoners, but this presented a problem for the Chinese and the leading nonrepatriates: if the men were given their mail, might they change their minds upon reading the words of their friends and families?[18] Fearing this, Chang hesitated to let them read the letters and warned the men that he had seen some of the letters and that they contained American propaganda and written statements from the explainers. When the letters arrived in the barracks, therefore, the men faced a dilemma as to what to do. Batchelor, Clarence Adams, and Larance Sullivan thought the men should be allowed to read the mail, but Condron, Corden, Veneris, and Belhomme opposed that option. Arguing that the letters should be put in a box next to Batchelor's bed and not given to the men, the four won their point, although Batchelor later wrote, "I still did not agree to this and I did not watch the box." Again, a new controversy had stirred resentments within the group and the next day Harold Webb "got into the box . . . and read his mail."[19]

With such challenges steadily dividing the group, Chang searched for a way to build cohesiveness while maintaining his influence. He contacted the hospital with his wish that Corden be admitted for a few days so that communiqués could be relayed between the two. When Corden rejoined his fellows three days later, he had Chang's plan to hold the group together committed to memory. Although the men already knew what Webb's mail contained, Chang insisted that the letters held articles and letters that violated the terms of the armistice. In protest, the group was to capture Major Kutki, the Indian officer who commanded the neutral camp, and hold him hostage until representatives from the Neutral Nations Repatriation Committee (NNRC) arrived on the scene.[20] When the NNRC officers responded to the emergency, the nonrepatriates would then state their charges against the UN for violating the armistice.

Planning such a move and convincing the others of its necessity were two entirely different propositions. Batchelor himself claimed to have gone along nervously fearing violence if the men went so far as taking the officer hostage. He further maintained that Morris Wills and Lewis Griggs were both strongly opposed to the controversial idea. The remaining men, however, followed Corden's lead and committed themselves. After a large meeting during which the men reaffirmed their support for the new strategy, both Wills and Griggs reluctantly acquiesced. Batchelor and the other representatives then took some of the mail to a different house. There, they selected parts to use in their formal protest. With this work done, Corden drafted the document accusing the UN of breaching the terms of the armistice.[21]

On the appointed day, Corden sent word that he would like to meet with Kutki. Obliging, Kutki, accompanied by a captain and a warrant officer, entered the compound and was directed to a house near the center of the grounds. Once inside, Corden announced that Kutki would not be allowed to leave until NNRC representatives met with the nonrepatriates. Although Cordon allowed the warrant officer to leave and deliver the message, the captain stayed behind with Kutki. It took about three hours for the NNRC to dispatch someone to meet with Corden and Condron, time during which the defectors lodged a variety of complaints against the Indian custodial troops. With their task complete, the defectors relented and allowed their hostages to leave.[22] Despite the theatrics, the complaints were generally either false or exaggerated, and the whole incident accomplished little more than creating publicity.

Growing more disenchanted with the general direction being taken by the group and his gradual marginalization, Batchelor secretly removed his letters from the box and took them to the latrine to read. After reading the letters from his mother, he opened several from schoolchildren, teachers, and other people who had taken it upon themselves to write the nonrepatriates hoping to convince them to return home. The letters from his hometown of Kermit, Texas, touched Batchelor most deeply. Men and women who had known him for most of his life wrote how the ordeal had taken a toll on the health and welfare of his parents.[23] These letters marked Batchelor's first steps toward home.

Back in the United States, relief for the Dickenson family had replaced the difficulty of the preceding months. Even before his decision to remain with the Chinese had been made public, the family had enjoyed hopeful visits from young men who had known Dickenson in prison. One, Alexander Luther, was among the first to be repatriated and returned home. During "Operation Little Switch," sick and wounded prisoners had been exchanged, including Luther, who was released from prison, repatriated, and returned to the United States on May 2, 1953. Shortly after his arrival home to Tom's

Creek, Virginia, only about twenty miles from the Dickenson farm, Luther received a letter from Dickenson's parents asking about their son. He drove down to visit the family and stayed only twenty or thirty minutes, then returned home with "two magazines, one of them was called People's China, and I don't remember the name of the other one . . . it was something similar to the other—China Review." A few days later, one of Dickenson's brothers wrote Luther asking him to return. Following this visit, Luther took another magazine and a few letters.[24]

While Luther attempted to appear naïve and innocent while testifying against Dickenson at the subsequent court martial, his testimony proved transparent. Within days of his first visit to the Dickenson home, he drove nearly three hundred miles to Fort Knox, Kentucky, where he met with agents of the Counterintelligence Corps and surrendered the magazines the Dickenson family had given him. Getting ready to go back home, a CIC officer asked Luther if he could get more evidence against Dickenson to which he replied that he "could probably get it." When Luther returned to Cracker's Neck, "I asked his mother first, and I got it; she gave me the letter and I turned it over to them [CIC]." Duplicitously, Luther accepted the Dickensons' hospitality, stayed overnight at their home, and reassured the grieving parents that all would turn out well for their son, yet secured evidence for the CIC that would later be used against him. At the trial, Luther alleged that his sole purpose in visiting the family was not to get the letter, but to offer friendship and moral support. But he acknowledged his impropriety when he refused to answer a question about the decorum of his visit while at the same time conspiring against the family's wishes.[25]

Alexander Luther's complicity in the Dickenson affair is curious. He apparently harbored no significant animosity toward the man against whom he gathered evidence, nor did he seem anything but sympathetic toward the family he manipulated. During the trial, however, Luther revealed what may have been his true motives. When asked about newsprint in the prison camp regarding germ warfare, Luther quickly acknowledged that he had seen such allegations "in some Communist papers, some China Review or Daily Worker papers—it was London Daily Worker, that's the British paper, and they put it in their magazines from China—People's China, China Review, or so on." Later, when asked about peace petitions that circulated through the camp, Luther acknowledged, "I signed a couple of them."[26] Although no direct conclusion can be drawn that Luther had himself been a Progressive, or at least susceptible to communist propaganda, his thorough knowledge of pro-communist literature and his signing of peace petitions may have motivated him to gather information on others in an effort to ingratiate himself with the army in the event his own loyalty ever came under suspicion.

This theory is bolstered by information obtained from the Federal Bureau of Investigation. On July 24, 1953, Special Agent George Hutchinson of the Louisville, Kentucky, field office received a package of unidentified documents suggesting Dickenson was sympathetic to the communist message while a PW. This information was delivered by "Confidential informant T-1, of known reliability . . . which he had received from Confidential informant T-2, of unknown reliability." Considering Luther's questionable background, it is unlikely that he was "T-1," but entirely possible that he was "Confidential informant T-2."[27]

Ed Dickenson also began thinking of ways to protect himself shortly after his return to UN lines. First, he started speaking freely about the remaining men and suggested a variety of methods that might help change their minds.[28] Second, he began to justify his reasons for remaining behind following "Operation Big Switch," including an outlandish story, which he later retracted, that he had stayed with the communists "to expose red lies."[29] Third, he became a propagandist for the United States, recording messages to be sent to the Neutral Zone, where they were broadcast over loudspeakers in an attempt to sway the remaining prisoners.[30]

During the month that followed Ed Dickenson's escape from the neutral camp, he and his family gained national celebrity status. Even during his stay in Tokyo, reporters had clamored for any comment from the recently freed soldier while the small mountain community of Cracker's Neck, Virginia, enjoyed unprecedented traffic. Indeed, the Dickenson case had become a *cause celebre,* and mail streamed into the family home from all over the nation, much of it commending Dickenson's wisdom in deciding to repatriate.[31] Major news magazines joined the fray and published articles not always generous to the family, who lived a simple and impoverished existence.[32]

In the onslaught of media attention, some newsmen became trusted friends of the Dickenson clan, if only temporarily. When news arrived that Ed would be flown back to the United States within days, Dave and Bessie Dickenson, who had never in their lives strayed more than a few miles from home, accepted an offer from the *Bristol Herald-Courier* to drive them to Washington, D.C., to meet their son.[33] At 1:40 A.M. on November 21, Ed stepped off the airplane at Andrews Air Force Base, just outside the District, and saw his parents for the first time in more than three years.[34] After getting a medical checkup at Walter Reed Army Medical Center and seeing the sights of D.C.,

Ed received a thirty-day furlough and the Dickensons began their long trip home. During the drive back to the mountains, Ed spoke about his captivity to his family and the newsmen who accompanied him on the trip.[35]

On the nearly five-hundred-mile drive, Dickenson's nerves began bothering him. Although most of the initial attention given him by the media and the general public had been positive since his decision to cross over to the UN lines, recent weeks had brought more media skepticism. In the same issue of the Big Stone Gap, Virginia, *Post,* in which a story from Dickenson's former squad leader appeared, praising him as "one of the best soldiers we had," an anonymous writer, claiming to be a veteran of World War II, publicly introduced the Dickenson case as a question for America's anti-Red crusaders. In McCarthyite tradition, the unidentified author damned Dickenson and the newsmen responsible for his story: "In our Country today we have many individuals of your type and his. Every day investigations are exposing a few, but we as a people will never know all the evil minded people among us."[36]

Once home, however, jubilation replaced Dickenson's trepidation as the small hollow roared in celebration. Associated Press reporter Don Whitehead described the community's reaction to the young man's return as "almost hysterical" and noted that Ed was nearly "mobbed by relatives and friends." Estimating that maybe one hundred people jammed into and around the family's four-room house, the reporter feared for a moment "that the little house might collapse under the weight."[37] Whitehead, who had been born only a few miles from the Dickenson farm but had traveled the world as a war correspondent, was by then a national celebrity. Unexpectedly, he filed a second, more critical story on Dickenson the next day. Whitehead began by reporting that a salesman had driven a second-hand Chevrolet up to the Dickenson place early on the morning following the young man's homecoming. Buying the car on the spot, the family piled in for a ride. The light nature of the story's introduction belied Whitehead's real purpose for writing the piece. He segued into a critical, although not damning, evaluation of Dickenson's history since his repatriation, noting the changes in the soldier's story and suggesting that the popular support for the young man was superficial. "The people in this region right now are divided into pro-Dickenson and anti-Dickenson groups. . . . On the surface the welcome given to Dickenson was wholehearted and without a trace of antagonism. Underneath, the communities of Crackers Neck and nearby Big Stone Gap are boiling with pro and con arguments. . . ."[38]

Whitehead's identification of anti-Dickenson sentiment proved true. Two days after his critical article appeared in print, Big Stone Gap's *Post* repeated

Whitehead's assertion that there existed significant pockets of the local populace critical of Dickenson, noting that the homecoming had become a "Circus Affair" when the *Bristol* (VA) *Herald Courier* took an active role in the corporal's return. Alleging that "a price tag was put on the event [the homecoming]" by the *Herald Courier,* the *Post* accused its much larger rival of using the Dickenson family as publicity pawns. Carl Knight, the editor of the *Post,* claimed that by adopting the Dickensons as local celebrities, the *Herald Courier* had driven a wedge in the community. Noting that the boisterous greeting given to Dickenson back in the hollow where his family lived was genuine, Knight also noted that in the town of Big Stone Gap, "the people gave the affair the 'silent treatment'." Phil Herndon, National Broadcasting Television and Newsreel's man in Lexington, Kentucky, drove over the mountains to get his share of the story, but "hit a blank wall." Knight reported Herndon's comments as, "In all my experience in covering news events, I have never run into anything so commercial and so revolting." When Herndon called his New York office and informed them of the price tag apparently applied to interviews and photo opportunities, "they literally blew their top. No news service pays for news coverage and we don't intend to start in Big Stone Gap."[39]

Just as the newsmen were angry with their colleagues and sometimes annoyed and stymied by the locals, the citizens of Big Stone Gap and its environs felt the same frustrations regarding the media horde. With the area flooded by people unfamiliar with the Appalachian region and its customs, more than one housewife became upset by the aggressiveness of the outsiders who often insisted on borrowing telephones for extended periods of time or did not use proper manners when making other requests.[40] A handful of vicious and condescending letters to the editor graced the pages of the *Post* commenting on the area and its people. Don Whitehead read the situation correctly when he surmised that the locals only wanted their lives, and Ed's, to return to normal, and agreed that Dickenson was just like the other soldiers who had returned: not a hero or a celebrity. Whitehead recorded that one woman, angry with the way the people and region had been portrayed in the national news, said, "You would have thought all of us were right out of a dogpatch cartoon." She took umbrage at the manner in which the colorful name of Cracker's Neck had been used and overused; in reality, she averred it was like any other small crossroads village in America.[41] Recalling some of the damage that local-color writer, John Fox Jr., and the more recent media trial of patricidal Edith Maxwell had done to the region, the *Post* published an editorial entitled "Now is the Time to Fight Back." Carl Knight's article described the Dickenson story as "originally . . . a perfect news story of a mother's joy of her son's return, was warped and twisted by daily newspapers such that local folks again experienced a growing indignation against certain city papers for their sensationalism and utter unreliability." Assuring his readers that "[p]eople in Big Stone Gap and nearby Cracker's Neck, in spite of the two colorful names, are no different from the residents of Bristol, Knoxville, Richmond, Washington, or New York," Knight accused overzealous reporters of "prostituting the profession of journalism" and called on local citizens to "fight back and let the individual newspapers and the news services know, their misrepresentations are not appreciated but actually resented."[42]

Although Knight, along with other local residents, would have liked the story to fade from attention and allow Ed and his parents to continue their lives in peace, it was not to be. During the first week of December, Ed Dickenson again became the subject of news for his December 5 marriage to Lottie Kate Laney, who lived only a few houses from the Dickenson clan.[43] Upon his release in late October, Ed cryptically suggested in several interviews that one reason for his decision to remain behind was a "Dear John" letter he had received from a girl back home. The subject in question was Laney, but she had not rejected Dickenson's interest outright—just attempted to slow the pace of the relationship. Although he and Lottie had known each other for several years, they had never dated nor had they discussed matters of romance until she began writing him while he remained a prisoner of war. Perhaps due to loneliness, Dickenson's replies became romantic and expanded to a discussion of a possible future together; in one such note, he asked Laney to marry him. Not ready to commit to marriage via long-distance correspondence, Lottie suggested they wait until he returned to the United States to contemplate their future.[44] In the meantime, newspapers clamored for a romantic angle to the Dickenson story. Although Lottie had probably not seriously considered a romantic connection with Ed, the media, beginning from the time that he announced the "Dear John" letter until his arrival back home in the mountains, suggested a torrid affair between the two. Whatever the nature of their relationship had been, it was formalized in marriage on December 5, 1953.

All was not easy for Ed Dickenson during those first weeks back home in Virginia, nor did he make them so. In November, Otho Bell's parents drove to Cracker's Neck from Hillsboro, Mississippi, to visit, hoping to gather any available information about their son. Inexplicably, Ed refused to see them. The Bells did meet Dave and Bessie Dickenson, but returned home crestfallen.[45] The Mississippi family would find persistent frustration in their attempts to bring their son home.

Thousands of miles from Big Stone Gap, the men that Ed Dickenson had left behind remained in a constant struggle confronting their plight. Claude Batchelor remembered that during November 1953, he suffered severely from homesickness and his growing disenchantment with Chang's promises. He also witnessed suffering among his comrades, as when Otho Bell fell into a deep depression. Bell, a husband and father of a child he had not yet seen, "stopped working around the place whereas before he was doing something. . . . He didn't do anything but mope around." Trying to console him, Batchelor noted that Bell would not open up about his problem. Then, one day, Bell began complaining about his back and sought aid at the hospital. After a week's absence, he came back to the group "happy as before and just an active person." Supposing that the smooth-talking Commander Chang had gotten to Bell and made promises regarding his family, Batchelor once more approached him. According to the convalescing Bell, "Chang had had quite a long talk with him and solved all his problems," the most important of which was his far-off wife and child. Chang promised him that he would get in contact with communists inside the United States and arrange for his wife and child to join him inside China very soon.[46] Despite Chang's promises, no evidence exists that Bell's wife was ever contacted about traveling to China.

Bell also informed Batchelor that Chang had divulged to him that Dickenson had fallen into serious trouble since returning home. Ostensibly, the ex-Progressives in the United States had turned on Dickenson and were pledging their support to the government in its efforts to prosecute the former PW. While this would later prove true, it was not so when Chang made the statement; indeed, no one had even suggested a prosecution for fear that such news would scare wavering PsW into remaining with the Chinese. Batchelor's critical mind read the situation properly when he wrote, "[i]t seemed to me that this would cause harmful propaganda to the group that was staying there and also on the Chinese communist forces in Korea."[47]

Claude Batchelor—January 1–24, 1954

The media spotlight that had shone so brightly on Ed Dickenson for the last two and a half months of 1953 was repositioned on New Year's Day, 1954, as a second nonrepatriate changed his mind and voluntarily returned to the United States. Claude Batchelor's defection was more surprising than Dickenson's since he had been possibly the most important individual within the group during the bulk of their time in the Neutral Zone. However, as Richard Corden became the group's leader, the recently replaced Batchelor began thinking about going home.

After Otho Bell's crisis in November, Batchelor, who was already growing critical of the Chinese and their promises, began rereading some of the staples of his recent political education. If Batchelor is to be believed, he picked up the old texts with a new skepticism and began taking apart those passages and theses that had earlier seemed so convincing to him. So engrossing was his reassessment of his readings, Batchelor noted, that he essentially withdrew from the group and even dismissed Lowell Skinner's news that Corden had been slandering him to Commander Chang. Although Corden had previously considered remaining behind in North Korea and was now apparently using his new leadership position to resurrect this plan, Batchelor "was not much interested in putting a stop to all this," although he knew that if he remained behind with the Chinese, he would have been recognized for doing so. Although no longer influential in the group, Batchelor and his longtime friend Andrew Condron spoke with Samuel Hawkins, who, like Skinner, had become a confidante of Corden, and asked him to visit the hospital and report Corden's suspicious behavior. Hawkins did as he was told and Chang responded by sending word back that Batchelor, Condron, and Hawkins should keep an eye on Corden, but to do so discreetly. Through a series of meetings with the other PsW, Batchelor and Condron effectively undermined Corden's plan to remain behind in North Korea and reestablished some of their lost credibility with Chang, although it was too little, too late.[48]

The month of December proved difficult for the group. On December 7, the Indian custodial force moved the nonrepatriates to a different camp in an effort to isolate them and to separate the men who had heard the UN explanations from those who had not. This new location created problems for the group. First, the compound was much smaller than the previous one. Second, the men no longer had the ability to cook for themselves and food had to be brought from the other camp. In the wake of the move, Claude Batchelor remembered that "the moral[e] of everyone went lower than it had ever been." He said, "The men argued more and the general atmosphere was getting worse and worse for men living together under these adverse circumstances. Fights almost broke out 3 or 4 times among the Americans and the men did nothing but complain all the time." The group would understandably grow more anxious as the January 22, 1954, repatriation deadline neared, but Batchelor saw other reasons for its uneasiness. He thought that some of the nonrepatriates, especially Lewis Griggs, Aaron Wilson, and William White, were beginning to have serious regrets about the course they had chosen.[49]

In the meantime, South Korean prisoners who were also refusing repatriation began hindering the explanation process by reciting long speeches, refusing to leave the explaining tent, and vacillating to the point that the Indians had to force them outside. The next day, the South Koreans refused to

In an obvious propaganda photo-op within days of their acceptance as defectors by China, Samuel Hawkins and Clarence Adams sing with their communist brethren. This photograph was taken in Panmunjom and shows Andrew Fortuna standing just next to Hawkins with North Korean flags prominently displayed. (UPI)

return to hear more explanations. On December 12, General K. S. Thimayya, of the neutral Indian delegation, met with the Americans and told them if they planned on copying the behavior of the Koreans, they should not attend the sessions. The group, now led by Condron and Corden, only asked that they be given the opportunity to explain themselves and their reasons for remaining behind to the press. Thimayya agreed and departed happy, with the promise that they would attend the explanations and behave properly.[50]

When news of the Korean near-revolt reached Commander Chang, he saw an excellent pretext to order the Americans to boycott the meetings. Through Richard Tenneson, who was at the hospital that day, Chang sent word to the rest of the men instructing them to refuse to sit through any future explaining sessions. Chang guaranteed the men that if they held steady until the end of the explanation period, they would not have to stay in the camp for a moment longer than necessary. Chang's new dictate put the men in an awkward position: they had already given Thimayya their word that they would attend the explanations but could not let on that they remained in contact with the Chinese; still they had to abide by Chang's orders and not arouse suspicion. Commander Chang had ordered the leaders not to allow any of the men to seek repatriation or attend the explanations and he further instructed them that if anyone suggested that they break these rules, that person should be ordered to the hospital where Chang could contact him. When the group met on the morning of December 13 to discuss their predicament, there was some debate as to whether they should go to the explaining sessions. Initially, William White, Morris Wills, Aaron Wilson, and Lewis Griggs felt that they should keep their word to Thimayya and attend the sessions, but after more discussion, all of the men, save the ever-petulant Griggs, dropped their opposition.[51]

If nothing else, Lewis Griggs could be stubborn. Committed to attending the explanation meetings, Griggs said he wanted to "tell off the explanation officer." Despite much argument by the others against hearing the explainers, Griggs would not be persuaded. Frustrated by this petty, but significant development, the nucleus group met to discuss Griggs's resistance. They felt that if they sent him to the hospital where the silver-tongued Chang could speak with him, he might be calmed. Seeing a potential embarrassment if news leaked that the group was not allowing Griggs to attend the explaining sessions, Batchelor convinced the group to let Griggs make his own decision, if only to show a level of freedom of choice among the men. All that day, the men doggedly tried to convince Griggs not to attend, but he remained firm. Some spoke softly, others harshly, a few even threatened him with violence if he stepped out of line. Batchelor claimed that while Griggs sat alone later that night, Lowell Skinner approached Batchelor asking permission to kill Griggs. Although he no longer held sway with Chang, Batchelor was respected by many of the men and he promised Skinner that "if he so much as laid a hand on Greggs [*sic*] that I would in turn take him on" and that "after we got out there would be Commander Chang to reckon with."[52]

Fearing that Griggs would leave in the middle of the night, John Dunn, Otho Bell, Albert Belhomme, Scott Rush, and Lowell Skinner took turns staying awake in case he tried to make a break. Batchelor remembered that he woke Griggs up the following morning in time for the explanations, but Griggs had changed his mind. Batchelor felt that the threats made the day before had done the trick. Still not trusting Griggs, the same men guarded against his escape the following night, but without incident. By the third day of the crisis, Griggs's depression had passed and he was back to his former self, playing ping pong with the others and renewing his friendships.[53]

Although Claude Batchelor had not mentioned it to anyone, the events of the preceding weeks had convinced him to leave the compound and accept repatriation. The Griggs incident had brought him closer to that final walk and he had prepared for his fateful decision by subtly working to ensure Griggs had his own freedom to choose. The arrival of mail a few days later afforded Batchelor an additional opportunity to rethink his earlier decision. This time, more of the men dug in and read their letters. Two of the group, Aaron Wilson and Richard Tenneson, were particularly swayed and this gave Batchelor an opening to plumb the depths of their commitment to stay in China. Hoping that he would not have to leave alone, Batchelor approached Wilson, who was stirred by his parents' poor health and angry at "how badly his folks were being deceived" by the United States. Seeing that Wilson was still spouting the traditional propaganda without question, however, Batchelor offered little more besides telling him that "he should be truthfull [*sic*] with himself and should think about what the letters said a bit more."[54]

Richard Tenneson's situation was different. When the news broke that he would remain behind, his mother, Portia Howe, began collecting for a trip to Japan, where she hoped to get permission to visit her son in Korea. While in Tokyo, Howe met Claude Batchelor's Japanese wife, Kyoko Araki. Sending messages indirectly through the letters of the other, Howe and Araki alternately wrote Tenneson and Batchelor. The overall stress of the situation, however, was overwhelming Tenneson. He had written a letter to his mother in Tokyo in which he supposed the "United States authorities . . . have probably told you that I was forced, doped, brainwashed or some other horse manure that they will use to slander and defile people like myself." Tenneson cautioned her, "[a]s soon as you read this you had better go over to GHQ and take a loyalty oath or you are likely to be arraigned before the House of Un-American Activities [House Un-American Activities Committee].[55] Looking past Tenneson's angry and paranoid commentary, his frustration with the term "brainwashing" speaks to an important point. Elizabeth Lutes Hillman explains that "[t]he brainwashing rationale effectively shifted blame from the American military, and from the United States itself, onto the deceptive tactics of the communist enemy."[56]

The turmoil of the previous months did not subside for the group as the New Year drew closer. Internal dissent had pushed group leader Richard Corden to the breaking point and he offered to step down; Corden's friend Albert Belhomme followed suit. Before any such decision was finalized, however, Commander Chang had to be consulted. Andrew Condron agreed to go to the hospital, where he could inform Chang of the deliberations occurring inside the camp. Two days later, Condron emerged from his meeting with Chang to announce that "new important developments were taking place" and no change in leadership was necessary. Chang's new tactics involved a series of broadcasts scheduled for the next few days. During these broadcasts, the men were to make noise and join in with the Korean PsW in a mocking song and dance routine. Although the nucleus group knew the full details of the ploy, the others did not know that the Koreans would be lined up between the Americans and the compound gate in an attempt to keep any of the remaining twenty-three from leaving. When the Americans were told of the plan, the story was altered to make it appear that the Koreans were afraid of one of their own making a run for freedom rather than one of the Americans or Condron. On the appointed day, all of the PsW gathered to hear the broadcast. Though occupying themselves by singing the *Internationale* and staging a "little show," the Americans became frustrated by the Korean troops' insistence on standing near the gate. Protesting that having the Koreans there looked as though force was being used to keep the others

The entire group, sans Edward Dickenson and Claude Batchelor, who had already been repatriated, poses with its mascot, Nonrepat, in the neutral zone. Top row, left to right: William White, Rufus Douglas, Albert Belhomme, Howard Adams, Samuel Hawkins, Larance Sullivan, William Cowart, James Veneris, Morris Wills, Andrew Fortuna, Aaron Wilson, Clarence Adams, Lewie Griggs, Harold Webb, and Richard Corden. Kneeling: Andrew Condron, Scott Rush, John Dunn, Richard Tenneson, Lowell Skinner, Arlie Pate, and Otho Bell. (CEGES-SOMA, Brussels, Belgium.)

inside, some of the men (those unaware of the full plan) motioned for the Koreans to step aside. Stubbornly, the Koreans stood their ground.[57] Despite the high level of commitment by several members of the U.S. nonrepatriate group, the actions of the defecting South Koreans illustrated that they were surrounded by parties skeptical of the Americans' motives and commitment.

On Christmas Eve, the group moved back to their original camp. Batchelor remembered that "[w]hen we got there we had several [bottles] of vodka and wine awaiting us along with towels, sweaters, socks, handkerchiefs, etc. which the Chinese had sent in for Christmas presents." After celebrating their "victory [over] the 'Imperialists'," Andrew Condron presented a report—given him by Chang—on the incredible progress being made by communism in England, France, and the United States. The exceedingly positive view of the world situation, as outlined by Condron, confirmed the righteousness of the actions of the men who remained behind.[58]

During the final week of 1953, several of the men were admitted to the camp hospital. Batchelor recalled that Larance Sullivan had tuberculosis, Rufus Douglas suffered from stomach trouble, and he suspected that Arlie Pate "had been falsely operated on for appendicitis." William Cowart was also a patient, although he "was not sick by any means." Visiting the men in the ward on the final afternoon of the year, Batchelor hoped for a moment of private conversation with Douglas, a man with whom he was very close and who possibly shared his interest in leaving, but that opportunity did not present itself. When Batchelor returned to the barracks, Corden approached him to say that Chang was very concerned about losing one of the men. Wondering who might be weakening, they settled on Lewis Griggs as the most likely candidate, followed closely by Otho Bell and Aaron Wilson. On Chang's orders, Corden was to send the likely candidate to the hospital and when the meeting broke up at 6:00 P.M., he promised to escort Griggs the next day.[59]

As Batchelor and the others slowly dispersed, Scott Rush came into the barracks and announced that Griggs had decided to go home. Rush explained that Griggs had been quietly lying in his bunk when "all of a sudden he just said 'fuck it, I'm going down to take a bath and then I'm going home'." Asking where Griggs was at that moment, Rush responded that he had gone in for his bath with Lowell Skinner, Sam Hawkins, and Clarence Adams in tow. Hoping to get a chance to talk with Griggs in the bathhouse, Batchelor gathered his own gear. He stepped inside just in time to see Griggs and the others preparing to leave. Trying not to look suspicious, he slipped into a tub and watched as the others left. However, after about ten minutes, Batchelor dried, dressed, and returned to the barracks to find Griggs the center of attention with some of the group's leaders giving him drinks of their vodka. Drinking quickly and heavily, it did not take long for Griggs to pass out on his bed. His inebriated state kept him subdued until he could be sent to the hospital the following morning.[60]

Claude Batchelor had thought long and hard about leaving the camp and was finally persuaded by an unlikely source. In the custodial camp, the men were given their mail, but agreed collectively to stash everything in bags under bunks and in trunks until after they were turned over to Chinese control. The idea was that if they waited until after the deadline, they would be unable to act on the emotions unleashed by the letters from home. With all of the men under constant surveillance from within their own group, the men seldom had a moment to seriously think about reading their mail, much less act on the urge. But one day, Claude Batchelor found himself alone in quarters and saw the edge of a *Reader's Digest* peeking out from within a pile of mail. He grabbed the magazine and found that it contained an article written by Whittaker Chambers on communism. Batchelor, who had harbored serious reservations about his role as a prisoner of war and the circumstances of his ideological interest in communism, read the article and found that "[w] hat he read conflicted so drastically with every word he had been hearing for several years that its effect was like a hammer blow. The multitude of concealed doubts and worries that had been torturing him settled into one clear thought. He had to get away."[61]

With his mind made up, he hoped to bring his very unhappy fellow Texan, Lewie Griggs, with him, but with Griggs passed out, he had to go it alone. Taking a long walk in order to devise a plan, Batchelor reentered the barracks at around 10:00 P.M. Sitting next to Otho Bell's bed, Batchelor talked briefly with him about Griggs, but could say very little without risking being overheard by the others. Batchelor asked Bell if he wanted to go for a walk, but Bell refused. Taking his solitary stroll around camp, Batchelor ambled toward the repatriation gate but he knew that some of the most committed Koreans lived in the house right next to the gate and were supposedly armed with clubs to be used on anyone seeking to leave. Batchelor neared their house, heard the drunken celebrants inside, but was afraid to take a chance. Returning to the barracks, he sat with Condron, who was the only man still awake, chatting about nothing of importance, just passing the time. Then, at around 1:00 A.M., he again headed toward the gate. Finding the Korean quarters quiet, he approached the Indian guard and asked for medicine. Knowing that a trip to the infirmary would get him closer to Indian officers who could then turn him over to the repatriation committee, Batchelor feigned sickness, but the guard stubbornly refused to believe him. Shocked and realizing that a failed attempt made public would make him persona non grata with the others, Batchelor argued with the guard until a second soldier emerged from the guard shack and allowed Batchelor through the gate. Several hours later, after a brief sleep, Claude Batchelor enjoyed the new year in the company of officers from the Neutral Nations Repatriation Committee as a free man. He spoke with General Thimayya and informed him that Griggs was to be sent to the hospital despite his wishes to return home. A few hours later, Griggs did arrive at the hospital, but the Indians could not help him.[62]

By the time Claude Batchelor left the communist camp, much of America had lost hope of seeing any of the men voluntarily repatriated. Ed Dickenson's early escape had given rise to the expectation that several of the men were on the cusp of returning, but after weeks and months passed, it seemed that no one else would leave. When news of Batchelor's repatriation reached the United States, therefore, some surprise was mixed with the happiness. No one was more amazed and happy than Claude's parents in Kermit, Texas.

It was still New Year's Eve in the West Texas oil fields when O. L. Batchelor drove forty-five miles from Kermit to Odessa to pick up his wife at the bus station. Mrs. Batchelor had been visiting relatives in Ballinger and when the bus arrived at the station, she could tell by the look on her husband's face that he had some news. At about 8:30 P.M., only minutes before the bus pulled in, Claude's father had taken a call at the station telling him of his son's turnabout. When his wife arrived and stepped off the bus, both stood in joyous amazement. Mrs. Batchelor remarked to reporters by telephone, "My husband and I are just standing here bawling like kids . . . I just feel like shouting here in this bus station." She had been at her lowest point when Christmas passed without word, conceding that it looked like "there's no hope." But, she remarked, "[r]eally . . . couldn't give up no matter how dark things look." Claude's father responded in a less emotional way. Speaking with a reporter shortly before his wife's bus arrived, O. L. said, "I never did give up. I think he was just brainwashed—a victim of war, that's all." "They were probably feeding him pretty good over there and he got to feeling better and saw where he had made a mistake."[63]

On Friday, January 1, the Batchelor house was alive with reporters and a ringing telephone. Dozens of people called offering their congratulations. Some were friends and neighbors while others called just to tell the family that they shared their happiness. Mrs. Batchelor received one call from a lieutenant colonel who had been in the prison camp with Claude to tell her "what a fine young man he was." Through it all, O. L. tried to get some sleep since he had to work the night shift as an oil driller.[64] As the Batchelor family and the community rallied around the news that Claude was returning home, journalists and army intelligence officers were equally excited about the prospect of talking with him.

Claude's first days of freedom were hectic. In his various media interviews, Batchelor recounted his time in the Neutral Zone. Proudly and unwisely, Batchelor trumpeted his leadership role within the camp and explained that he had waited a month to leave out of fear that the others might assault or kill him if he tried. Claiming that some of the men were armed with knives, a contention the Indian troops questioned, the Texan suggested that there was a well-developed culture of threats and coercion inside the camp. Later, the Indians confirmed that prisoners had fashioned crude weapons out of scrap metal. Like Ed Dickenson a few months before, Batchelor offered some general information to the media and journalists grew frustrated by his repeated refusals to answer more specific questions.[65]

Although much of Claude's attention had been required for news conferences and debriefing sessions, the primary focus of his return home was on his wife Kyoko. Crediting her letters to him during the explaining period as giving him the strength to return, Claude hurried to Japan to reunite with Kyoko. This would take time, as Batchelor spent his first days of freedom meeting with counterintelligence officers in Tokyo, discussing his former comrades one by one. Harried by the sudden media attention and constantly ringing telephone, Kyoko Batchelor went into seclusion behind her father's stern façade. One reporter noted that an army officer even had difficulty getting a message from Claude past the older man.[66]

On January 3, the couple was reunited at Tokyo Army Hospital, where Claude asked Kyoko to play a role in enticing the others back to the West. He asked her to "[w]rite letters to my buddies just like those you wrote to me. You can tell them how happy I am in the reunion with my wife. Some of them have wives. Maybe your letters will make them want to come back." Kyoko dutifully complied, writing the men, including one, in particular, who Claude thought might be very close to crossing over. While he never made the name public, the man was most likely Otho Bell, who had agonized over his decision to abandon his wife and baby for life in China.[67] Kyoko's efforts produced no results.

Batchelor seemingly always had a soft spot for the gentle and timid Bell and had hoped that Bell would leave with him. Upon hearing of Batchelor's repatriation, Jewell Bell wrote her husband Otho asking about the circumstances of their captivity. She wanted to know the credibility of the rumors that the men had been drugged by the Chinese to keep them behind. Batchelor responded that the men "were duped rather than doped," and that Otho remained behind out of fear rather than political conviction. He noted that Bell "had done nothing to be afraid of," but that he remained scared of what awaited him should he return. By way of illustration, Batchelor informed Jewell of what the Chinese were disseminating about him, telling her "Radio Peiping says I am undergoing third-degree methods of torture to extract information and atrocity stories from me, which is an outright lie." He disclosed to Jewell that her husband had suffered from severe depression during their time in the neutral zone, that he had been sent to the hospital, "which is completely staffed by Chinese and North Koreans," and returned the next week appearing to be perfectly content. Describing Bell as being driven by a fear instilled by both the communist captors and his fellow prisoners, Batchelor wrote, "he, like myself, was one of those prisoners of war who, wanting to do good for the American people, fell for a bit of the Chinese propaganda and became what was known as Progressives."[68]

Although his correspondence with Jewell Bell can be described as insensitive at points, his most notable blunder came in the form of an inexplicable request he made to the military shortly after he accepted repatriation. Apparently not fully understanding the breadth and depth of Joseph McCarthy's domestic influence, Batchelor asked that he be assigned to army intelligence. Citing his more than three years as a prisoner in North Korea, his acceptance of the Chinese propaganda efforts, and his leadership of the procommunist nonrepatriates while imprisoned, he argued that his background made him intimately familiar with "the tactics of the communists and their purposes." With that knowledge, he could "be of valuable assistance to our country and Govt."[69]

During the weeks that followed his repatriation, Claude remained in Tokyo undergoing mental and physical evaluations while American media outlets told his story. Granting interviews, Batchelor used the attention to his benefit. Unlike Ed Dickenson, who seemed unwilling or overly guarded when questioned about his life behind the "bamboo curtain," Claude Batchelor relished the attention and spoke openly with newsmen. He wrote his life story for the Associated Press, which ran the short autobiography in hundreds of newspapers.[70] For the Counterintelligence Corps, he produced a single-spaced, typewritten document of 148 pages explaining his life, military service, and captivity, which an army psychiatrist who interviewed him before his trial considered a form of self-criticism similar to that taught to him while in Chinese custody.[71] The Batchelor family also tried to help answer some of the media's questions. Claude's brother Oliver made himself available to reporters while his mother traveled to Chicago, Illinois, for a television appearance.[72]

With the January 22, 1954, deadline for repatriation looming, the initial excitement of Batchelor's return tempered and reserved optimism for the fates of the remaining men followed. The United States Army, happy that it had enticed two of its own back home, still hoped that the others would reconsider their stance during these final weeks. None of the nonrepatriates would rethink their decision and on January 22, the rules changed.

EIGHT

Dickenson's Reckoning

> "I sold my soul for a blanket that smelled of fish and urine and three lousy hours of uninterrupted sleep. You know what else colonel? At the time, I thought I was getting one hell of a bargain."
>
> —Paul Newman in *The Rack* (1956)

> "Always remember one thing. Never forget the people, they reared you and they can destroy a traitor."
>
> —Richard Tenneson's advice to his younger brother.

For more than four months, the world watched to see who would flinch in the small neutral compound at Panmunjom. In October, the West won a small victory when Ed Dickenson requested repatriation. The floodgates did not open thereafter, as many Americans had hoped. New Year's Day saw Claude Batchelor, a former PW leader, cross over, but again, little activity followed. With the deadline for repatriation fast approaching, both sides worked frantically in their last-ditch efforts to either maintain control or entice the returnees, while at the same time, preparing for the moment when the standoff would finally end.

Although the Americans who remained in Korea did not know it, an event was taking place halfway around the world that would spell trouble for the now free Dickenson and the soon-to-be free Claude Batchelor. Private Robert Blevens had arrived for duty with the army in West Germany in January 1953. Having avoided Korea, the near-certain destination of most young American soldiers, one would think that Blevens would have been thankful for his relatively good duty in Europe. However, he quickly found himself at odds with military authorities for fighting and drinking. While jailed, he learned of his pending court martial and directed his German girlfriend to locate the Soviet embassy in East Berlin, which she did. With promises of Soviet appreciation and respect, Blevens escaped his cell and crossed into East Germany. Once there, he wrote pro-communist articles, but refused to entice other American soldiers to defect to the East. Blevens then escaped back to the American lines in West Berlin and was rearrested. Through his girlfriend, he remained in contact with the Soviets and effectively used his captivity as a bargaining chip. With certain assurances of future treatment in East Germany, Blevens received a smuggled saw and again escaped the custody of the U.S. Army. Once back in East Berlin, he stole a sheaf of documents from Soviet files and was arrested. Remanded to a political education school, Blevens had taken enough of the Soviet punishment and left the communist bloc for the second time. When he returned to Berlin, he did so within the French zone of occupation. Within hours, he was arrested and given over to the Americans. Back in jail for the third time, Blevens was not going to be given another chance to escape custody. He was held fast until his court martial could be convened. On December 21, 1953, Blevens was sentenced to a dishonorable discharge, forfeiture of pay, and thirteen years in a military prison.[1]

Two days later, on December 23, the explaining period for the Korean War PsW ended thereby leaving both sides without a voice with which to reach their reluctant soldiers. That morning, the Americans heard their last army broadcast. The most important, and later controversial, statement within that announcement centered around an implied promise of immunity from prosecution if they decided to come home. Using Dickenson as bait to lure the others out, Major Edward Moorer announced, "Cpl. Edward Dickenson returned home to his loved ones and enjoyed a combination 30-day leave and honeymoon. This fact explodes the Communist charges that you and your family will be harmed if you return." He closed his announcement by reiterating, "[t]he fact that you have not elected repatriation prior to this time will not be held against you."[2] The implied promise of immunity became one of the most controversial issues surrounding the repatriation question.

A few months later, army attorneys would successfully argue that the statement did not promise immunity from prosecution for crimes committed while a PW. In a strictly legal sense, the statement was an accurate and effective technique for enticing the men back. However, for the twenty-one remaining nonrepatriate PsW, most of whom had never graduated from high school, such a promise was solid in principle. As soon as the army broke this implied promise, the remaining men jumped on the fact as an example of American duplicity.

Indeed, American duplicity was at work during those final weeks of repatriation. In Washington, D.C., the army's Judge Advocate General's Office was busily preparing briefs on each of the men. Giving a short background of their military service, most of each report was devoted to citing the individual's transgressions while in captivity. Interestingly, the final notes of the reports suggest a sinister motive behind the work. With both Claude Batchelor and Edward Dickenson having voluntarily returned to the United States as free men and with no overt threat of prosecution, the army began exploring how to use the prisoners' relationships with one another to entice more of the men back to face prosecution. Since Batchelor had been very close to several of the men, the army determined that his friendship with Corden might make the latter "change his mind and follow Batchelor back to United States control."[3] The army determined that Rufus Douglas, one of Batchelor's close friends and a fellow Texan, "might be persuaded to follow Batchelor's return to United States control" as "he depends on Batchelor for advice and counsel."[4] Andrew Fortuna's report read, "He is believed to be a weak character who is susceptible to influence of liquor and women. It is thought that he might accept repatriation if confronted by a beautiful woman and if assured that he would not be prosecuted for his acts while a prisoner of war."[5] Samuel Hawkins, it was determined, had "refused repatriation because the Communists had promised him an education in the field of aviation. . . . It is possible that he might be persuaded to accept repatriation if promised an aviation education in the United States."[6] The army concluded that Scott Rush was "fond of luxury and good times" and that "he might be persuaded to be repatriated if promised the kind of life he desires."[7] Lewie Griggs "might change his decision and accept repatriation if he could be convinced of the futility of the Communist promises."[8] The army believed that if they could eliminate Otho Bell's fear of reprisals from former prisoners for his behavior while a PW, he too might be enticed back home.[9] Despite the army's contention that it never offered the men immunity from prosecution and that the possibility of legal action always remained a viable course of action, this statement clearly announces a willingness to obscure the line of immunity in order to entice the men back to face charges.

As the deadline drew near, the Chinese repeatedly lodged complaints hoping to place the neutral Indian delegation in a difficult position. Arguing that the free release of prisoners on both sides violated the original armistice agreement, Chinese representatives sought to have an international conference decide the men's fates. They also understood that while winning the minds of twenty-one Americans, one Brit, a handful of Turks and Belgians, and 325 Koreans was impressive, it paled in comparison to the more than 21,000 former Chinese and North Korean soldiers who had eschewed communism during their imprisonment and now wished to live as free men.[10]

While the Chinese postured, General K. S. Thimayya, commander of the Indian forces responsible for the prisoners, readied his men for the completion of their duty. Warning the petulant Chinese and North Koreans that his men would withdraw from the compound at midnight on January 23, Thimayya planned to abandon the prisoners to their own devices. As promised, the Indian troops withdrew from their positions at midnight, leaving only a small guard of twenty men behind a knoll out of sight of the neutral camp to provide one final watch.[11] Morris Wills remembered that "[w]e woke one morning and the gates were open, and there was not a soul in sight." Realizing that the Indians had abandoned their posts, the Chinese moved in and welcomed their new charges.[12] The front page of the January 23 *New York Times* told the full story of the ideological struggle. The report, "Anti-Red Captives Are Freed By U.N.," explained the withdrawal of the Indians and the resultant liberation of the prisoners to take their chosen path. Directly underneath that article and below the fold, the most recent occurrence in Ed Dickenson's life was told in "G.I. Who Chose Reds, Then Quit, Is Seized in Court-Martial Case."[13] The army had used Dickenson and, to a lesser degree, Batchelor to lure their fellow prisoners back to the United States, all the while planning to exact revenge upon the passage of the repatriation deadline.

After spending two months at home in Virginia, Ed Dickenson boarded a bus early on January 21 for his trip to Walter Reed Army Medical Center in Washington, D.C. Lost on Dickenson was the fact that his leave expired on the same day that the Indians were to abandon the neutral zone thereby turning the nonrepatriates over to whomever would accept them. After checking into the medical center, Dickenson settled into what he expected would be several days, if not weeks, filled with medical examinations and treatments for the lingering effects of his imprisonment. Instead, he was visited that first night by officers who placed him under arrest on charges that during his time as a prisoner of war, he violated Articles 104 and 105 of the Uniform Code of Military Justice. The Article 104 charge addressed giving aid to the enemy and carried a possible sentence of death while the second charge related to prisoner misconduct and left open the possibility of punishment but not as a capital offense.[14]

As one might expect, the news shook his supporters. When informed of her son's situation, Bessie Dickenson broke down in tears, asking, "Why did they want these other boys back if they were going to court martial him?" His father announced, "He is no more of a Communist than I am" and offered to take his son's punishment.[15] Although Dickenson was in no condition to address the media in regard to his arrest, his defense counsel, Lt. Col. Edward W. Hendrick, relayed that Dickenson was "a sick man and very nervous" and that "[h]e was shocked by his arrest."[16] However, Claude Batchelor spoke from Tokyo saying that he was not surprised by Dickenson's arrest and suggested that he might also be arrested on similar charges.[17]

Support came from higher levels, too. Congressman William C. Wampler, a Republican who represented the Ninth District of Virginia, promised to contact the Secretary of the Army on Dickenson's behalf. Although the two had probably never met, Wampler confidently announced, "I don't believe he is any more Communist than you or I" and estimated that the charges would be dropped before the issue ever went to trial.[18] The congressman backed off his position rather quickly, though. Two days later, on January 26, Wampler denied that he had promised any assistance or had asked the army to drop the charges against Dickenson and called the case, "a top policy decision above my realm of jurisdiction."[19] Although Wampler did not say so, his change of heart was likely motivated by politics because his early conciliatory position would not fit with Congress, which had recently began retrenching on the subject of communism.

Apart from tearing at the fabric of the Dickenson family and complicating the political career of his congressman, Dickenson's arrest also illuminated a schism between the Department of Defense and the Department of the Army. On January 23, a spokesman for the Defense Department claimed that the army's haste to act on the Dickenson case "had upset a last-ditch psychological warfare campaign to induce twenty-one other American prisoners of the Korean war to return home." The army responded that it had received advance permission for the Dickenson arrest from Assistant Defense Secretary for Manpower, John Hannah. The Department of Defense countered that the army's claims were patently false and were in violation of Defense Secretary Charles Wilson's policy on prisoners of war. The *New York Times* tracked Hannah down at his East Lansing, Michigan, home where he refuted the army's claim that he had given permission, stating that "it was not up to him to approve the Army plans in the Dickenson case." He did reveal that he had been contacted previously regarding a fact-finding committee that planned to investigate the Dickenson case, "[b]ut whatever the Army decides to do does not need my approval."[20]

Undersecretary Hannah acknowledged that "it was the timing, not the action itself [arrest] which caused some consternation."[21] Across the nation, the coincidence of Dickenson's arrest and the expiration of the neutral period shook Americans' faith in the honor of their political system, causing some to beg, plead, and even threaten violence on behalf of the poor boy from Cracker's Neck. Colonel Norman Sprowl, a public information officer for the Military District of Washington, received the brunt of these early complaints. Of the five telephone calls he took on January 24, three were threatening. Fearful, Sprowl requested and received permission to wear his sidearm. Feeling that four of the calls were the product of cranks, Sprowl did take seriously a call from "an ex-Army sergeant who said he came from the same part of the country as Dickenson and wanted to talk to him in person to straighten him out."[22]

On January 25, the army acted on the twenty-one men who remained in Korea. Secretary of Defense Wilson, understanding that the men would not return, sent Acting Secretary of the Army John Slezak a memorandum requesting that the men be struck "from the rolls as dishonorably discharged." Later that day, the Assistant Secretary of Defense for Legislative and Public Affairs released a brief statement announcing that Secretary Wilson "had taken the Dickenson case 'under advisement.'"[23]

In the meantime, Dickenson was having a difficult time dealing with his arrest. His young wife, his brother Grover, and a brother-in-law drove to Washington, D.C., to visit him after the family's attempts to contact him through Walter Reed Army Medical Center failed.[24] Friends both near and far offered support and encouragement, from anonymous letters to small-town newspaper editors to the surprise registered by President Eisenhower when he heard of Dickenson's arrest.[25] Former PW Donald Dumas knew Dickenson at Camp Five and told a newspaper reporter, "[h]e didn't do anything more than I did myself, except to decide to stay" and defended Dickenson's actions based on the fact that "[f]or two years, we were taught nothing but Communism. . . . It was that darned stupid schooling they gave us that made some of the boys stray. I can understand it, although someone who hasn't been through it all might not."[26] A former Marine and PW wrote the Dickenson family to show his support, assuring them that Ed responded to his captivity in the same way that others had responded.[27] Retired army Brig. Gen. Herbert C. Holdridge even telegraphed the family from his home in Van Nuys, California, offering to defend Dickenson against the charges.[28]

Charged with mistreating fellow prisoners and being "allied to treason," Dickenson was quickly transferred from the medical center to a jail at Fort Belvoir, Virginia. There, he met his appointed attorney, Lt. Col. Edward Hendrick, who would handle the preparation for the pretrial investigation and the full defense if Dickenson decided to retain him.[29] By February 18, the charges had been focused to a violation of Article 105 of the Uniform Code of Military Justice, informing on his fellow prisoners in such a way that he caused hardship, and a similar violation of Article 104 for collaboration based on the first charge.[30]

While the nonrepatriates either adapted to Chinese life or refused it and returned home, Ed Dickenson's and Claude Batchelor's individual dramas kept unfolding. By early April 1954, the army had arrested and charged Batchelor and had scheduled Dickenson's court martial for April 19. By that time, Guy Emery had replaced Hendrick as Dickenson's defender. Emery, a retired army colonel and a West Pointer, took his charge seriously and took the army to task for refusing to provide him with copies of the collected evidence. The army had secured 400 statements against Dickenson, but had classified their contents, including the name of the interviewee, as secret. Unable to prepare for the individual witnesses or their written statements, Emery was forced to issue a plea to men who had served with Dickenson who might be sympathetic to his plight to offer their assistance. Although Emery had sent a letter to the Secretary of the Army requesting the names and locations of the men who had been imprisoned at Pyoktong with Dickenson, the army refused his request, leaving him with little hope of finding strong defense witnesses.[31]

On Monday, April 19, 1954, Ed Dickenson's trial began at Fort McNair. The first day was primarily occupied with opening statements, during which the prosecution outlined the charges against Dickenson and Guy Emery assailed the army's accusations. A central component of Emery's argument was Dickenson's allegation that the army had broadcast promises of immunity to the men while they were in the neutral camp. Emery asserted that "[s]trong assurances were made by spokesmen in Washington inviting the prisoners to come home, that no harm would come to them. If these specious promises were merely propaganda, why didn't the Army repudiate them?"[32] Dickenson himself told the court, "I was promised immunity if I would come back to the U.S. if I had committed any crimes against the U.S. government. But they didn't keep their promise." Raymond Lech agreed with Dickenson's position, reminding readers that Maj. Edward Moorer had given the men the perception of immunity when he spoke over the loudspeaker: "Corporal Edward Dickenson returned home to his loved ones and enjoyed a combination thirty-day leave and honeymoon. This fact explodes communist charges that you and your family will be harmed if you return." Lech also boldly identified the hypocrisy in the army's assertion that it had not promised any of the men immunity yet called on several admitted Progressives to testify against Dickenson and Batchelor, with the implication being that their cooperation would assure their forgiveness of wartime indiscretions.[33]

Despite the anticipation of the trial's opening day, the subsequent days stole the show with detailed testimony and sometimes crippling cross-examination. April 20 opened with Cpl. Thomas A. Carrick of Blacksburg, Virginia, testifying that he and Dickenson had shared a foxhole in the days before the Chinese overran their unit in the fall of 1950. From there, the two men had both been imprisoned at Camp Five, where Carrick allegedly heard Dickenson tell a Chinese officer about the escape plans of others.[34] However, on April 27, Carrick was cross-examined by Emery and the story changed dramatically. Seeking to place Dickenson as the informant, Emery asked if the witness was sure the voice he heard telling a Chinese guard of the plan was that of Dickenson's. To that, a clearly confused Carrick replied, "I'm not sure. . . . It could have been Dickenson. I'm not sure about the general nature of the incident. I've been trying to remember. It's been almost three years." Pressing further, Emery asked Carrick if, in light of this revelation, he would be willing to withdraw his testimony. Carrick agreed and the presiding officer concurred and ordered the testimony stricken. The prosecution, however, was not going to allow Carrick's vivid information to go for naught. Objecting to the striking of the evidence and characterizing Carrick as a hostile witness, prosecuting attorneys attacked him for his motives in recanting his testimony. Carrick had been scheduled to be married on that very day; however, the Dickenson case had kept him in Washington long enough to force a postponement. Inexplicably, the court decided that Carrick's initial testimony was more reliable than his recanting and allowed it to stand.[35]

In addition to Carrick's testimony, the court heard from four other prosecution witnesses. Corporals Johnny Moore of San Pedro, California, and Franklin Barrett of Richmond, Virginia, testified that they had shared a room with Dickenson at Camp Five, where he attempted to spread communist propaganda. Former Sgt. Barney M. Younce Jr. stated that he heard Dickenson's voice over the camp public address system promising that he would "fight for peace" and witnessed him smoking Chinese cigarettes and in possession of Chinese money.[36] This testimony cannot be considered damning given the Chinese habit of offering such rewards as a way to breed paranoia among the prisoners.[37] Sergeant Dominic Cantillo of Boston, Massachusetts, recalled that Dickenson had gone around his room once trying to get the men to sign a camp petition called the "Asiatic Peace Pact." Cantillo said that he signed it without reading it for fear the Chinese would put him in "jail."[38]

Curiously, Cantillo knew more about Johnny Moore than came out in the testimony that day. In his debriefing, Cantillo identified Moore as having "sincere leanings toward Communism" and having attempted "to influence other prisoners to follow and accept communistic theories" while the latter served as an informer for the Chinese and made propaganda recordings.[39]

The next day, April 21, saw Dickenson return some of the fire that had been sent his way. Capt. Bert Cumby had been the lead agent in Dickenson's post-repatriation debriefing and while the young soldier knew Cumby was an army officer, the civilian clothes he wore and the easy nature of "Captain Bert," as Dickenson called him, belied the officer's true motives. Dickenson testified that when he met him for debriefing sessions, Cumby did not inform him that he was under suspicion of any crime.[40] Also on the stand that day was S.Sgt. John A. Davis of Niagara Falls, New York. Davis testified that in February 1951, he witnessed an argument between Dickenson and another soldier over food. Dickenson was serving as cook in the sick compound at that time and a severely emaciated man approached him asking for additional food. Alleging that Dickenson was in the habit of trading extra food for cigarettes, Davis testified that he saw food in the pot while Dickenson claimed that none was left after the meal. Arguing with the man, whom Davis remembered as 5' 9"and approximately 105 pounds, Dickenson pushed him backward out of the door, down three steps. Falling hard, the man lost the use of his legs for the remainder of that day. Within two days, he was dead.[41]

On the trial's fourth day, April 22, the army introduced a letter Dickenson had written to his hometown newspaper, the Big Stone Gap, Virginia, *Post*.[42] In that letter, dated February 23, 1953, Dickenson spoke of peace and the hope of his fellow prisoners to return to their homes. By modern standards, questions such as "Is peace good or bad?" and statements like "I am sure that we want peace and happiness in our beloved country" hold no negative connotation, however, during the politically contentious early 1950s, the word "peace" became a codeword for communist subversion.[43] After the introduction of Dickenson's letter, Sgt. Lyle W. Jacobson of Butte, Montana, took the stand and testified that the accused revealed the escape plans of eight prisoners of war. Noting that the next "morning he was quizzed by a Communist guard who threw their escape plans 'right back in my face—more or less as if he had been there himself,'" Jacobson felt confident that Dickenson had been the man who squealed because he had been seen standing near an open window at the time the men were discussing their plan. "The subject was changed promptly . . . because Dickenson had the reputation of being an informer." Following his conversation with the guard, Jacobson promised

Dickenson that retribution would follow him out of the prison camp, but was warned later by a guard to stop "threatening Progressive students." Although Roy H. McClain of Rochelle, Illinois, did not appear in Washington for the trial, the army did enter a statement from him into the record. In it, he alleged that Dickenson spent considerable time around the Chinese headquarters, especially the office of an officer known as "Screaming Skull," and was seen conversing with the Chinese on many occasions.[44]

The first week of the trial ended on April 23, with several highly contentious moments focused around two different escape attempts (the first of which was examined in chapter 4). In July 1952, Dickenson had successfully escaped Camp Five with three other men. During the trial, the three testified that he had informed on them. Virgil Rutherford, from Tulsa, Oklahoma, known as "Okie" while a PW; Fred Obroff of Wheelwright, Kentucky; and Martin Christensen of Hammond, Indiana, all told similar stories of how they successfully escaped camp with Dickenson and remained at large for approximately eighteen hours before being recaptured. Suggesting the presumption and paranoia many of the men felt during their imprisonment and after their release, Christensen swore that when the Chinese patrol recaptured the men, they "appeared to know where we were exactly."[45] Other inconsistencies in the stories hint at the state of mind of the men while prisoners. Fred Obroff identified Dickenson as a Progressive who "hung around Chinese Headquarters" and wrote propaganda articles for the Chinese. However, when Dickenson, a man whom Obroff should not have been able to trust, asked Obroff to join him and Virgil Rutherford in an escape attempt, Obroff quickly agreed. Following their recapture, all of the men were interrogated, beginning with Dickenson, who apparently revealed the full story under pain of death. Obroff paraphrased Dickenson's justification: "The Chinese put a gun in my face and threatened to kill me so I told them everything." Curiously, Dickenson's apparent cooperation did not make his life easier. Obroff's statement noted that Dickenson was jailed for twenty-five days, part of which was spent with his former partners, who now suspected him as an informant, while Christensen did thirty days; however, Obroff was jailed only twenty-one days and Rutherford from ten to fifteen days.[46] While imprisoned and even afterward, speculation and paranoia ruled the day.

That day's testimony had begun with Edward M. Gaither taking the stand. Gaither, a Philadelphia, Pennsylvania, native relayed that in July 1951, he and Robert Lauri had been busily making arrangements for an escape attempt. Claiming that Dickenson was trusted by the men at that time, Gaither told him of a stash, including a homemade compass, waterproof bag, matches, and other useful items he had buried under his bed. Gaither recalled that after Dickenson's escape attempt with Christensen, Obroff, and Rutherford, he was called in and questioned about his own plan. The Chinese had already dug up his supplies and showed them to him during questioning. Gaither alleged that "[a]s a result of Dickenson's squealing I was put before a mock firing squad three times, jailed for seven months and beaten with clubs and kicked by the Chinese." He then discussed his imprisonment, however, and mentioned only fifty-five days of jail time, during which he recalled Dickenson bringing food to the prisoners, looking nervous and afraid and having "a guilt complex."[47] Although he offered no concrete evidence that Dickenson had ratted out his plan nor seemed to understand that at least Lauri and possibly Dickenson's fellow escapees knew of his stash of supplies, he vehemently defended his assumptions at the court martial, one time leaning forward in his chair and screaming at Dickenson, "Don't you like it?" Both Gaither and Guy Emery traded contentious barbs, "which left the record of the court-martial pretty well muddled," Emery asking the witness if he had a good memory "in connection with people you want to get." Gaither responded, "Yes, sir, if they deserve it."[48]

The testimony of Friday, April 23, carried over to the Monday session with dramatic results. Christensen's charge that Dickenson had informed on their escape attempt was thrown out of court on the basis that Christensen was not competent to testify that questionable documents he swore were in Dickenson's handwriting actually were written by the defendant. Emery attempted to have Gaither's more damaging testimony dismissed, arguing that no solid evidence had been submitted by the witness, only hearsay and speculation. The judge, however, decided to allow that testimony to stand.[49]

On April 27, the seventh day of the trial and the very day that a court of inquiry decided not to pursue charges against Col. Frank Schwable for signing germ warfare confessions while a prisoner of war, Thomas Carrick was recalled by the defense. While on the stand, he broke down and admitted that he was extremely confused about the testimony he had given a week earlier and wanted it to be withdrawn. Despite Carrick's uncertainty and his pivotal position as the only witness to personally hear Dickenson's supposed informing, the court allowed the statement to stand, just as it had Gaither's testimony of the previous day. During a break in the proceedings, however, all eyes were on Bessie Dickenson, Ed's mother, who collapsed outside of the courtroom from what newspapermen deemed a "nervous attack." Guy Emery had intended to call Mrs. Dickenson to the witness stand later that afternoon, but a physician ordered her to leave the proceedings and get some rest.[50]

With Bessie Dickenson unavailable, Emery called Dr. Philip Bloemsma, a physician with a special interest in the psychological effects of captivity. In 1942, Bloemsma, then a member of the Dutch military, was captured by the Japanese on Portuguese Timor and spent the next three years imprisoned along a railroad between Bangkok, Thailand, and Rangoon, Burma. When he was released, he devoted considerable time to the study of the mental challenges he witnessed as a prisoner. While on the stand on Dickenson's behalf, he gave the most important psychological testimony of the trial.[51]

Bloemsma introduced the court to the term "fence complex." As he explained it, after a few months of captivity, a man becomes "only interested in the means to prolong his life" and he becomes mentally focused on "food, work, and bed space, and diseases." Bloemsma noted that the fence for which the syndrome was named was that of the prisoner's mental self-restriction:

> "his interest and his field of vision becomes narrower and narrower; because of his concentration on the means to prolong his life in prison camps, he becomes egoistic and he becomes very much nonsocial. Social consciousness doesn't exist after a long time of imprisonment in prison camps in many cases. . . . Then the usual development is that these patients, these prisoners of war, get limited in their power of expression. They cannot talk normally, because they lose interest in those things that lie outside the fence, because of the necessity of maintaining themselves alive. Most of them have monosyllabic conversation. They practically all lead a very shallow mental life; and because there is an equilibrium in normal life between thoughts and words, this equilibrium becomes disturbed in a prisoner of war."

All of these symptoms combined to make prisoners very paranoid. Bloemsma's opinion was that Dickenson's life was "threatened from day to day," as was that all of the PsW, and, as a result, he became "very suspicious." He noted that "[r]umors are always believed; and if a rumor hasn't been in a camp for a certain time, rumors are made up; and this is a typical thing of an advanced fence complex patient."[52] Bloemsma explained, "nearly every POW 'loses his sense of right and wrong' after he is held captive behind a fence for any length of time," making a compelling case for Dickenson and his defense counsel.[53]

The next day, April 28, more evidence as to Dickenson's mental health while a captive was submitted in the form of testimony by three psychiatrists. Giving credence to Bloemsma's "fence complex" assertion, Morris Kleinerman described Dickenson as being 'emotionally unstable' and irrational while a prisoner. Winfred Overholser, who was superintendent of Washington, D.C.'s, St. Elizabeth's Mental Hospital, agreed with Kleinerman and offered that "the type of treatment given some prisoners 'could be pushed to a point where almost any one would submit'." To no one's surprise, army psychiatrist and colonel Emmet Litteral held Dickenson responsible, testifying that he could in fact distinguish right from wrong while imprisoned and did possess the strength to do right. Moreover, while neither the court nor the defense saw the importance of this, Litteral, rightly or wrongly, suggested that severe paranoia drove Dickenson to see the army as seeking to destroy him and that "every order given him was an insult." Steeling himself against the pitfalls of interpretation, Litteral stuck strictly with the legal definition of sanity as written into military regulations and declared Dickenson to suffer from 'acute situational maladjustment." Kleinerman and Litteral agreed that Dickenson had a passive aggressive personality, but differed otherwise with the former arguing, along with Overholser, that the corporal exhibited a great level of dependency, particularly when presented with harsh circumstances.[54]

With recent and similar charges against Frank Schwable and William Dean, both officers, Guy Emery attempted to introduce General Dean's testimony on life in a prisoner of war camp. Calling Dean an "expert witness" on the conditions, Emery was disappointed when the court took a narrow view and found the general's information to be "wholly immaterial."[55] Emory had hoped that the court would afford his client the same opportunity at defense given to Schwable and Dean, both of whom had chalked up their own behaviors to the desperation that resulted from the poor conditions of imprisonment. Unfortunately for the enlisted men of that era, the army had grown exceedingly rank-conscious and that custom extended into the realm of military justice. Although the separation of officers and enlisted men in the military is supported by considerable reason, the Dickenson and Batchelor cases saw two different laws being applied. For officers who broke protocol and committed crimes while imprisoned, lenience and compassion was practiced, but for enlisted men, severe punishment was demanded.

On Thursday, April 29, the court relented and allowed the Dean deposition to be read aloud. The Medal of Honor winner and former PW had testified that the Chinese threatened their families if they refused to cooperate and because of the rigors of captivity, the men were weakened enough and the Chinese appeared strong enough that nothing was impossible for them. Dean's account also told of the ability of the Chinese to use threats of cold and starvation to get information and cooperation from the men, and since virtually all of the prisoners had seen their comrades die from those causes, the threats were effective. That day, the court also heard testimony from four men who had known Ed Dickenson since childhood. They offered further evidence of his dependent nature. With the testimony now complete, Dickenson had to decide if he would testify. After being assured that his silence would not be viewed as an admission of guilt, he deferred, allowing the testimony phase of the trial to close.[56]

Closing arguments were made on Friday, April 30. Eight army officers sat in judgment hearing defense attorney Guy Emery describe Dickenson as the army's "Judas goat (which) had outlived its usefulness." Alleging that Dickenson had been used to lure his fellow prisoners back to the United States where they would then be prosecuted, Emery accused the army of prosecuting the defendant based on assumption and circumstantial evidence. Calling the trial a "'garbage can' of suspicion, innuendo, rumor, and hearsay" and "not so much of a trial of law as a preparation for crucifixion," Emery asked the officers to acquit Dickenson of the charges against him. Prosecuting attorney Col. Robert Bard essentially agreed with Emery's evaluation of the case as one based on circumstantial evidence when he offered the confusing, "Fact plus the accused equals result." Explaining the statement, Bard meant that Dickenson heard the facts of escapes from his fellow PsW, then the hopeful escapees were called to headquarters by the Chinese. Ed Dickenson left the courtroom that day hopeful that a two-thirds majority to convict was not possible and he would not have to face the possibility of life imprisonment.[57]

After spending the weekend locked in a ward of the hospital at Fort Belvoir, Virginia, Dickenson woke on Monday morning, May 3, for another ride to the courtroom at Fort McNair in Washington. That day, the presiding officer of the court gave the eight-man tribunal their instructions and then dismissed them to deliberate. Although Dickenson spent most of the day at court, no news was forthcoming.[58] The deliberations continued the next day before Dickenson was summoned back to Fort McNair that afternoon to hear the verdict. Dickenson stood as his conviction was announced. Listening silently and without emotion, he heard the sentence of ten years at hard labor and a dishonorable discharge announced by the court.[59] On the same day that saw the U.S. Air Force clear sixty-nine airmen of misconduct while prisoners of war, Ed Dickenson was held to a much higher standard. Elizabeth Lutes Hillman astutely notes, "If the 'very survival of the nation' hinged on prosecuting the likes of Batchelor and Dickenson, American democracy . . . stood on shakier ground than military leaders could afford to admit."[60]

A distraught Dickenson returned to the locked hospital ward that had been his home for the previous weeks and seethed. One week later, he wrote a letter to the *Washington Post and Times Herald* in which he bared his post-conviction thoughts. Writing, "I went to Korea to fight for my country and

I carried out my duty to the best of my ability and now I have received my reward," he bitterly accused those who testified against him of lying.[61] Indeed, many of the men who returned to the United States as former PsW and heroes misbehaved while in Korea.

Cpl. Harold M. Dunn had been known as a Progressive while a PW, but quickly became a patriot upon his return home. While at Camp Five, "Dirty" Dunn, as he was called, was the camp's librarian and recorded propaganda for the Communists. When he came home, however, that part of his life was forgotten. Shortly after getting back to New York, he was honored as the king of the state fair and became a minor celebrity. In January 1954, the army was gathering evidence against Dickenson and sought out the men who had known him in prison. Dunn was a Progressive while in Camp Five and CIC agent Stanley Gedney surely knew that when he took Dunn's statement after repatriation. As Lech notes in his book, Dickenson's trial gave former prisoners plenty of opportunities to get even. Dunn stated that he and Dickenson first met sometime in the summer of 1952, but the two were never friends "because I did not like him." Remembering Dickenson as "a weak-willed individual, who was not too intelligent," Dunn added that he was "an escapist from reality" and "a coward." Curiously, Dunn acknowledged, "I became a Progressive, as far as the other prisoners in the camp were concerned, shortly before Dickenson." Apparently feeling confident that no mention had been made of his friendliness with the Chinese during captivity, Dunn made a mistake in January 1954 when he wrote an article entitled, "I Was a Progressive POW in Korea" for *Pageant Magazine.* Within months, the army was gathering evidence against Dunn and in June he pleaded guilty to charges that he collaborated while a prisoner of war and that he gave aid and comfort to the enemy. He was given an eight-year sentence, dishonorable discharge, and forfeiture of all pay and allowances. The next year, Dunn's sentence was reduced to two and a half years.[62]

Harold Dunn was not the only former Progressive to turn on Dickenson during his trial. The inter-camp Olympics held at Pyoktong in 1952 identify hundreds of men who participated in the games in various ways, some of whom later claimed to be staunch Reactionaries. Although not a sign of outright collaboration, joining in such games certainly did not constitute resistance. Johnny Moore, who testified that Dickenson tried to spread the communist line, was in the "entertainment" group at the Olympic games, along with fellow accusers Donald Sherrick and Wallace Dunham. John Davis's testimony that he saw Dickenson shove a severely ill man down steps rather than give him food was damning, but scarcely two years before, Davis had been a member of the "cheering" section at the Pyoktong games. William Hansen, who also testified against Dickenson, had participated as "working personnel." Those not called to Fort McNair, but who had given written statements as to Dickenson's Progressive leanings, included Nick Berchem and John Megyesi, who took the stand against Batchelor, of the "cheering" section; Ronald Lovejoy of "entertainment"; and Richard Holmquist of "working personnel."[63]

Of all the participants in the inter-camp Olympic games, only a handful of the nonrepatriates appear, although prominently. In the athletic events, only two of the men were represented, with Clarence Adams boxing and Larance Sullivan on the parallel bars. Several other nonrepatriates participated, but not as athletes. On the sixth night of the games, a theater group put on "Golden Boy," the story of a young man whose boxing career comes to a tragic end in a car accident. The commemorative book described Claude Batchelor as "very convincing as the manager of Golden Boy Joseph Bonaparte" and lauded Dickenson prosecution witness, Robert Lauri's work as Bonaparte Sr. Howard Adams, Ed Dickenson, and Bennie Smith were cast members. "Entertainer" and prosecution witness, Johnny Moore, served as the play's master of ceremonies. Official photographers Scott Rush and Albert Belhomme can be seen in pictures intently watching the boxing matches, while Andrew Condron; Scott Rush; Bohus Janda; the notorious James Gallagher, who had thrown two sick men out into the cold where they froze to death; and Larance Sullivan participated in a general physical training demonstration.[64]

More damning, considering the overwhelmingly convincing evidence offered against Batchelor and Dickenson, was the participation of many of their accusers in the games. Dominic Cantillo, who sat in an office on Governor's Island, New York, and gave an extensive deposition about the conditions of camp and the main collaborators, played football in the 1952 inter-camp Olympics, along with Bobby DeGraw, who had sought to remain behind with the other twenty-three and had served as the leader of the cheering section for the Camp One basketball team.[65]

While it is clear that many of the men who agreed to testify against Dickenson and Batchelor had their own past behavior to hide, the question of whether or not the army knew about that behavior at this point is most important. As the former prisoners returned to the United States after their release, the army's Counterintelligence Corps busied itself conducting interviews in an attempt to reconstruct the PW experience. As part of these statements, soldiers were asked to identify those who collaborated with the enemy. Although historians agree that the total number of collaborators was much higher, 256 men were identified as the worst offenders by their comrades. Interestingly, only twenty-one of the twenty-three nonrepatriates were listed; the names of Aaron Wilson and John Dunn were conspicuously absent. Of the seventy-four former prisoners who wrote statements against Dickenson in preparation for his court martial, six of them made the list. During the trial, only one, Harold Dunn, was brought in to testify along with the twenty-seven prosecution witnesses.[66]

Clearly, the army knew that some of the men upon whom it was depending to provide damning evidence against Dickenson and Batchelor were guilty of the same crimes and used that knowledge to compel them to testify. Knowing that these men were susceptible to coercion and that the Chinese had already attained their cooperation while prisoners, the army simply provided them an opportunity to show themselves to be good Americans, most likely with the idea of their personal immunity implied. Raymond Lech contends that the army used information gained during repatriation to coerce former prisoners to testify against Dickenson and Batchelor, knowing that they would agree to do so and hoping that they would not be questioned about their own behavior. Upon his release from prison in 1957, Ed Dickenson said, "[t]he only difference between me and a lot of others is the others have not been caught."[67] As Raymond Lech pointed out, "[t]he others were caught; the army had the goods on everyone."[68]

Although it was clear that Dickenson was not part of any pro-communist conspiracy, the FBI suspected that the Dickenson Defense Fund Committee was a pro-communist front. The DDFC had been founded in Orangeburg, New York, by a group of sympathetic citizens shortly after Dickenson's conviction. Over the coming months, it mailed thousands of letters requesting donations and copies of an issue of *True* magazine that told the corporal's story. The FBI estimated that from late 1954 until April 1955, the DDFC distributed more than 1,000 copies, most of them to Dickenson's home state. By July 1955, the Dickenson Defense Fund Committee was cleared and the FBI discontinued its investigation.[69] More than two years later, Dickenson would again become a free man.

The most unfortunate aspect of Ed Dickenson's court martial was its timing. Although Dickenson probably never saw his situation as part of a broad national movement, it certainly was. A fight had been brewing between Joe McCarthy and the army for more than six months. He had blamed the army for covering for its own while protecting those whom McCarthy sought to expose. In early March 1954, the army had flung charges back at McCarthy, threatening to expose him and his cohorts to the nation. Within a month and a half, the Army-McCarthy hearings began.[70]

Only two days after Ed Dickenson's trial had begun at Fort McNair, the Army-McCarthy hearings started on Capitol Hill, only a half mile north. On Capitol Hill, the army's lawyers could argue points of law and politics in the hopes of discrediting Joe McCarthy's seemingly unending litany of charges, but at Fort McNair, the army could speak directly to the worried citizens of the United States by showing how tough it could be on communism. Through Edward Dickenson's trial, the army fought McCarthy's charges. Sadly for Dickenson however, the Army-McCarthy hearings outlasted his court martial. By the time Joe McCarthy had been embarrassed in front of the entire nation in mid-June, Dickinson had already been convicted, and Batchelor, a worse offender and easier prosecution, was already scheduled for trial.[71] One can only wonder how the courts martial would have turned out if the Army-McCarthy hearings had been decided in advance of the Dickenson court martial.

NINE

Batchelor's Reckoning

"The court deliberated only thirty minutes before passing the sentence. Just long enough to smoke a cigarette and come back to throw a young man's life away."
—Mrs. Edward Frazier on Claude Batchelor

"The American prisoners of war court-martialed after being released from POW camps were among the most unlikely military criminals of the twentieth century."
—Elizabeth Lutes Hillman in *Defending America*

Having convicted and sentenced Edward Dickenson, the army then turned its attention to Claude Batchelor. As an admitted former leader of the nonrepatriates, Batchelor was considered to be a much easier prosecution for the army and a serious liability for a defense attorney. Fearing his fate if he allowed a military attorney to defend him, Batchelor arranged with Joel Westbrook for representation. Westbrook was a fine attorney and partner in one of San Antonio's most prominent law firms. More importantly, he was very well connected politically and counted Senator Lyndon Johnson as a personal friend.[1] If Claude Batchelor had a chance to escape the charges before him, Joel Westbrook was it.

Maintaining that his client's case was "basically different" from that of Ed Dickenson, Joel Westbrook was cautiously optimistic about Batchelor's future.[2] On June 22, the army announced that Batchelor would be tried on charges of consulting "with the enemy concerning a subversive organization to be established in the United States after the . . . armistice," making speeches and writing "articles in an attempt to persuade fellow prisoners . . . to believe the enemy propaganda and accept Communist doctrine," and writing "letters to promote disloyalty among the civilian population."[3] With these charges hanging over his client, Westbrook began maneuvering for as much time to formulate a defense as he could arrange. On August 3, he complained that the army investigator assigned to the case was "intemperate and hostile" to Batchelor's cause.[4] A few days later, he alleged that the army still had not supplied him with information that he had requested three months earlier and that the pretrial investigation had been shoddily conducted.[5] In light of Westbrook's concerns, the army delayed Batchelor's court martial two weeks.[6]

On August 30, 1954, at Fort Sam Houston in San Antonio, Texas, Claude Batchelor's trial began. Flanked by his mother and Portia Howe, who came from Minnesota to lend her support, Batchelor felt cautiously confident that the coming days would allow him to clear his name. However, the proceedings got off to an inauspicious start when Medal of Honor winner 1st Lt. Edward R. Schowalter Jr. stood and asked to be recused from the trial because of his preconceptions of Batchelor. He told the court, "I challenge myself on the grounds that I am hostile to the accused and prior to the convening of this court, formulated the opinion and expressed the opinion that the accused is a traitor."[7] Although Schowalter was dismissed from the proceedings and was reportedly berated by an army colonel for his courtroom display, his statements set the tone for what would become a highly contentious trial.[8]

On September 1, testimony began in earnest. Bohus Janda took the stand first and testified that he got to know Batchelor in November 1952, around the time of the inter-camp Olympics. If anything, Janda did more to harm his own credibility than that of Batchelor. He acknowledged that Batchelor was active in the Chinese propaganda efforts at Camp Five, but also admitted that he had been brought from Camp Three to attend the same meetings as Batchelor. One aspect of the Camp Five meeting involved the creation of an organization named "Ex-Prisoners of War for Peace," which would be started secretly within the PW camps, but be made public once the men returned to the United States.[9]

The second witness called was Harold "Dirty" Dunn. After testifying against Dickenson, he traveled to San Antonio, where he also went on record for the prosecution against Batchelor. Acknowledging his own progressive stand, he noted that he and Batchelor were cohorts in a study group and that they had met, along with Lowell Skinner, Howard Adams, and Donald Disney, during the repatriation process to further discuss the concept of organizing pro-communist groups within the United States.[10] More flatteringly, Dunn recalled that Batchelor did a lot of work on behalf of his fellow prisoners and "looked after sick prisoners without showing partiality."[11]

Attorneys spent the next several days reading into the court record the statements Batchelor wrote from the army hospital in Tokyo after his repatriation.[12] However, on September 8, the testimony resumed with allegations that Batchelor played the role of informant being discussed. John Megyesi started the day by telling the court that he had gotten hold of an 8-mm motion picture camera while in the PW camp. Having used up all the film, he then found the camera useless. In late June or early July 1952, a British soldier named Buckley approached Megyesi about the camera and asked if he could have it for a souvenir. As there was no more film and the camera could get Megyesi in serious trouble with the Chinese, he gave it to the Brit. Later that day, however, Buckley returned and asked for the film spool. Megyesi did not mind giving him the spool, but his film was still on it. When Buckley revealed that he was going to give the camera and spool to 1st Lt. Walter Mayo, a fellow prisoner at Camp Five, Megyesi spent that night stripping off the film and handed the spool over the next day. About a month after giving the camera to Buckley, Megyesi was called into camp headquarters where Lin, better known to the prisoners as "Screaming Skull," interrogated him for three hours about the source of the camera. Megyesi gave no statement, nor could he tell who might have informed on him. He spent the next two months and eight days in "the hole," the prison camp's internal jail.[13]

The next man to take the stand was Lieutenant Mayo, who could continue the camera story from where Megyesi left off. Mayo had a canister of film, but without the spool the camera was useless. He gave Buckley the empty canister and when Megyesi took his film off, he kept the canister and sent the empty spool to Mayo, who then added his film and, like Megyesi before him, began recording brief segments of Chinese atrocities until he ran out of film a couple of months later. In late August 1952, about the same time that Megyesi was questioned by the Chinese regarding his involvement with the camera, Lin called Mayo in and told him point-blank, "We know you have the camera and the camera is in your room." Mayo immediately confessed, hoping to end the inquiry and save others who might have been involved. For the next nine weeks, Mayo was locked away in solitary confinement. Like Megyesi, Mayo did not identify the informant who caused his suffering.[14]

The day's final witness was Sgt. Bernard Buli. Having gotten in trouble with the Chinese for stealing a blanket, Buli was remanded to confinement in a cell that adjoined Lin's office. He recalled that Lin met with Andrew Condron and Claude Batchelor and asked them who had a camera in the compound. Neither had any knowledge of a camera, but they promised to find out and report the culprit. Three days later, Batchelor returned and told Lin that Megyesi was the transgressor. With his ear pressed to the mud wall, Buli was confident that the voice he heard talking with Lin was that of Batchelor.[15]

With Buli's testimony, Batchelor's name had finally been tied to the camera incident, but only tenuously. Neither Megyesi nor Mayo even suggested Batchelor as the informant and Buli fingered Batchelor after hearing a muffled conversation through a dirt wall. If that were not speculative enough, all those present in the courtroom missed that fact that if Buli were telling the truth, his statement would partially exonerate Batchelor. When Batchelor and Condron met with Lin, the Chinese commander already knew about the camera while neither of the men standing before him did. If Batchelor did indeed report back to Lin, he gave the commander erroneous information, since Megyesi had already traded the camera to Mayo. All of this points to an informer other than Batchelor. Since the officers and enlisted men were separated and each company lived apart, it would have been highly unlikely that anyone outside of Mayo's company could know much about the camera, particularly the exact location of Mayo's hiding place.

On Thursday, September 9, more witnesses took the stand on behalf of the army. John Fields opened that day's testimony with a story about an apparently innocuous rock-throwing incident. In the late summer of 1952, around the same time that the Megyesi/Mayo camera issue arose, Billy Clark and John Fields were walking across the compound when Fields picked up a rock and threw it against the side of a building under construction by a group of Progressive prisoners. Clark and Fields returned to their room and soon, Claude Batchelor and Johnny Moore appeared. Moore had a long and difficult history with "Pappy" Fields and told Batchelor that he had seen Fields throw the rock in question. Fields and Moore began arguing and Moore promised, "If I ever see you in the States, I will get you." Batchelor and Moore left and reported the incident to Lin. Later that day, Fields, Clark, and a few others were sitting around when a runner came and ordered Fields to report to headquarters. When he arrived at company headquarters, Lin ordered a soldier to escort Fields to regimental headquarters about a half mile away. Once there, Tong, the Chinese interpreter for the regiment, asked why he had been sent there. To that, Fields replied, "I don't know." Tong kept asking and Fields kept repeating the same answer, finally frustrating the interpreter. He ordered Fields to stand at attention outside and after about two hours, he came out and threw down a file at the prisoner's feet and explained that all of Fields's transgressions were documented there. By the time Tong returned with the folder, it was after 9:00 P.M., but Tong had plenty of time. He read off that day's charge of throwing the rock, and again, Fields denied it. Tong slapped him in the face with a wet grass rope he was carrying. For the next three hours, Tong would ask, Fields would answer, and Tong would slap him in the face with the length of wet rope. Tong kept after Fields to admit his culpability and sign a confession to that effect, but Fields stood his ground. Finally, Tong grew tired of the game and placed Fields in jail. Pappy Fields remained in jail for sixty-one days, except for the times Tong took him out to question and beat him.[16]

Billy Clark was up next. His day on the stand would be short. In his sworn statement, he corroborated Fields's story about the rock. The larger content of Clark's statement, however, indicates the speculative nature of much of the testimony. Clark noted several instances of his involvement with Batchelor, including his first meeting when he saw Batchelor "issueing [*sic*] chow." He added, "From this time on I had many occassions [*sic*] to see Batchelor and hear of his actions and form an opinion of him." Clark recalled that from early 1951 until 1952, the prisoners were required to attend communist lectures and participate in study groups. Each man was given a small notebook in which to record his thoughts and document his participation. Although he remembered Batchelor as a discussion leader, he could not recall much else, only adding that "he was stating things that were against the US [*sic*] but I can't remember what things he said." After a long discourse on Batchelor and Chinese indoctrination, Clark could only state that he was once put to hard labor because he had failed to pay attention in class, but, "I do know know if Batchelor causing my punishment. . . ." Surprisingly, Clark added that he did not "know of any times that Batchelor caused punishment to PW's except" in regard to the rock-throwing incident. However, Clark supplied no eyewitness evidence of Batchelor's culpability in his or Fields's punishment, only noting that the accused had come to their room to question them about the incident. According to the evidence offered by Clark, Moore could just as easily have effected their punishment. Clark continued on with an allegation that Batchelor had caused the men to be given less food and put to hard labor after they had refused to sign a petition he had brought around to the company. Again, he could not conclusively say that Batchelor had brought on the punishment and wrote, "I never heard Batchelor ever come out and say we would be punished if we didn't sign nor were we told by the Chinese why we were being punished." Regarding an argument several men had with Batchelor when he visited with a peace petition, Clark could only recall that the men were chastised by a Chinese official, who threw their words to Batchelor back at them and "stood us at attention a few minutes and told us not to do it again." Clark did recognize Batchelor's voice from propaganda announcements over the camp public address system.[17]

However weak Clark's allegations, another aspect of these claims should be evaluated. Many of these men were put to hard labor for breaking camp rules; however, Clark's definition of hard labor hardly matches what most people would picture in their mind's eye: "Hard labor that I had to perform and others also included hauling wood, digging and cleaning latrines, and moving rocks from one spot to another for no constructive purpose." He added that routinely, "the whole company was detailed to haul wood or we were given latrine duties as a regular duty rather than punishment." Clark contended that "[t]he hauling of wood and latrine duty was also hard labor for punishment when it was given as extra duties at a time others weren't working."[18] By having the same types of duties as both punishment and regular labor, the allegation of hard labor as punishment is somewhat undermined.

Robert McGreevey also took the stand on September 9 and rounded out the rock-throwing story. Verifying the details already presented by Fields and Clark, McGreevey's real purpose was to place Batchelor and Johnny Moore at Chinese headquarters. However, all McGreevey could do was testify that they "went right up the path toward headquarters over the hill." Adding to the inconclusive nature of his observation, he said, "I took it for granted, and I figure I am pretty well right that they did go to headquarters."[19]

The day's final witness was Robert Ghyers, who verified the information that the other men had failed to confirm. As a PW platoon leader, Ghyers was called to headquarters to meet with Lin and was ushered into a room next to one where Lin was concluding a meeting with Batchelor and Bennie Smith. As he sat there waiting for Lin, Ghyers listened in on the conversation next door. He heard Batchelor name Fields and Clark as the throwers of the rock. Armed with this information, the Chinese administrators then went to work on Fields, who was still standing at attention outside. Ghyers testimony was the only account identifying Batchelor as an informant.[20]

Although Robert Ghyers gave the prosecution what it wanted in his testimony against Batchelor, under cross-examination, he ran into problems. First, one must question Ghyers's level of credibility considering his high-level position within a Chinese-created PW hierarchy. Second, Joel Westbrook broached the subject of Ghyers being a leading Progressive during his cross-examination. Identifying him as a member of the "central committee of United States and British P. O. W.'s for Peace Committee," Westbrook pressed Ghyers on his stand and behavior while a prisoner of the Chinese. Ghyers refused to answer Westbrook's more difficult questions, on one occasion reminding the defense suspiciously, "After all, I'm not on trial here." Westbrook argued his points of law and was able to force Ghyers to identify himself in a photograph along with a peace dove and Korean communists.[21]

September 10 saw John Wells speak regarding statements made by Batchelor while in Camp Five. Wells had first met Batchelor in March 1952 and had been in the same company as the accused until Operation Big Switch. Wells recalled Batchelor actively participating in study groups, making announcements over the camp's public address system, circulating peace petitions, and writing articles for the inter-camp propaganda magazine, *Toward Truth and Peace*. Wells also placed Batchelor as Chairman of the Camp Peace Committee and Chairman of the Daily Living Affairs Committee of his company. He also provided details regarding Batchelor's public address announcements, recalling phrases like "Wall Street warmongers" and identifying American military failures as "intentional blunder[s]."[22]

That afternoon, Shirley Grimmette entered the courtroom with more information about Batchelor's activities while a prisoner of war. Grimmette and Batchelor had been in the same company and were captured by the Chinese on the same day. Grimmette remembered that Batchelor was a frequent announcer on the camp's public address system and that he wrote articles for *Toward Truth and Peace*. Like Billy Clark, Grimmette remembered Batchelor carrying around a peace petition and asking men to sign it.[23]

When Clarence Peterson took the stand on September 13, he continued with the theme of Batchelor's role in study groups, on the public address system, and as a petition circulator. However, what Peterson added to the proceedings was speculative. He alleged that during a card game, Batchelor told him that the Chinese paid him for writing pro-communist articles for *Toward Truth and Peace*. Under cross-examination, the law officer of the court, Lt. Col. Donald Manes, pressed Peterson for details and the sergeant exploded at the colonel, "Where the hell else would he get Chinese money in prison camp?" After the tensions lifted, the defense counsel asked about Batchelor's activities on the public address system. He asked if Batchelor ever played music and Peterson replied that he played "communist music." When pressed to elaborate, Peterson recalled "The East is Red" as one tune and "Old Man River" as another.

> The east is red, the sun is rising.
> China has brought forth a Mao Zedong.
> He amasses fortune for the people,
> Hurrah, he is the people's saving star.
>
> Chairman Mao loves the people,
> He is our guide,
> To build a new China,
> Hurrah, he leads us forward!

The Communist Party is like the sun,
Wherever it goes, there is light.
Wherever there is a Communist Party,
Hurrah, there the people are liberated!

Although "The East is Red" was a Chinese communist anthem after Mao's rise to power, the mention of "Old Man River" struck the attorney as odd. Clarifying his mention of the last song, Peterson noted that Paul Robeson, whose leftist stance on many issues, particularly on racial equality was well known, sang it.[24]

After an hour devoted to fruitlessly arguing for the dismissal of many of the charges against Batchelor, the last prosecuting witness took the stand after lunch. Wilburn Watson had testified against Dickenson and came to San Antonio to tell essentially the same story about Batchelor. He claimed that upon his capture early in the war, the Chinese tortured him because he was carrying papers noting that he was a deputy sheriff in Mississippi. As a result of this torture, he signed a confession that he was an American spy and "was forced to sign a request to remain behind" with the other nonrepatriates more than two years later. Watson remembered that he signed the paper refusing repatriation because he had only recently been released from a six-month stint in solitary confinement. Soon thereafter, he and several others were transported from Camp Two to Camp Five, where they met the rest of the men committed to go to China. However, once at Camp Five, the Chinese set up the infamous trial of Watson, during which several of the other nonrepatriates, including Batchelor, reportedly urged the Chinese to kill him, before Andrew Condron intervened on his behalf.[25]

The next day, September 15, saw the seating of witnesses for the defense. Joel Adams was the first to be called and testified that during his captivity in Camp Five he was leader of a Reactionary group and knew Claude Batchelor even before the Chinese captured them. He spoke of the culture of duplicity that captivity bred in the men. Like countless others, Adams noted "that it was generally agreed to go along with the Chinese, with the thought living conditions might continue to improve." He continued, "the monitors—who didn't believe what they heard at the lectures—began to tell the Chinese what they wanted to hear."[26]

That day also saw the introduction of the argument that "brainwashing" was a viable defense against Batchelor's collaboration. Joel Westbrook, Batchelor's defense counsel, contended that the unrelenting communist indoctrination his client had endured for more than three years had twisted Batchelor's sense of right and wrong. He suggested that the camp conditions had convinced the normally loyal soldiers that collaborating with the enemy was an acceptable course of action providing it was done with the best interest of the American prisoners in mind. In Batchelor's mind, Westbrook argued, the accused "simply tried to get a little better treatment and had no idea of hurting his country."[27] Astutely, Westbrook argued that as a result of the years of brainwashing, Batchelor suffered "a mental derangement which acted on his conduct."[28] The next day, the court ruled that brainwashing was not a suitable defense and was unrelated to Batchelor's collaboration.[29]

The next day, Sergeant Robert Vincent took the stand and corroborated Westbrook's theory. He outlined how Batchelor came to be his squad's representative and evaluated his performance of his duties. Vincent testified, "he [Batchelor] was elected by the company. . . . He helped a great deal in improving the chow in the company, more medical attention for the sick, more improvement on the sanitary conditions of the company, improvement on better standard of morale." When asked for specific examples of Batchelor's using his position for the benefit of those whom he represented, Vincent told the story of Billy Ray, who could not handle the harsh food supplied by the Chinese. Batchelor came to the man's aid and "got the Chinese to give him eggs for his meals, and at times, powdered milk."[30]

John Edward Owens took the stand to close the day and affirmed Vincent's interpretation of Batchelor's admitted cooperation with his Chinese captors. Living in utter squalor, Owens contended that he and the other men saw the order to elect a representative to the Chinese peace committee as an opportunity to place someone in a position to improve conditions within the camp. His group gathered and chose Batchelor. He explained that "the nature of that discussion was more or less the men were trying to get a man into that particular committee there that would do the men more good in the company and at the same time get somebody in there that could be responsible for themselves and not get entirely involved with the Chinese." When asked, "How did the men look upon Corporal Batchelor at that time?" Owens confidently responded, "the majority of the men that I knew liked Corporal Batchelor."[31]

Westbrook ended the day emboldened by the testimony that he had heard, but also disappointed by the lack of scientific evidence. He had called two renowned experts on the psychology of brainwashing: Dr. Joost Meerlo, who formerly headed the Dutch army's psychological division, and Dr. Leon Freedom, coauthor of *Brain-Washing in Red China*. Unfortunately for Batchelor, neither of the men agreed to fly to San Antonio to testify in the case, but a determined Westbrook vowed to have at least one of the experts answer hypothetical questions via airmail and present those conclusions as evidence by the end of the trial.[32]

Despite the methodical progress being made by Westbrook in defense of Batchelor, September 17 was a big day. The first witness was Claude's mother, who offered the court a family history replete with affirmations of her son's good citizenship, right upbringing, and Christian morality. Clara Mae Batchelor explained to the court that she anticipated the Chinese would not allow any disagreeable mail to get either in or out of the prison, so she took Claude's "peace" writings with a grain of salt and tried to respond as ambivalently as possible. "I did agree that war was terrible, and that the world should work for peace, but, of course, I had no idea what the Communists were doing with the Peace Movement and so forth."[33]

One of the central issues Westbrook had to refute was the testimony of Bernard Buli, who had fingered Batchelor as the informant in the camera episode. Edward Clevinger had told the court on September 15 that Buli, rather than being confined as he had earlier testified, was with a group of Progressive soldiers rehearsing Konstantin Simonov's *The Russian Question,* a play about an American journalist who embraces communism.[34] Clevinger's testimony not only cast doubt on Buli's, but also brought his loyalty into question. Two days later, Sgt. William Skipper was brought to the stand for more Buli-related testimony. Although Buli had told the court that he had been confined in a camp kitchen when he overheard Batchelor reveal the name of the man in possession of the camera, Skipper remembered talking to Buli just after his release and being told that he had been jailed in a bathhouse too far away from the kitchen to have overheard Batchelor's alleged informing.[35]

On September 16, the prosecuting attorneys successfully lobbied the court to make Claude Batchelor's CIC statement public. Taken during his stay in the army hospital in Tokyo just after his repatriation, the candid soldier had made some ill-advised statements. Although the whole document cast Batchelor in an unflattering light, the prosecution ostensibly opened it to discredit defense witness William Skipper. In discussing the Ex-Prisoners of War Welfare Association, which was to be set up inside the United States as a pro-communist cell, Batchelor confessed that he had been selected by the Chinese to head it, but when he chose to remain behind, a new man had to be found. The Chinese concluded that "William C. Skipper was the best qualified prisoner to take my place on this special project."[36]

In addition to the information provided to the court, the opening of Batchelor's classified statement helped turn a moderately sympathetic public into a fearful mass. In their eyes, Batchelor was no longer an intimidated and well-meaning leader of his fellow prisoners, but a hand-picked communist operative who willingly accepted the job of returning to the United States to set up covert organizations to bind together camp Progressives once they had returned home. The fear in people's minds, however, was of the capabilities of these men if indeed their brainwashing had been successful. As covert operatives for communist China, they could then effectively help China fight the Cold War. Perhaps hoping to shift the focus away from himself, Claude Batchelor suggested the possibility of such operations when he stated during the interview, "If there are any Americans who have missions for the Communists, I feel certain that the above named persons are the ones."[37]

September 17 saw Claude Batchelor take the stand in his own defense. Much of his testimony centered on one of the most damning, and controversial, witnesses. Wilburn "Clue" Watson had offered the same testimony against both Dickenson and Batchelor regarding the death sentence reportedly imposed by his fellow prisoners. However, as Batchelor openly revealed in court that day, Watson's credibility should have been considered worthless because of his own behavior while a prisoner. In the statement he made shortly after his repatriation, Batchelor specifically named him as a Progressive who would play his guitar and sing the song "Panmunjom," whose lyrics suggested that American negotiators were at fault for prolonging the war. He also told the court about Watson's wish to stay behind with the group, but "they [the Chinese] would not permit Clue Watson to remain."[38] Although he confessed that he had made compromises during his captivity, Claude Batchelor passionately denied ever informing on a fellow prisoner.[39]

After a weekend spent in the stockade at Fort Sam Houston, Claude Batchelor returned to the witness stand on the morning of September 21.[40] At the request of the prosecution, Batchelor revisited the idea that communists might be under orders from China and presently at work within the United States. He elaborated by explaining that those agents would attempt to infiltrate "sensitive spots" such as police departments, federal agencies, and plum military positions. Both Dickenson and Batchelor had asked to serve within the army's Counterintelligence Corps shortly after their release and such a request, particularly coming from a leader of the group like Batchelor, was suspicious at best. He explained that his inquiry into the CIC had not originated from him, but came as a result of "the encouragement of two U.S. intelligence officers."[41]

After Batchelor left the stand, celebrated Associated Press photographer Frank "Pappy" Noel stood to testify on his friend's behalf. Frank Noel had arrived in Korea at the behest of his company in 1950 and was captured along with about 120 other men on November 9, 1950. Treated as a military prisoner from the time of his capture until early 1952, when the Chinese realized who he was, Noel's newly found celebrity made him a valuable commodity to his captors. At this point, the Chinese gave him a camera with instructions to take pictures for those back home. In reality, his captors wished to use his photographs for propaganda purposes, and Noel knew it, but he saw his photography as a way of providing a diversion for other prisoners.[42]

On the stand, Noel spoke warmly of the trust he had in Batchelor. He explained that in early June 1953, Batchelor had managed to save an estimated two dollars and had received permission to buy some white wine and throw a "Texas party." The men had asked if Noel could join them with his camera and he happily obliged. Noel remembered that "we would sit around and chew the fat about Texas and one thing and another," but the Chinese moved the group, first to a small club room, and then to a different room. Noel remembered walking in seeing "linen on the table, knives, dishes, loaded with food. They also had these studio lights in the corner of each one of these rooms. They had newsreel cameras set up. They had Chinese photographers all over the place." Seeing the bounty laid out before them and the cameras, the men knew that they had walked into a propaganda session: "Batchelor and several of us said 'Well, what cooks on this?' We knew it was a propaganda deal the minute we spotted it, but at that time we couldn't care less, because we were after the food. They had canned chicken, canned duck, boiled peanuts, cigarettes."[43]

Noel continued and explained to the court how he had grown to trust Batchelor while they were both prisoners. When the Chinese gave selected prisoners marked newspaper copy to be read over the camp loudspeakers, Batchelor and Preston Ritchie would often slip copies to Noel, who would read them with his eye for news. By doing so, Noel found that what had been marked was read verbatim by whichever prisoner gave the day's broadcast. When pressed, Noel clarified that the Chinese left no room for individual commentary; only the direct reading was allowed.[44]

Finally, Noel recalled for the court how he had come to trust Claude Batchelor. Noel had planned four separate escape attempts during his time as a prisoner, one of them resulting in a successful absence of three days. As a result of his behavior, the Chinese had him under individual guard and housed him within the Chinese camp. This gave him infrequent contact with the American prisoners, so he only came to know a few of the men. He remembered that "they let me up to headquarters there one day a week for about an hour, and I had the opportunity to talk to the accused and also these other men up there briefly, very briefly. At the early stages there, I had this guard on top of me all the time." However, he did find time to talk with Batchelor about a proposed escape and soon Batchelor stole a map from headquarters and secretly delivered it to Noel. Batchelor and Noel began planning their escape in April 1953 and set the date for August 1, in the midst of the monsoon season so as to cover their trail. However, they did not embark on the attempt, as that day became the first day of Operation Big Switch.[45]

While emotions welled up inside the courtroom, the motley collection of both prosecution and defense witnesses who spent those weeks in San Antonio made their personal beefs public. On the evening of September 23, a prospective defense witness and rumored camp Progressive, Robert Hickox, walked into the Merry-Go-Round, a downtown bar. Looking around, he saw prosecution witnesses Bernard Buli, John Fields, and Clarence Peterson sitting at a table with defense witness John Owens. He approached the group and said, "Hello boys, how are things going?" Peterson angrily warned Hickox, "Get out of here, we don't want your kind around." With that, Hickox returned to his table and after a few minutes looked up to see Fields and Peterson approaching. The pair began cursing Hickox, Fields saying "you guys are trying to tear up the testimony of good men." One of the men then threw a drink in Hickox's eyes, while the other grabbed him by the necktie and started choking him. The bar's bouncer, a part-time policeman, held off the pair while Hickox made his escape.[46]

The next day, Joel Westbrook revealed that he had heard an unsubstantiated report that such tactics were behind the changing testimony of William Skipper. When initially called to the stand, Skipper confidently refuted Bernard Buli's testimony that he had overheard Batchelor informing on a fellow prisoner. However, after a few days, the prosecution briefly recalled Skipper, who could no longer remember where Buli had told him he was confined when he heard Batchelor.[47]

The final phase of the defense's case began when Dr. Leon Freedom took the stand to offer testimony about brainwashing. Freedom, a Baltimore-based psychiatrist, was a leading expert on the psychological effects of communist indoctrination on prisoners of war and testified that the intense pressure that the Chinese placed on Batchelor resulted in a form of temporary insanity.[48] "The case of Claude J. Batchelor presents one of the most outstanding examples of what I have chosen to call an induced political psychosis that I have seen. This lad actually was deluded into believing he was a potential savior of humanity and that his efforts were devoted to the good of his fellow man."[49] To support his argument, Freedom explained the very simple, yet effective, methods that the Chinese captors used on their prisoners: "Indoctrination begins the moment of capture. To put POWs in the proper frame of mind at the beginning, they use the fear technique of delaying medical attention, exposure to the cold, solitary confinement for minor offenses and little or no food." Illustrating the niche that Batchelor fell into, Freedom informed the court, "As indoctrination begins to take hold on more susceptible prisoners, the condition of the prisoners gradually gets better."[50] Freedom's conclusions supported those offered by Dr. Philip Bloemsma, a Washington, D.C., psychiatrist who had spent five years during World War II a prisoner of the Japanese.[51]

Army psychiatrists stood in court on September 28 and attempted to refute the testimony of Freedom and Bloemsma. Maj. Henry Segal told the court that Batchelor was sane at the time he collaborated with his Chinese captors. Somewhat dismissive of the brainwashing-induced insanity defense, Segal admitted that he had written a paper on brainwashing and stubbornly crafted his psychological pronouncements to mirror the definition of insanity as written in the Uniform Code of Military Justice. Capt. William Mayer offered similar conclusions. Mayer had been busy since the close of the war personally testifying in over 100 courts martial and offering written depositions in 450 others. "It is my opinion that then and now, and during Batchelor's confinement in prison camp, he was able to distinguish between right and wrong, and is able to adhere to the right. There is no such thing as 'political psychosis.'" The final psychiatric witness was Col. Albert Glass, who offered conclusions predictably similar to those of Mayer and Segal.[52]

The final witness of the trial was the previously convicted Edward Dickenson, who spoke for the prosecution. Having been sentenced to ten years in prison only five months before, Dickenson offered damning testimony, which might have been construed as ethically questionable, considering his potential to ingratiate himself with the army by helping to convict Batchelor. The most damning part of Dickenson's trial had been the story about Wilburn Watson narrowly surviving a PW trial for his life. The most specific information Dickenson provided was his allegation that Batchelor, who at the time was the PW leader, stood during Watson's trial and told him, "Master Sergeant Watson, if I had the final say-so, you would be shot."[53] In McCarthy's America, the naming of names was an effective, if not accurate, method of securing justice in the face of scant evidence.

Dickenson's willingness to testify against Batchelor raises some interesting issues. First, it can be surmised by his testimony and contemporary interviews, that Dickenson and Batchelor did not like each other. Although no explanations were given for this animosity, it is likely that Batchelor looked down on Dickenson for being less committed to the wishes of the group than he thought Dickenson should be. Whatever their personal feelings about one another, Dickenson played the same card against Batchelor that many other soldiers had played in the courts martial. Hoping that his testimony against Batchelor would help him in his legal challenges, Dickenson agreed to testify. By speaking against Batchelor, Dickenson joined three others, who had been identified as collaborators, who offered testimony for the prosecution. In all, of the fourteen fellow prisoners who testified against Batchelor, four of them, or more than 25 percent, were identified as prison camp collaborators. As for those who provided evidentiary statements against Batchelor, two of the thirty-six had been identified by fellow prisoners as collaborators.[54]

As the trial testimony ended, one final question remained: Was Claude Batchelor a sane man either while a prisoner or during the present trial? Lt. Col. Donald E. Manes Jr., the court martial's law officer, gave a mixed ruling when he found that Batchelor was sane enough to stand trial on the collaboration charges, but did not offer any specific guidance regarding Batchelor's state of mind during his admitted collaboration—the latter question being more important than that of whether or not he was fit to stand trial. With the one ruling made and the other left open, the court of eight commissioned officers, all veterans of Korea, retired to judge the case.[55]

After an adjournment of only two hours and fourteen minutes, the men returned to the court and announced a verdict of guilty. After another thirty minutes, they returned with a life sentence for the twenty-two-year-old corporal. The announcements turned the courtroom into a madhouse for several minutes and sent shockwaves across the Pacific. Confidently stating, "I can take it," when the sentenced was announced, Batchelor remained composed for reporters until his mother began crying. Joel Westbrook, Batchelor's defender and a lieutenant colonel in the Texas National Guard, told newspapermen that he was very disturbed by the way the court was conducted and the decision it reached. Always considering himself a loyal officer, he announced "now I'm cynical about the Army." The next day, he stated, "My only comment is in connection with the obvious shock which ran through the courtroom last night. My concern is not with Corporal Batchelor's personal failure but with our Army's understanding of the evil and insanity of communism."[56]

Westbrook pointed to one of the first moments of the trial as the turning point, when 1st Lt. Edward R. Schowalter Jr., a Medal of Honor winner, stood and told the court, "Sir, I challenge myself on the grounds that I am hostile to the accused and that prior to the convening of the court, I formulated the opinion and expressed the opinion that the accused is a traitor." Raymond Lech astutely notes that the court even allowed the prosecution to use the word "treason" until the defense counsel took issue. When Westbrook asked for clarification regarding the use of the word "treason," the opposing counsel stated, "I merely made the general statement that the acts with which Batchelor is being charged are treasonable in nature." In reading the prosecution's words, Lech identified "treason" and "treasonable in nature" as two vastly different concepts and determined that "the case should not have been tried in a military courtroom."[57]

Almost forgotten in the astonishment at the sentence was Batchelor's wife, Kyoko, who had remained in Tokyo where she hoped Claude would return after the trial. When she heard the news of her husband's conviction and life sentence, she immediately went into hiding, offering only a brief comment to newsmen: "The life sentence seems to me to be very, very harsh, I simply hadn't expected that he would have to stay for life." As Kyoko began to recover from the initial shock, she grew angry and announced that "she was sorry that she wrote a letter to her husband when he was with the Reds" and called the life sentence, "harsh and unjust."[58]

Those involved in Batchelor's prosecution became targets for men and women sympathetic to the corporal's situation. Bert Cumby, the CIC agent who questioned both Dickenson and Batchelor and later testified against both, received two death threats while at Fort Sam Houston. The army prosecutor reportedly received twenty-five hostile letters per day. After the trial ended, he immediately went on a long leave to allow sentiments to calm down.[59]

The remaining months of 1954 passed with Claude Batchelor in confinement at Fort Crowder, Missouri, and later, at nearby Fort Leavenworth, Kansas, where Dickenson was also jailed. As Westbrook filed petitions on his client's behalf, many segments of American society rallied to Batchelor's cause in much the same way as they had for Dickenson only months before. A concerned citizen from Texas wrote that "the penalty handed down by the officers with shiny buttons (none of whom . . . were prisoners of war) is not justified."[60] Another called the proceedings, "one of the most unjustified violations of military justice, Americans ever beheld."[61] H. W. Wright, the chairman of Big Spring, Texas's, draft board, went one step further, resigning his position because "My conscience will not let me be a part of drafting young men who might later be subject to the severe punishment that was rendered Cpl. Claude Batchelor."[62] Although this did not help Batchelor's cause in any meaningful way, his former comrades, now living behind the Bamboo Curtain, spoke out against his conviction. Richard Corden read a broadcast statement from the group, which was undergoing political reeducation at the time, condemning Batchelor's conviction and sentence.[63]

By late October, the army reduced Batchelor's sentence to twenty years, drawing the ire of his supporters even more. Westbrook likened the reduction to "chopping a man's head off at the eyebrows rather than the neck." Perceptively, Clara Mae Batchelor attributed the case's the reduction in Batchelor's sentence to recent publicity, saying, "I have read many newspaper editorials and letters people have written to newspapers saying Claude got a raw deal. I think the majority of the people feel that he was treated too harshly by the Army and those opinions had something to do with the reduction of the sentence."[64] By December, Clara Mae and her husband wrote President Eisenhower asking him to intervene on their son's behalf because, as she concisely put it,

> Claude went into the Korean War with practically no combat training, no training for conduct as a prisoner, and completely ignorant of communist beliefs. He was young and impressionable. Chosen by the Communists to be a leader of their study groups and given a place of leadership within the camp where he was respected for his concern and assistance to fellow prisoners, they subjected him to a rigid system of indoctrination, which he was not able to withstand. At last, however, he began to see the flaws in the Communist propaganda. Their methods employed to hold twenty-three Americans in Korea were revolting to his ideas of fair-play and freedom of choice.
>
> So he decided to throw them over and come home. Coupled with his mistrust of the Chinese was the letters from many people in the United States and the pleas of his government to come home.
>
> When he came back, he spent a month in Tokyo giving the Army all the information about the Communists, their methods, plans, etc. . . .

Astutely, she reminded the President that the case was not about "one insignificant American boy," it "involves more than just the case of one person."[65]

As 1954 turned to 1955, both soldiers who had taken America at its word had returned home, been arrested, tried, and convicted for their actions while prisoners of war. In the meantime, several of those men who had repudiated their country in preference for China were reconsidering their decisions. One year later, both Dickenson and Batchelor would remain in prison while three of their fellow nonrepatriates would return to the United States and be treated as free citizens.

TEN

Men Jailed . . . and Walking Free, 1954–1957

> "We listened to a re-broadcast of an appeal directed to the 21 men who were prisoners of war in which they were promised that there would be no action taken if they changed their minds and returned to the United States. It seems to us that the United States has broken faith with this boy."
>
> —Dugald Satterfield and J. A. Allverson on Claude Batchelor

From early 1954 through the end of 1957, many things changed for the non-repatriate group. The two returnees were convicted and sentenced to long prison terms, while those who emigrated to China struggled to carve out a place for themselves in their adopted country. Of those in China, several went to school, married, and moved into various state-ordered jobs. However, that transition was not a completely happy one as several of the men began filtering back to the United States and one of their comrades died. By the end of 1957, Mao's changing China became a much more difficult place to live.

While Ed Dickenson languished in a cell at Fort Belvoir, and Claude Batchelor continued his counterintelligence interviews in Tokyo waiting for the hammer to fall on him, those who remained with the Chinese were initially treated like celebrities. Although several of the men still harbored hopes to go either to the Soviet Union or remain in Korea, the Chinese handlers spoke with them individually and convinced them that emigration to China was the wisest course. Morris Wills remembered that at some point, "Commander Tien read a little speech accepting us, as free citizens of America, for China. We signed papers saying we wanted to go to China. And we had a party, and we and the Chinese all got very drunk."[1]

The men spent the next several days in Kaesong, where they walked around the city, had clothes made, and enjoyed the hospitality of the Chinese. In their first interview after being accepted by the Chinese, Richard Corden read a prepared statement that he said had been approved by the group. It read, "We are not Communists, though some of us hope to be." As the men stepped forward individually, their personal motives, although sometimes scattered and inadequately explained, became clearer. Clarence Adams explained, "The main reason we are staying is to draw the attention of the people of the United States and the whole world to the need for world peace and we can't do that as long as [Senator Joseph] McCarthy and McCarthyism exist in the United States." Larance Sullivan added, "The American people know how the Negro is treated in the United States. Definitely this is one of my reasons. Of course, my desire to work for world peace is the main reason. I can't speak

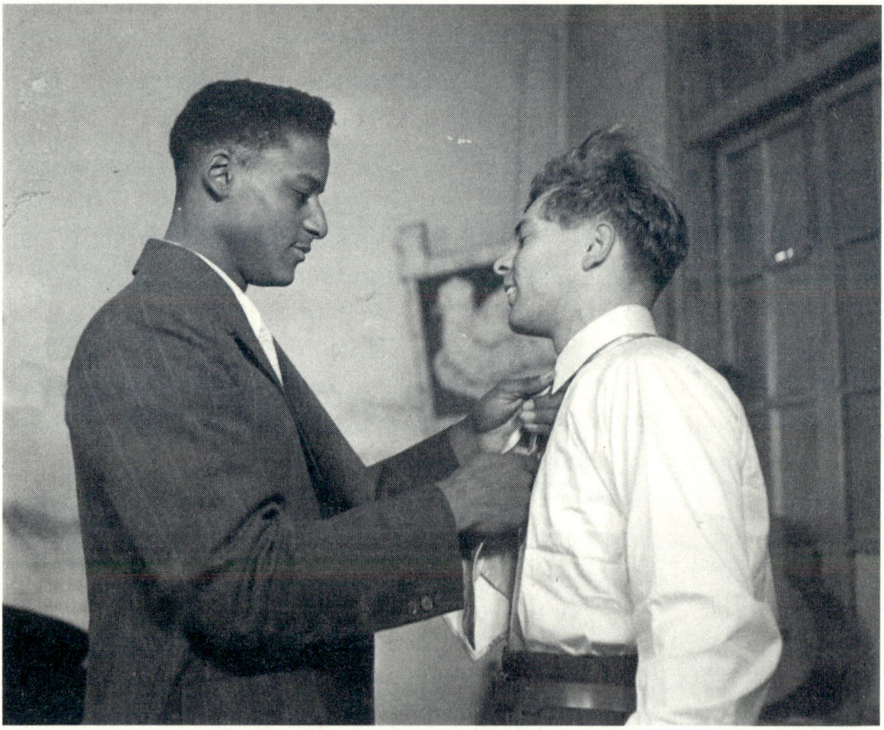

Larance Sullivan helps Otho Bell with his tie during the group's first days in China. This is one of the few spontaneous images of their Chinese lives. This and several other photos were taken by Louis Verdyck, a Belgian photographer who also refused repatriation after the Korean War. (CEGES-SOMA, Brussels, Belgium.)

out for peace in America without being prosecuted." Focusing on the McCarthy issue better than some of his colleagues, Morris Wills said, "People who voice an opinion for peace in the United States are persecuted and their voices suppressed. There is not a democratic government in the United States as long as McCarthyism and [Nevada Senator Pat McCarran] McCarranism are allowed to exist."[2] Three of the men claimed that they had been sent to Korea to "plunder, rape, burn, and kill" in support of "the greedy American billionaires" and that their commanders had ordered them "to commit atrocities." One unidentified soldier, likely Howard Adams, claimed that as a child "we used to go to the bakery in Houston to ask for stale, broken bread unfit for sale" and vowed that he was remaining behind "to help do away with poverty and hardships of the working people of the U.S."[3]

Wishing to exploit the nonrepatriates for public relations purposes, the Chinese secured a private train for the men consisting of an engine, a dining car, two coaches, and two flatcars, with Russian Jeeps for excursions. Traveling through North Korea, the men saw the devastation of the war and Wills noted that some Pyongyang refugees were living in caves. At nearly 4:00 A.M. on February 24, the train carrying the men approached the Yalu River and the Chinese border. Wills remembered, "I looked out of the window; it was misty and cold—very dark, very gray, very cold."[4]

Their entry into China would have to wait. Halfway across the bridge, the train stopped and the men were told that a planned reception at the next town, Antung, was being organized for them. Sitting there on the bridge, straddling the Yalu River, the men had about half an hour to consider the path that had brought them to China. Shortly, however, the train began rolling again and pulled into the station, where the men traded the train for limousines. After meeting several city officials, and eating a Western-style breakfast of eggs, bacon, and coffee, the nonrepatriates returned to their train and continued their journey into the interior of China.[5]

Arriving in Taiyuan, an industrial city 200 miles southwest of Beijing, in late February, the Americans met representatives of the Red Cross Society of China, which had agreed to sponsor the Westerners for the duration of their stay.[6] About this time, several members of the group began to realize that the initial excitement of their defection was beginning to wane. Morris Wills wrote, "we were a liability for the Chinese; they really didn't know what to do with us." Likening the celebrity of their arrival in China and then the disappointment of Taiyuan to having entered "the U.S. at New York and been sent to a city in Wyoming," Wills described the dismal scene: "It had just snowed an inch or two, and on top of the snow was a thin film of dust. It

This small group picture shows Samuel Hawkins, Richard Tenneson, and Aaron Wilson standing over Roger Devriendt (Belgian defector) and James Veneris. At the time the photograph was made, the men were at Taiyuan undergoing intense indoctrination to life in Mao's China. (CEGES-SOMA, Brussels, Belgium.)

gave the city a very dirty look. Taiyuan has a miserable climate, and because you are close to the desert, terrible dust storms."[7]

After their initial welcome in Taiyuan, the men were given medical examinations, and acclimated to Chinese life while China decided what to do with them. During the exams, one of the black soldiers, Larance Sullivan, was discovered to have a serious case of tuberculosis. After three months in a sanitarium, Sullivan had fought off the disease and was able to return to the group. Rufus Douglas was not so lucky. Wills recalled that Douglas "had a heart defect caused by a disease he contracted in Japan." Without treatment in the PW camp, Douglas's condition had degenerated and by the time the group had moved into the neutral camp, he was constantly ill. Admitted to the hospital in Taiyuan, Douglas worsened over the course of several weeks. He died on June 8 at the age of twenty-seven. More recently, another of the nonrepatriates remembered Douglas's death differently. Despite Wills's detailed recollection of Douglas's heart ailment, another man recalled that Douglas had a large tumor on his side and that was the cause of his death. Whatever the cause, the way the Chinese handled Douglas's death struck Wills as odd. They insisted on having a Christian funeral although Marxist doctrine saw no need for religious formality: "They had a Chinese minister come and he read passages from the Bible in Chinese." After the funeral, they took Douglas's body to a cemetery outside of the city.[8]

Clarence Adams remembered that after a great feast given by the Red Cross, the men were all asked what they wanted to do with their lives. Most of the men "just wanted to work for world peace and to become friends with the Chinese people," but Lowell Skinner saw his opportunities differently. Adams remembered Skinner as "kind of crazy," a view that was reinforced when he told the Chinese, "[h]e figured that an American corporal was smarter than a Chinese general." "Make me a general and give me some weapons," Skinner said.[9] Rather than becoming a general, Skinner ended up working in a factory.

The nonrepatriates remained in Taiyuan from the end of February until October and experienced life on the semi-isolated Chinese frontier. Morris Wills's and Clarence Adams's memories of Taiyuan differ greatly. Wills claimed that the city's residents had very little experience with foreigners and that on their first Sunday in Taiyuan, the group went for a walk downtown and was followed by a large crowd, mostly peasants, who had never seen a foreigner: "We headed for the center of the city and fled into a department store. The mob crashed in right behind us. They broke windows and glass cases." Fearing his store would be destroyed, the store's manager pulled the men upstairs and put them in a small room until the crowd dispersed. A couple of weeks later, Wills, Aaron Wilson, and Clarence Adams had another run-in with the Chinese. After dinner, the three took a short walk. With a policeman standing nearby unoccupied, a Chinese man walked up to the group, circled them, and kicked the African-American Adams in the rear. The man cursed at Adams and shook his fist, while a small crowd gathered; Wills was surprised when the policeman paid no attention to the incident. Wills and Wilson had to drag Adams away and the three men ran back to their dormitory.[10]

During the seven months the group spent in Taiyuan, they underwent a course in Chinese political and social education. Different from the indoctrination they received in prison, these lectures were intended to enable them to function within traditional Chinese society. After a series of political lectures, at that time dealing mainly with communist motives in Vietnam, the group embarked on an emotionally painful system of criticism and self-criticism. One of the tenets of their reeducation held that the path to true harmony depends on man's ability to both levy criticism upon his fellow man when he is wrong and to accept the criticism of others and change one's behavior as a result. The Americans and Briton suffered through this period of having their closest friends and confidantes attack their lives.[11]

When Wills wrote that the Chinese did not know what to do with the men, he was right. However, by the time their political training in Taiyuan ended in October 1954, the men were parceled out to their new lives.

During the course of their political training, the men were to learn four things: (1) to become a "peace fighter," (2) to become a good communist, (3) to become a good revolutionary, and (4) to give cadre training to others. Throughout the training period, members of the group were classified as "far advanced, advanced, and backward" based upon their progress. Bell recalled that he, Lewie Griggs, William Cowart, and two Belgians fell into the "backward" category. Interestingly, this group was called "reactionary," the term that was used to identify the strongest opposition to indoctrination while in prison and was now given to those who refused to commit themselves to further indoctrination. The "advanced" group included Arlie Pate and Richard Tenneson. The remaining men were classified as "far advanced."[12]

After an examination, which tested their language skills and general aptitude, the men left on their new assignments. Wills and ten others were sent to the People's University in Beijing, a few others were assigned to a collective farm, and the remainder to a paper factory.[13] At the university, the Westerners were first enrolled in preparatory training. Wills remembered that the place was very cold, requiring the students to wear cotton padded clothing all the time, even in the classrooms. The People's University was China's premier institution for political education and it was quite an honor for the men to be sent there, particularly with a monthly stipend of ninety yuan [about $40] a month. There, the nonrepatriates were mixed in with Czechs and Russians who were studying at the university. The group had their own dining hall and separate dormitory space where the Americans and Briton lived in three rooms. The university also provided a janitor to help the men keep their rooms, maintain the coal fire in each room, and heat water. Wills noted incredulously, "The university had about 5,000 students and more than 740 janitors."[14]

In February 1955, Richard Tenneson elaborated on his factory group's living conditions in a letter to his mother. Portia Howe, who had traveled to Japan during the explaining period in the hopes that she could visit with her son personally, had sent coffee. Although Tenneson would have refused to see her, even if the U.S. Army had allowed her onto the Korean peninsula, he would drink her coffee. He wrote, "Your coffee to me Lowell [Skinner] and Jimmy [Veneris] reminds me to tell you that we've moved into a bigger room and there are 5 of us now." Continuing, he said, "Arlie [Pate]" along with the fifth member of their group, an unnamed Chinese, likely an imbedded

James Veneris and Arlie Pate pose together in this photograph taken while they were working at the Shantung West Paper Mill. (CEGES-SOMA, Brussels, Belgium.)

handler, "doesn't like coffee, but thought it was pretty swell that we could receive things like that thru the mail." He closed his note by complaining that "it was still powdered coffee."[15]

In July 1955, French journalist Jacques Locquin spent a day with Lowell Skinner and filed his story with Skinner's hometown newspaper, the Akron *Beacon-Journal.* In what was generally a very sympathetic story, Locquin noted that Skinner and three other Americans (Veneris, Pate, and Tenneson) all worked in a Jinan factory that made thin paper for cigarettes and typewriters. He outlined Skinner's daily routine, giving readers an idea what daily life in communist China was like. Skinner woke at 7:00 A.M. and had a free breakfast of bread, two raw eggs, and a pint of milk in a factory canteen. Staring work at 8:00 A.M., he and an experienced mechanic made rounds until quitting time at 4:00 P.M. Lunch was purchased at the factory and eaten on the floor between jobs. Workers had a choice between a lunchtime meal with meat and a cheaper one with vegetables and tofu. After work, Skinner spent much of his time window-shopping, walking around the neighborhood, visiting with some of his Chinese friends from work, and drinking beer in a local bar. In all, Skinner's life as a factory worker in China appeared to be very similar to that of an American worker.[16]

Now that the men were being introduced into Chinese society, several of them began trying to develop independent lives for themselves. As they were all young, they were interested in establishing relationships, but because of the strict social rules in China, it was difficult, although not impossible, for the Americans to find Chinese girlfriends. In spring 1956, two of the men did marry Chinese women. After long courtships and numerous permissions, Lowell Skinner and Albert Belhomme married their partners. At the time, both men were working in a paper mill in Jinan and wanting to build typical lives. Skinner married Chi Hsiao-fei, a schoolteacher from southern China whom he had met the previous winter. In a letter to his parents, he explained the challenges of simple communication. His new wife spoke the Nanking dialect and understood Shantung, while Skinner could speak Shantung and only comprehend Nanking. Albert Belhomme married what he called "a very ordinary country girl."[17]

The rules regarding fraternization between Chinese women and American men were stringent, but relationships with Russian or European women were not strictly governed. The youngest of the group, Samuel Hawkins, began dating a Russian woman, whom he later married, while a student at the university. Hawkins, a bright and motivated student, only spent a few months in school and excelled in his academic studies. However, his behavior did not fit well with the reserved Chinese and after several infractions concerning dormitory life, he was permanently expelled. Once out of school, Hawkins was assigned to be a driver and later a mechanic in Beijing and Wuhan.[18]

Despite Hawkins's confession of his own poor behavior in the restricted university setting, Morris Wills suggested that his colleague's leaving the institution might have centered more on his growing political disenchantment. Writing years later, Wills noted that all of the men quickly grew tired of their required self-criticism, with Hawkins and possibly Scott Rush leading the way. Specifically regarding Hawkins, Wills wrote, "One or two found themselves White Russian girl friends in town and would stay away two or three days at a time." In early 1956, Wills and several others approached their handler at the university and asked that they be allowed to leave the institution and take factory jobs in the countryside in order to enjoy more freedom and get to know the common Chinese. Reacting quickly, the Chinese sent Fortuna, Rush, Hawkins, and Sullivan to factories in Wuhan and Beijing, while Clarence Adams, Corden, and Webb remained in school, but were transferred to Wuhan University to study Chinese language and literature. The Scotsman, Andrew Condron, became an English teacher at the Foreign Language Institute in Beijing. As one of the most frustrated of the Americans, Morris Wills was perfectly willing to go anywhere in China to get away from the group of men with whom he had lived closely for nearly two years. Surprisingly, the Chinese segregated Wills by allowing him to remain in place at the People's University, where he was the only American student.[19]

While Morris Wills and the ten others in Beijing were studying at the university, the five men who had been sent to the state farm and the factory were considerably less satisfied. On June 18, 1955, Beijing radio announced that three of the American nonrepatriates, along with two Belgians, had decided to leave China. Otho Bell, William Cowart, and Lewis Griggs had not

Occasionally, particularly early in their stay, Chinese officials would take the men on short vacations and other travels around China, primarily showing off sites that highlighted Chinese cultural and technological advancements. Here the men are in Hangzhou. Standing, left to right: Lowell Skinner, James Veneris, unidentified Westerner, Howard Adams, and Louis Verdyck. Sitting: Roger Hoste (Belgian nonrepatriate). This trip was organized as a going-away tour for Verdyck. (CEGES-SOMA, Brussels, Belgium.)

been selected to receive a college education. Instead, as members of "the dummy bunch," Bell, Griggs, and Cowart were sent to a collective farm "cuz we wasn't educated enough to learn Chinese. We were way out in the country—the people there thought we was from outer space."[20]

Living for a year in Henan province, about 800 miles south of Beijing, the men, along with two of the other Americans, spent their days working on the farm and their nights living in substandard conditions. Cowart told of how he and the two others had been sent to a farm where they were put to work repairing tractors although none of the three knew anything about tractors. "It was hell. . . . The conditions were like nothing I had ever seen or heard tell of before. We ate like dogs. We slept in a barn. We burned up in summer and we froze to death in winter. I froze both my feet." Cowart recalled that he made the equivalent of twelve U.S. dollars a month, of which half went for food and one-third for cigarettes. Frustrated, the group rebelled against Chinese authority. Fearing that if they acted individually, the Chinese might punish them severely, they decided to resist as a group and insist on being sent home. First, they abandoned the farm. Bell and Cowart likely left the farm together, but Griggs and a deserter from the Belgian army "resigned" the state farm and lived in the countryside for a while.[21] Tired of the social and cultural isolation in Henan, Bell, Griggs, and Cowart, along with Roger Devriendt and Louis Verdyck—both Belgians—ran away and trekked ten days to Beijing, where they sought assistance from the British Embassy.[22] While the trio was in Beijing, the Americans there met with them, a few of the men attempting to talk Bell, Griggs, and Cowart out of leaving.[23] It was for naught. The three simply had had enough of life away from their families and a nation familiar to them.

Apart from the frustrations created by the difficulty of life in China, Otho Bell confided in a 1991 interview that the defining factor for him was the fact that he had been promised before he even left Korea that his wife would be in China to meet him when he arrived. With no other corroborating source, Bell's memory must be questioned. Adam Zweiback notes that Bell's assertion was probably false since he did not insist on leaving as soon as he arrived and Jewell Bell was not there.[24] In reality, Bell's fear of retribution if he returned home drove his decision to go to China and his frustration with the hard life there ultimately drove him home.

The level of the men's frustration did not change the fact that they would likely be tried and convicted, as Dickenson and Batchelor had been, if they returned to the United States. On June 7, the five men arrived in Beijing and were guests of the Red Cross Society of China until their departure could be arranged through government channels. They immediately drew the interest of Chinese officials by staying out late, drinking to excess, and drawing attention to themselves. Ignoring the advice of the Red Cross to moderate their behavior, a couple of the men became well-known nuisances. Louis Verdyck was arrested by Beijing police for "disturbing public order." Otho Bell had pretended to commit suicide by cutting himself with a knife and then bragged that once he was away from China he would allege that the cuts were the result of Chinese mistreatment.[25]

In a June 18 broadcast from Beijing, Lewis Griggs and Otho Bell were identified as wanting to return to their home country, while William Cowart supposedly wished to emigrate elsewhere. The Belgian Devriendt also asked for permission to go to the United States while Verdyck asked permission to enter Laos. Lewie Griggs took the remarkable step of writing directly to President Eisenhower asking for his help in bringing himself and Bell home, sending Cowart to India, and accepting Devriendt into the United States.[26] Wishing to avoid the type of controversy engendered by Dickenson's prosecution, newspapers ran articles discussing the likelihood of prosecution that might follow the men's expected return.[27] After nearly a month of waiting, the three Americans were granted permission to leave China, but only to return to the United States. Fittingly, they walked out of China together in the rain on July 10, 1955.[28]

That night, the men enjoyed Hong Kong's nightlife. Given money by the British Red Cross to buy Western clothing and dining with two reporters, Griggs, Cowart, and Bell spent the remainder of the evening in the company of another reporter visiting nightspots. Their nightlife was short-lived, however, since they were given third-class passage on the *President Cleveland,* which departed shortly after midnight on July 11 en route to the United States. Staying in a fifty-bed open bay dormitory, which the sailors called the "Marco Polo Room," the three were surrounded by Chinese, leaving just as they had lived.[29]

After nearly two weeks at sea, the men arrived on U.S. soil at Honolulu, Hawaii. Not allowed to leave the ship during the fourteen-hour stopover, the men met with reporters who came aboard, where William Cowart led a short news conference. Acknowledging that they had heard a speech by President Eisenhower early in the year that focused on international trade, Cowart claimed that he and the others were heartened by the "peace plans" within it. Apparently already considering leaving China, Cowart, Griggs, and Bell were motivated by Eisenhower's speech, despite the possibility that they would be prosecuted if they returned home. Cowart spoke about that likelihood, too.

William Cowart, Lewis Griggs, and Otho Bell stand aboard the S.S. *President Cleveland* as the ship makes its way through San Francisco Bay on July 29, 1955. The three men were arrested by military police when the boat docked and held for several months until the U.S. Supreme Court intervened. Looking over their shoulders in the distance is Alcatraz Federal Penitentiary. (UPI)

As all three men declared themselves to be "anti-Communists," Cowart optimistically stated that "if a trial is held it definitely will be fair."[30]

The next day, the U.S. Army announced plans to arrest the three men upon their arrival. The most important sticking point had been the fact that the army had discharged all of the remaining men when they refused repatriation for the final time. Now civilians, they were no longer under military jurisdiction and could not legally be arrested, tried, or convicted by court martial. With its lawyers at work, the army found a legal precedent in Article 3A of the Uniform Code of Military Justice, which allows the military to regain control of soldiers who have been discharged, but have subsequently been linked to crimes committed while members of the armed services. Because both sides had agreed to allow prisoners to choose during the explaining period, the men could not be tried on charges of desertion. They could, however, be held accountable for their behavior while prisoners of war, including giving aid to the enemy.[31]

On July 26, the army revealed a letter that had been sent to Brig. Gen. Archelaus L. Hamblen during the explaining period. Signed by all of the nonrepatriates except William Cowart, the note asked General Hamblen to desert the army and come to the communist side. Hamblen, who was serving in Korea at the time, saved the letter, which ultimately surfaced at the Pentagon where the cases against the three men were being built.[32]

On July 29, Bell, Cowart, and Griggs arrived in San Francisco. There to greet them were several relatives, who spent about an hour and a half on board the ship with their loved ones. The group then disembarked and passed through customs, where the three were placed under arrest by the army, loaded into the back of a truck, and driven to the stockade at nearby Fort Baker. Charged with betraying others while prisoners to improve their own conditions and, in the case of Bell and Griggs, "soliciting a general officer of the United States Army to desert," the men stood silently in a pier shed. The only betrayal of any emotion came when Otho Bell blinked repeatedly when he heard the charge that he had deprived his fellow Americans of food while in the prison camp.[33]

After more than a month and a half in jail, the men, through their attorneys, submitted an appeal directly to President Eisenhower requesting a hearing with him during which they promised to provide information that would "enable our Government to strike an effective counter-blow at Communist propaganda." Attorneys George T. Davis and Harold C. Brown had been retained by the three nonrepatriates shortly after arriving in the United States and were notified later that same day that the Oval Office had referred the case to the Secretary of the Army and that the attorneys should refer all communication to that office.[34] Seemingly rebuffed by the President, Bell, Cowart, and Griggs remained in the guardhouse at Fort Baker. During the bleak months that followed their arrival in San Francisco and brief reunion with their families, the three nonrepatriates sat quietly waiting for some hopeful word about their case.

With the White House refusing to become involved, all appeared lost; however, the three were saved by a Pittsburgh steelworker accused of murdering a Korean civilian. Robert W. Toth was a member of the U.S. Air Force in Korea in 1952 when the incident took place. Brought up on charges along with two other servicemen in 1954, Toth, who had been discharged from the army before being charged, argued that he could not be tried by court martial if he no longer had any connection to the military. U.S. Supreme Court Justice Hugo Black agreed, and in a 6–3 decision, the court declared that once discharged from their military obligations, former servicemen could only be tried in civilian courts.[35] For Griggs, Bell, and Cowart, the news was miraculous.

After the Toth decision, a federal judge ordered the three men released and on November 9, they walked out of the guardhouse unfettered, as free men for the first time in five years. From there, Otho Bell went to Olympia, Washington, to join his wife and four-year-old daughter, whom he had only met for the first time during the brief homecoming aboard ship in late July. William Cowart announced plans to move back to Monticello, Arkansas, where he would stay with his mother and stepfather. Lewis Griggs was more ambiguous, saying that he would return to Texas and go to school.[36]

Many of the men would find their returns to the United States difficult. Within six months of his release from the stockade at Fort Baker, Bell and his wife were both in trouble. At some point in early April 1956, a drunk Otho Bell apparently visited Dorothy Hamilton, a neighbor in East Olympia, Washington, and attempted to seduce her. Hamilton rebuffed him, which made Bell angry, and he pulled a pistol from his pocket, handed it to the woman, and begged her to shoot him. She refused, returned the gun, and convinced Bell to go home. For weeks, nothing came of the incident until Hamilton was visiting the home of a neighbor on the evening of April 29, and Bell and his wife walked in. Jewell Bell accused Hamilton of giving her husband wine to drink earlier that evening and violently attacked the woman, beating her until subdued by the neighbor. At this point, Otho, who had apparently placed the blame on Hamilton and stood back watching the fight, threatened to "cut her heart out and drink the blood" and shoot her if Hamilton reported the incident to authorities.[37] Although Otho was not a violent man nor was Jewell Bell normally a violent woman, Otho's drinking was always the catalyst to his self-destruction. Hamilton put it simply, and apparently accurately, when she said, "he goes nuts on a stubby of a beer."[38]

In the midst of the Griggs, Bell, and Cowart drama, Richard Tenneson chose to leave China. In mid-September 1955, he wrote his mother of his intentions. Fully aware that the army was preparing a case against the other returnees, Tenneson wrote, "I am coming back to the States, coming home, but my friend, the Army, will see to it that I don't get that far." Apparently, he had been exploring the possibility of returning for quite some time. He described how he had recently met with a representative of the Red Cross General Society, who told Tenneson that "it wouldn't be too long" and that "preparations were already being made."[39]

Despite the assurances by the Red Cross, Tenneson's trip home would be delayed. Although those following his case probably expected him to appear at the Chinese border with Hong Kong shortly after his letter home, technicalities kept him waiting until late November. On November 30, it was reported that Tenneson had arrived at the border and filled out the requisite paperwork, but was forced to spend one last night in China before leaving the country the next day.[40] However, that information was erroneous. In reality, Tenneson was just across the border in China, but the Chinese were apparently dragging their feet at letting him leave. The American Red Cross sent a representative to the border checkpoint twice each month with parcels and mail for Westerners living in China, but on this day, November 30, a Chinese official stepped forward and offered to turn over Tenneson. Since the Red Cross representative had no authority to repatriate Tenneson to a British colony, he turned the matter over to the appropriate authorities, who sent diplomatic representatives to the checkpoint each day hoping to take charge of the American.[41] Tenneson wrote his mother, "on the 30th we went to the actual border contact point, but the American Red Cross representative refused to accept the responsibility of assisting my return."[42]

On December 10, Tenneson finally crossed the border into Hong Kong. With his repatriation complete, he called his mother and spoke with her directly for the first time in nearly five years. After he checked into his hotel room, he held a press conference in his room during which he tried to explain his motives for refusing repatriation and his timing in returning to the United States. He acknowledged that he had believed the germ warfare charges that the Chinese leveled against the United States during the Korean Conflict and that the photographs and other evidence his captors had presented were convincing to him. Although he refused to discuss his reasons for leaving China, he compared his nearly two years there to "something like attending school" and added that he would return home with an "open mind" to start his "postgraduate course." Revealing a sentiment that would be echoed during the next decade as the other nonrepatriates trickled home, Tenneson said "none of them [Chinese] tried to keep me back; they wanted to get rid of me."[43] He later cryptically elaborated on his decision to leave, "certain weaknesses in my character make it very uncomfortable and impossible to stay."[44]

As the nonrepatriate question was significant politically, Tenneson addressed some of those issues. He claimed that during his time in China, he had read both Chinese and American newspapers and thought the political climate had moderated enough to warrant his return. This was likely related to the embarrassment of Senator Joseph McCarthy during the army hearings in the summer of 1954. Taking the middle road, Tenneson freely explained that he understood "communism today, more than in 1951" and noted that he was "not fighting against communism, nor am I against it." For Tenneson, President Eisenhower's 1955 meeting with Soviet Premier Nikita Khrushchev in Geneva signaled progress and allowed the American to surmise that the "whole [international] spirit is different now."[45]

On December 15, Tenneson boarded an airplane in Hong Kong for his long flight home. With stopovers in Tokyo, Japan; Shemya, Alaska; and Seattle, Washington, he finally arrived in Minneapolis before 9:00 A.M. on December 16. After a reunion with his mother and twin brother and sister, Tenneson met reporters in the terminal. In the barrage of questions, one in particular proved troublesome. While in Hong Kong, he told reporters that he had become an atheist because he "kept praying and praying and nothing ever happened."[46] When he arrived home, reporters questioned him vigorously about his abandonment of God. He responded that he planned to attend church the coming Sunday, but was standoffish when pressed if he would "pray to God." Defiantly, Tenneson reiterated, "I'll be in church." Pushing again, reporters wished to know if he believed in God, but again Tenneson stood firm and responded "I want to . . . think things out."[47] With the atheism question garnering no substantial answers, reporters moved on to other topics.

One of the most sensational reports regarding Tenneson's reason for staying behind with the communists suggested that an abusive stepfather had driven the young man away. Although Portia Howe admitted that her husband Ebenezer had whipped Richard just as he did the other children, she did not consider the treatment abuse. While in Hong Kong and upon his arrival in Minneapolis, Richard sought to put these rumors to rest. He claimed that while he was young, he resented these punishments, but that he had grown out of that resentment and did not think much about those memories.[48] Halfway through the interview, Richard looked up to see his stepfather and brother Nathan come in the rear door. Stopping the reporters, Tenneson yelled to Ebenezer, "Come on in, man with the big hat." Striding to the front of the room, the older man, bedecked in a cowboy hat, shook hands with Richard and the two then embraced. Enjoying the timing of his stepfather's arrival, Tenneson told the reporters, "Remember that radio broadcast. You guys want to remember this."[49] After a few more questions, Richard Tenneson left the media circus and returned home.

Not long after Tenneson's repatriation, Lois Mitchison, a British reporter whose father represented the Labor Party in Parliament, wrote a story after meeting six of the men during her travels in China. Her report illustrated the extent to which the Chinese controlled the minds of the men. Spending several days with the men, all of whom were students at the People's University in Beijing, Mitchison noted that all the men she spoke with were certain that they would one day return to the United States. Larance Sullivan expressed his intention of "waiting until conditions are ripe" for his return as "a good revolutionary" who could "serve those people in America, white as well as Negro." A much more cynical Scott Rush agreed that he would return, but only "when I'm sure no men in leather jackets are going to beat me up."[50]

Their answers as to why they had chosen to stay in China varied. Addressing the pivotal issue of germ warfare, Samuel Hawkins told of a "large bomb . . . found in our camp" by some of his fellow prisoners. Inside of the capsule, the men found "insects . . . mashed a bit and couldn't escape . . . there were a lot of them lying around for us to see." However naïve, Hawkins's story illustrated the profound results of the Chinese indoctrination effort. Rush added that he signed numerous peace petitions while in the prison camp, but after "Little Switch" he heard that those signers who returned to the United States "were summoned by Sen. Joseph R. McCarthy and the un-American committee. I just wanted peace, and I didn't want to be persecuted. So, naturally, I stayed." Sullivan and Clarence Adams claimed that they stayed because "Negroes were oppressed in America for economic reasons."[51]

On the issue of communism, the men confessed that while they were not yet good communists, they hoped to grow into that role one day. Sullivan did not have "the qualifications for a Communist party member, but I'm working toward the qualifications. It's a glorious thing to be a member." Andrew Fortuna, who grew up on the mean streets of Detroit, contended that "Marxist philosophy solved my basic problems."[52]

Just as hiding one truth in preference for a second, safer truth, was beneficial during their days in the prison camps, the conversations with Mitchison painted a pretty picture over a more unpleasant truth. Morris Wills recalled that during the latter months of 1955, dissent steadily grew among the Beijing group primarily because of the Americans' isolation from the Chinese and the ongoing self-criticism that inevitably wore all the men down. Although Sam Hawkins and Scott Rush were the first to see the glimmer wear off the Red Chinese dream, the others began seeing the same. Wills remembered that some of the men found girlfriends off campus and would sneak away for a few days.[53]

In early 1956, several of the men requested that the group be split up. In Wills's opinion, the Chinese eagerly complied, "Hawkins, Rush, Sullivan, and Andrew Fortuna were sent to factories in Wuhan and Peking." From those initial assignments, some of the men later transferred to Hankou; Sullivan became a lathe operator and Fortuna an automobile mechanic. Clarence Adams, Richard Corden, and Harold Webb enrolled at Wuhan University, while Wills transferred across town to Beijing University.[54]

Breaking up the group took time, however, and in the summer of 1956, Morris Wills, Andrew Fortuna, William White, and Andrew Condron spent almost a month on vacation at Dalian. Surrounded by Russians, because of the large Soviet naval base there, the men felt a bit more at ease than they did in Beijing. Wills noted that the men had complete freedom there as the Chinese still had some confidence in the group at that time.[55]

In the fall, when Wills started classes at Beijing University, he found himself the only American there, but, more pleasantly, surrounded by many other foreign students. In addition to the students, the university's faculty impressed him greatly. As China's flagship institution of higher education, Beijing University could count the nation's best minds as members of its academic corps. For Morris Wills, his college experience was particularly enjoyable because of his size and athletic ability. He began playing basketball for Beijing University and, although he was a mediocre player in high school, became the best player on the team. He recalled that he "used to average 26, 27 points, sometimes 35 or 40" and that although foreigners never fully fit into Chinese society, while playing basketball, he was treated as an equal by his teammates.[56]

The year 1956 was a transitional one in the communist world as new Soviet Premier Nikita Khrushchev opened the year with a speech denouncing Joseph Stalin's cult of personality. Just as the speech shocked the world and began thawing the image of the Soviet Union, it also sounded a word of caution to other nations with similar cults. Nearby, China and Mao Zedong listened intently as their Marxist neighbor made statements potentially harmful to Chinese success.[57]

That year also proved an important one back home for the nonrepatriates. For years, FBI Director J. Edgar Hoover had been conducting illegal investigations into the lives of private citizens, but with permissive and like-minded friends in the White House, he began expanding his own personal program of rooting out communists. In January 1956, William F. Tompkins, Assistant Attorney General for Internal Security, ordered copies of the Department of the Army files on the nonrepatriates who remained in China. Having been frustrated by the recent returnees who had been protected by the Supreme Court, Tompkins agreed to assist Hoover and the FBI in their amassing of evidence for possible future prosecutions under the laws of treason and sedition. By late June 1956, Tompkins sent a detailed directive complete with individualized instructions stressing specific concerns upon which the attorney general thought he might one day be able to base a prosecution. Throughout the late summer and fall of 1956, Hoover put his plan into action. In the coming months, he ordered FBI offices nationwide to locate and interview hundreds of former PsW about the activities of the nonrepatriates while in captivity.[58]

As part of this program, FBI agents visited Arlie Pate's parents. Of primary concern to the Bureau were the activities of the Save Our Sons Committee, an organization initially created to draw these nonrepatriates back to the United States. Hoover's men felt that the SOSC could be acting as a communist front, particularly since Arlie had been vocal about his willingness to donate any military back pay to pro-communist organizations in the United States.[59] Upon meeting with the Pates, the agent reviewed fifteen letters that Arlie had written to his family since he had entered China. Generally, they sought to portray Chinese communism in the most favorable light and placed much of the blame for global problems on the United States and capitalism.

In November 1956, news broke that two more nonrepatriates planned to return to the United States. Just before Thanksgiving, Aaron Wilson's mother reported that her son had written her a letter in which he told her that he had applied to the Chinese government for permission to return home. Although neither federal, civil, nor Red Cross officials knew anything of Wilson's efforts, his family excitedly prepared for their reunion.[60] Within a few days, it was revealed that Wilson would not return alone. Illinoisan Arlie Pate had also made the necessary arrangements to come home after hearing that one of his teenaged brothers had drowned in the summer of 1956.[61]

On December 2, one year after Richard Tenneson had made his preparations to depart China, Wilson and Pate crossed into Hong Kong. As was the custom by now, the American Red Cross took them to their hotel, where they met with reporters, and the U.S. government began arranging their transportation back to the States.[62] At the news conference, Pate did most of the talking, announcing that he "went to China because I wanted peace . . . I did not find it there, and will now go back to lead a peaceful life with my family." Regarding his time in China, Pate noted that he did not fit in partly because of his difficulties with the language. "In fact, you can't consider me a worker because I was handicapped by the language. In the paper factory in Jinan where I was a third-grade lathe operator, the Chinese did most of the heavy work while I watched." It seems that all Pate did was have as much fun as he could. "At night I ran around and went to dances and movies, having a good time." He noted that he "didn't bother to listen to newscasts or the radio from the Voice of America or read Chinese Communist news sheets," but "just went to dances."[63]

Departing Hong Kong on December 5, Pate and Wilson spent the long flight anticipating the receptions they would receive upon their arrival in their hometowns. For Pate, his family's hard times would require much work from him to help alleviate some of his mother and father's financial troubles. Upon Arlie's arrival in Milwaukee and his transfer to a bus that would take him through the day's heavy fog to the airport in Chicago, a reporter introduced him to the types of questions he would have to answer in the coming days. Upon being asked if he betrayed the United States, Pate replied, "No sir, I have never thought of myself as a traitor."[64] After a long and arduous trip that included airplane flights, bus rides, and finally a jolting drive down rough and muddy lanes in a rainstorm, Arlie Pate finally arrived at the family farm at 2:00 A.M. on December 7, 1956. With newsmen in tow from Chicago, he saw his family for the first time in more than six years.[65]

Although Pate did most of the talking on his way home, allowing Wilson to be nearly anonymous, his skill with the media was severely lacking. Upon his arrival home, reporters remarked that Pate seemed to revel in his celebrity status and acted 'cocky' on the drive down. Before turning in for the night, Arlie scheduled a 9:30 A.M. press conference for the following morning. However, the hour came and went without his appearance. An older lady who acted as the family's spokesperson announced that Arlie did not show up at the conference because he "has his own newspapermen now and he's not going to talk to anyone but them."[66] Despite Arlie's public missteps, the people of southern Illinois rallied around him. On the day after he arrived home, a neighbor, who was an army veteran and had returned from occupied Germany only one year before, drove up to the Pate house to visit with Arlie. Although the two did not know each other well, their military background provided a common bond that allowed them to meet for quite a while and part as if old friends.[67] In the Carbondale *Southern Illinoisan,* letters to the editor were decidedly sympathetic. After a vicious letter from a man claiming to be a World War II veteran condemning Pate and calling him a traitor, a flurry of letters arrived in Arlie's defense. One written by a group of five men who had fought in World War II and in Korea expressed sympathy for Pate, considering the conditions of his imprisonment. Others asked for compassion during the coming holiday season.[68]

For the Pate family, Arlie's return was a godsend. His father's epilepsy did not allow him to work very hard on the family's seventy-nine acres, of which about thirty were farmed. He supplemented his corn and soybean crops with a $22 per month relief check from the state of Illinois. Farming was tough, particularly with Arlie being away. During those years, even Arlie's eleven-year-old brother Harold, who had to walk a mile each way to catch the bus to school, grew sixteen acres of corn in order to help the family. Additionally, Arlie's younger sister suffered from rheumatic fever. Daniel Pate's farm also had two twenty-four-year-old plow horses, three cows, and sixteen hogs.[69]

With such a large tract and little with which to work it, Arlie promised to throw himself into becoming a farmer in order to help out his parents. Although a neighbor had spoken with a company in East St. Louis, Illinois, that had previously employed Arlie as a truck driver, the company refused to rehire him. This did not dampen Pate's spirits, though, and he steadfastly stuck to his promise to "stay here and work on the farm, and try to straighten it out."[70]

Visitors, once rare at the Pate household, began to appear regularly. Within only a few days of Arlie's return, Richard Tenneson came for a visit. Having been home for a year, Tenneson spent a couple of days with his old buddy hoping to help him adjust to life in the United States. Speaking to reporters briefly, Tenneson addressed the difficult adjustments that he had had to make upon his return.[71] Just before Christmas, another man arrived on the farm. Harry Moreland had driven from Tulsa, Oklahoma, in search of information about his son, who had been shot down over North Korea in late 1952. Although Pate was not able to give the man the information he sought, Moreland left town just as optimistic about his son's fate as he had been when he arrived.[72]

With the coming and going of the holiday season, Arlie Pate's bucolic life on the farm turned ugly. On January 22, 1957, Arlie got into an argument with his father, which resulted in the twenty-six-year-old son badly beating his fifty-year-old father. The older man, sporting knots on his head and black eyes, watched as local police took his son away. Later, he agreed to drop the charges if Arlie would pack his belongings and leave. Joining Arlie was his brother Donald. It is unknown what Donald's role was in the fracas, but he accompanied Arlie to the police station and returned to the house to pack his things along with his brother. The two then cashed a check and took a cab to St. Louis in search of a new life.[73]

When Arlie first arrived home, he planned to turn the struggling family farm around and provide for his parents. With a $580 bill arriving any day from the State Department, however, demanding that Pate repay the government for his transportation from Hong Kong, Arlie apparently sold most of the family's livestock to cover part of his debt. The sale only brought $280 and likely drew Daniel Pate's paternal ire upon his realization that the lion's share of his farm had been sold to pay less than half of the debt.[74]

Once in St. Louis, Arlie's problems continued. On April 15, he married Barbara Jones, who was sixteen at the time, although he did not confess the marriage for three days. He claimed that he and Jones were engaged, but would not marry until he found a job. He did this because he still owed the government money for his return trip and "was afraid they wouldn't think I was doing the right thing in getting married while I owed the money." Pate expected the interest in him to die down, but it only grew. It was revealed that his new bride was actually the daughter of his mother's twin sister. When Arlie's father read an article announcing the marriage, the shocked old man exclaimed, "My God, he's married his cousin." Claiming ignorance, Arlie promised to check with the judge who married the two while his mother-in-law/aunt contended that she did not "know that would make the kids cousins."[75]

With the social firestorm at full strength, both Arlie and his father sought out advice as to how best to end the marriage. Arlie inquired of a local sheriff, "how do I go about getting this marriage stopped?" to which the officer responded, "I'm not telling you a thing! I didn't marry you" and hung up on him. Daniel Pate, still angry with his son for his treatment earlier in the year, told the county prosecutor that Arlie knew full well that he was marrying his first cousin and asked if criminal charges would be proffered. The attorney informed the angry man that the marriage was null and void in the state of Missouri and that the only punishable crime might be if the two lied on their marriage application, which they had done by affirming that they were not closely related.[76] However, within two weeks, Arlie had changed his mind and was seeking a way to legally marry Barbara. The judge who had married the two in April checked the various state statutes and found that Tennessee might allow a marriage between two first cousins.[77] Arlie's vacillation and uncertainty on the issue of his marriage may have indicated that he still thought with a prisoner mentality. After marrying his cousin and finding that he was scorned because of it, he sought to satisfy those critical of him, even to the point of taking a personal role in dissolving the marriage, but later, he again thought of himself and his own feelings and returned to his initial position.

As summer wore on, Arlie's dissolved marriage dimmed in the public light, but the media remained focused on the family for another reason. When Arlie and Daniel left the family farm in January over the sale of livestock, the family suffered irreparable damage. Within days, the two other children in the household left home along with Arlie's mother. Daniel Pate spent that winter and spring living by himself on the farm while the rest of his family was parceled out to family members in the St. Louis area. On July 6, Zady Ann Pate, Arlie's mother, filed for divorce from Daniel and Daniel filed a suit a few days later asking that the farm be divided between the two.[78] Within a few months, the court confirmed through the divorce proceeding and Arlie Pate finally removed himself from the public eye.

For the family of Aaron Wilson, his projected homecoming was particularly sweet. On November 28, 1950, the U.S. Army had declared him dead, but in late July 1951, the family received a letter from Aaron telling them that he was in a prison camp.[79] Enduring the long imprisonment and their son's refusal to return home, the Wilsons likely thought they would never see him

Aaron Wilson of Urania, Louisiana, sits on an airplane during a layover in Memphis on his way home for the first time in six years. The stress and strain of his experiences is obvious. (UPI)

again, but in the early hours of December 7, 1956, they finally got their wish. After traveling thousands of miles from Hong Kong with Arlie Pate, the two met Portia Howe, Richard Tenneson's mother, at the airport in Minneapolis, Minnesota, before going their separate ways homeward. The anticipation at the Wilson home in the lumber town of Urania, Louisiana, was increased by the recent arrival of Tenneson, who had come to visit to help Aaron, who struggled socially and intellectually, adjust to his new life at home and the treatment he would be given by the media.[80] Confirming some of the problems that Arlie Pate would soon have, Tenneson said that Wilson would find it hard to make decisions for himself because "he hasn't made a decision for himself in six years except the one to come home."[81] Upon landing in New Orleans, Aaron Wilson was met by his mother and sister, who then hurried him to a car where his father and other family members were waiting, along with Richard Tenneson.[82]

Always likeable, Aaron Wilson did nothing to complicate his already smooth homecoming. Perhaps he benefited from the fact that he had little to say under normal conditions and even less under the stress of his return, or maybe Teneson's influence helped him to avoid the same mistakes he had made a year earlier. More likely was the fact that the people of Urania, Louisiana, were sympathetic to Wilson's plight and made a conscious attempt to give Aaron a wide berth on his return. However, on the day of his arrival, a drunken visitor from Arkansas who had driven down to "tend to this" shocked the town. The man, who identified himself as a sergeant in the army, asked around town for "the Wilson boy," but apparently left after getting little cooperation from the townsfolk.[83]

Although the tight-lipped and naturally reserved Wilson avoided the self-imposed difficulties of his friend Arlie Pate, trouble came to him in the form of a government inquiry. Since Wilson had been declared dead as of November 28, 1950, the Veterans Administration had paid Aaron's family survivors benefits in the form of a $10,000 life insurance policy and a monthly pension of $35. Aaron's father had bought a 100-acre farm with much of the money from the policy portion of the settlement on July 28, 1951, only two days before he received the letter from his son confirming that he was still alive. The next February, the V.A. investigated the claim and found that Aaron was alive, but the family was in no position to repay the insurance money. Although the agency did forgive the $10,000 lump sum, it did stop the monthly pension payment.[84]

Into the fray stepped Congressman George S. Long, brother of Louisiana political legends Huey and Earl and representative from Louisiana's Eighth District. Offended that the Wilson family was found unable to repay the sum when land prices had skyrocketed since they bought the farm, Long sought to force them to either sell the farm or to come up with the money in another way. The representative contended that the V.A. should reclaim the money "if it is legally and physically possible to do so" and noted that "[t]he veterans of my state will not condone regulations which set up in business any man who has been guilty of such traitorous action as has Wilson."[85] Texas congressman Olin "Tiger" Teague, a highly decorated World War II veteran who had ridden his military reputation to the nation's capitol, affirmed Long's belief that the Wilson family should have to repay the money.[86] However contentious the initial debate, the federal government put a stop to the proceedings on December 21 when it revealed that the Veterans Administration had attempted to recover the money from the family in 1953, but an internal board had ruled in favor of the family.[87]

The attempt by the V.A. and two congressmen to recoup the life insurance money paid to the Wilson family was not the only governmental failure to impact Wilson. Although Wilson never knew it, the army had restarted their efforts to prosecute the nonrepatriates in January 1955. Led by the influential army attorney George S. Prugh Jr., the military began organizing prosecution files and Prugh began making his own determinations as to the viability of the army's cases against each of the men. For Aaron Wilson, Prugh found one instance of circulating petitions, three of making recordings, one of collaboration, two of receiving preferential treatment from the Chinese, one of selling food and water to sick PsW, and three of informing. Prugh determined that Wilson's was "a weak art 105 case, and one of the weaker treason cases, but further investigation ought to develop sufficient leads to convict this backward and spineless offender."[88] Wilson may indeed have been backward, but for Prugh, the army lawyer who fought so hard for Vietnam era PsW, Wilson's perceived weakness was apparently part of the reason for his possible prosecution.[89]

Otho Bell's life was also becoming complicated. In late spring 1956, Bell granted permission to Ethel Knight of Taylorsville, Mississippi, to write his biography. Seeking to be straightforward in her intentions with such a controversial subject, Knight had her attorney contact the Department of Justice offices in Jackson, Mississippi, and request that agents visit her so she could lay out her intentions with this project. In her letter to the FBI, Knight revealed that Bell planned to come to Mississippi and live at her house while the book was being written. Knight's sole question of the FBI was whether Bell's California attorney was linked to communism as she did not want her name unknowingly dragged into such a circle.[90]

On August 21, 1956, Knight wrote the FBI directly. She wrote that she was "one of the first to go to the home of Mr. Elbert Bell . . . seeking an interview with the 'Turncoat'," but Bell did not appear at the time. The family did promise Knight exclusive rights to the story if and when Bell returned to Mississippi and after some waiting, Knight received from the family the promised full account of Bell's experiences upon which to base her book.[91]

As usual, however, Bell's drinking got in the way. In August, Bell arrived at Ethel Knight's home unannounced asking for a $150 advance on the sales of the book which had not yet been written, much less sold a single copy. Bell promised to furnish Knight newspaper clippings and photographs, but after he sobered up, he apparently forgot about the incident. Bell kept his distance from Mississippi from that point forward, returned to Washington, and the book never appeared in print.[92]

In January 1957, while the nation was still in the wake of the recent flurry of returnees, Samuel Hawkins's mother announced that a letter she had recently received from her son told her to expect him to return soon along with his Russian wife, Tonya, and their infant son.[93] On February 27, Hawkins crossed the border into Hong Kong alone. He had no trouble getting permission to leave, saying to reporters, "[t]hey gave me my exit visa fifteen minutes after I applied. They made no attempt to dissuade or discourage me from coming out." However, his wife and son had to stay behind because of trouble with their exit visas. The separation scared Tonya, who thought the Chinese might be more than willing to let Sam leave, but hold her and her child once he was gone.[94]

Sam Hawkins's return had been precipitated by his growing disenchantment with life in China and his realization that the Communist utopia he thought he would find there did not exist. When he heard about the "wanton killing by Soviet troops in Hungary," he began to see the hypocrisy of his position. Regarding his reason for going to China initially, the intelligent and affable Hawkins explained, "I halfway believed what I was told—we were brainwashed and I was afraid."[95]

Hawkins's wife's situation was considerably different than that of her husband. Tonya had been born in Harbin, Manchuria, and after her parents died, she was reared and educated in a French convent. In 1947, she applied for and received a passport from the Soviet Union, but her husband at the time affirmed that she was not a communist.[96] Having started dating in 1955, Samuel and Tonya, now divorced, were married in June 1956. Finally, one year after their marriage and after nearly four months of separation, she and her son were allowed to cross into Hong Kong on June 14, 1957, on their way to the United States.[97]

When Hawkins left Hong Kong en route to the United States on March 1, he did so on a ticket bought for him by an Oklahoma oilman sympathetic to his cause. M. H. Champion was rich and influential. When he heard that Hawkins was planning to return home, Champion offered to pay for his ticket. The oilman even escorted Hawkins's mother, Carley Jones, to Will Rogers Airport to welcome her son home. The sympathetic philanthropist promised Hawkins a job with his company and confidently took on Tonya's immigration situation by saying that the United States would not guarantee an entry visa for the woman and child, but "we're going to work on it in Washington."[98]

Champion's help eased Hawkins's transition back into American life. He went to work for his patron's company, welcomed his wife and child a few weeks later, and in June, he appeared on *The Mike Wallace Interview,* a television program dedicated to newsmakers of the day. The interview reveals much about mainstream perceptions of the nonrepatriates. During the course of the show, Wallace used the recently popularized term, "turncoat," on thirteen different occasions, periodically interspersing it with "traitor." Wallace, like most Americans at the time, had a difficult time comprehending how Hawkins could have considered his childhood unhappy because he had a nice home and received a high school education. He further noted that Hawkins's mother had raised him strictly, hoping to shelter him from "worldly things outside of Church and Boy Scouts" and wondered how those institutions could "turn you against the United States." Hawkins defended his actions and attempted to make Wallace understand his motivations. Wallace closed the interview with, "After the Korean War, Marine General Lemuel Shephard said that our ultimate weapons against communism were, as he put it, "Faith and Courage." Those weapons obviously couldn't be issued by the army to David Hawkins when he went into battle, and was captured. Faith and courage are instilled by home, in church, in school, and in that sense David Hawkins' problem certainly has become our own."[99] Using phraseology popular in the ultra-righteous 1950s, Mike Wallace echoed the sentiments of countless others who had not spent three years in a prisoner of war camp.

Only months after Hawkins's repatriation, Andrew Fortuna decided to return home. Having been reared on the streets, both his stepfather and mother dead by the time he went to China, Fortuna had little reason to come back to the United States. His half sister told reporters, "he doesn't have much to come home to but I'm certainly glad he's coming home." Apart from the half sister, Fortuna's only living relative was a half brother serving a term in prison. Despite these concerns, Andy gave a simple, yet effective explanation for his return: "I was homesick. I guess you can say it was just plain homesickness that is making me go back." During his three years in China, Fortuna had not been given the educational opportunities that many of the others had enjoyed. Rather, he had lived in Hankou, where he worked as a government mechanic earning about $40 per month.[100]

Andrew Fortuna entered Hong Kong at noon on June 15. After examining his paperwork and issuing even more, the British officials moved quickly to secure him transport back to the States on the *President Wilson,* scheduled to leave that very evening. By nightfall, he was aboard ship and on his way home.[101] Meanwhile, his sister offered to extend any help possible. Guessing that Andy did not know that his mother and stepfather had both died and the family home had been sold, Viola Van Oast announced that she would open her home to Andy to allow him to get back on his feet: "He's a good brother but he never had a chance."[102] Nor would Fortuna make the most of his limited opportunities upon his return.

Like Otho Bell, Fortuna's personal habits caused him significant problems when he returned to the United States. Unlike other PsW who came back to consternation in their hometowns, Fortuna had very few relatives left in Detroit and disembarked on the West Coast en route to his aunt's house in Kellogg, Idaho.[103] Fortuna's time in Kellogg was short and unproductive as he abruptly quit his job and left for Chicago after only a few weeks.

By the end of 1957, Fortuna was in Kankakee, Illinois, where he spent his time drinking, drawing the shades in fear that he was being watched by the FBI, and developing a brief relationship. He had recently met Mary Mills, who had allowed him to move into her house, and told her that the FBI had chased him out of Idaho. After promising to marry the woman after only a few weeks of living together, Fortuna abruptly disappeared, not paying his rent or any other bills and not even taking his clothes, sending Mary on a desperate search for him. She wrote the FBI asking why they would not let him hold a job and why agents had run him out of Idaho. Although she was naïve enough to take up with Fortuna and take his marriage proposal seriously, she acknowledged to agents that "he insists he is not a Communist but all he can talk about is the Chinese people" and suggested they search for him at his grandfather's farm in Kentucky.[104] In February, Fortuna turned up in Lucasville, Ohio, living with his grandfather for the rest of the year before disappearing again.

To make money, Fortuna had tried to shop his life story to editors of the *Saturday Evening Post* while living in Kankakee, but the magazine politely turned him down. Later, he wrote a short autobiography and had a friend, Jack Ellis of Colma, California, submit it to *Reader's Digest*. Ellis was the desk clerk at the San Francisco YMCA where Fortuna spent his first days back in the United States in the summer of 1957. An aspiring writer, Ellis found a good subject when he secured permission for an article on Fortuna's life story. However, nothing ever came of the endeavor.[105]

Fortuna quickly sank into a pattern of alcoholism and unemployment. It took only a few months for him to be arrested for the first time for an alcohol-related offense. After an initial arrest in 1957 in Kellogg, Idaho, Fortuna was arrested in Arroyo Grande, California, in May 1959; Salem, Oregon, in August 1959; Turlock, California, two consecutive days in September 1959, for drunk driving and being drunk in public. On October 11, 1961, by order of San Francisco County, Fortuna was admitted to California's Mendocino State Hospital as an alcoholic. After two weeks of treatment, he was transferred to Napa

State Hospital. Fortuna remained a patient there for two months and was released in late January 1962. Less than two months later, he was readmitted to Mendocino because of his alcoholism. After sixty days, he was deemed "improved" and released. By 1963, "T.B. carrier" was added to police warnings about Fortuna's alcoholism. That spring, he was an isolated patient in the San Mateo County Sanitarium from which he walked away in late June after having a lung removed.[106] From California, Fortuna moved back east to Detroit briefly, and then to Chicago, Illinois, and Gary, Indiana. In both places, he became dependent on Salvation Army shelters and worked for the company as a truck driver.[107]

Meanwhile, Mao's China was reveling in its recent successes and slowly beginning to tire of Soviet supervision. In May 1956, Mao Zedong announced the "Hundred Flowers Campaign," a movement intended to open free discourse among intellectuals. For a year, those invited to voice their concerns had kept their mouths shut out of fear that their complaints would come back to haunt them, but in May 1957, their venom spilled forth. The nation erupted in widespread criticism, with most of it directed at the Chinese Communist Party. Morris Wills was a student at Beijing University when the reaction struck. He recalled that many of the young and idealistic students leaped at the opportunity to criticize and covered the campus in provocative posters. The Chinese had taught Wills pragmatism in prison, however, and he kept his mouth shut on the issues.[108]

With his experiment in free speech backfiring and the Communist Party bearing the brunt of the open criticism, Mao quickly put a halt to the movement, but the gates of change were already opened. This period, known as the Anti-Rightist Movement, began in early June and struck back at those who had taken Mao so literally. Mao theorized that the Hundred Flowers Movement was successful up to the point where it had been hijacked and corrupted by a handful of Rightists who took advantage of the climate of openness. To counter this corruption, the party forced everyone to cover each critical poster with one praising the party and implemented more stringent self-criticism meetings than had been seen in years. Wills remembered the campus experiencing several suicides and witnessed one himself while walking across campus one evening. He looked up and saw a student leap out of a third-floor window. Wills later learned that the man had committed suicide in the middle of a criticism meeting.[109]

In the summer of 1957, Morris Wills left cosmopolitan Beijing to visit Howard Adams in Jinan. He found Jinan "remote and primitive." The town was "scorching hot in the summer and floods every year" and "[t]he people were filthy and ragged and very rough." Adams and Wills toured the city and factory and observed the changing nature of the Americans' existence in China. Noting that the situation was not good at all for the Americans, Wills surmised that "they had been given over to this factory to look after them and the Red Cross had washed its hands of them." Wills said, "The Americans did their eight hours of drudgery each day at the factory and rode back home by bicycle." Once home, "[s]upper was whatever their wives could throw together. . . . Then they would lie around with their ears glued to the Voice of America." Day to day, little changed.[110]

The men in Jinan were anxious to learn all they could about Wills's comfortable life in Beijing and questioned him relentlessly about the amounts of food he received and his general living conditions. Shortly after he returned to Beijing, "the thing blew up." The Americans apparently struck for more money and food, and some became violent in the process. Wills heard that "[o]ne or two were thrown into jail by the police because the Party Secretary said they had to be intimidated a bit, so throw them in jail." The the men's wives were then interviewed and threatened, followed by some of the men being jailed again. With conditions worsening, several of the men announced that they wished to leave China. This got them into even more trouble. Wills recalled that early on the Chinese had refused to allow anyone to leave, an account confirmed by the trouble Griggs, Bell, and Cowart went through to leave the farm. Hoping to forestall the departures, Chinese officials attempted to keep the Americans out of Beijing, where the office of the British Charge d'Affaires was located.[111]

Hoping to put the strikers in their place, the government grew more rigid and the men responded similarly. On numerous occasions, some of the men were jailed, sometimes for months, in an attempt to calm their emotions. The always-obstinate Lowell Skinner earned his jail time by punching the Party Secretary and getting into a fight with the police commissioner. Wills claimed that "[a]ll except one of them was in jail at one time or another" and that "two or three of them had been held . . . for a few days before leaving China" because after asking for permission to leave and being refused, they "decided to walk out of China . . . and were picked up by the Red Army and thrown into jail and finally taken back to the farm."[112]

On September 11, 1957, Richard Corden, Harold Webb, Clarence Adams, and Scott Rush met with a group of visiting Americans in Hankou. Speaking highly of Chinese communism, Corden told the visitors, "I am impressed with

Socialism but I was not brainwashed" and Adams contributed that he expected to marry the next year and "remain indefinitely in China." Despite their sunny outlooks, the reality of the situation was far different. Recent social reforms in China was making the lives of foreigners more difficult day by day.[113]

The men had found a small group of fellow Americans in China. The most important to them were Robert and Jean Hodes. Robert had been a pathologist teaching at Tulane University and his wife was a member of the Sachs (of Goldman Sachs) family. Both had become active in leftist politics and emigrated to China with their children, where they enjoyed one of the few free-standing houses in Beijing. The Hodes home became the center of activity for many of the Americans, including the more established and doctrinaire Marxists, like Sidney Rittenberg, Israel Epstein, and Sidney Shapiro.[114]

Personally, several of the men were establishing good lives for themselves. Scott Rush, who worked in Wuhan as a lathe operator in a textile factory, married a Chinese woman and settled into a comfortable routine. Although by Western standards, a sparsely furnished, two-bedroom apartment seemed poor, Rush noted that his living conditions compared favorably with those of factory managers and Communist Party officials. Rush earned 45 yuan (about $18.90), and received 50 yuan from the Red Cross each month. Although his wife worked and earned 45 yuan a month, all of her pay went to support her parents.[115]

Clarence Adams was also growing more comfortable with life in China. After arriving at Wuhan University in 1956, he met Lin Ling Feng. Lin had graduated from Wuhan University the year before Clarence arrived and was teaching Russian at nearby Wuhan Polytechnic University. Lin came from an influential family. Her father had been a regional warlord who became Hubei Province's governor after he surrendered his army to Chiang Kai-shek. After dating for several months, Clarence and Lin announced their intention to marry. On December 20, 1957, they were married at Wuhan University and honeymooned in a small house on campus. Adams later wrote that "[t]he foreign students had put wines, candies, and cigarettes in the guest house for us." Old friends Harold Webb and Richard Corden joined the newlyweds. Clarence confessed that "[t]hey drank up the wine and ate all the candy before I told them they had worn out their welcome and kicked them out."[116] James Veneris had also found a bride during the preceding year. He married a Chinese woman who had contracted tuberculosis in 1949. Although her health was strong early in their marriage, by 1966, he was a widower and looking to remarry.[117]

For the nearly four years that Ed Dickenson was jailed in the United States, his attorneys constantly filed motions seeking reconsideration of his conviction and sentence. Time after time, those requests were turned down, but Guy Emery's persistence and the change in America's political climate combined to spell success. By mid-1956, both Joe McCarthy and his crusade were slowly dying; the former from acute alcoholism and the latter from the unrealistic ambitions of its namesake. On May 2, 1957, "Tailgunner" Joe passed from this Earth and took with him much of the anxiety of the 1950s.[118]

Unexpectedly, on April 16, 1957, the army announced that Ed Dickenson's sentence of ten years would be halved, therefore making him eligible for parole in January 1958.[119] With time off for good behavior, Dickenson was released from confinement at Fort Leavenworth, Kansas, on November 23, just in time for him to return home for Thanksgiving dinner for only the second time in nearly a decade. As he left the prison, Dickenson spoke frankly about his treatment by the United States. By that time, it was apparent to him that before his court martial the army had "held him up . . . as an example of how a turncoat could return to freedom without punishment for having defected." He further noted that he had been exploited for political purposes: "The only difference between me and a lot of others is the others have not been caught."[120] Considering the myriad credibility questions surrounding those who testified against him, Ed Dickenson was certainly right. In all, Dickenson served three and a half years in Fort Leavenworth, the same amount of time Lt. William Calley served in house arrest at Fort Benning, Georgia, as a result of his conviction on charges of premeditated murder of twenty-two Vietnamese men, women, and children.[121]

As for his future plans, Dickenson told reporters that he wished to enroll at Free Will Baptist College in Nashville, Tennessee, and eventually return home as a minister of the gospel. In the meantime, he began practicing for a ministerial career. En route home, he stopped at a Raytown, Missouri, Free Will Baptist church, where he was invited to speak about "the dangers of Communist infiltration into our churches and schools."[122] Although he felt he had been called by God while in prison, his fifth-grade education, and prison-produced high school diploma did not meet the minimum standards for admission to the college, nor could he afford the tuition.

On the evening of November 27, Dickenson finally returned home to the Virginia mountains. This homecoming differed dramatically from the frenzied affair that had followed him back to Cracker's Neck in the fall of 1953 as the family hoped to keep the outside attention to a minimum.[123] However, frustrations boiled over at the Dickenson house on Thanksgiving morning, and Ed left angrily. His mother explained that the family was listening to radio news reports of Ed's return when one broadcaster classified him as a "returned jailbird, not welcomed by the people of Cracker's Neck or Big Stone Gap." At this, Dickenson began angrily pacing the floor and asked his brother to drive him to Knoxville, and the two departed.[124] After the news broke that Dickenson had left the area to avoid what was erroneously being publicly advertised as widespread criticism, a groundswell of support flooded the newspaper offices with letters of support for him, criticism of the newspaper and radio coverage, and cash donations to help him get back on his feet.[125]

Within weeks, Dickenson had again quietly returned home. Following him from a safe distance was the FBI, who continued to harbor suspicions that he and the other nonrepatriates were part of a grand conspiracy. Beginning in February 1958, investigators began compiling a dossier on Dickenson. As he had done during his initial trip home after accepting repatriation, he married quickly and went to work as a laborer at a quarry. On February 12, 1958, the day after his wedding, Dickenson met with a special agent and answered his questions. Of particular interest that day was pro-communist literature that had been sent to him by an unknown person during his initial time home after repatriation, during his confinement and trial, and while he was incarcerated at Fort Leavenworth. Dickenson had alerted authorities to the material and had turned it over to them. He also affirmed that he had not received any such materials since his release from prison.[126] Shortly afterward, the FBI closed its file on Ed Dickenson.

By early 1958, the complexion of the once solid expatriate group had changed dramatically. Those who had returned home found their lives difficult, particularly Dickenson, who had only recently been released from prison, and Batchelor, who remained behind bars. However, those men still in China were about to begin one of the most difficult challenges of their lives as their adopted nation embarked on a series of catastrophic reforms. Sadly, just as the political separation from the Soviets would bear fruit, those domestic reforms would take China on a sobering trip back in time by reminding it of the limitations of a preindustrial society.

ELEVEN

Outcasts in Life and Death since 1958

> "When we first went to China, they called us comrades. And after some years in China, they switched from comrades to calling us Peace Fighters. . . . Then later on, the worst thing to be called in China is to be called a mister. Then they started addressing us as mister Adams, then you know you're completely out."
>
> —Clarence Adams in *They Chose China*

> "When I asked him why he had written so negatively about his experiences in China, he said, 'Now that you are in Rome again, you'd better act like a Roman.'"
>
> —Clarence Adams on Morris Wills

For those men who remained in China after 1957, conditions changed dramatically. With Mao Zedong's Great Leap Forward, the already stressed nation spasmed as it severed its relationship with the Soviet Union and exercised true independence. At Mao's urging, China embarked on a wide-ranging economic and social overhaul in the hopes that the immense population could rapidly transform the traditional, agrarian nation into a modern, industrialized one. For the next three years, China would be wracked by food shortages that resulted in millions of deaths. Although the Americans enjoyed more food because of extra rations, they were not immune to the problems of a transitional nation and several reached their breaking points.

After spending four years behind the Bamboo Curtain, Larance Sullivan, the first of the black expatriates to leave China, arrived in Hong Kong on March 30, 1958. Although Sullivan was tight-lipped about his motives for going to China, William Cowart had said in 1955 that "LaRance wanted to go to China to emphasize how bad things were for Negroes here in the United States . . . but he soon found out things were no better in China." Sullivan affirmed Cowart's statement when he claimed that discrimination in America was the root of his dissatisfaction. In an Associated Press interview in 1956, Sullivan said, "There's going to have to be some changes in the States first, before I go home."[1]

Previous returnees had described Larance as the most bitter of the group and his behavior during his return affirmed his state of mind. When Sullivan arrived in Hong Kong, he visited the consular section to arrange the details of his departure from China, but refused to meet with representatives from the political section stating, "as for politics . . . I want to be considered dead."[2] It was clear that Sullivan was operating under a great deal of strain during the process and the behavior of the Chinese officials illustrates the level of mental games being played on the nonrepatriate. In what may have been a demeaning racist gesture, Chinese officials handed him a bunch of bananas as he stepped across the border, which did not happen to any of the other men.[3]

In early December 1958, a news story appeared in American newspapers featuring Morris Wills. Wills talked candidly about his own experiences and his observations of the experiences of others. Living within China during one of its most anti-American periods put Wills and other Westerners in a difficult position. Wills acknowledged that it "always hurts a bit" when he passed the anti-Western banners that line the streets, but he also felt "ashamed every time Dulles blows off in Washington." Standing with a foot in each world, Wills, like most of the other Westerners in China, was caught between the appeal of his traditional home and that of his adopted one. Wills also offered updates on the status of his fellow Americans. With several of the men having recently gotten married, Wills erroneously noted that the Chinese policy of not allowing native Chinese to leave the country would probably prevent the men from returning to the United States with their wives. He elaborated on the social life that he and a few others enjoyed with the Hodes family, Iona Kramer, Bertha Hinton, and Marcella Vance, all Western expatriates living in Beijing.[4]

The new year of 1959 saw the return of Richard Corden. As one of the most doctrinaire of the expatriates, Corden remained steadfast in his support of Marxism and agreed to sit for interviews while shipboard. On December 19, 1958, Corden emerged from China "spouting the Communist line full blast." "I firmly believe there is more democracy in Communist China than in the United States," he said before predicting that the United States would eventually succumb to socialism.[5]

It took nearly two weeks, but Corden secured passage out of Hong Kong on the *President Cleveland* on New Year's Day.[6] When the ship stopped in Honolulu on January 14, he got another chance to relate his experiences, although he was under orders not to leave the ship until it arrived in San Francisco.[7] He told a Honolulu reporter, "I believe that communism is the long range goal" for America, but that it would not be realized during his lifetime. He thought that the slow descent into socialism had to be all-encompassing and complete before a nation could move into the realm of true communism. However troubling Corden's prediction of America's eventual political direction might have been, he made additional enemies when he volunteered these comments on the American GI: "The American soldier is soft—pretty soft. The majority went right along when they started banging our ears. Some guys just gave up and died. Pulled the blankets over their faces and died." He added, "He [the American GI] lives good. So when he runs up against a tough situation like that he buckles easily. You switch him from C rations to soupy rice—he just can't take it."[8]

When he arrived in San Francisco on January 19, he intended to continue on to Providence, Rhode Island, to be with his family.[9] However, two months passed and he had only made it to Los Angeles. Although he still planned to visit his hometown, he spent the summer of 1959 giving lectures to a variety of organizations in the city, including the Los Angeles Committee of Young Socialist Supporters.[10] When he spoke to a meeting of the Southern California District of the Communist Party, he said that upon his arrival in San Francisco, he "had meetings there for nearly 30 days," presumably with fellow radicals.[11] Corden contacted the local Communist Party when he arrived and volunteered to give lectures on behalf of the group.[12]

Corden, who had been rumored to be a homosexual while in prison camp, wasted little time securing a social life. In the summer of 1959, he met a woman at a communist picnic. After a short but intense courtship, they married in October. By December, however, their impulsive union was broken and Corden moved out.[13] After escaping his marriage, he also set out to leave Los Angeles. He left the city in March 1960 and found work for two months on a New Mexico ranch before moving on to Milwaukee, Wisconsin.[14]

For all of Richard Corden's openness with political subversives and media organizations, he flatly refused to speak with any representatives of the U.S. government. By late 1960, he was in Milwaukee and had contacted the local FBI office seeking "to clarify all his previous actions which included his refusal to talk with the FBI in California." Corden then contacted the Adjutant

General of the Army to get documentation of his dishonorable discharge, guidance on the possible reinstatements of his rights, and even the possibility of rejoining the army.[15]

In 1958, Mao Zedong announced his second Five-Year Plan, more popularly known as the Great Leap Forward. It came in the wake of China's realization that the Soviet formula for communist success would not work with such a large population and comparatively small landmass as China's. To address this problem, Mao refocused Chinese attention on agricultural and industrial production; his ambitions were allowed to run amok because of the previous year's suppression of economists and other professionals during the Anti-Rightist campaign. In the coming years, Chinese agriculture rapidly moved into hundreds of thousands of communes, which worked with machinery when available and with bare hands when unavailable. Hundreds of miles of irrigation canals were dug, mostly by hand, to turn previously marginal farmland into more productive soil. More than a million furnaces popped up in backyards throughout the nation and began to produce iron, albeit in small quantities.[16]

Despite the country's ambitious hopes, its reality was much different. After a semi-successful first year, 1959 proved to be the beginning of a long failure because of the dual weaknesses of Mao's limited economic knowledge and the inability of the farmers to harvest all that they had grown . . . and reported to the government. The results were disastrous. In the famine that stretched from 1959–1962, an estimated twenty million Chinese died, not counting the toll longtime malnutrition took in the years thereafter.[17]

Morris Wills participated in the Great Leap Forward. His college basketball team and hundreds of thousands of other Chinese, including Mao Zedong and Zhou Enlai, built an earthen dam near the site of the Ming Tombs, about thirty miles north of Beijing. Wills spent a few days there living, eating, and working as the common Chinese did. When he returned to Beijing, he saw that those who had remained behind were putting their energies to work eradicating "the 'four pests': sparrows, flies, mosquitoes and rats." Later in the fall, a full-scale effort began to rid China of sparrows. Convinced that the birds ate too much grain, the Chinese people refused to let them land for three days while vigilantly watching for one to grow overcome by exhaustion and fall to the ground. When the bird hit the ground, several men and women would descend on it and beat or stomp it to death. Wills was awakened in his dormitory at 4:00 A.M. on the first day by gunshots, fireworks, and any other noise-making apparatus. Each building had someone stationed on top and after the three-day battle ended, virtually all birds had been eliminated. He sarcastically recalled that "the next year the Chinese privately admitted that they lost tremendous amounts of grain to the insects which the sparrows had been eating."[18]

In the midst of the unrest of 1959, Albert Belhomme took a stand against Chinese coercion. As anti-foreign sentiment was rising at the time, Belhomme petitioned the government to allow him and his family to leave. His request was denied, however. Frustrated by the government's answer, he refused to go to his job as an electrician in a paper mill, thus beginning a strike that would last for nearly ten months. During the stoppage, some of his fellow Americans in Jinan joined in his strike. Lowell Skinner refused to work for three months and Howard Adams and James Veneris, who worked at the same mill, walked out in support. However, the men began to drop out as their finances began to tighten. Belhomme himself had to end his strike in order to feed his family: "By going on strike I didn't get paid and we needed money to buy food."[19]

From Richard Corden's return in early 1959 until the summer of 1963, only one man left China, but he did not return to the United States. Harold Webb had married a Polish woman who was in China likely as part of a communist-bloc exchange program. In 1960, the two left China and settled in Poland, where they remained until the mid-1980s.[20]

Those who had returned before 1959 continued to try to rebuild their lives in America. Otho Bell had returned in 1955 and attempted to settle into a quiet life, but his alcohol addiction would not allow an easy transition. In January 1956, he was ticketed for drunk driving; in March 1958, he was jailed for ten days for striking a man on the head with a .22 rifle; then, on the last day of 1958, he was arrested for taking indecent liberties with a fourteen-year-old girl and remanded to the mental health ward for evaluation at Western State Hospital in Steilacoom, Washington. During his month in treatment, Dr. Giulio DiFuria diagnosed Bell as having a "paranoid personality with psychotic reaction."[21] Bell still harbored "an abnormal fear that the Chinese Communists were after him" keeping him in "an extremely fearful state." At the time of Bell's admittance, there was a Chinese American in the ward, but the doctor had to transfer Bell because he "believed that the other patient had been sent to the hospital 'to get him'." Although DiFuria did not consider Bell violent, he did acknowledge that if another episode struck, Bell "could be capable of inflicting bodily harm to any person whom he suspected of trying to harm or kill him and would probably try to kill such a person."[22]

Larance Sullivan also had a difficult transition back in the United States. In June 1958, he married, but the couple fought constantly, mainly because of his drinking, which had started shortly after returning home. On three different occasions, his wife had him committed to state mental health facilities. On the evening of December 16, 1959, a drunk Sullivan came into his grandmother's house, where he had lived since the demise of his marriage, and began arguing with the older woman. A neighbor reported that Sullivan screamed, "Mama, I'm sick and tired of you running my life" and then he began choking the eighty-year-old woman. As he "was shaking the daylights out of her," the neighbor broke up the fight by pulling Sullivan off his grandmother. The next day, a judge remanded Sullivan to his fourth facility in less than two years.[23] Two weeks later, a judge considered the mental health report from Sullivan's recent stay at Napa State Hospital, where Andrew Fortuna would be committed two years later. Although the counselors considered him to have "schizophrenic reactions" and be "of a paranoid type," the judge, who was impressed by Sullivan's intelligence and clarity regarding his own condition, ordered him to spend another thirty days at the facility for a complete evaluation.[24]

Over the course of the coming years, Sullivan completely succumbed to the bottle. He spent several stints in mental health facilities, sometimes self-committed for his alcoholism, and was arrested numerous times for drunkenness and begging. Until the FBI lost interest in him in 1967, Sullivan lived in squalid hotels and existed on welfare benefits. Various FBI contacts described Sullivan's drinking problem as so debilitating that it made him "unemployable."[25]

Indeed, former prisoners of war suffered terribly from mental illness after returning home. Kathleen Taylor found that the efforts of PsW to resist or even deal with the stresses of indoctrination often left them so severely traumatized that they could not function in their own society.[26] Otho Bell, as a prisoner of war, had suffered from bouts of insanity and after his return to the United States, his mental health continued to lapse periodically. Lowell Skinner's postwar violence and mental illness was well-documented as was that of Larance Sullivan. Virgil Rutherford, who had attempted an escape with Edward Dickenson while at Camp Five, broke under the stress of FBI interviews. In Spring 1956, when FBI agents attempted to contact him to gather information about the nonrepatriates, his father turned them away. Telling the agents to leave his son alone, the old man said, "on each occasion after his son has been contacted regarding his experiences as a prisoner of war he becomes upset, nervous and sits around the house crying and wringing his hands . . . it usually takes several weeks . . . to get over this extreme nervousness."[27] Leonard "Lucky" Bell also left Korea mentally ill. By late April 1956, when FBI agents questioned him about the behavior of other PsW in camp, Bell had been given a medical discharge from the army. After a nervous breakdown in the summer of 1954, Bell spent seven months in the hospital at Fort Sam Houston, Texas, during which he received twenty-one electric shock treatments.[28]

In late 1959, Morris Wills met Li Kai-yen and the two began a romantic relationship. Dating between Chinese women and foreign men was not officially forbidden, but the practice was certainly frowned upon and discouraged. Wills remembered the difficulties associated with their relationship and wrote, "In 1958 and '59 it could still be done if one was careful." Several of his fellow Americans had already married and many had dated Chinese girls, but by the time Wills began seeing Kai-yen, the practice was slowly being restricted. Wills recalled that the two had been seeing each other for several months when Kai-yen's uncle, the Red Cross, Beijing University, and the girl's school met and agreed to send Kai-yen away to Tientsin after the school term ended. In the fall of 1960, Kai-yen was sent away as planned, but between Morris's money for train fare and her willingness to return to Beijing every weekend, the geographic separation mattered little. Within a few weeks however, Kai-yen's uncle found out about her return trips to the city to visit Wills and asked the authorities to intervene. One evening after leaving Morris's dormitory, she was arrested and sent to prison for ten months. Officials told Wills that she had been caught stealing—the exact sum he sent with her for train fare. Morris Wills then embarked on a personal mission to harass the Chinese Red Cross, which had played a major role in Kai-yen's arrest. He stormed in and out of their offices and even wrote scathing letters to politicians, including Zhou Enlai, and the commandant of Kai-yen's prison camp. Finally, on September 23, 1961, Kai-yen was released and reunited with Morris. Not wishing to waste time, Morris and Kai-yen went about securing official permission and once that was granted, they married the next evening. The date was November 23, 1961, exactly two months after her return.[29] By Christmas 1962, Wills's life had stabilized. He wrote his father that he and Kai-yen were happy and that he intended to remain in China for the remainder of his life. With a university degree in hand and a job at the Foreign Language Press as a translator and writer, Wills was stable.[30]

Back in the United States, Otho Bell, Lewie Griggs, and William Cowart were still fighting for money owed them by the army while they were prisoners of war. On January 11, 1961, attorneys argued the case in front of the U.S. Supreme Court and after months of waiting, the court returned a decision for the plaintiffs. Associate Justice Potter Stewart wrote the unanimous decision, which awarded Bell $1,455.00, Griggs $2,810.00, and Cowart $4,951.00. Although many people thought the men were being paid for their traitorous activities, the court held that the army had willingly entered into a contract with the men and could not abandon it, particularly in light of the controversy surrounding so many of their fellow PsW.[31]

In the spring of 1963, William White, Morris Wills, and Clarence Adams helped the Foreign Languages Press commemorate the fifth year of one of its publications. Chinese Premier Chou Enlai attended the celebratory dinner and the three Americans were honored when he stopped by their table to talk to his foreign guests. Recalling the occasion, Clarence Adams remembered that the premier asked the men how they liked their lives in China and if there were any issues that his office might help repair. The three Americans went home that night feeling "almost as important as the old-time foreigners in China, such as [Israel] Epstein and [Sidney] Rittenberg."[32]

By late summer 1963, the Chinese wanted to get rid of Lowell Skinner as badly as he wanted to leave. Both he and Howard Adams had been jailed for months for their factory strike. Skinner refused to go when offered the chance, however. He had a wife whom he did not want to leave behind. Understanding that, the Chinese promised Skinner's wife a monthly stipend if she would encourage Lowell to go ahead without her and told her she could join him later. Morris Wills knew the Skinners well and noted that the Chinese did not live up to their end of the bargain. When he left China, she was still in Jinan, by then nearly crippled by a lingering childhood malady and "barely existing."[33]

Finally free to return to the United States and expecting that his wife would soon follow, Skinner said little upon crossing into Hong Kong other than "It's about time I go back and my parents are getting old."[34] The next day, he sat down for an extended interview during which he touched on various issues during his life in China and his decision to return home. Skinner's story was of a man whose disillusionment had grown from the innocence of his initial decision to go to China to his realization that the Chinese system was far from a utopia. He lamented the "lack of individual freedom" in China and the fact that living conditions there were not higher than in the United States, nor could he travel freely or pursue an education, all of which he had been promised in 1953. Despite his criticisms, Skinner never felt harassed by the Chinese and regarded his stay as a learning experience, stating, "I don't think I lost anything by staying in China. I soon gained a knowledge of the country, its customs and language." Regarding the label "turncoat" that had been commonly applied to the men, Skinner optimistically thought, "It might wear off."[35]

One important result of Lowell Skinner's repatriation was his offering updates on the handful of men who remained in China. Of the group, Clarence Adams and William White worked at the Foreign Language Press, China's publishing house for English-language propaganda literature along with children's stories and some classics. Both Clarence Adams and William White were married to Chinese women and had children. Howard Adams was married, with one child, and working as a chemist in a paper mill in Jinan. Albert Belhomme was also in Jinan working as an electrician, as was James Veneris, who was a lathe operator and married. Scott Rush was also a lathe operator, but was living in Wuhan with his wife and child. Two of the other men had abandoned China for communist-bloc eastern European nations. John Dunn had married a staff member of the Czechoslovakian embassy and relocated with her to her homeland, while Harold Webb and his Polish wife had gone to Poland.[36]

After waiting several days in Hong Kong while his parents scraped together the $725 necessary to bring him home, Skinner boarded a plane to Tokyo and then to New York.[37] Traveling under an alias, he arrived at Idlewild Airport at 1:00 A.M. on August 9, where he met briefly with reporters. Despite the openness of his interviews while in Hong Kong, Skinner put on a "curt almost surly" face for the media. His reason rested in the fact that he had agreed to sell the exclusive rights to his story to a New York television station. When pressed for details, Skinner stood tall and accused the reporter of asking an unfair question before a group from the television network whisked him away from the other reporters.[38]

During his taping for the Metropolitan Broadcasting Company's television special, Skinner told a very revealing story. Skinner explained that during his time in the PW camp, "I had studied just about everything they had." Having studied communism at the behest of his captors and fellow prisoners, Skinner feared retribution, acknowledging that "I had a certain amount of apprehension about going back at that time." When interviewer David Schoenbrun asked him to explain his answer, Skinner responded, "They had a word, 'progressive.' If you just read anything, even magazines. It was 'progressive.'" Furthermore, he felt a significant amount of alienation from the United States due to his captivity. During his time as a prisoner, Skinner "gradually lost some contact with the United States" while growing close to and increasingly dependent on his Chinese captors.[39]

Despite his salty mood while in New York City, he was very happy once he got back home to Akron, Ohio. After some hesitation, he sat down in his mother's kitchen, drinking coffee and speaking freely to reporters from the local newspaper. Confidently, he explained, "I would do it over again under the same conditions that existed at the time." Staying true to the sentiments that both sent him to China and kept him there, he relayed stories of a more permissive government than had many of his fellow returnees. He noted that Chinese authorities "paid no attention if I went fishing, or hunting or had a few beers with the boys" and that conditions in China were "generally good, but . . . there were two 'bad' years." An uncowed Skinner took particular issue with his being referred to as a turncoat and argued that he had researched the word and "It does not express what I am. I am what the Government says is a voluntary nonrepatriate."[40]

Almost immediately upon his return to Akron, Skinner began to run into problems. First, the U.S. Army owed him $1,705, minus allotments already sent to his parents, for his time as a prisoner of war. However, the army had a ten-year statute of limitations on such claims, which had expired on August 4, 1963, five days before he landed in New York City. Skinner did file the appropriate paperwork on August 12, a week later than allowed, but Secretary of the Army Cyrus Vance refused to make an exception on his behalf. Denying Skinner his back pay was a small but sweet victory for the Pentagon, which had attempted to refuse pay to the previous returnees, but had been forced to by a decision of the U.S. Supreme Court. However, the disappointment of missing out on the opportunity to collect the pay owed to him paled in comparison to the struggles the coming years would bring.[41] Lowell Skinner's homecoming had been tense from the first moments. He had hoped to bring his ill wife from China, but that plan never materialized and Lowell apparently quickly lost interest in trying to bring her to America. Within months, he found himself in serious legal trouble and over the coming year and a half was arrested five times.

On the night of November 18, 1963, Skinner's legal odyssey began. Apparently involved with a woman whose husband was serving a term in the state penitentiary, Skinner came into her house one evening to find two teenaged boys sitting on the sofa. Inexplicably, he erupted in anger, pulled a pistol, and fired a round into the couch between them. He then put the gun to one of the boys' heads and told them to get out. Jealousy may explain Skinner's reaction, but in fact, the woman had asked the boys in to watch her children while she ran out for a few moments.[42] Four months later, Skinner was given two years' probation.[43]

In October 28, 1964, police were called to a private dwelling where one of Skinner's friends lived. The newspaper identified the man as having "been linked with [Skinner] in prior escapades." The lady of the house claimed that Skinner had broken the window in an attempt to burglarize the dwelling, but Skinner claimed to have not been there. When an officer arrived, Skinner told him that the woman had been making harassing telephone calls to him and soon became embroiled in an argument with the police officer. Skinner alleged that the officer "called him a traitor who ought to be shot," to which he responded by calling the man a fascist.[44] After spending a few days in jail, the charge of malicious destruction of property was dropped because "Mr. Skinner has an emotional problem."[45]

Within days of Skinner's release, he managed to get into serious trouble. On the evening of November 20, 1964, Lowell began flirting with eighteen-year-old Cheryl Hashman at an Akron bar. Her refusing his advances enraged Skinner who responded by punching her in the face, ultimately breaking her nose and bruising her badly. Hashman fought back with a beer bottle and Skinner backed off. The young woman required eleven days of hospitalization to recover from her wounds. Since Skinner was already on a two-year probation for firing at the two youths, his assault on Hashman threatened to send him to the state penitentiary.[46]

A week later, he was arrested for violating his probation by drinking. On December 10, Skinner stood in court and admitted to the judge presiding over his probation violation hearing that he had violated the proscribed terms more than twenty times since the sentence was imposed earlier that same year. Summit County Common Pleas Judge L. A. Lombardi had initially sentenced Skinner to probation in the shooting episode and found him in violation of his probation on this occasion. Skinner's attorney, A. P. Feldman, asked the judge to have his client examined by a mental health professional to determine the root of Skinner's antisocial behavior. Feldman argued, "My observation and reading of police reports indicate that he actually is begging police to beat him. . . . In my honest opinion he is always asking for punishment." The attorney elaborated: "He knows he's on probation. He's inviting the court to revoke it by his actions. To me that doesn't make sense. . . . There very definitely is something wrong with Skinner that causes him to do these things."[47] Judge Lombardi, apparently sympathetic to Skinner's circumstances, told him, "We had a long talk the last time you were here didn't we? I had a great deal of faith and confidence in you then."[48]

After more than two months in jail on the charge of beating Hashman, Judge Lombardi released Skinner in order to allow Probate Judge Nathan Koplin to immediately place him in the custody of Hawthornden State Hospital for psychiatric treatment. Koplin asked Skinner if he thought he needed psychiatric treatment and he responded that he did. After three psychiatrists examined Skinner, they agreed that he was "emotionally disturbed." Two of them traced his condition to his service in the army while the third determined that his difficulties predated his enlistment. Skinner's attorney had filed the motion for his client's committal and after receiving the psychiatric results, began pressing the Veteran's Administration to take responsibility and accept him as a patient at one of their facilities.[49]

One wishes that Lowell Skinner's sad story had ended with his successful treatment at Hawthornden, but the reality was not so rosy. On May 18, 1965, he walked away from the facility, prompting a regional manhunt for him and two others who left later that day. The hospital superintendent noted that Skinner had not been locked up and could have left long before he actually did. Furthermore, he revealed that the patient "had not responded well to treatment" and that "We didn't seem to be able to do much with him. His attitude didn't make it very easy. We had him on intensive treatment and we gave him considerable attention." Skinner's attorney stated that his client "preferred the penitentiary" to the mental hospital.[50] After only one day at liberty, Skinner was recaptured and remanded to the Summit County Jail until he could be returned to the institution.[51]

Albert Belhomme appeared at the famous Hong Kong border crossing on August 30, 1963, accompanied by his Chinese wife and their four children. Having grown up in Belgium and emigrated to the United States after World War II, Belhomme probably had less of an adjustment to life in China than his fellow nonrepatriates considering his previous moves. Knowing the difficulties met by previous returnees, Belhomme decided to use his Belgian passport rather than go back to America.[52] However, Belhomme's departure from Hong Kong was delayed. He and his family sat on the island until November 2, when they were finally allowed to borrow money for passage from the Belgian government.[53] After arriving in Brussels on November 5, Albert Belhomme dropped from sight.[54]

Only a week after Belhomme's entry into Hong Kong, Scott Rush passed out of China with his wife and daughter. Since the Belhomme family remained stuck in the British colony until November, it is likely that the families had a brief reunion before the Rushes left for America on September 14.[55] Speaking freely and critically, Rush called his decision to refuse repatriation to the United States "a foolish mistake" and offered no specific reason for his decision. He did say, "During the three years I was in a prison camp I had it pumped into me that Communism was such and such and such. I was curious and wanted to see what it was."[56] However, the reality of life in China could not live up to the promises made by the Chinese.

Whereas Skinner had stubbornly defended his decision to go to China, Rush sought acceptance through voluntary self-criticism. Within days of his return, he stated to news reporters, "Frankly, I wouldn't let a person such as myself keep his citizenship." Putting himself before a group of newsmen and retired military officers, Rush answered the media's questions and humiliated himself for the officers' benefit. When stung by the statement, "The truth is that you aided and abetted the enemy," Rush, as he had learned so well as a prisoner of war, meekly responded, "Yes, sir, that is the truth." Just as the Chinese had taught him in the camp, Rush allowed his pragmatism to take over in the hopes of surviving the moment at hand.

Upon his return to the United States, Scott Rush wasted no time embracing capitalism. After their initial arrival in Los Angeles, the Rush family flew to Tucson, Arizona, to visit Scott's mother. While in Tucson, veteran KTTV-Los Angeles television journalist Paul Coates called Rush asking if he would be willing to fly back to the West Coast for a prime time interview. Rush agreed, saying, "I don't want to see other kids making the same mistake I did," but within a few minutes, Rush called Coates back telling him "I don't think we got all the details worked out. Maybe you better talk to my agent." A surprised Coates was then greeted on the telephone by John Bilby. Whoever Bilby was, he had been quickly hired by Rush to act as a talent agent, a fact that shocked Coates. While Bilby was asking for an appearance fee, Coates was reminding him that Rush should probably be happy just to have a chance to tell his story. When Bilby told Coates that they had other offers waiting in the wings and if not properly managed, Rush was "liable to come out without making a dime from this whole thing," Coates found his opening: "if you send him down here to Hollywood for an interview, some movie mogul might see it and decide to make his life story."[57] Scott Rush began making travel plans.

The remaining nonrepatriates in China struggled with the deprivations of the time. Because of their foreign status, the Americans were not as restricted as the Chinese in what they could buy or in what quantities, although the time was difficult for all. Morris Wills wrote that in 1957, times were tough, but food was available. However, by 1959, nothing was for sale. He remembered that "[i]n town long lines of people waited to get just a leaf of cabbage, and the people at the end of the line got nothing." Party officials and foreigners were partially exempt from the suffering, but the Chinese knew it and antagonism grew. Wills recalled how his Chinese friends would drop by for a visit and tell him about their starving families and then ask that he buy a simple can of sardines for the family.[58] By the time Morris Wills left China in 1965, conditions were just beginning to stabilize.

In other ways, the Americans shared the sufferings of the common Chinese. Scott Rush, who had spent his youth in Depression-era Akron, noted, "in all the depression years, living conditions in the United States were never as low as they are in China." He and his wife had also endured personal loss as a result of the industrialization movement in China. They had lost one child, who had only lived one day after being born in a factory clinic, and Rush believed that had the baby been delivered in a proper hospital, it would have lived.[59] Although he did not specifically name Scott Rush, Morris Wills wrote that "[o]ne of the men from our group had an infant that died. . . . He told me that the child died from a lack of nourishment. . . . The baby's death made him very bitter."[60] Other notes about China affirmed what many of the other men would say. After the Soviets left, Chinese industrialization came to a complete halt and the average Chinese harbored a severe hatred for the Russians as a result.[61]

Until 1963, James Veneris worked in a Jinan mill that converted old and worn-out shoes into toilet paper. However, that year, his fortunes turned. The People's University in Beijing offered him admission and he spent the next three years there studying Marxism, Leninism, and Maoism, in addition to playing basketball on the university team as his friend Morris Wills had a few years before.[62]

One of the more interesting events occurred while Clarence Adams was hospitalized with an ulcer in 1963. He was on a semi-private hospital ward with a servant of Pu Yi, the last Manchu emperor. During Adams's stay there, the former emperor visited several times and was known to Adams as Henry Puyi. He recalled that Pu Yi was once surrounded by a group of young patients who harassed him about his imperial background, but the ex-emperor "smiled politely the whole time, and tried to give the answers as best he could." Adams learned from the servant that Pu Yi had struggled with his role as an "average" Chinese and when he returned to society, he could not even catch a bus. The ex-emperor would wait at the stop with the crowd. When the bus stopped and the mass pressed forward, he would step back and wait for the bodies to clear, but by then, the bus would pull away leaving him standing alone on the sidewalk.[63]

In the late 1950s and early 1960s, William White and Morris Wills worked together and were neighbors in Beijing. They spent a majority of their time together and had established reputations as black marketers. Clarence Adams remembered that the two "made money 'hand over fist'" during the Cultural Revolution, and when he arrived in Beijing, he joined in their venture. Adams said he had gotten in on the end of the black marketing heyday and could sometimes double his monthly salary dealing goods on the side, but when Chinese officials became suspicious of the men's spending habits, the three agreed to stop dealing for a year. Although Wills and Adams maintained their end of the agreement, "White could not resist, continued his activities, got caught, and ultimately was expelled penniless from China."[64] White's expulsion from China was not that simple: in addition to his black marketing, he also had "a series of incidents involving fighting with his wife, [and] immoral ralations [*sic*] with numerous other women."[65] When William White left China, he appeared to do so with the least financial support of any of the group.

Upon Morris Wills's repatriation, he provided the State Department with considerable details about William White's life in China. Calling him a "habitual liar," Wills explained how White had involved numerous African embassies in their black marketing activities by helping embassy personnel do "a very brisk business in watches, phonograph records and other contraband that they bought by the case when they came on leave to Hong Kong."[66] In contrast to White's relative poverty upon his exit from China, Wills had used his connections with the Ceylonese embassy to secure a bank account in Hong Kong, which he used to launder Hong Kong dollars into Chinese yuan for embassy personnel.[67] Upon his earlier repatriation, Scott Rush confirmed the existence of the bank account and relayed that Wills had recently earned a substantial sum of money for acting in the propaganda film *After the Cease Fire*.[68]

While White's black marketing activities caused concern, his personal behavior was more problematic. In 1964, White had struck up a friendship with a rather shady African named Amos Obote. Wills described him as moving from one university to another with little motivation and a man who "signed chits whenever he wanted something but never paid up." Gravitating to White for his abilities with the Chinese language and "his list of girlfriends," Obote used his friend to arrange sexual liaisons between himself and Chinese women, a practice frowned upon if not officially forbidden in China. In December 1964, one of these arrangements went wrong when Wills locked Obote and a Chinese woman in White's apartment for the afternoon. After locking the door, Wills returned to work at the Foreign Language Press while the two were left alone for their tryst. At around 3:00 P.M., a disturbance got the staff's attention and Wills went out into the street to see about the commotion. A bystander told Wills that a Chinese woman wearing only high heels and a scarf had fallen out of a fourth-floor apartment. Wills immediately realized that the apartment in question was White's and that the woman was the one he had locked in with Obote earlier in the afternoon. The police located White, got his key, and opened the apartment to find Obote "lying on a bed pretending to be asleep." Both White and Obote were arrested and released.

For the Chinese, this was the last straw in regard to William White. Wills said that White returned to work at the Foreign Language Press for about two weeks before he found a note on his desk telling him that he had been fired. Afterward, White moved his family into a small, simple apartment and sought to make ends meet with black marketing activity. Expecting that White would return to illegal activity, the Chinese police set up a sting to catch him in the act and set the stage for his official expulsion. He was arrested and jailed for several weeks until he agreed to leave the country.[69]

With a wife and two children, White had thought about returning to the United States since the previous year, but his behavior provided the impetus behind his departure. On August 17, 1965, White and his family requested admission to Hong Kong en route to America. As expected, he answered a handful of questions, although his quiet demeanor made the responses notably brief. He credited his wish to visit his family, particularly his mother in Kansas City, Missouri, as the deciding factor in his return. Regarding his refusal to return to the United States in 1954, he said "Curiosity" was the key to his going to China, that he wanted to "see what life was really like in Communist China." Answering the question about the term "turncoat" being applied to him, he explained, "I have not betrayed my country . . . I have always been an American. I still am an American."[70]

White and his family met the same financial crisis as many of their predecessors. Since Chinese authorities would only allow the men to leave the country with a limited amount of property, his diary, law books, and only $18.50, he was stuck in Hong Kong until passage could be arranged by either his family, the State Department, or some other source. His family back home was unable to finance his return and Georgia Senator Richard Russell wrote President Lyndon Johnson urging the federal government to offer no assistance whatsoever to White. After waiting a week and a half, another source of funding came through. White told newspapermen that he had been offered a job in Honolulu, Hawaii, and that after a few months visiting the mainland, he would start work the following April. Although he did not tell the media where his passage came from, he simply announced that the money problem "has just been solved."[71]

During the middle of September, the White family made its way from Hong Kong to Honolulu and ultimately to Kansas City, where he spoke with reporters again. At the airport, he reiterated his feelings on the word "turncoat" and the reason behind his going to China, but also spoke about the fundamental reason he chose to come back home: "I am an individual and I want to be treated as one. But all they talk about is collectivism." With the Chinese focus on conformity, White surmised, "They don't want people who think." An intelligent man, White had studied law for three years at People's University and completed his degree. Understanding the limitations an Eastern degree would place on him, he voiced his wish to get a degree from an American institution.[72]

As William White's family waited in Hong Kong for their passage, Morris Wills crossed the bridge to freedom with his wife and daughter. In his autobiography, *Turncoat,* Wills offered the most detailed discussion of his life in China and the process of repatriation. He remembered that within China's structured society, an astute observer could see when his importance was diminishing. In descending order, the Chinese identified men as Lao, Comrade, Fellow Student, Friend, and at the bottom of the order, Mister. In 1957 and 1958, Morris Wills slipped from Comrade all the way down to Mister, until he complained to the Red Cross and became Comrade again.[73] Toward the end of his stay in China, he had returned to Mister. In an interview, Clarence Adams echoed Wills's observation: "When we first went to China, they called us comrades. And after some years in China, they switched from comrades to calling us Peace Fighters. . . . Then later on, the worst thing to be called in China is to be called a mister. Then they started addressing us as mister Adams, then you know you're completely out."[74]

By 1964, Wills began to realize that he was of no more use to the Chinese and started thinking of returning to America. In June, his two-year contract with the Foreign Language Press was to expire and when Wills asked about an extension and a raise, he was rebuffed. In January, he made up his mind to return and visited the British Consulate, through which he contacted the American delegation in Hong Kong. In February, Wills made an appointment with the Red Cross to speak with his handler. Coming clean about his intentions, Wills told the bureaucrat, "I'm telling you now so that when the time comes for them to go, I don't want you to say that you haven't had enough time."[75]

With his plans to return home underway, Wills was offered a plum job. The Foreign Language Press set up a school and asked him to teach English to Chinese soldiers. His colleagues at the language school were Betty Chan (formerly Betty Chandler) and Sidney Shapiro. In September, he gave the school notice that he would be leaving on October 10 and sent Kai-yen to the local police station to request an exit visa. Wills recollected that "[u]sually, if any Chinese would walk in and ask for an exit permit, they would bully him. But Kai-yen told me later that she felt they already knew she would be coming." Uncharacteristically, the clerks at the police station were helpful and

Kai-yen had no trouble obtaining her exit permit. Then Morris went to the police station that handled alien residents' business. Expecting some trivial difficulty, he, too, was surprised when they happily served him. When he returned a couple of days later to pick up the paperwork, the clerks returned to their petulant habits, ultimately drawing Wills's ire. However, he did receive the necessary paperwork in time for his departure, apparently because the Chinese wanted him to go as badly as he did.[76]

As his time in China dwindled, he and Kai-yen made their final visits with her family and prepared to leave. On October 17, the Wills family left Beijing en route to Canton, where they spent two days visiting with Kai-yen's father and brother. By 10:30 A.M. on October 19, the Wills' arrived at Hong Kong and made the slow walk across the famous covered bridge.[77]

Shortly after Morris Wills's return, Clarence Adams began making the news in America. During the early days of American involvement in Vietnam, Adams began broadcasting antiwar messages aimed at black soldiers in southeastern Asia. Foretelling the ultimate defeat of American forces in Vietnam, he reminded the soldiers that he had fought in a similar conflict. Asking to "have a heart-to-heart talk," Adams challenged the black soldiers to evaluate their condition in the United States. "Fellows, are you on the right side of this?" asked Adams, "The Vietnamese are not bombing your churches and killing your children." Finishing his broadcast, he told the soldiers, "You are in the wrong battle here . . . You are fighting the wrong war. Brothers, go home. The Negro people need you back there."[78]

When Morris Wills returned to the United States, he confirmed that the course taken by Clarence Adams had been laid out as a comprehensive plan to influence American involvement in Vietnam. In the spring of 1965, British expatriate Michael Shapiro staged a teach-in for Westerners living in China, during which he urged them to write letters and record broadcasts condemning American interference in Vietnam. In attendance were the remaining American nonrepatriates Wills, Clarence Adams, Howard Adams, and James Veneris, along with Anna Louise Strong, Anna Pu, Israel Epstein, Frank Coe, George Hatem, Sidney Rittenberg, and Dorothy Adler.[79]

Despite the aplomb and conviction of Adams's message, he, too, was growing tired of life in China. Married for several years and by now the father of two, Clarence began making plans to return to the United States the following spring. After several delays waiting for his family's exit documents, the small family crossed into Hong Kong on May 26, 1966. Refusing to elaborate on his reasons for returning to the United States, Adams simply stated, "I wanted to see my mother," whom he had not seen in sixteen years.[80]

Upon crossing the border into Hong Kong, Adams felt like he was "moving from one world to another." Indeed, he was. He returned to a nation far different from the one he had left more than fifteen years before. As a young black man in Memphis, he had grown up with few opportunities; now he returned with the ability to teach the Chinese language. He also returned to a nation that was much more contentious than the one he had left. With the American Civil Rights Movement in full swing and many people aware of his anti-war speeches while still in China, Adams also came back under significant scrutiny. Answering for his anti-war speeches, Adams refused to back down. He admitted that he had recorded two such messages to African American troops, both along the same intellectual lines and defended his actions saying, "the United States is involved in a war there which is not in the interests of the country." He added, "Negroes are fighting for the freedom of other peoples when they themselves are not free—not totally free."[81]

Although the Adams family had crossed into Hong Kong ready to travel to America in late May, delays kept them well into the next month. During that time, he and his family waited for his mother to gather enough money for their passage, which finally took place on June 22.[82] On Independence Day, the family arrived in San Francisco and Adams again spoke to the media: "I never considered myself a Communist" and "always considered myself a loyal American citizen."[83] His statement surely took many people aback, with all that had been reported about him, but in Adams's mind, he was working toward the goal of becoming a communist in China and had not wholly succeeded in that pursuit. In addition to that failure, he had also considered his ability to go to China to be one of the great benefits of living in a liberal society and since he thought his stay there could eventually benefit blacks in the United States, he did feel very patriotic in his long-term intentions.

He attributed his decision to go to China to his "curiosity and to get an education," and stood firm on the statement that "I never turned my back on my own country, and in that sense I'm not really a turncoat." Responding to the question whether a specific event had convinced him to return to the United States, he added a hint that the Senate's Foreign Relations Committee's hearings on Vietnam may have helped motivate him to return and said of the war only, "We have to find some way to solve it."[84]

Regardless of the mixed signals Clarence Adams sent on his reasons for returning, the Civil Rights Movement was at the top of his list. Once back in Memphis, Adams was optimistic: "The racial situation . . . gives me a new hope for the future." Seeing the changes that had taken place in his hometown since he left sixteen years before, he praised the progress saying,

"Things are moving now and I'm happy about it." Later, when asked about black-white relations in Memphis, he replied, "I'm amazed they are as good as they are." Adams also confessed that the Chinese government often used the racial situation in America to its "advantage."[85]

Within a few months, the former expatriate offered his services as an anti-communist propagandist to the United States. Adams noted the high standard of living and credited the democratic political system with achieving the personal freedoms Americans enjoyed. "I conducted a sort of personal referendum between Communism and democracy by seeing both first-hand and making up my mind the hard way," he said, adding, "I like all this but there's something I like better. . . . In China I learned you don't want your mind dominated or subjugated to somebody or some system. To be able to talk freely is wonderful." Expanding on his earlier thoughts on America's racial progress, he was particularly complimentary of Memphis, saying "As a boy, I thought of Chicago as a mecca for Negroes. Memphis is working out its problems better than Chicago."[86] Clarence Adams was the last of the nonrepatriates to return permanently to the United States.

While all of the men had a difficult time assimilating into American society, Clarence Adams faced particular challenges. Although he had been initially excited about the racial progress within the United States, he came to realize that long-festering racial concerns lay just beneath the surface, particularly in a place like Memphis, Tennessee. For the first year back home, Adams struggled to make a living and support his family. He hoped to write a memoir of his time in China, have Chinese prints reproduced and sold through upscale department stores, and get a government job, but all he could do was work as a salesman by day and drive a truck by night. That first year was a difficult one. The FBI informant T-1 relayed that Adams had "lost much of his 'devil-may-care' attitude" and was growing depressed.[87]

One of the things the repatriates needed least was to be embraced without their knowledge or consent by radical groups within the United States. Although Lewie Griggs spent much of his life back home requesting and receiving a variety of international literature, some of it of a Marxist nature, he also found himself on the mailing list of the Christian Nationalist Crusade, which credited an international Jewish conspiracy with having created the ills of modern society.[88] Clarence Adams also found himself loosely linked to controversial figures. In 1967, Robert F. Williams, the former head of Monroe, North Carolina's, NAACP branch, who had fled to Cuba after being accused of the armed kidnapping of a young white couple, wrote Adams in Memphis. While the content of the letter is not known, the FBI learned about the correspondence through their informer, T-1. Within two weeks of the Williams letter, Adams was contacted by the daughter of Dr. Robert Hodes, whom he had known in China. The Hodes family had left China and returned to the States several years before, and now Hodes's daughter wanted to drive to Memphis to meet Adams. He welcomed her as he had known her when she was a young girl, but was skeptical of her motives when she brought a suspicious man with her. Peculiarly, Adams confided in a man he knew as a friend, but whom the government called "T-1," that he worried that the girl might have been a government "plant" when indeed he was talking to one all along.[89]

Morris Wills returned to the United States with a complete plan for future success. Understanding that his in-depth knowledge of Mao's China was a valuable commodity in academic and intelligence circles, he had been positioning himself professionally for months preceding his return. He had offers from both Harvard University's East Asia Center and "a 'branch' of UCLA." Although the Harvard job was clearly a research position, the UCLA offer suggested more dramatic work. When Wills's father asked his son what kind of work he would be doing at UCLA, Morris responded, "translating, analyzing, and interpreting Red Chinese literature." The senior Wills pressed him further, asking "if he were going to do 'spy' work, to which Morris responded 'sort of'." Clearly, Morris was more taken with the possibilities of working at UCLA and stated that if their offer matched that of Harvard, he would gladly move to California.[90] By spring 1966, UCLA had fallen out of contention and Morris began looking for an apartment in Boston.[91]

Wills came home with a much better financial future than any of his cohorts. He had already negotiated a contract with *Look* magazine to serialize the story of his life behind the Bamboo Curtain. As part of the deal, his return was financed by the magazine and he and his family flew the San Francisco to New York leg of their return flight as first-class passengers. *Look* had given Wills a $1,200 advance for his story and had committed to paying "living expenses for himself and his family for the next two years in the event he does not obtain suitable employment."[92] Taking care of business first, Morris and his family remained in New York City for several weeks, living at the Hotel Bretton Hall while presumably working on the magazine articles.[93] He did sneak home shortly before Thanksgiving in the company of two representatives from *Look*.[94] By the end of January 1966, the Wills family left Manhattan and traveled to Fort Ann, where they planned to live with Morris's father for a few weeks.[95]

In the months that followed his return, Wills stayed busy marketing his life story. He appeared on several television programs, gave radio interviews, and accepted speaking engagements. In early March, he traveled to Washington, D.C., where he met in closed session with one of Senator J. William Fulbright's diplomatic committees and discussed the prevailing sentiments in China toward American involvement in Vietnam. He returned to Capitol Hill in early April to meet formally with the Senate Foreign Relations Committee. He also began working on a book about his experiences, which would eventually be released as *Turncoat: An American's Twelve Years in Communist China.*[96] The aggressive marketing of his experiences drew the ire of many, including Paul Harvey, who contributed a radio report on December 7, 1965, entitled "The Defective Hero," in which he described Wills as "the bad guy wearing the white hat," whose new home was on "a red carpet, basking in limelight and with a guaranteed livelihood."[97]

Wills's celebrity peaked in February with the publication of the two articles he had been writing. The first, entitled "Why I Chose China," detailed the path that had led him to his fateful decision to remain with his captors. He discussed the brainwashing that took place within the prison camp and attempted to explain his decision to refuse repatriation.[98] The second article appeared two weeks after the first and caused a firestorm. "Why I Quit China" focused on the years Wills spent in China and chronicled his slow disillusionment with the communist system and his ultimate decision to return home. In that article, Wills revealed that a group of fifteen English-speaking men and women lived and worked in China undermining the interests of the United States and England.[99]

The allegation that some of the reactions to the Vietnam War and race relations within the United States were being directed from China surprised many Americans who could not imagine how society could be influenced from so far away. Wills identified British-born Michael Shapiro as the leader of the English-speaking element in China and included Sidney Shapiro, Dr. George Hatem, Sidney Rittenberg, Anna Louise Strong, and Israel Epstein as members of the group. When the United States started bombing North Vietnam in 1965, Michael Shapiro called a meeting of all the Americans in Beijing and told them that the Communist Party wanted to see and hear more vocal support of North Vietnam coming from the Americans. He noted that Epstein was an organizer of "campus sit-ins and demonstrations" and that he was able to affect these activities through longstanding relationships back in the States: "The Chinese Party envisioned the Vietnamese war coming to a halt because of this movement in America."[100]

The notoriety that Morris Wills received as a result of the *Look* articles brought some unwanted attention. The White House asked the FBI to forward as much information as was available on the Americans who were working within the Chinese propaganda machine, particularly on those who had influence within American campus movements. Marvin Watson, Lyndon Johnson's Chief of Staff, coordinated with the FBI's Cartha "Deke" DeLoach to gather enough information to brief White House officials.[101] Wills also found enemies in two former PsW who were put off by his profiting from what they considered treasonous behavior. Although they did not know Wills personally, his hero's welcome angered them. Robert Stringer and Kenneth Eaton wrote a rebuttal to Wills's well-received *Look* articles, dismantling some of the more redemptive elements of his story.[102]

Wills's homecoming was filled with the same challenges that faced many of the other nonrepatriates. He returned to a nation that had changed dramatically during the fifteen years he had been gone. Although his father had maintained contact with him through letters and had provided his son magazines and books that were difficult to obtain in China, Morris's brothers and sisters refused to even mention him in conversation.[103] While some members of his family avoided him, others did not. Shortly after his return to New York, his father reported receiving a letter addressed to Morris from a former PW. The man wrote that Wills had been his best friend while a PW and that he had been a "source of strength when he was wounded and he expressed that he would have never survived the ordeal if it had not been for the subject [Wills]." When Morris read the letter, he immediately recognized the man and promised his father that he would write the fellow soon.[104] Curiously, while Wills was corresponding with his father, his father was keeping close contact with the FBI. While this seems duplicitous on the surface, it is likely that the senior Wills cooperated with the FBI in an attempt to be transparent about his son's intentions, perhaps even with Morris's blessing.[105]

In 1966, Morris and his family moved to Boston, where he went to work as a research assistant at Harvard University's East Asian Institute. Working closely with John King Fairbank, Frank Friedel, Oscar Handlin, Ernest May, and Ezra Vogel, Wills put his knowledge of China to good use in the academy. His experience was a valuable commodity, particularly in an era when little information escaped Mao's China. For a year, he worked under Vogel on a paper about Beijing University and gave the scholars at Harvard valuable information about life behind the Bamboo Curtain. Vogel remembered Wills as a poor farm boy who probably received more opportunities in China than he would have in the United States.[106]

Wills advocated a stronger policy against China in a letter to Lyndon Johnson. In his letter to the President, he wrote, "your policy [in Vietnam] is a correct one as viewed from the interests of the United States and the free nations of Asia." He warned that a strong hand must be employed in dealing with

China as perseverance and a full-scale military commitment were the keys to victory in southeast Asia.[107]

While less willing than Wills to "act as a Roman" while in Rome, Clarence Adams still sought to put a positive face on his return to the United States. Seeking to have a law passed making Americans' cooperation with an avowed international enemy a crime, the House Un-American Activities Committee subpoenaed Adams, who spoke freely about his experiences in Korea and China. Speaking without an attorney, he discussed the broadcasts he had made directed toward black American soldiers in Vietnam and told the committee that the idea had been his and his alone. He had approached the National Liberation Front Office in Beijing and acted on his own, even so far as writing the text of the announcements. By the time Adams left Washington, he had impressed the legislators with his candor and knowledge.[108]

By the end of the 1960s, Richard Corden's life was falling apart. Upon moving to Milwaukee in 1960, he got a job at the Schroeder Hotel, where he remained for more than two years. Despite his recent history of steady work, Corden had developed a serious drinking problem and soon left his job and the city.[109] He landed in Chicago in May 1964, only days after leaving Milwaukee, and went to work in a factory that made automotive seatbelts. While remaining wedded to his alcohol addiction, he was made a foreman and "[tried] to do a good job and [was] successful in satisfying the needs of the company."[110] In February 1966, however, Corden's stable employment fell apart. He had gone into debt and when the creditor pursued garnishment of his wages, he flew into a rage and quit his job.[111]

The next years would not be kind to Corden. In late January 1967, a confidential informant reported to the FBI that the alcoholic Corden "appears to be deteriorating more rapidly in recent weeks" and described his drinking as "constant." The informant said that Corden had been trying to stop drinking, but was "obviously meeting with no success."[112] For the next several months, he worked in a variety of part-time jobs with little responsibility until he attacked his drinking again and went back to work full-time.[113]

In the summer of 1969, Corden was living with friends in a rough neighborhood in Chicago when he was accosted by a group of youths. In the fight, he was stabbed several times and his right arm was badly damaged. Reports note that he nearly bled to death after the attack and spent six weeks in the hospital. With his arm partially paralyzed, he began a rigorous schedule of physical therapy, but ultimately remained disabled by the injury.[114] In the coming years, Corden's lingering injury and escalating alcoholism turned him into a sad figure who was often described as "almost unable to walk." He had found a common-law wife who enjoyed drinking as much as he did and the couple lived off monthly welfare payments.[115] In November 1975, Corden wrote the FBI requesting copies of the information on him.[116] Richard Corden then faded from history.

In 1966, China's Cultural Revolution derailed James Veneris's educational plans by forcing the closure of universities and soon he was back at the factory. The combination of a university education and a factory setting mixed with the ongoing civil strife to make a combustible environment. Shortly thereafter, he "wrote a big-character poster criticizing one of the cadres for following the revisionist line of Liu Shao-chi," the former Chinese president. His political protest drew unwanted attention and Veneris cryptically explained the consequences as "[s]ome people tried to isolate me," but rumor placed him in prison for a time.[117]

Sidney Rittenberg remembered Veneris as the group's only true ideologue: "Among all of the ex-POWs, the outstanding thing about Jim was that he really, enthusiastically accepted the ideology, Mao Zedong thought, I would put him . . . in terms of Chinese politics . . . definitely on the left. I think he was very sincere." Rittenberg was not as confident about the commitment of some of the others. He said that Howard Adams was a "straight shooter . . . not terribly interested in politics" and noted that "he didn't talk an awful lot about ideological issues." Although he did not know Clarence Adams and Morris Wills very well, he did not recognize much dedication in them. Considering the two of them very friendly but lacking commitment, "I used to think to myself, 'goodness knows what they're really thinking.'" In retrospect, Rittenberg surmised, "[t]hey were sort of freeloading, they didn't have to work really, they had an easy time, they were treated as guests." Rittenberg saw race as the one thing that Clarence Adams truly cared about: "I couldn't see that they were serious about anything except Clarence Adams, being black, did seem to be interested, or seemed to appreciate, the fact that the Chinese were supporting the Black Nationalism at the time."[118] As far back as his time in Camp Five, Adams had been considered lackadaisical about communism. In an FBI interview, a former PW said that Adams often "did not appear too enthused to attend these lectures, in that he appeared to have a 'don't care' attitude and on occasions was late for meetings."[119] In Wills's case, Rittenberg may have been fundamentally correct. An unidentified former PW recalled that Wills was a squad leader and enjoyed the benefits of hanging out with the progressives, but "even though Wills did do the things I have said, I was always under the impression he was 'pulling the leg' of the Chinese Communists."[120] Synopsizing the interview responses of returning PsW, a federal attorney found that Wills was frequently described as "not as intent on influencing fellow POW's to cooperate with the Chinese as were other members of the Study Group" and that they had been surprised to learn that Wills had decided to remain behind rather than return home.[121]

Clarence Adams viewed the Rittenbergs, Epsteins, and Shapiros with the same kind of derision with which they viewed him and Morris Wills. Adams called them "200 percenters," meaning they "were foreigners who are going to stay there and doing 100 per cent to make them welcome is not enough for them. They go 200 percent." He chastised James Veneris for toeing the party line and hanging "around the ragged edge" of the group. In Adams's eyes, "they let him tag along with the group but never give him anything significant to do."[122]

After Clarence Adams returned to Memphis, he gave an extended interview to the FBI during which he spoke candidly about the two American soldiers who remained in China. He suggested that Howard Adams might be the next to come back. Clarence thought that Howard's wife had developed a "taste of affluence" and was pushing her husband to take the family to the United States. Clarence Adams saw two major obstacles to Howard's departure though: He was older than the rest of the men when they left and would have a difficult time finding work, and he had adopted a daughter through unorthodox channels that would require much legal wrangling to get her out of China. Of James Veneris, Clarence was less complimentary: "Veneris and I never set horses. . . . He is a crier and a whiner . . . a shifty guy who will always agree with everything you say whether he believes it or not." He did not expect that Veneris would leave China in the foreseeable future.[123]

After the death of his first wife in 1966, Veneris remarried. His new wife worked in the same paper factory as Veneris and was widowed. With her four children and the two others that she and James added after their marriage, their four-room apartment made for a bustling household. However, all was not happy and during the late 1970s, the marriage became strained and he was granted a rare state-sanctioned divorce.[124]

In 1976, James Veneris began making news in the United States. He had not left China since his arrival more than twenty years before, but he was ready to return home, if only temporarily. After asking the Department of State for permission to visit his family in the States, Veneris began making his travel plans. On July 31, Veneris arrived in California, where he planned to spend part of his five-and-a-half-month vacation. While in the United States, he spent time with his mother and siblings in Hawthorne, California, and returned to his childhood hometown of Vandergrift, Pennsylvania, where he hoped to reconnect with some of his old friends. He spent Christmas and New Year's Day in the United States and returned home to Jinan sometime in 1977.[125]

James Veneris and his wife pose with Louis Verdyck along with Howard Adams, his wife, and his stepdaughter. The two men flanking the group are Chinese communist officials. (CEGES-SOMA, Brussels, Belgium. All rights reserved.)

Upon Veneris's return to China, he disappeared from view for several years. However, in 1981, he resurfaced in a news story updating his life since his visit to America. After suffering from cataracts and having corrective surgery for them, he returned to his factory job in 1977, but broke his leg in a 1979 accident that ended his time on the factory floor. When he recovered from his injury, his eye problems returned and Veneris left his longtime vocation and took a position at Shantung University in Jinan, teaching English. He also got married for a third time, to a botany professor at Shantung University. Old friend Harold Gayle Adams was teaching at a nearby medical school.[126]

The most recent news story regarding the men was on the return of Harold Webb. Although he had gone to Poland in 1960, he returned to the United States for good in 1985. Upon his arrival, he went to Louisville, Kentucky, where he lived with relatives for a time. In an interview, he confessed that he had wanted to return to the United States immediately after he had made his decision to go to China, but waited more than thirty years to act on his urge. After arriving in the Soviet-bloc nation in 1960, Webb applied for Polish citizenship in order to protect himself and his family during troubling times, finally receiving it in 1970. When he returned to the United States in 1985, he sought to renew his U.S. citizenship, which the government considered to have been renounced when he accepted Polish citizenship. The Department of State finally relented and Webb brought his wife and daughters to the United States. He is now retired in the South and lives anonymously among his friends and neighbors.[127]

And thus ends the story, as far as it is known. As of 2007, Gayle Adams remains in Jinan, a retiree from the medical school where he taught for decades. In spring 2006, he left China for a vacation to California and Texas, where he reunited with old friends and family.[128] Unlike the outgoing James Veneris, who died in the early 2000s, he does not speak about the past.[129] Reportedly, John Dunn married a Czechoslovakian woman and emigrated to that nation sometime during the 1960s, where he completely dropped from view. Similarly, Albert Belhomme disappeared into Belgian society upon his return. Scott Rush has also retired and lives a quiet life in the Midwest.[130] Samuel Hawkins succeeded in bringing Tonya to Oklahoma. By 1959, he was working and attending night school in the hopes of gaining admission to the University of Oklahoma. His marriage fell apart, however, and Tanya and the children moved in with a sympathetic friend. After years of work, he became a physician's assistant.[131] In the early 2000s, he returned to China for a visit and participated in the documentary, *They Chose China*. During the filming, he revisited the factories in which he had worked, the university where he was schooled, and James Veneris's family and grave.[132] Aaron Wilson took a job as a heavy equipment operator after his return to the United States and was employed for a time in New Orleans.[133] He is now retired and living in the South. Claude Batchelor still lives in Texas, and like Gayle Adams, refuses to speak about his experiences.[134]

Most of the group are now dead. Ed Dickenson returned to the Virginia mountains after his release from Fort Leavenworth in 1957. Having been divorced by Kate Laney while in prison, he returned home and struck up a romance with a teenaged girl, Alice Begley, with whom he had several children and lived out the rest of his life.[135] Attempting to fulfill a promise he had made to himself shortly after his release from prison, in the early 1990s, he petitioned the Secretary of Defense to have his case retried in the hopes of receiving an honorable discharge. Although officials refused to take up the case again, they urged him to apply for a presidential pardon.[136] He refused to do so and lived a quiet life until he died in 2002; his obituary proudly acknowledged his service in Korea.[137]

Otho Bell returned to Washington state, where he finally met and reared his baby daughter. He spent several years working at a mushroom farm, then as a handyman in Olympia. He often ran afoul of the law, with most of his trouble traced to alcohol. Sometime before 1975, he and Jewell divorced and he got remarried to a registered nurse in Walla Walla, where he became active in the Seventh Day Adventist Church. It is unknown if either the marriage or the sobriety worked out for Otho. He died in 2001.[138] Like Otho Bell, Larance Sullivan developed a serious problem with alcohol when he returned to the United States. Over the course of the coming years, he was either self-committed or court ordered to mental health facilities several times until his death in 2001.[139]

William Cowart returned to his hometown in northern Georgia, where he lived out the remainder of his life. He died in Dalton, Georgia, in 1984.[140] Lewis Griggs entered Stephen F. Austin University and graduated with a degree in psychology in 1959. Upon his graduation, he returned to Neches, Texas, where he lived a simple lifestyle without a car or friends. Not having a job, he began raising chickens to provide himself with a little money. He died in 1984.[141]

The tumult surrounding Arlie Pate's return moderated somewhat in his later life. In the years immediately following his fight with his father and marriage to his first cousin, Pate attempted to settle down into a predictable pattern. He spent some time living in St. Louis, but occasionally took temporary jobs like cutting wood.[142] By 1958, his first marriage had ended in divorce and he had begun a new relationship.[143] The two were expecting a child.[144] Frustrated by his postwar life, Arlie began entertaining the idea of rejoining the army. He told FBI agents that he had "learned to hate Communism, and that it is his desire to get back into the armed services of the U.S. to prove his patriotism and loyalty."[145] Pate's life in Missouri stabilized for a time but debt was a constant problem for him, particularly that which he owed the U.S. State Department for his travel home. In 1965, Pate moved to Tucson, Arizona, with his wife, three children, and a brother-in-law.[146] Taking a job driving a truck locally, he and his family only stayed in Arizona over the summer. By October 1965, they were in back in Missouri and the next year he left his family to take a new job in Oklahoma, quickly returning to Missouri where he continued skipping from job to job.[147] With nothing working in his life, Pate left Missouri and, presumably, his family behind and returned to Arizona. By 1970, the FBI either lost interest in Pate or tired of following him across America. Three years later, he remarried in Las Vegas, Nevada. He died in Tucson on October 11, 1999.[148]

Lowell Skinner bounced around when he returned to the States, including stays in jail and in mental facilities. In the mid-1960s, he left northern Ohio and began using the alias of Larry David Sims to avoid the scrutiny his time in China brought. For a time, he lived in Cincinnati and worked in steel. It appeared that he would finally achieve some measure of stability until his alcohol abuse and FBI harassment undid his progress. He applied for a Federal Housing Administration loan, but the FBI was watching "to determine whether possible FHA violation occurs." Skinner did violate the terms of the loan when he applied under his alias and the agency rejected his application. The FBI sought prosecution of Skinner because of his use of the alias, but the United States Attorney's office declined to pursue the charge. Shortly afterward, he moved to Phoenix, where he remained under FBI surveillance, and later to San Bernadino, California. He died in 1995.[149]

Richard Tenneson, who was one of the first to return, had a very difficult transition. One man who worked with Tenneson described him as "a confused, unsettled, individual" who had been "unable to establish for himself a place" in his hometown upon his return.[150] A newspaper editor who employed Tenneson as a proofreader said, "he seemed like a confused individual who was attempting to work himself out of a fog."[151] After returning home in late 1955, Tenneson worked a variety of jobs in and around his hometown of Alden, Minnesota, with a brief hiatus in the summer of 1956 when he went to Hampton, Iowa, to work for three months before returning to Alden.[152] He tried to join local society and became active in the Hopkins, Minnesota, Junior Chamber of Commerce, but his reputation limited the amount of trust people were willing to place in him. By 1957, Tenneson was shopping a manuscript through a literary agent in New York City.[153] By the late 1960s, Tenneson had moved to Massachusetts and embarked on a career in film. Working behind the scenes, he served as a production assistant on the film version of Arlo Guthrie's *Alice's Restaurant* and later with the Berkshire Theater Festival.[154] Tenneson finally settled into life as a dealer at a casino in West Wendover, Nevada, just across the state line from his home in Wendover, Utah. He died in 2001.[155]

Morris Wills rejoined American society with considerable success. Upon his return, he took a job in Harvard University's East Asian Reading Room and later graduated from Columbia University with a Master's in Library Science. He spent the next twenty-five years as the Cataloguing Librarian at Utica College, periodically teaching Chinese language courses at area colleges and universities. Always curious, Wills continued to seek out adventure and was a frequent international traveler. He died in 1999.[156]

Of all those who returned and whose stories are known, Clarence Adams enjoyed the most success. A spitfire who could have likely done anything he put his mind to, he and his wife struggled for their first few years back in the United

States. He drove a truck, sold insurance, and worked at whatever he found until they saved enough money to open a Chinese restaurant. Within a few years, the Adams's owned a chain of eight Chop Suey houses scattered throughout Memphis, Tennessee. By the time of his death in 1999, they still owned one of the restaurants, which remains open on Elvis Presley Boulevard.[157]

Rufus Elbert Douglas's body still lies in a common grave near Taiyuan.[158]

Either seeking anonymity or personally lost, some of the men disappeared after their return; a few later resurfaced. William White, who took his college degree back to the United States and reportedly worked for a time on a farm in upstate New York, remains lost. In Spring 1966, Stephen Jacoby purchased an estate in South Kortright, New York, with the intention of building a nondenominational, coeducational school. Naming it John Brown College, after the famous abolitionist, Jacoby appointed White to head the language department. Although plans were underway to accept the first students in the Fall, the college failed and White and his family dropped from sight completely.[159]

TWELVE

Lessons, Learned and Ignored

> "The Government may have me up on something before this is through. . . . We all probably did something wrong at some time while we were over there."
>
> —Former PW John R. Worley

> "In making my most difficult decision to seek the 'only way out,' my primary consideration was that I would be of greater value to my country in exposing this hideous means of slanderous propaganda than I would be by sacrificing my life.
>
> —Colonel Frank Schwable, U.S.M.C.

Fundamentally, the question that remains is one of loyalty, but this cuts both ways. While the men who were PsW had a responsibility to their nation and their service, they also had a responsibility to themselves. Similarly, their nation and their military also had a responsibility to stand by, protect, and defend those who served under their auspices. Clearly, both entities failed each other, and in the end, failed themselves.

Winning Hearts and Minds in History

Historically, reeducation has been an important element in the reconciliation of nations and peoples after civil wars. In almost every intra-national conflict, the victors are met with the formidable postwar problem of bringing their former enemies around to an accepted way of thinking. In international conflicts, however, combatants are "foreigners" and "outsiders" not to be accepted, and presumably, not morally, socially, or politically equipped to join the society of the other. In the ancient world, Rome invented the tactic that would later become brainwashing through its dealings with the Latin League. After Rome's policy of forced inclusion through territorial expansion, most attempts at "winning the hearts and minds" of the vanquished came as a result of religious wars. Obviously, such conflicts lend themselves to conversion of the former enemy, indeed, the Christian tradition of forgiveness essentially dictates that the militarily defeated be offered salvation by the victor and suggests that the victors have a moral responsibility to save the soul of the men whom they had previously tried to kill. Wars of religion notwithstanding, the history of international warfare shows only isolated incidents of what became known as "brainwashing."

World War II provides the modern foundation of reeducation. Unlike the Axis powers, who held prisoners without any intention of indoctrination, the Allies, particularly the United States and the Soviet Union, sought to replace the fascism that had permeated German thought during the prewar years with their own respective political philosophies.[1] The United States brought more than 430,000 German, Italian, and Japanese prisoners of war over to live out the duration of the war. Once transferred to prison camps scattered throughout the United States, these prisoners began the reeducation process. Like the so-called brainwashing of American PsW in Korea, the indoctrination of German PsW during World War II was considered sufficiently controversial that an internal memo was produced that warned staff not to use the words "reeducation" or "reorientation," but instead call the plan the "'I.D. Program' (Intellectual Diversion)." Regardless of what the process was called, it qualified as reeducation, reorientation, and brainwashing. The Germans lived a relatively comfortable existence alternating between working for pay and attending classes on American history, civics, and a variety of other topics. The University of Kansas even accredited the coursework at Camp Concordia and as the prisoners were preparing to return home, the university presented those whose academic records warranted it with a wax-sealed academic certificate.[2] Although Americans decried the Chinese efforts to indoctrinate prisoners to communism, the U.S. Army had created the modern means and justification for such indoctrination only a decade before.

Preparing Soldiers for Possible Captivity

In the summer of 1949, the Third Geneva Convention met and announced the drafting of a document outlining the rules regarding capture and treatment of prisoners of war. However well intentioned the resulting rules were, they also suggested to potential prisoners of war that they were assured of fair and generous treatment. In reality, such treatment is likely impractical and expectations that wartime captivity would be governed by such rules unrealistic. Only a year later, the regulations were put to the test in Korea. With Chinese intervention in November 1950, thousands of UN soldiers were quickly taken prisoner, most of whom had a vague expectation that they would be treated humanely. They would be sorely disappointed. By 1954, the war in Korea was over and Americans were coming to grips with the great failings of hundreds, if not thousands, of soldiers who had been prisoners of the Chinese. Some, like Dickenson and Batchelor, were punished. Others, like the dozens of Air Force officers who had collaborated with the enemy, including Lt. John Quinn, who had been an internationally known spokesman for the fictional U.S. Air Force bacteriological warfare program, were forgiven by their branch of service. But the problem was apparent to officials in Washington, D.C.: The American soldier had to be properly trained to deal with the possibility of capture and deprivation.

President Dwight Eisenhower understood the problem better than most. He convened a board to develop a policy on the behavior of American prisoners of war. Throughout the Korean War, the only instruction given to American soldiers came from the Third Geneva Convention, which required prisoners of war to provide only their name, rank, service number, and unit information. Eisenhower's commission would spend the early part of 1955 crafting a more specific set of standards. In August, their work was complete and Eisenhower announced the new military Code of Conduct. On the little cards that were distributed to all servicemen, it read:

> I
> I am an American fighting man.
> I serve in the forces which guard my country and our way of life.
> I am prepared to give my life in their defense.
>
> II
> I will never surrender of my own free will.
> If in command I will never surrender my men while they still have the means to resist.
>
> III
> If I am captured I will continue to resist by all means available.
> I will make every effort to escape and aid others to escape.
> I will accept neither parole nor special favors from the enemy.

IV

If I become a prisoner of war, I will keep faith with my fellow prisoners.
I will give no information or take part in any action which might be harmful to my comrades.
If I am senior, I will take command. If not I will obey the lawful orders of those appointed over me and will back them up in every way.

V

When questioned, should I become a prisoner of war,
I am required to give name, rank, service number, and date of birth.
I will evade answering further questions to the utmost of my ability.
I will make no written statements disloyal to my country and its allies or harmful to their cause.

VI

I will never forget that I am an American fighting man, responsible for my actions, and dedicated to the principles which made my country free.
I will trust in my God and in the United States of America.[3]

Although the adoption of the code signaled a newly recognized responsibility on behalf of the nation to its men in uniform, its mere existence suggested a failing on the part of the nation in preparing its fighting men for the rigors of captivity. The failure of the United States military to train these men for possible imprisonment is indicative of the larger problem of the day: As Ben Shephard wrote, "Washington sent to Korea 'one of the least professional, least motivated armies America had ever put into the field."[4]

The Officers and the Enlisted

The fundamental problem for both Dickenson and Batchelor was voiced by William George Richards, a Texas attorney who wrote then-Senator Lyndon Johnson, "During my four years of service, I heard a great deal about the type of military 'justice' handed out to enlisted men." Richards's concerns cut to the core of the collaboration issue that damned both Dickenson and Batchelor. The segregation of military society places commissioned officers in positions of influence and power, but generally holds enlisted men to a higher standard of behavior. In his letter, Richards offered several affirming examples of what he sarcastically called "military justice."[5] Although such stories dot the memories of enlisted veterans nationwide, the military did nothing to show any sense of fairness in this regard. Marine Col. Frank Schwable confessed to helping administer a high-level program that used bacteriological bombs on Korean civilians but was allowed to continue his career and retired a brigadier general.[6] Army Brig. Gen. William Dean violated the ironclad nonintercourse rule by being photographed playing chess with his Chinese captors, reportedly drinking with them on occasion, and writing his fellow army commanders letters with strategic advice at the urging of the Chinese. Upon his release, he returned home a hero and retired a major general.[7]

The officer corps stuck together, even across services. In a widely read article, Lt. Col. Thomas Harrison strongly defended the discipline and ethics of the officer corps while identifying enlisted men as easily duped Progressives. To be sure, many enlisted men did collaborate and earned an "extra ration of rice if they would defuse some unexploded bombs" or read some Marx or Lenin because "It will get you a lot better chow than the garbage you've been eating." While countless similar instances existed, Harrison held his fellow officers to a much lower moral and ethical standard. In discussing officers who confessed, Harrison explained that they "should not, under any circumstances, be placed in the same classification as 'Progressives' who turned to the enemy of their own free will." As officers and enlisted men were held together and not segregated from one another, how would free will affect only one segment of the population? He claimed that Air Force officers should be excused from their disloyalty because they had been "given a fearful choice—Confess or die!" No evidence suggests that officers and enlisted men were given different types of punishment based upon rank. If one was threatened with death if he did not confess, were they not all threatened with death by starvation and neglect throughout their imprisonment? Were those enlisted men not gaining additional food in order to survive in the same way the Air Force pilots were signing false germ warfare confessions? For Harrison, the key to resisting indoctrination was to be "older, better educated and strongly religious . . . [with] a background of happy family life" . . . qualifications more frequently found amid the white middle class from which military officers have traditionally been chosen.[8]

Homer Parks of Kerrville, Texas, spoke to the same problem when he reminded Senator Johnson that Batchelor was "a boy that was not yet through high school" when he enlisted "when the army brass stayed at home and some of them have partly accepted communism themselves." In Parks's estimation, the officers who wavered in the prison camps were being protected by their fellows "so they can get a big pension when they retire."[9] V. J. Holmes echoed the same sentiment: "Cpl Dickenson and Claude Batchelor may have been guilty as charged, but if so, then the U.S. Army does not even conform in the severity of sentence with the U.S. Marines and the Air Force. Should any branch of the service have a special justice of their own? I say no! Was Gen. [William] Dean's rank what protected him from receiving similar treatment? Is the U.S. Army afraid to charge him? I think that possibly this is a very grave matter as serious as the question of firing Gen. MacArthur was. . . ."[10] Raymond Lech agreed with the premise that a standardized policy among all the branches would have prevented these disparities of justice.[11] Another noted, "Claude Batchelor probably did no more than the Lt. Colonel from Wisconsin [Schwable], whom the army gave the well-known slap on the wrist."[12] Yet a third wrote, "As a former soldier I am well aware of army methods . . . of 'white washing' officers and condemning enlisted personell [*sic*]."[13] Robert Alferi of Kingsville, Texas, described the duty of lower-ranking men as "[b]eing the apparent scapegoat for the higher echelons" and noted that it served as "the supreme example of the expendability of the U.S. enlisted GI."[14]

Without doubt, military rank played a major role in saving some former PsW from penalty and dooming others. An editorial in the *Christian Century,* the "Quality of Mercy is Strained by Rank," succinctly argued this point. Comparing the crimes of Cpl. Edward Dickenson and Col. Frank Schwable, the article concluded that the differences in treatment that the two men endured should not have "made the difference between ten years in prison and none."[15] To further illustrate the difference that rank made, only two weeks after Dickenson had been placed under arrest in his hospital room, the Air Force cleared sixty-nine officers suspected of collaborating with the enemy. The fourteen that remained on the Air Force list were identified as warranting further investigation, resulting in six of the men requesting and immediately receiving honorable discharges. The final eight reported to Scott Field, Illinois, where they were given the chance to convince a board of five generals that they could show that "they could still effectively serve their country in the USAF." Raymond Lech notes that "[t]he worst that happened to any of them was receiving honorable discharges and having to find a new line of work."[16]

In all, fourteen men stood trial for collaboration. Of this number, nine were enlisted and five were officers. Eight of the nine enlisted men were convicted and received sentences ranging from two years to life imprisonment. Five officers stood trial and three were convicted. Major Ronald Alley received a ten-year sentence at hard labor. Alley considered his harsh sentence at least partially the result of his being a reserve officer and not a West Pointer like the other two convicted officers. The other officers received much lighter sentences than any of the enlisted men or Alley. One was drummed out of the service, while the other was reprimanded with no possibility of promotion for two years. While Eugene Kinkead was writing *In Every War But One,* he met with Lt. Col. Charles Trammell and asked about the disparity between rank and punishment. Trammell pointed out that a military court considered crimes against other prisoners to be more serious than collaborating with the enemy and that the enlisted men were exclusively responsible for the most serious crimes.[17]

The Chinese astutely separated officers from enlisted men thereby destroying any hope of the prisoners maintaining military order and discipline. With the ranks separated, the enlisted camp imploded into chaos because the army never prepared its enlisted men to retain their military discipline and demeanor while prisoners of war. Claude Batchelor noted the influence of officers who sanctioned cooperation with the Chinese when he wrote: "After we heard this plea from the officers . . . we felt that if it was approved by our former officers, it was perfectly allright [*sic*] for the enlisted men to go ahead with the committees. These officers told the enlisted men that the United States wanted peace, and that they, the officers, saw no harm in forming the committees. In my opinion, this was the real start of the peace committee movement. Frankly, I don't think they would have started if the officers had not urged that they be formed."[18] Just as the men in the enlisted ranks failed themselves, the officer corps failed both themselves and the enlisted men with whose security they were entrusted. The army failed them all.

Collaboration as a Way to Help Others

The theory that some prisoners collaborated with their captors in order to save the lives of their fellow prisoners first appeared in Claude Batchelor's court martial. Batchelor defended his collaboration with the Chinese by claiming that he cooperated not to gain favor for himself, but to help the men in his squad. Two defense witnesses testified to this effect, with Robert Vincent reminding the court that Batchelor had been elected by the squad to represent them and that in one specific case, he had used his influence with the captors to get one of the men placed on a special diet, which saved him from starvation.[19] John Owens recalled how the squalid conditions of the camp fomented disease and that, he, along with others, had elected Batchelor to help get the filth cleaned up. Owens testified that Batchelor was popular within his squad and apparently acted unselfishly.[20]

Even after Batchelor's humanitarian argument failed, Lt. Cols. Harry Fleming and Paul Liles tried it. As officers, they claimed to have been attempting to restore order to the chaos of the prison camp. Theorizing that discipline would restore self-interested individuals as members of their military society, Liles and Fleming both compromised with their captors in an effort to gain access and influence with the men. Fleming was overwhelmingly elected to represent the officer corps at Valley Camp and used that position to visit the enlisted compound. Over the course of the coming months, Fleming instituted a very strict sanitation regimen and an equally strict disciplinary code. Raymond Lech wrote that "when Fleming caught them defecating anywhere else in the compound he forced them to clean up their mess—and he didn't care how they did that." Most of the men living in those camps, however, did not respect any authority, and soon Fleming was hated by many of his fellow prisoners. Despite his efforts, Fleming was fighting a losing battle. As a powerless man caught between those whom he was supposed to lead and those who held his survival in their hands, he soon realized that the men who resented him were lodging complaints with the prison administrators and undermining everything he was hoping to accomplish. By February 1951, the rumor and innuendo had grown to such a degree that an "anti-Fleming" group had developed and began to seriously undermine the colonel's credibility among the men.[21]

Despite Fleming's efforts to improve the cohesiveness of the men, his 1954 court martial resulted in his conviction as a collaborator and his dismissal from the army.[22] Similarly, Liles was convicted and given a two-year suspension in rank and a terse reprimand.[23] Regardless of the intensity of the reprimand, suspended promotions, or even outright dismissal, Fleming and Liles, both commissioned officers, did not go to prison. Echoing a previous point, those sentences were reserved for the lowest level of military man, one who possessed no important information, was least trained to resist captivity, and ultimately, held to a much higher standard than his own commanders.

During the FBI's attempts to build a case against the nonrepatriates, the Bureau interviewed hundreds of former PsW. Michael Cornwell remembered that Richard Corden, his squad leader, used his position on behalf of the men under him. Describing Corden as "a super-intelligent person . . . an absolute intellectual," he noted, "Corden could get more out [of] the Chinese than any of us because he could be so diplomatic."[24] Clarence Adams told a similar story: "I sensed that if conditions were to improve we were going to have to cooperate with the Chinese. They kept telling us that we ought to cooperate . . . after thinking about it for some time, I took it upon myself to cooperate." Adams contended that his cooperation had nothing to do with selfish motives: "it was not a matter of personal gain. The Chinese didn't have a damn thing to give you." He contended that he "cooperated with them for the good of everybody" and insisted that he never "ratted or squealed on any of my fellow soldiers."[25] Similarly, Bob Price told CIC interrogators that Albert Belhomme "acted as speaker for the men when they thought they needed something bad enough."[26] When questioned about the behavior and motives of Lowell Skinner while imprisoned, an unidentified veteran stated that "SKINNER and the other nonrepatriates . . . were all primarily interested in the welfare of the other prisoners of war (POW's) and themselves and that what they did they did in an effort to improve conditions in the camp." His sympathetic depiction of the entire group does note that in Camp Five, where much of the collaboration occurred, there was a significantly higher living standard than in many of the other camps. He "felt SKINNER and other POWs were chosen by the communists to cooperate with them and that they individually had no other choice but to cooperate." The investigating officer closed the statement by noting that the man felt "that he would make a better witness for the defense than for the prosecution."[27]

Historically, the experiences of slaves can illustrate the philosophical challenges surrounding the concept of collaboration. In writing of Gabriel's Rebellion, James Sidbury pointed out that "[s]cholars have generally analyzed informers through moral categorization" because "[s]uch moral categorization creates comfort, neatly classifying those who lived in Gabriel's world according to modern observers' sympathies." Although focusing on early nineteenth-century slavery, Sidbury illustrates the historical relevance of his idea: "This comfort is purchased, however, at a cost that few stop to acknowledge. Ascribing betrayal to simple cowardice and venality—to bad personal qualities—allows historians to sidestep" the reasons underlying the controversial behavior.[28] In Gabriel's case, the slave was correct in using violence to right a moral wrong. The same would have been considered proper if American prisoners had violently risen up against their captors in an effort to regain their freedom. Indeed, the later decisions of the U.S. Army, and to some degree American public opinion, demanded such aggressive action be a main line of defense against wartime captivity.

Sidbury also speaks to the realities of the powerlessness of individuals in captivity: "Slaves' lives consisted of endless compromises with the master class, and it is hardly surprising that such compromises also characterized attempts to build an oppositional movement." He continues, "Such compromises need not indicate sympathy with the status quo. One survival lesson that members of subordinate groups learn in oppressive societies is how and when to cut their losses and settle for partial victories." Sidbury surmises that because several black informants revealed the details of Gabriel's plan, many other black men and women lost their lives.[29] The easy criticism of this comparison is that the two instances are not comparable. On a philosophical level, however, they are perfectly matched for an examination of the power of individual moral values juxtaposed against society's contemporary sentiments.

The experience of being unfree, whether enslaved or held as a prisoner of war, is philosophically unifying. Eugene Genovese adds to this line of argument when he suggests that collaboration is not the result of "moral degeneracy," but the product of measured reality. A man in this condition truly understands the tenuous nature of his existence and is perhaps closer to death than ever before. His acceptance of his captor's point of view and his own powerlessness is therefore a strength rather than a weakness. He will not be free to make a difficult decision about his condition until "the cost of collaboration rises to the level of the cost of rebellion. For only then will people be free to choose sides on grounds of duty."[30]

In the twenty-first-century business world, this idea of "coercive persuasion" has spawned "Change Management Theory." This concept was pioneered by Kurt Lewin of the Massachusetts Institute of Technology, whose work influenced psychologist Edgar Schein, who based a significant portion of his professional work in the field of organizational management on studies of American PsW in Korea and the conditions in which they were held.[31] In the end, Chinese methods of torturing American PsW have informed new trends in the free market through the works of Lewin, Schein, and others who study organizational behavior.

Men as Bait

One of the most controversial aspects of this tragic episode is the possibility that the United States used the early repatriates as bait to lure the other men back home where punishment awaited them. When Ed Dickinson returned home, he was photographed with nice cars and pretty girls. Nowhere was there even a suggestion that he might come under scrutiny. On November 4, the *Korean Republic* included a story that stated that the men who remained behind did so out of fear that they would "be prosecuted for articles they wrote and broadcasts they made during up to three years of captivity."[32] A much more skeptical Claude Batchelor accepted repatriation seemingly expecting to be arrested at any time, but hoping his cooperation might save him in the end. However, while the Chinese were accepting the remaining twenty-one PsW, Dickenson was placed under arrest. Batchelor was arrested a few weeks later.

With the arrests and charges against these two men, whom the U.S. Army had enticed home with seeming sincerity, came a flurry of complaints from private citizens who saw it as an official "railroading" of the already tortured former PsW. Mrs. Edward Frazier wrote to Senator Lyndon Johnson complaining about exploiting family members: "I specifically wish to protest the Army's use of the nonrepatriates' families to attempt to persuade the boys to 'return to freedom.' Their mothers little expected that the Army intended to prosecute while deliberately creating the opposite impression in the public mind. Never once did anyone think that these boys were to be used for intelligence purposes and then promptly imprisoned."[33] Another wrote Johnson, "those boys were told that if they were to come back, they would not be punished. I heard these promises being made to them direct by radio."[34] Major Edward Moorer, who made many of the army's announcements over the loudspeakers near the neutral camp, addressed this issue in his final broadcast. He reminded the men that "Dickenson returned home to his loved ones and enjoyed a combination 30-day leave and honeymoon" and offered that "This fact explodes Communist charges that you and your family will be harmed if you return. I assure you that nothing will happen to your family at the hands of the United States government regardless of your decision."[35] Despite Moorer's assurances, he skirted the issue of whether or not the men would be punished; he only assured the men that the government would not harass their families. The U.S. Army always denied that it had promised amnesty to any of the nonrepatriates, and in a purely legal sense, the army did not renege. The denials may be considered accurate if the men were told that they would not be prosecuted for remaining behind, but ultimately they were prosecuted for their behavior while prisoners.

Raymond Lech examined this concern extensively. He found that the army had allowed the men to believe that they would not be prosecuted for any crimes if they returned. However, it simply intended to absolve the men from the responsibility of remaining with the enemy after the conclusion of Operation Big Switch, not from crimes committed while PsW. He illustrated the level of official deception by quoting Moorer, whose broadcasts avoided directly addressing the issue of immunity to prosecution. Army broadcasts bear out allegations that immunity, as far as could be reasonably understood by men as educated as those who remained behind, was promised to the men.

The Role of the Army-McCarthy Hearings

Perhaps the most obvious element tying the case of these twenty-three PsW to the broader anti-communism movement in the United States is the timing of the Army-McCarthy hearings. As thousands of fighting men languished in Chinese PW camps, one of America's most important political transitions occurred back home. With the rise of Joe McCarthy and his anti-communist crusade, the political climate within the United States became much more stringent and unforgiving than anything those men could remember.[36]

In the midst of the nonrepatriation crisis, McCarthy was preparing for a fight with the U.S. Army. If there was one personal thing that Roy Cohn, McCarthy's chief counsel, was interested in at this time it was a young man named David Schine. Having caught Cohn's eye, Schine was given a consultant position on McCarthy's staff as a way to keep him close to the gay, but closeted, Cohn. When Schine was drafted in late 1953, Cohn began frenetically lobbying army officials to allow his young interest to remain on McCarthy's staff. Finding no cooperation within the army's bureaucracy, Cohn then asked McCarthy to intercede, which spurred the now famous showdown. If the army would not release this young man from his military commitment in order to remain part of the most effective anti-communism crusade in world history, perhaps the army itself was soft on communism. It was under this guise that Joe McCarthy altered the course of American history.[37]

After months of attempts by both Cohn and McCarthy, the duo was no closer to securing Schine's release than when they had begun. On March 11, 1954, while Edward Dickenson sat in jail at Fort Belvoir, Virginia, the war between McCarthy and the U.S. Army began. After a long day of questioning a poor black woman named Annie Lee Moss, who had recently lost her job as a result of McCarthy's allegations, the army released a report outlining forty-four instances, over the course of the preceding eight months, of McCarthy's and Cohn's attempts to improperly influence the Schine case. Having clearly crossed the line, the army girded itself for McCarthy's coming assault.[38]

On the morning of April 22, 1954, the Army-McCarthy hearings began in the Senate chamber, only three days after Edward Dickenson's court martial had been called to order at Fort McNair and one half-mile south of the Capitol. By the time McCarthy had been permanently subdued in mid-June, the convicted Dickenson was imprisoned for his crimes. It appears that while Joe McCarthy was attacking the army for being soft on communism, the army was attempting to show all those interested that it could be tough on communism. Unfortunately for Edward Dickenson, his court martial and conviction served as the army's gambit and it came in advance of McCarthy's public repudiation.[39]

The Credibility of Witnesses

One of the most controversial aspects of the Dickenson and Batchelor trials was the participation of Wilburn Watson, Bobby DeGraw, and Wesley Biers. All three initially refused repatriation and remained with the others until ordered out of the group. Once they returned to U.S. lines, the army had three guaranteed prosecution witnesses, if they were to avoid prosecution themselves. The three attempted to explain away their remaining behind with the Chinese by claiming that they planned to play along with their captors and lull them into complacency. All the while, they would be talking to the other prisoners trying to convince them to return home. If true, this plan would suggest a superhuman level of commitment to the anticommunist cause on the part of these men, who had been imprisoned for nearly three years, and who would nonetheless take it upon themselves to volunteer to remain behind, in a potentially life-threatening situation. While marginally plausible on the surface, one must wonder why the Chinese would allow these three men to remain with the others and refuse repatriation if the communists were not convinced of their sincerity.

Other questionable witnesses also testified. Corporal Harold Dunn was a wartime Progressive who became a staunch Reactionary once he got home. After testifying against Dickenson, Dunn sold an article, "I Was a Progressive POW in Korea," to *Pageant Magazine*. With a star prosecution witness publicly confessing his own shortcomings while a prisoner of war, the army gathered enough evidence to prosecute Dunn. It convicted him of collaboration and gave him a sentence of eight years at hard labor, but only after it used his testimony against Dickenson.[40]

Additionally, the credibility of the army investigators must also be examined. It is likely that Capt. Bert Cumby consciously avoided divulging that the army was collecting evidence from Edward Dickenson that might be used against him in the future. In his book on Maj. Ronald Alley, Don Snyder uncovered the fact that Lt. Col. Charles Trammell, the lead investigator of all the army's collaboration cases, "plugged (accusations) into reports wherever they could do the most damage to the POW," and that, "Trammell had a job to do. . . . The Army had decided to get the Korean War POWs, and the Army made it clear that the prosecutions had better end in convictions." Apparently, Trammell "was going around G-2 [Intelligence], doing things his own way," which resulted in his superiors launching a year-long investigation against him in 1955.[41]

Stockholm Syndrome

It is also necessary to examine a clinical reason behind the widespread cooperation of PsW during their captivity in North Korea. The Chinese use of indoctrination is reminiscent of Jaycee Dugard's kidnapping or Patty Hearst's involvement with the Symbionese Liberation Army. In those cases, the victims did not try to escape, either, because of fear, conditions, inculcated obedience, or a combination of factors.

From the first day of captivity, the Chinese made sure the Americans understood their level of seriousness. Along the march route, when a man fell, he was shot without hesitation. Once in camp, starvation, disease, and exposure killed even more of the men and left those who survived in a terrible, emaciated condition. Throughout it all, the Chinese did nothing to ease the situation. Although the prisoners did not know it, the Chinese barely had enough for their own survival, much less to provide for those under their charge, but the message of starvation and casual mistreatment was clearly received by the PsW, who could only see their own condition. As a result of the terrible conditions, prisoners began to learn, and the Chinese began to teach, that when supplies were limited, those who cooperated got preferential treatment.

Cooperation is one thing, but dependency is another. A certain number of prisoners became completely dependent on their captors. Apart from having to depend on the Chinese for food and medical treatment, they also suffered from a lack of information. For the three years that most of the men were prisoners, they were deprived of news by the Chinese, and what little they learned came from recent captives who generally brought the true, yet depressing news of a bogged down war replete with UN defeats. For most of the prisoners, the idea that the good guys would win the war was an unlikely proposition. With this realization, the prisoners wondered if they would ever return home. They knew that the Soviets had not yet returned German prisoners of war from World War II and had heard of the atrocities perpetrated by the Japanese upon the Chinese during the 1930s so their impression of the Asian way of war was overwhelmingly negative.

As a result of physical deprivations, mental torture, and omnipresent uncertainty, a sizable portion of the UN PW contingent cooperated with its captors. These men saw that their best chance for survival was to cooperate and bide their time until freed. Once the Chinese began procuring enough food for the prisoners, they started an indoctrination program that espoused utopian communism. Virtually all the prisoners were forced at one time or another to attend, but soon a small cadre of PsW began regularly meeting out of their sincere belief in the communist system or their wish to ingratiate themselves with their captors. In return for attendance, they earned small rewards such as extra rations, medicine when needed, and protection against Reactionary prisoners, if necessary. It was not long until many of these men had accepted enough from the Chinese to earn their alienation from only the most cooperative of PsW. Once a man crossed the Rubicon of disloyalty, there was only one way to live. Like Jaycee Dugard and Elizabeth Smart, many prisoners came to believe that the only way to survive was through cooperation and even that their captors were somehow on the side of right in this conflict.[42] Although most Americans had never heard of it, in January 1954, Stockholm Syndrome hit home.

Notes

Introduction

1. The abbreviations PW, for Prisoner of War, and PsW, for Prisoners of War, are used rather than the traditional POW and POWs. This is in keeping with Department of Defense usage.

2. Thomas D. Harrison, "Why Did Some GIs Turn Communist?" *Collier's,* Nov. 27, 1953, 25.

3. John W. Blassingame, *The Slave Community: Plantation Life in the Antebellum South* (New York, N.Y.: Oxford Univ. Press, 1972, reprint 1979), 284–322.

4. John Marks, *The Search for the "Manchurian Candidate": The CIA and Mind Control* (New York, N.Y.: Times Books, 1979), 126.

5. Marks, *"Manchurian Candidate,"* 125–26.

6. Virginia Pasley, *21 Stayed: The Story of the American GI's Who Chose Communist China—Who They Were and Why They Stayed* (New York, N.Y.: Farrar, Straus, and Cuhady, 1955); and Tape #118, *Firing Line* television program collection, Hoover Institute, Stanford University, Stanford, California; hereafter cited as Stanford-*Firing Line.*

7. Abbott Gleason, *Totalitarianism: The Inner History of the Cold War* (New York, N.Y.: Oxford Univ. Press, 1997), 101.

8. William Lindsay White, *The Captives of Korea: An Unofficial White Paper on the Treatment of War Prisoners* (Westport, Conn.: Greenwood Press, 1957).

9. Eugene Kinkead, *In Every War But One* (New York, N.Y.: W. W. Norton, 1959). Kinkead's book was also published in 1959 with the title *Why They Collaborated.* See also Clara Amelia Copa, "American Prisoner of War Behavior in the Korean War," M.A. thesis, Utah State University, 1970, 9–10.

10. Albert D. Biderman, *March to Calumny: The Story of American POWs in the Korean War* (New York, N.Y.: MacMillan, 1963).

11. Kinkead, *In Every War But One,* 25.

12. *The Manchurian Candidate,* movie poster, 1962.

13. Charles S. Young, "Missing Action: POW Films, Brainwashing, and the Korean War," in Lori Lyn Bogle, ed., *The Cold War,* vol. 5: *Cold War Culture and Society* (New York, N.Y.: Routledge, 2001), 195–96; Susan L. Carruthers, "*The Manchurian Candidate* (1962) and the Cold War Brainwashing Scare," *Historical Journal of Film, Radio, and Television* 18:1 (Mar. 1998), 75–76; and John Loken, *Oswald's Trigger Films: The Manchurian Candidate, We Were Strangers, Suddenly?* (Ann Arbor, Mich.: Falcon Books, 2000), 2–12.

14. Morris Wills and J. Robert Moskin, *Turncoat: An American's 12 Years in Communist China* (New York, N.Y.: Prentice-Hall, 1968).

15. William Adams, "Vietnam Screen Wars," in Nicolaus Mills, ed., *Culture in an Age of Money: The Legacy of the 1980s in America* (Chicago, Ill.: Ivan R. Dee, 1990), 156–74.

16. Raymond Lech, *Broken Soldiers* (Urbana: Univ. of Illinois Press, 2000), 3.

17. Lewis H. Carlson, *Remembered Prisoners of a Forgotten War: An Oral History of Korean War POWs* (New York, N.Y.: St. Martin's Press, 2002).

18. Lech, *Broken Soldiers,* 3.

19. Adam J. Zweiback, "The 21 'Turncoat G.I.s': The Political Culture of the Korean War," *The Historian* 60 (Winter 1998): 345–62.

20. Gary Harold Rice, "The Lost Sheep of the Korean War," Ph.D. diss., University of Texas at Austin, 1998.

21. Clarence Adams, *An American Dream: The Life of an African American Soldier and POW Who Spent Twelve Years in Communist China* (Amherst: Univ. of Massachusetts Press, 2007).

22. Elizabeth Lutes Hillman, *Defending America: Military Culture and the Cold War Court-Martial* (Princeton, N.J.: Princeton Univ. Press, 2005), 47–48, 54.

1. Beginnings and Backgrounds

1. Clarence Adams, *Clarence Adams and the American Dream: The Story of an African American Korean War Combat Soldier and POW Who Spent Twelve Years in Communist China* (original, unedited, manuscript version), 39.

2. Pasley, *21 Stayed,* 245–48. Most of the biographical information contained in this chapter is derived from Pasley. Where possible, however, it has been supplemented by newspaper and other reliable accounts.

3. Federal Bureau of Investigation Form FD-263, Dec. 28, 1956, pages 2, 10, Andrew Fortuna FBI File, United States Department of Justice, Washington, D.C., hereinafter cited as FBI-Fortuna. Various records state the subject's birth year as 1926 and 1927.

4. *Detroit News* (Mich.), Apr. 29, 1956.

5. Federal Bureau of Investigation Form FD-263, Dec. 28, 1956, pages 3, 4, FBI-Fortuna.

6. *Detroit News* (Mich.), Apr. 29, 1956.

7. Harold Lavine, "Twenty-One G.I.'s Who Chose Tyranny: Why They Left Us for Communism," *Commentary* (July 1954), 42–43.

8. Pasley, *21 Stayed,* 151–54; *Dallas Morning News* (Tex.), Sept. 23, 1953; July 13, 1966; "Case Histories of Those 21," *Newsweek,* Jan. 18, 1954, 56; and Summary of Information (Adams, Howard Gayle), NARAII-153-Summary.

9. Pasley, *21 Stayed,* 221–25; *Houston Chronicle* (Tex.), June 2, 1985; and "Case Histories of Those 21," *Newsweek,* Jan. 18, 1954, 54.

10. Edward Swanson Dickenson Statement, Nov. 6, 1953, 1 of 9, Edward S. Dickenson Court Martial Records, copy in the possession of Sheila Miyoshi Jager, Oberlin, Ohio. Hereinafter cited as Dickenson Court Martial; and Review of the Staff Judge Advocate, undated, 56, Dickenson Court Martial.

11. Pasley, *21 Stayed,* 29–30, and "Case Histories of Those 21," *Newsweek,* Jan. 18, 1954, 54–55.

12. Pasley, *21 Stayed,* 30–31.

13. Pasley, *21 Stayed,* 31–32; Special Agent Report, Oct. 2, 1956, 3–4, Richard Guy Corden FBI File, United States Department of Justice, Washington, D.C., hereinafter

cited as FBI-Corden; and Summary of Information (Corden, Richard Guy Joseph), NARAII-153-Summary.

14. Pasley, *21 Stayed,* 33–34; and Background Material on Non-Repatriated Prisoners, 3, NARAII-319(G-2)-Background Material.

15. Pasley, *21 Stayed,* 159–64; "Case Histories of Those 21," *Newsweek,* Jan. 18, 1954, 55; and Summary of Information (Douglas, Rufus E.), NARAII-153-Summary.

16. Claude Batchelor Social History, Jan. 22, 1954, Claude J. Batchelor Court Martial Records, copy in the possession of Sheila Miyoshi Jager, Oberlin, Ohio. Hereinafter cited as Batchelor Court Martial.

17. Claude Batchelor Social History, Jan. 22, 1954, Batchelor Court Martial.

18. Pasley, *21 Stayed,* 93–95; "Case Histories of Those 21," *Newsweek,* Jan. 18, 1954, 54; *Los Angeles Times,* Nov. 3, 1963; Summary of Information (Belhomme, Albert G.), NARAII-153-Summary; and *The Spokesman-Review* (Spokane, WA), Nov. 3, 1963.

19. Federal Bureau of Investigation Form No. 1, May 31, 1956, page 2, Otho G. Bell FBI File, United States Department of Justice, Washington, D.C., hereinafter cited as FBI-Bell. Interestingly, on his birth certificate, the child (Otho Bell) was identified by the attending physician as "still-born". The certificate would not be filled out for Bell until a school official did so when Bell was eight years old.

20. Pasley, *21 Stayed,* 81–86; Background Material on Non-Repatriated Prisoners, 3, NARAII-319(G-2)- Background Material; "Case Histories of Those 21," *Newsweek,* Jan. 18, 1954, 55; *The Clarion-Ledger* (Jackson, Miss.), Oct. 1, 1953; and Summary of Information (Bell, Otho G.), NARAII-153-Summary.

21. Pasley, *21 Stayed,* 141–42; and "Case Histories of Those 21," *Newsweek,* Jan. 18, 1954, 54.

22. Pasley, *21 Stayed,* 141–42; and "Case Histories of Those 21," *Newsweek,* Jan. 18, 1954, 54.

23. Pasley, *21 Stayed,* 144–46; "Case Histories of Those 21," *Newsweek,* Jan. 18, 1954, 54; and *Southern Illinoisan* (Carbondale, Ill.), Nov. 29, 1953; and Mar. 1953. Newspaper date undistinguishable.

24. Pasley, *21 Stayed,* 169–70.

25. Report Form, FD-263, May 21, 1956, FBI-Griggs.

26. Pasley, *21 Stayed,* 170–71; and "Case Histories of Those 21," *Newsweek,* Jan. 18, 1954, 55–56.

27. Pasley, *21 Stayed,* 43; and Summary of Information (Cowart, William A.), NARAII-153-Summary.

28. Pasley, *21 Stayed,* 45–46; and "Case Histories of Those 21," *Newsweek,* Jan. 18, 1954, 56.

29. Pasley, *21 Stayed,* 55–56.

30. Pasley, *21 Stayed,* 56–57; "Case Histories of Those 21," *Newsweek,* Jan. 18, 1954, 55; and Memorandum from SAC, Cleveland, July 17, 1956, p. 12, hand numbered, upper right, Lowell Skinner FBI File, United States Department of Justice, Washington, D.C., hereinafter cited as FBI-Skinner.

31. Pasley, *21 Stayed,* 75–76.

32. Summary of Information (Rush, Scot Leonard), NARAII-153-Summary.

33. Pasley, *21 Stayed,* 76–77; and "Case Histories of Those 21," *Newsweek,* Jan. 18, 1954, 55.

34. Pasley, *21 Stayed,* 125–27; and "Case Histories of Those 21," *Newsweek,* Jan. 18, 1954, 55.

35. Pasley, *21 Stayed,* 111–13; and "Case Histories of Those 21," *Newsweek,* Jan. 18, 1954, 56.

36. Pasley, *21 Stayed,* 119–22; and "Case Histories of Those 21," *Newsweek,* Jan. 18, 1954, 57.

37. While Adams was living in China, his home became Memphis's best New Orleans–style French restaurant, Justine's. It would remain the preferred gastronomic destination of Memphians for the next forty years.

38. Pasley, *21 Stayed,* 133–35; and Adams, *An American Dream,* 8–22.

39. Report Form, Aug. 9, 1956, pages 1–3, Larance V. Sullivan FBI File, United States Department of Justice, Washington, D.C., hereinafter cited as FBI-Sullivan; Pasley, *21 Stayed,* 63–69; and "Case Histories of Those 21," *Newsweek,* Jan. 18, 1954, 56.

40. Pasley, *21 Stayed,* 71, 134.

41. Pasley, *21 Stayed,* 188–90.

42. Pasley, *21 Stayed,* 190–93; "Case Histories of Those 21," *Newsweek,* Jan. 18, 1954, 56; and FBI Form No. 1, May 25, 1954, pages 1–3, Richard R. Tenneson FBI File, United States Department of Justice, Washington, D.C., hereinafter cited as FBI-Tenneson

43. Pasley, *21 Stayed,* 192–93.

44. Pasley, *21 Stayed,* 99–102; and "Case Histories of Those 21," *Newsweek,* Jan. 18, 1954, 54.

45. Pasley, *21 Stayed,* 102–4; and "Case Histories of Those 21," *Newsweek,* Jan. 18, 1954, 54.

46. Pasley, *21 Stayed,* 178; and Morris R. Wills, *Turncoat: An American's 12 Years in Communist China* (New York, N.Y.: Prentice-Hall, Inc., 1968), 21–22.

47. Wills, *Turncoat,* 23–25; and "Case Histories of Those 21," *Newsweek,* Jan. 18, 1954, 57.

48. Clay Blair, *The Forgotten War: America in Korea, 1950–1953* (Annapolis, Md.: Naval Institute Press, 1987), 7–8.

49. Pasley, *21 Stayed,* 200–201; "Case Histories of Those 21," *Newsweek,* Jan. 18, 1954, 55; and *Baltimore Sun* (Md.), June 6, 1954.

50. Pasley, *21 Stayed,* 201–2.

51. Pasley, *21 Stayed,* 203; and *Baltimore Sun* (Md.), June 6, 1954.

2. *The Short Careers of Soldiers*

1. Special Agent Report, June 8, 1965, 13, 25, FBI-Skinner.

2. Special Agent Report, June 8, 1965, 14, 25, FBI-Skinner.

3. *Bristol Herald Courier* (Tenn.), Nov. 22, 1953; James L. Stokesbury, *A Short History of the Korean War* (New York, N.Y.: William Morrow, 1988), 66–75; and Pasley, *21 Stayed,* 59.

4. Review of the Staff Judge Advocate, undated, 56, Dickenson Court Martial.

5. *The Post* (Big Stone Gap, Va.), Nov. 5, 1953.

6. Ibid.

7. Cpl. Edward S. Dickenson, USA, Transcripts, 4:215, in Raymond B. Lech, *Broken Soldiers* (Urbana: Univ. of Illinois Press, 2000), 36–37.

8. Lech, *Broken Soldiers,* 39–41; and Review of the Staff Judge Advocate, undated, 23, Dickenson Court Martial.

9. Prosecution Exhibit #4, undated, 1, Batchelor Court Martial.

10. Prosecution Exhibit #4, undated, 1, Batchelor Court Martial; and Claude Batchelor Military History, Jan. 22, 1954, 4, Batchelor Court Martial.

11. Claude Batchelor Military History, Jan. 22, 1954, 4, Batchelor Court Martial.

12. Prosecution Exhibit #4, undated, 1, Batchelor Court Martial.

13. Prosecution Exhibit #4, undated, 1–2, Batchelor Court Martial.

14. Prosecution Exhibit #4, undated, 2, Batchelor Court Martial; and Edward Hunter, *Brainwashing: The Story of Men Who Defied It* (New York, N.Y.: Farrar, Straus and Cuhady, 1956), 216–17.
15. Prosecution Exhibit #4, undated, 2, Batchelor Court Martial.
16. Prosecution Exhibit #4, undated, 2, Batchelor Court Martial.
17. Prosecution Exhibit #4, undated, 2, Batchelor Court Martial.
18. Adams, *An American Dream,* 20–22.
19. Adams, *An American Dream,* 23–31.
20. Adams, *An American Dream,* 30–34.
21. Adams, *An American Dream,* 35–36.
22. Adams, *An American Dream,* 36.
23. Adams, *An American Dream,* 36–37.
24. Adams, *An American Dream,* 37.
25. Adams, *An American Dream,* 37–38.
26. Adams, *An American Dream,* 40–46.
27. Transcript of Richard Corden interview on KPFA-FM, San Francisco, aired 9:45 P.M., Feb. 23, 1959, p. 4, FBI-Corden.
28. Corden interview, Feb. 23, 1959, pp. 4–5, FBI-Corden.
29. Corden interview, Feb. 23, 1959, pp. 6–7, FBI-Corden.
30. *The Spokesman-Review* (Spokane, WA), Nov. 3, 1963.
31. Wills, *Turncoat,* 26–28.
32. Wills, *Turncoat,* 28–30.
33. Wills, *Turncoat,* 30–31.
34. Wills, *Turncoat,* 31–33.
35. Wills, *Turncoat,* 33–34.
36. Wills, *Turncoat,* 34–35.
37. Wills, *Turncoat,* 36–37.
38. Wills, *Turncoat,* 36–37, 40.
39. Wills, *Turncoat,* 38–39.
40. Wills, *Turncoat,* 40–41, 49.
41. Wills, *Turncoat,* 42, 44.
42. Wills, *Turncoat,* 48–50.
43. Memorandum, SA (Classified) to SAC, Minneapolis, Apr. 21, 1958, pp. 2–3, FBI-Tenneson.
44. Memorandum, SA (Classified) to SAC, Minneapolis, Apr. 21, 1958, pp. 2–3, FBI-Tenneson.
45. *Baltimore Sun* (Md.), June 6, 1954.
46. *Houston Chronicle* (Tex.), June 2, 1985.
47. Director, FBI, to SAC, WFO, Oct. 5, 1956, p. 2, FBI-Fortuna; Memo, re: Andrew Fortuna, Aug. 28, 1964, p. 1, FBI-Fortuna; Andrew Fortuna, "I Never Skinnied . . . ," pp. 2–3, FBI-Fortuna; and Lavine, "Twenty-One G.I.'s Who Chose Tyranny," 43.
48. Pasley, *21 Stayed,* 211–13; Background Material on Non-Repatriated Prisoners, box 7, folder 1-A, Geog V Korea 386.6—Non-Repatriated POWs, U.S. Army Center of Military History, Department of the Army, Fort McNair, DC, Record Group 319, Records of the Army Staff, Records of the Assistant Chief of Staff for Intelligence (G-2), G-2 Decimal File, Textual Records, National Archives and Records Administration II, College Park, Maryland, hereinafter cited as NARAII-319(G-2)-Background Material; "Case Histories of Those 21: What Their Lives Show," *Newsweek,* Jan. 18, 1954, 52–53; Summary of Information (Fortuna, Andrew), box 1, volume 1, 1–108, RECAP-K Program, Records Pertaining to U.S. Army Personnel who Refused Repatriation in Korea ("Voluntary Non-Repatriates"), 1953–1957, Record Group 153, Office of the Judge Advocate General

(Army), Textual Records, National Archives and Records Administration II, College Park, Maryland, hereinafter cited as NARAII-153-Summary; Director, FBI, to SAC, WFO, Oct. 5, 1956, p. 2, FBI-Fortuna; and Memo, re: Andrew Fortuna, Aug. 28, 1964, pp. 3–4, FBI-Fortuna; and Lavine, "Twenty-One G.I.'s Who Chose Tyranny," 43.

3. Captivity and Compromise

1. J. A. C. Brown, *Techniques of Brainwashing: From Propaganda to Brainwashing* (Baltimore, Md.: Penguin Books, 1963), 256–57.

2. "U.S. Prisoners of War in the Korean Operation: A Study of Their Treatment and Handling by the North Korean Army and the Chinese Communist Forces" (Fort George G. Meade, Md.: Army Security Center, 1954, photocopied), 92–93, U.S. Army Center of Military History, Department of the Army, Fort McNair, DC, Record Group 330, Records of the Office of the Secretary of Defense, Records of the Defense Prisoner of War/Missing in Action Office, Copies of Records Relating to POW/MIAs, 1951–1958, Textual Records, National Archives and Records Administration II, College Park, Maryland, hereinafter cited as NARAII-330(POW/MIA)-POW Manuscript; and William Shadish with Lewis H. Carlson, *When Hell Froze Over: The Memoir of a Korean War Combat Physician who Spent 1010 Days in a Communist Prison Camp* (New York, N.Y.: iUniverse, 2007), 25–28.

3. "U.S. Prisoners of War in the Korean Operation," 92–93, 109, NARAII-330(POW/MIA)-POW Manuscript. To put the two-month 50–70 percent mortality rate into perspective, Raymond Lech notes that of the 7,190 American soldiers who became PsW, an estimated 3,000 (43 percent) died during captivity, mostly from starvation. In comparison, only 4 percent of Americans held by Italians and Germans during World War II and 34 percent of those taken by Japan met the same end. He notes, "The only theater of operations that came close to comparing with Korea was the Eastern Front during World War II. There, the German POW casualty rate under the Russians was 45 percent, and that for Russians under the Germans was 60 percent." In comparison, 32 percent of Union prisoners at Andersonville, Georgia, died and those Americans held during the 1960s and 1970s by the North Vietnamese died at a rate of 14 percent.

4. Lech, *Broken Soldiers,* 42–43.

5. "U.S. Prisoners of War in the Korean Operation," 93.

6. "U.S. Prisoners of War in the Korean Operation," 109, NARAII-330(POW/MIA)-POW Manuscript; and Lech, *Broken Soldiers,* 43–45.

7. "U.S. Prisoners of War in the Korean Operation," 93, NARAII-330(POW/MIA)-POW Manuscript.

8. "U.S. Prisoners of War in the Korean Operation," 93, NARAII-330(POW/MIA)-POW Manuscript; and Shadish and Carlson, *When Hell Froze Over,* 31–32.

9. Lech, *Broken Soldiers,* 39–40.

10. The supposition that Arlie Pate was held at Peaceful Valley is based upon the fact that the camp opened only days after Pate was captured and his transfer to a permanent camp coincided with the closure of Peaceful Valley.

11. "U.S. Prisoners of War in the Korean Operation," 93–94, NARAII-330(POW/MIA)-POW Manuscript; and Lech, *Broken Soldiers,* 86.

12. "U.S. Prisoners of War in the Korean Operation," 94–95, NARAII-330(POW/MIA)-POW Manuscript; and Lech, *Broken Soldiers,* 48–51.

13. Richard L. Walker, *China under Communism: The First Five Years* (New Haven, Conn.: Yale Univ. Press, 1955), 57–59, 70–71; and William Sargant, *Battle for the Mind* (Garden City, N.Y.: Doubleday, 1957), 167–68.

14. Debriefing of Morris R. Wills, Nov. 19, 1965, Department of State Airgram, p. 27, FBI-Wills.

15. "U.S. Prisoners of War in the Korean Operation," 95–97, NARAII-330(POW/MIA)-POW Manuscript.

16. "U.S. Prisoners of War in the Korean Operation," 95–97, NARAII-330(POW/MIA)-POW Manuscript.

17. Adams, *An American Dream,* 46.

18. Adams, *An American Dream,* 46–47.

19. David Rees, *Korea: The Limited War* (Baltimore, Md.: Penguin Books, 1964), 332–33.

20. Sworn Statement (classified), Apr. 21, 1956, Lewie W. Griggs documents, United States Army Intelligence and Security Command, Fort George Meade, Maryland; hereinafter cited as USAISC-Griggs.

21. Eugene Kinkead, *In Every War But One* (New York, N.Y.: W. W. Norton, 1959), 142–43.

22. "U.S. Prisoners of War in the Korean Operation," 391–92, NARAII-330(POW/MIA)-POW Manuscript.

23. Kinkead, *In Every War But One,* 143.

24. H. C. Gibson, et al., "Repatriated American POWs with Special Reference to Avitaminosis, Tuberculosis, and Intestinal Parasites," *Medical Bulletin of the United States Army Far East* (Aug. 1953), 154, 158, 159. Much of the medical information given was gleaned in conversations with Dr. Melanie Skeen, an internal medicine physician in Norton, Virginia.

25. Kathleen Taylor, *Brainwashing: The Science of Thought Control* (Oxford, UK: Oxford Univ. Press, 2004), 90–91.

26. Copa, "American Prisoner of War Behavior in the Korean War," 10.

27. "Why Did Many GI Captives Cave In? Interview with Major William E. Mayer," *U.S. News & World Report,* Feb. 24, 1956, 56.

28. Claude J. Batchelor Statement (voluntary, typewritten, double-spaced), 9, Batchelor Court Martial.

29. Adams, *An American Dream,* 49.

30. Adams, *An American Dream,* 50.

31. Shadish and Carlson, *When Hell Froze Over,* 33.

32. Adams, *An American Dream,* 50.

33. Robert J. Berens, *Limbo on the Yalu . . . and Beyond* (St. Petersburg, Fla.: Southern Heritage Press, 2000), 55.

34. Quoted from Robert J. Lifton, "Home By Ship: Reaction Patterns of American Prisoners of War Repatriated from North Korea," *American Journal of Psychiatry* 110 (Apr. 1954): 733.

35. Sgt. Robert I. Banks statement, Dec. 9, 1953, pp. 2–3, Dickenson Court Martial. Leonard Bell's PW experience left him mentally ill. By late April 1956, when FBI agents questioned him about the behavior of other PsW in camp, Bell had been given a medical discharge from the army. After a nervous breakdown in the summer of 1954, Bell spent seven months in the hospital at Fort Sam Houston, Texas, during which he received twenty-one electric shock treatments.

36. Adams, *An American Dream,* 50.

37. Adams, *An American Dream,* 50–51.

38. John A. Davis sworn statement, Jan. 18, 1951, Dickenson Court Martial.

39. John A. Davis sworn statement, Jan. 18, 1954, Dickenson Court Martial.

40. Steve Glowacki sworn statement, Jan. 9, 1954, Dickenson Court Martial.

41. Federal Bureau of Investigation report form, Oct. 4, 1956, p. 5, FBI-Sullivan.
42. Shadish and Carlson, *When Hell Froze Over,* 41.
43. Lifton, "Home By Ship," 733.
44. Claude J. Batchelor Statement (voluntary, typewritten, double-spaced), 10, Batchelor Court Martial. The Army formed a composite biography of Lin based on interviews of returned PsW. He was about thirty-five years old, stood 5 feet 2 inches, weighed about 130 lbs, and had a very large head. A native of Malaya, his English was good and he likely earned the nickname "Screaming Skull" from the volume at which he spoke.
45. *American POW's Calling From Korea* (Peking, China: Foreign Languages Press, 1951), 1–39.
46. Claude J. Batchelor Statement (voluntary, typewritten, double-spaced), 11, Batchelor Court Martial.
47. Brown, *Techniques of Persuasion,* 262–63.
48. O. John Rogge, *Why Men Confess* (New York, N.Y.: Thomas Nelson & Sons, 1959), 122.
49. Lech, *Broken Soldiers,* 92–93; and "U.S. Prisoners of War in the Korean Operation," 678, NARAII-330(POW/MIA)-POW Manuscript. Wong or Wang was a field-grade officer in the CPV who served as an interrogator and interpreter at Pak's Palace, Camp Two, and Camp Five. A native of Beijing, he allegedly worked for the United States intelligence service in China during World War II. He also claimed that his father had worked at the U.S. embassy in Beijing. Standing 5' 11" and weighing 175 lbs, he was about thirty years old, athletically built, stood ramrod straight, and had a large, square head and sallow complexion. American PsW remembered him as speaking perfect English, likely learned in an American university, and being clever, ruthless, arrogant, and bellicose. A similar story of the meeting appears in Thomas D. Harrison, "Why Did Some GIs Turn Communist?" *Collier's* 132, no. 13 (Nov. 27, 1953), 28.
50. Claude J. Batchelor Statement (voluntary, typewritten, double-spaced), 11, Batchelor Court Martial.
51. Kinkead, *In Every War But One,* 144.
52. Claude J. Batchelor Statement (voluntary, typewritten, double-spaced), 11, Batchelor Court Martial.
53. Claude J. Batchelor Statement (voluntary, typewritten, double-spaced), 12, Batchelor Court Martial.
54. Federal Bureau of Investigation report form, May 25, 1956, 6, FBI-Bell.
55. United States Department of Justice, Federal Bureau of Investigation, June 18, 1956, 15, FBI-Bell.
56. Claude J. Batchelor Statement (voluntary, typewritten, double-spaced), 12, Batchelor Court Martial.
57. Claude J. Batchelor Statement (voluntary, typewritten, double-spaced), 15, Batchelor Court Martial.
58. Claude J. Batchelor Statement (voluntary, typewritten, double-spaced), 15–17, Batchelor Court Martial.
59. See the testimony of Joel Adams, Robert Vincent, and John Edward Owens in Batchelor Court Martial.
60. Federal Bureau of Investigation Report Form, Oct. 3, 1966, 31, FBI-Clarence C. Adams.
61. Carlson, *Remembered Prisoners,* 205.
62. Berens, *Limbo on the Yalu,* 97–98.

63. Carlson, *Remembered Prisoners,* 205.

64. Berens, *Limbo on the Yalu,* 97–98.

65. CHECK LIST ON RECAP-K CASES, Cpl Albert C. Belhomme, continuation sheet (Price, Sfc Bob E. statement), NARAII-153-CHECK LIST.

66. FBI Report Form, Sept. 3, 1956, 3, FBI-Sullivan.

67. Lifton, "Home By Ship," 735.

68. Report Form, Sept. 18, 1956, 109–10, handwritten, upper right corner, FBI-Skinner.

69. *Baltimore Evening Sun* (Md.), Oct. 3, 1953.

70. *Baltimore Sun* (Md.), June 6, 1954.

71. Carlson, *Remembered Prisoners,* 206.

72. Richard Peters and Xiaobing Li, *Voices from the Korean War: Personal Stories of American, Korean, and Chinese Soldiers* (Lexington: Univ. Press of Kentucky, 2004), 232.

73. CHECK LIST ON RECAP-K CASES, Cowart, William A., box 1, volume 1, 1–108, RECAP-K Program, Records Pertaining to U.S. Army Personnel who Refused Repatriation in Korea ("Voluntary Non-Repatriates"), 1953–1957, Record Group 153, Office of the Judge Advocate General (Army), Textual Records, National Archives and Records Administration II, College Park, Maryland, hereinafter cited as NARAII-153-CHECK LIST.

74. Kenneth E. Spingola statement, DA form 19–24, May 18, 1956, FBI-Bell.

75. Federal Bureau of Investigation Form No. 1, May 24, 1956, FBI-Bell.

76. Federal Bureau of Investigation report form, May 28, 1956, FBI-Bell.

77. Report Form, Aug. 2, 1956, 37, handwritten, upper right corner, FBI-Skinner.

78. Report Form, Sept. 18, 1956, 106, handwritten, upper right corner, FBI-Skinner.

79. Claude J. Batchelor Statement (voluntary, typewritten, double-spaced), 17–18, Batchelor Court Martial.

80. Claude J. Batchelor Statement (voluntary, typewritten, double-spaced), 19–20, Batchelor Court Martial.

81. Claude J. Batchelor Statement (voluntary, typewritten, double-spaced), 21–22, Batchelor Court Martial.

82. Claude J. Batchelor Statement (voluntary, typewritten, double-spaced), 23–25, Batchelor Court Martial.

83. Claude J. Batchelor Statement (voluntary, typewritten, double-spaced), 28, Batchelor Court Martial.

84. Claude J. Batchelor Statement (voluntary, typewritten, double-spaced), 28–29, Batchelor Court Martial.

85. Claude J. Batchelor Statement (voluntary, typewritten, double-spaced), 29, Batchelor Court Martial.

4. Winning Captive Hearts

1. Kinkead, *In Every War But One,* 104.

2. Edward Hunter, "Our POWs Are Not Traitors," *Combat Forces Journal* (Oct. 1953), 37.

3. Kinkead, *In Every War But One,* 112.

4. Claude J. Batchelor Statement (voluntary, typewritten, double-spaced), 30–31, Batchelor Court Martial.

5. Claude J. Batchelor Statement (voluntary, typewritten, double-spaced), 31–32, Batchelor Court Martial.

6. Claude J. Batchelor Statement (voluntary, typewritten, double-spaced), 33–34, Batchelor Court Martial.

7. Rees, *Korea,* 346.

8. Claude J. Batchelor Statement (voluntary, typewritten, double-spaced), 37, Batchelor Court Martial.

9. Claude J. Batchelor Statement (voluntary, typewritten, double-spaced), 38–39, Batchelor Court Martial.

10. Claude J. Batchelor Statement (voluntary, typewritten, double-spaced), 40, Batchelor Court Martial; *New York Times,* May 2, 1953; June 30, 1953; "Without Honor," *Newsweek,* July 13, 1953, 30; and Memorandum on Paul Frederick Schnur Jr., Apr. 25, 1953; folder, FBI S (1); box 3, FBI Series; White House Office, Office of the Special Assistant for National Security Affairs: Records, 1952–61; Dwight D. Eisenhower Presidential Library, Abilene, Kansas.

11. Claude J. Batchelor Statement (voluntary, typewritten, double-spaced), 40, 43, Batchelor Court Martial; and Federal Bureau of Investigation Report Form, Feb. 28, 1957, 3, FBI-Clarence C. Adams.

12. Claude J. Batchelor Statement (voluntary, typewritten, double-spaced), 44, Batchelor Court Martial.

13. Report Form, Aug. 2, 1956, 37–38, handwritten, upper right corner, FBI-Skinner.

14. "U.S. Prisoners of War in the Korean Operation," 124–26, NARAII-330(POW/MIA)-POW Manuscript.

15. Lloyd W. Pate, *Reactionary* (New York, N.Y.: Vantage Press, 2001), 130.

16. Pate, *Reactionary,* 110.

17. "U.S. Prisoners of War in the Korean Operation," 129–31, NARAII-330(POW/MIA)-POW Manuscript.

18. "U.S. Prisoners of War in the Korean Operation," 125–27, NARAII-330(POW/MIA)-POW Manuscript.

19. Claude J. Batchelor Statement (voluntary, typewritten, double-spaced), 44, Batchelor Court Martial.

20. *Bristol Herald Courier* (Va.), Apr. 23, 1954; *Roanoke Times* (Va.), Apr. 28, 1954; and Edward M. Gaither Sworn Statement, Jan. 13, 1954, Dickenson Court Martial.

21. Lech, *Broken Soldiers,* 155–56.

22. Cecil Mark Ingram, *A Celebration of Life: A Prisoner of War's 54 Year Journey Since the Korean War* (Xulon Press, 2006), 159.

23. James Thompson, *True Colors: 1004 Days as a Prisoner of War* (Port Washington, N.Y.: Ashley Books, Inc., 1989), 51–52.

24. Lech, *Broken Soldiers,* 156.

25. Claude J. Batchelor Statement (voluntary, typewritten, double-spaced), 43–44, Batchelor Court Martial.

26. Report Form, FD-263, Mar. 27, 1956, p. 5, FBI-Tenneson; and Report Form, FD-263, Apr. 20, 1956, p. 6, FBI-Tenneson.

27. An example of these propaganda letters is Dear jewell & paula, Dec. 26, 1951, FBI-Bell.

28. Federal Bureau of Investigation report form, June 25, 1956, 3, FBI-Bell.

29. United States Department of Justice, Federal Bureau of Investigation, interview report, June 18, 1956, 15, FBI-Bell.

30. SAC, Louisville to Director, FBI, June 12, 1956, FBI-Bell.

31. CHECK LIST ON RECAP-K CASES, Corporal Otto [Otho] G. Bell, continuation sheet (Beers, Capt John D. statement), NARAII-153-CHECK LIST.

32. CHECK LIST ON RECAP-K CASES, Corporal Otto [Otho] G. Bell, continuation sheet (Mizoguchi, Sgt Aryanari statement), NARAII-153-CHECK LIST.

33. CHECK LIST ON RECAP-K CASES, Corporal Otto [Otho] G. Bell, continuation sheet (Naito, Cpl Tadao statement), NARAII-153-CHECK LIST.

34. CHECK LIST ON RECAP-K CASES, Corporal Otto [Otho] G. Bell, continuation sheet (Dominguez, Cpl Willie statement), NARAII-153-CHECK LIST.

35. CHECK LIST ON RECAP-K CASES, Corporal Otto [Otho] G. Bell, continuation sheet (Rivera-Perez, Sgt Pedro statement), NARAII-153-CHECK LIST.

36. Rick to Dear Mother, Apr. 7, 1953, transcript included with FBI Form No. 1, Aug. 19, 1953, 6–7, FBI-Tenneson.

37. Rick to Dear Mother, June 29, 1953, transcript included in FBI Form No. 1, Aug. 19, 1953, 5, FBI-Tenneson.

38. Rick to Dear Mother, Apr. 14, 1953, transcript included in FBI Form No. 1, Aug. 19, 1953, 8, FBI-Tenneson.

39. Virgil Rutherford's postwar story is a sad one. In Spring 1956, when FBI agents began trying to contact him to gather evidence on the Americans, who by then were in China, they were turned away by Rutherford's father. Agents reported that the old man did not want them to talk to his son because "on each occasion after his son has been contacted regarding his experiences as a prisoner of war he becomes upset, nervous and sits around the house crying and wringing his hands . . . it usually takes several weeks . . . to get over this extreme nervousness." See Director, FBI, to Assistant Attorney General William F. Tompkins, Apr. 26, 1956, FBI-Bell.

40. Fred Obroff Sworn Statement, Jan. 21, 1954, Dickenson Court Martial.

41. Fred Obroff Sworn Statement, Jan. 21, 1954, Dickenson Court Martial.

42. Fred Obroff Sworn Statement, Jan. 21, 1954, Dickenson Court Martial.

43. Fred Obroff Sworn Statement, Jan. 21, 1954, Dickenson Court Martial.

44. Tong was the Provost Marshall and chief investigator of PW infractions at Camp Five. Former prisoners remembered him as speaking English methodically, but well, and claiming to have been educated in the United States. Since he asked all the questions, they nicknamed him "Dick Tracy." In his mid-20s, Tong was 5' 8" and 165 lbs, with a heavy build, excellent posture, and a crew cut.

45. Martin Christensen sworn statement, Jan. 7, 1954, Dickenson Court Martial.

46. Federal Bureau of Investigation Form No. 1, Apr. 10, 1956, pp. 4–5, FBI-Tenneson.

47. Federal Bureau of Investigation Form No. 1, Aug. 15, 1956, p. 5, FBI-Fortuna; and Report Form, FD-263, Aug. 29, 1956, p. 14, FBI-Fortuna.

48. Memo, Re: Andrew Fortuna, Aug. 28, 1964, FBI-Fortuna.

49. Report Form FD-263, Oct. 17, 1956, pp. 5–6, FBI-Fortuna; Federal Bureau of Investigation Form No. 1, Nov. 21, 1956, p. 16, FBI-Fortuna; Report Form FD-263, Oct. 29, 1956, p. 3, FBI-Fortuna; and Report Form FD-263, Sept. 24, 1956, p. 6, FBI-Fortuna.

50. Lech, *Broken Soldiers,* 4; and Carlson, *Remembered Prisoners,* 200.

51. Carlson, *Remembered Prisoners,* 200.

52. Pate, *Reactionary,* 97.

53. Pate, *Reactionary,* 86.

54. Federal Bureau of Investigation report form, Oct. 23, 1956, 4, FBI-Sullivan.

55. Federal Bureau of Investigation report form, Nov. 7, 1956, 2–3, FBI-Sullivan.

56. Federal Bureau of Investigation report form, Oct. 23, 1956, 5, FBI-Sullivan.

57. Claude J. Batchelor Statement (voluntary, typewritten, double-spaced), 47, Batchelor Court Martial.

58. Federal Bureau of Investigation, Form No. 1, Nov. 1, 1956, 3, FBI-Clarence Adams.

59. Claude J. Batchelor Statement (voluntary, typewritten, double-spaced), 47–48, Batchelor Court Martial.

60. Interview of Unidentified Former PW (name classified), Aug. 8, 1956, 9, Morris Robert Wills FBI File, United States Department of Justice, Washington, D.C., hereinafter cited as FBI-Wills.

61. Interview of Unidentified Former PW (name classified), July 24, 1956, 4, Arlie Howard Pate FBI File, United States Department of Justice, Washington, D.C., hereinafter cited as FBI-Pate.

62. Lech, *Broken Soldiers,* 157.

63. CHECK LIST ON RECAP-K CASES, Corporal Otto [Otho] G. Bell, NARAII-153-CHECK LIST; Interview of Unidentified Former PW (name classified), July 2, 1955, 3, FBI-Wills; and interview transcript, subject unidentified, questioners: Lt. Glenn and Mr. Montgomery, undated, FBI-Griggs.

64. Federal Bureau of Investigation, Form No. 1, May 23, 1956, 11, FBI-Bell.

65. Tape #118, Stanford-*Firing Line.*

66. Claude J. Batchelor Statement (voluntary, typewritten, double-spaced), 48, Batchelor Court Martial.

67. Claude J. Batchelor Statement (voluntary, typewritten, double-spaced), 49–50, Batchelor Court Martial.

68. Claude J. Batchelor Statement (voluntary, typewritten, double-spaced), 50–51, Batchelor Court Martial.

69. Claude J. Batchelor Statement (voluntary, typewritten, double-spaced), 53, Batchelor Court Martial.

70. Claude J. Batchelor Statement (voluntary, typewritten, double-spaced), 53–54, Batchelor Court Martial; and Lech, *Broken Soldiers,* 158–59; and Sworn Statement of Lieutenant John S. Quinn, Series, S-0846, Box 2, File 4, Political Matters-China-Secretary General's Visit to Peking 1954–55-Basic Documents-Korean Prisoner of War; Subject Files of the Secretary General: Dag Hammarskjold, 26/10/1953–10/01/1955, pages 17–18, United Nations Archives and Records Management Section, United Nations, New York, New York; hereinafter cited as UN-Political Matters, 1954–55.

71. Interview of Unidentified Former PW (name classified), Oct. 19, 1956, 4–5, FBI-Pate.

72. Interview of Unidentified Former PW (name classified), Aug. 13, 1956, 3–4, FBI-Pate.

73. Interview of Unidentified Former PW (name classified), Nov. 27, 1956, 3, FBI-Pate.

74. Interview of Unidentified Former PW (name classified), Jan. 8, 1957, 2, FBI-Pate.

75. Interview of Unidentified Former PW (name classified), Jan. 8, 1957, 5–6, FBI-Pate.

76. Interview transcript, subject unidentified, questioners: Lt. Glenn and Mr. Montgomery, undated, FBI-Griggs.

77. Federal Bureau of Investigation report form, May 31, 1956, 2, FBI-Bell.

78. Federal Bureau of Investigation report form, May 31, 1956, 4, FBI-Bell.

79. Federal Bureau of Investigation report form, May 31, 1956, 2, FBI-Bell.

80. Federal Bureau of Investigation report form, June 7, 1956, 2, FBI-Bell.

81. Federal Bureau of Investigation Form No. 1, May 9, 1956, 2, FBI-Bell.

82. United States Department of Justice, Federal Bureau of Investigation, Re: Otho Grayson Bell, June 18, 1956, FBI-Bell.

83. Tong served as Provost Marshall at Camp Five and was in charge of investigating all infractions among the PsW. Variously known to prisoners as "Dick Tracy,"

"Bill," and "Tom," Tong spoke broken, but good, English and claimed to have been educated in the United States. See "U.S. Prisoners of War in the Korean Operation," 672, NARAII-330(POW/MIA)-POW Manuscript.

84. "U.S. Prisoners of War in the Korean Operation," 660, NARAII-330(POW/MIA)-POW Manuscript. Quan was likely Kwang, nicknamed "Mulehead" by the PsW. PW comments described him as "somewhat milder than 'Screaming Skull' in manner." Federal Bureau of Investigation report form, May 16, 1956, 3, FBI-Bell.

85. Federal Bureau of Investigation Report Form, Aug. 20, 1956, 5, Clarence C. Adams FBI File, United States Department of Justice, Washington, D.C., hereinafter cited as FBI-Clarence Adams; and Federal Bureau of Investigation, Form No. 1, Sept. 27, 1956, 8, FBI-Clarence Adams.

86. Federal Bureau of Investigation, Form No. 1, May 29, 1956, 4–5, FBI-Bell; Federal Bureau of Investigation, Form No. 1, May 24, 1956, 4, FBI-Bell; and Federal Bureau of Investigation Report Form, Aug. 24, 1956, 2, FBI-Clarence Adams.

87. Albert D. Biderman, *March to Calumny: The Story of American POWs in the Korean War* (New York, N.Y.: McMillan, 1963), 57–58; and "U.S. Prisoners of War in the Korean Operation," 346–47, NARAII-330(POW/MIA)-POW Manuscript.

88. *"United Nations" P.O.W.'s in Korea* (Beijing, China: Chinese People's Committee for World Peace, 1953), 73–89.

89. *Olympics: Inter Camp Olympics, 1952* (Pyuktong, D.P.R.K., 1953). A copy of this publication is held at the New York Public Library and is scanned and transcribed online at: http://www.kmike.com/POW_Olympics/pow/index.htm

90. *Olympics, 1952.*

91. Claude J. Batchelor Statement, continuation (A), 2–3. One of the popular propagandists who broadcast daily was Anna Wallace Suhr, who became known as "Seoul City Sue." She was born in Arkansas in 1898, and her family moved to Johnson County, Oklahoma, a socialist stronghold. Married and divorced, she went to Korea in 1930 as a Methodist missionary and met her future Korean husband while working in Shanghai, China. She was arrested by the Japanese during World War II and after her release, she and her husband returned to Korea. They worked at a mission school until the outbreak of the Korean War. Although most GIs hated Sue, evidence supports the contention that she was forced to make her propaganda broadcast first by the North Koreans and later by the Chinese. Reports indicate that Sue and her husband aided in the reeducation efforts at Camp Twelve. In 1962, she was photographed with U.S. Army deserter Larry Abshier. Another American defector, Charles Jenkins, claimed to have met her by chance in 1965 in the "foreigners only" section of a department store. She was reportedly executed as a double agent in 1969.

92. Claude J. Batchelor Statement, continuation (A), 3–5.

93. Federal Bureau of Investigation, Report Form 1, Aug. 17, 1956, 4, FBI-Clarence C. Adams.

94. Claude J. Batchelor Statement, continuation (A), 5–6.

95. Report Form, FD-263, Apr. 25, 1956, pp. 4–5, FBI-Tenneson.

96. Interview of Unidentified Former PW (name classified), Aug. 31, 1956, 3, FBI-Pate; and Interview of Unidentified Former PW (name classified), Oct. 4, 1956, 7, FBI-Pate. The subject of the Oct. 4 interview was George A. West.

97. Claude J. Batchelor Statement, continuation (A), 7; and Synopsis of the Frank Noel Story, box 24, Record Group 319, Records of the Army Staff, Army Intelligence Document Files, 1950–1955, Textual Records, National Archives and Records Administration II, College Park, Maryland, hereinafter cited as NARAII-319(AID Files)-Noel.

98. George Burchett and Nick Shimmin, eds., *Memoirs of a Rebel Journalist: The*

Autobiography of Wilfred Burchett (Sydney, AU: Univ. of New South Wales Press, 2005), 382–85; Harry Spiller, ed., *American POWs in Korea: Sixteen Personal Accounts* (Jefferson, N.C.: McFarland, 1998), 57; and John Faber, *Great News Photos and the Stories Behind Them* (New York, N.Y.: Dover Publications, 1978), 112–13.

99. Francis E. Noel testimony, Sept. 21, 1954, Batchelor Court Martial.

100. Francis E. Noel testimony, Sept. 21, 1954, Batchelor Court Martial.

101. John Toland, *In Mortal Combat: Korea, 1950–1953* (New York, N.Y.: Quill, 1991), 561.

102. William C. Hansen sworn statement, Jan. 11, 1954, Edward Dickenson Court Martial.

103. Claude J. Batchelor Statement, continuation (A), 8.

104. Claude J. Batchelor Statement, continuation (A), 8–9.

105. Rick to Dear Mother, Apr. 14, 1953, transcript included with FBI Form No. 1, Aug. 19, 1953, 6–7, FBI-Tenneson.

106. Toland, *In Mortal Combat,* 561; and Biderman, *March to Calumny,* 201.

107. Trip Report of Robert H. Beezer, undated; folder, PSB 383.6 [Prisoners of War] (2); box 26, Psychological Strategy Board (PSB) Central Files Series; White House Office, National Security Council Staff: Papers, 1953–61; Dwight D. Eisenhower Presidential Library, Abilene, Kansas, hereinafter cited as Eisenhower-PSB; and Burchett and Shimmin, *Memoirs of a Rebel Journalist,* 414–15.

108. *New York Times,* Apr. 29, 1953 and May 2, 1953.

109. *New York Times,* May 2, 1953; and Trip Report of Robert H. Beezer, undated, folder, PSB 383.6 [Prisoners of War] (2); box 26, Eisenhower-PSB.

110. *New York Times,* May 3, 1953.

111. *New York Times,* May 4, 1953.

112. These men, along with more than 250 others, were identified by the U.S. Army, based on counterintelligence interviews with returning PsW, as having collaborated with the enemy during their captivity. Appendix B, Counterintelligence Report, box 24, Record Group 319, Records of the Army Staff, Army Intelligence Document Files, 1950–1955, Textual Records, National Archives and Records Administration II, College Park, Maryland, hereinafter cited as NARAII-319(AID Files)-Appendix B.

113. Biographical sketches of repatriates, folder, PSB 383.6 [Prisoners of War] (3); box 26, Psychological Strategy Board (PSB) Central Files Series; White House Office, National Security Council Staff: Papers, 1953–61; Dwight D. Eisenhower Presidential Library, Abilene, Kansas, hereinafter cited as Eisenhower-WHO/NSCS-PSB 383.6.

114. Biographical sketches of repatriates, folder, PSB 383.6 [Prisoners of War] (3); box 26, Eisenhower-WHO/NSCS-PSB 383.6.

115. *Pravda,* Oct. 31, 1954; and Albert D. Biderman, *March to Calumny: The Story of American POWs in the Korean War* (New York, N.Y.: MacMillan, 1963), 217–19.

116. Gibson, et al., "Repatriated American POWs," 157; and Henry A. Segal, "Initial Psychiatric Findings of Recently Repatriated Prisoners of War," *American Journal of Psychiatry* 111, no. 5 (1954), 358–59.

117. Claude J. Batchelor Statement, continuation (A), 10–11.

118. Claude J. Batchelor Statement, continuation (A), 11–16.

5. Politicians and Their Careers

1. Quotes taken from David M. Oshinsky, *A Conspiracy So Immense: The World of Joe McCarthy* (New York, N.Y.: Free Press, 1983), 16–17.

2. Oshinsky, *A Conspiracy So Immense,* 29–32.

3. Oshinsky, *A Conspiracy So Immense,* 34–52; and Michael O'Brien, *McCarthy and McCarthyism in Wisconsin* (Columbia: Univ. of Missouri Press, 1980), 55.

4. Michael J. Ybarra, *Washington Gone Crazy: Senator Pat McCarran and the Great American Communist Hunt* (Hanover, N.H.: Steerforth Press, 2004), 55, 64, 66–67, 111–12, 123–25.

5. Ybarra, *Washington Gone Crazy,* 485.

6. Kenneth W. Vickers, "John Rankin: Democrat and Demagogue," M.A. thesis, Mississippi State Univ., 1993, 96–98.

7. Roger Morris, *Richard Milhous Nixon: The Rise of an American Politician* (New York, N.Y.: Henry Holt, 1990), 258.

8. Morris, *Nixon,* 293–94.

9. Morris, *RMN,* 393–94; and Oshinsky, *Conspiracy So Immense,* 98–99.

10. Whittaker Chambers, "Big Sister is Watching You," *National Review,* Dec. 28, 1957, 594–96; Ted Morgan, *Reds: McCarthyism in Twentieth-Century America* (New York, N.Y.: Random House, 2004), 274.

11. Morgan, *Reds,* 304–5.

12. Oshinsky, *A Conspiracy So Immense,* 61–66, 73.

13. Morgan, *Reds,* 358–60.

14. Morgan, *Reds,* 362–63, 365.

15. Morgan, *Reds,* 364–65.

16. Oshinsky, *A Conspiracy So Immense,* 77.

17. Oshinsky, *A Conspiracy So Immense,* 108–12; Michael O'Brien, *McCarthy and McCarthyism in Wisconsin* (Columbia: Univ. of Missouri Press, 1980), 99.

18. Morgan, *Reds,* 393–98.

19. Ybarra, *Washington Gone Crazy,* 570.

20. Morgan, *Reds,* 393.

21. Oshinsky, *A Conspiracy So Immense,* 117–78.

22. Oshinsky, *A Conspiracy So Immense,* 172, 191–93; O'Brien, *McCarthy and McCarthyism,* 100.

23. Athan Theoharis, *The FBI and American Democracy: A Brief Critical History* (Lawrence: Univ. Press of Kansas, 2004), 88.

24. Theoharis, *The FBI and American Democracy,* 88–89; and Ellen Schrecker, *Many are the Crimes: McCarthyism in America* (Boston, Mass.: Little, Brown, 1998), 215.

25. Oshinsky, *Many are the Crimes,* 257–58.

26. Ybarra, *Washington Gone Crazy,* 547–48; and Schrecker, *Many are the Crimes,* 215.

27. Ybarra, *Washington Gone Crazy,* 720.

6. The Shocking Refusal

1. Clay Blair, *The Forgotten War* (New York, N.Y.: Times Books, 1987), 975; William Stueck, *The Korean War: An International History* (Princeton, N.J.: Princeton Univ. Press, 1995), 341; and *Military Armistice in Korea and Temporary Supplement Agreement,* Treaties and Other International Acts 2782, Washington, DC: Department of State, undated, in Series, S-0846, Box 2, File 6, Political Matters-Korea-UN Military and Korean Prisoners of War, vol. I, Subject Files of the Secretary General: Dag Hammarskjold, 01/12/1654–30/12/1954, page 28, United Nations Archives and Records Management Section, United Nations, New York, New York; hereinafter cited as UN-Political Matters, 1955.

2. In addition to the twenty-three American soldiers who voluntarily spent the coming months in Chinese custody, there was one British marine, and three other American soldiers who attempted to remain behind but were quickly expelled by the group.

3. Edward Swanson Dickenson Statement, Nov. 6, 1953, 3–4 of 9, Dickenson Court Martial; and Federal Bureau of Investigation Form 1, Aug. 15, 1956, 4, FBI-Fortuna.

4. Edward Swanson Dickenson Statement, Nov. 6, 1953, 4–5 of 9, Dickenson Court Martial.

5. Interview of Unidentified Former PW (name classified), Aug. 13, 1956, 6, FBI-Pate.

6. Interview of Unidentified Former PW (name classified), Oct. 5, 1956, 3, FBI-Pate. Although the name of the interviewee is classified, it is clear that he is Edward Dickenson.

7. Assistant Attorney General William F. Tompkins to Director, FBI, Nov. 26, 1956, FBI-Pate.

8. Federal Bureau of Investigation Report Form, Mar. 19, 1957, 3, FBI-Clarence C. Adams.

9. Interview of Unidentified Former PW (name classified), Oct. 19, 1956, 13, FBI-Corden.

10. Federal Bureau of Investigation Form FD-263, Sept. 6, 1956, 7–8, FBI-Fortuna.

11. Claude J. Batchelor Statement, Continuation A, 27, Batchelor Court Martial.

12. Tape #118, Stanford-*Firing Line.*

13. Sandy Strait, *What Happened to American Prisoners of War in Korea* (Unionville, N.Y.: Royal Fireworks Press, 1997), 162–63.

14. Adams, *An American Dream,* 68; Clarence C. Adams FBI debriefing, A-61, July 29, 1966, United States Department of State.

15. SAC, Philadelphia to Director, FBI, Mar. 30, 1954, 1, FBI-Tenneson.

16. United States Department of Justice, Federal Bureau of Investigation, interview report, June 18, 1956, FBI-Bell.

17. Jose G. Navarro statement, DA form 19–24, June 12, 1956, 3, FBI-Bell.

18. Federal Bureau of Investigation, Form No. 1, May 24, 1956, 3, FBI-Bell.

19. *The Korean Republic,* Nov. 4, 1953, in William S. Lawton Papers, Box 2, Folder 2, "Korean Prisoner of War Repatriation," United States Army Military History Institute, Archives, Carlisle, Pa.; hereinafter cited as USAMHI-Lawton.

20. Tape #118, Stanford-*Firing Line.*

21. Tape #118, Stanford-*Firing Line.*

22. CHECK LIST ON RECAP-K CASES, Corporal Otto [Otho] G. Bell, continuation sheet (Stone, Cpl. Willis J. statement), NARAII-153-CHECK LIST.

23. CHECK LIST ON RECAP-K CASES, Corporal Otto [Otho] G. Bell, continuation sheet (Godlewski, Pfc. Richard W. statement), NARAII-153-CHECK LIST.

24. CHECK LIST ON RECAP-K CASES, Corporal Otto [Otho] G. Bell, continuation sheet (Taylor, Cpl Charles E. statement), NARAII-153-CHECK LIST. Mao was described by the men as being effeminate and believed to be a homosexual.

25. CHECK LIST ON RECAP-K CASES, Corporal Otto [Otho] G. Bell, continuation sheet (Lam, Cpl Leroy V. statement), NARAII-153-CHECK LIST.

26. CHECK LIST ON RECAP-K CASES, Corporal Otto [Otho] G. Bell, continuation sheet (Dixon, Sgt John Lewis statement), NARAII-153-CHECK LIST.

27. CHECK LIST ON RECAP-K CASES, Sullivan, Larance V, NARAII-153-CHECK LIST; and Summary of Information (Sullivan, Larance V.), NARAII-153-Summary.

28. Anonymous interview #1, Nov. 15, 2007, recording and transcript in possession of the author.

29. Interview of Unidentified Former PW (name classified), July 20, 1956, 4, FBI-Corden.

30. Interview of Unidentified Former PW (name classified), Aug. 13, 1956, 15, FBI-Corden.

31. Interview of Unidentified Former PW (name classified), Nov. 13, 1956, 10, FBI-Corden; and Interview of Unidentified Former PW (name classified), Feb. 18, 1957. Homosexuality was widespread among a portion of the men in the PW camps. Robert I. Banks's statement, Dec. 9, 1953, Dickenson Court Martial, illustrates the pervasive nature of homosexuality within the camp.

32. *Washington Post,* Dec. 29, 1953, in Box 1, Folder 1, "Official Papers and Diaries Concerning Repatriation of Korean War Prisoners," Ralph E. Pearson Papers, United States Army Military History Institute, Archives; hereinafter cited as USAMHI-Pearson.

33. *Baltimore Sun* (Md.), June 6, 1954.

34. Claude J. Batchelor Statement, Jan. 28, 1954, 5 of 11, Batchelor Court Martial.

35. Wills, *Turncoat,* 64–68.

36. Interview of Unidentified Former PW (name classified), Nov. 19, 1956, 3, FBI-Pate; Federal Bureau of Investigation Report Form, Apr. 12, 1957, 3, FBI-Clarence C. Adams. Although the name of the interviewee is classified in both documents, it is clear that he is Wesley P. Biers.

37. Federal Bureau of Investigation Report Form, May 3, 1956, 3, Lewie W. Griggs FBI File, United States Department of Justice, Washington, D.C., hereinafter cited as FBI-Griggs.

38. Federal Bureau of Investigation Report Form, Apr. 7, 1956, 3, FBI-Griggs.

39. Report Form, Nov. 30, 1956, 191–92, handwritten, upper right corner, FBI-Skinner.

40. Unknown (classified Secret Service agent) to Mr. Harry Morgan, July 9, 1968, FBI-Skinner.

41. FBI Report Form, Aug. 31, 1956, FBI-Corden.

42. Wills, *Turncoat,* 68–70.

43. Adams, *An American Dream,* 68.

44. Spiller, *American POWs in Korea,* 65.

45. Despite FBI censoring, this unidentified nonrepatriate appears to have been Wilburn Watson.

46. Report Form, Nov. 30, 1956, 193, handwritten, upper right corner, FBI-Skinner.

47. Wills, *Turncoat,* 70.

48. Report Form, Nov. 30, 1956, 193, handwritten, upper right corner, FBI-Skinner.

49. Wills, *Turncoat,* 71.

50. Edward Swanson Dickenson Statement, Nov. 6, 1953, 8 of 9, Dickenson Court Martial.

51. *The Korean Republic,* Nov. 4, 1953, in Box 2, Folder 2, USAMHI-Lawton.

52. Edward Swanson Dickenson Statement, Nov. 6, 1953, 8 of 9, Dickenson Court Martial.

53. Claude J. Batchelor Statement, Jan. 28, 1954, 4 of 11, Batchelor Court Martial.

54. Edward Swanson Dickenson Statement, Nov. 6, 1953, 6 of 9, Dickenson Court Martial.

55. Claude J. Batchelor Statement, Jan. 28, 1954, 5 of 11, Batchelor Court Martial. Biers was Pfc. Wesley P. Biers, who later joined Wilburn C. Watson and Bobby R. DeGraw in testifying against Claude Batchelor. DeGraw was killed in an automobile accident in Hillsborough County, Florida, in 1954.

56. Claude J. Batchelor Statement, Jan. 28, 1954, 5 of 11, Batchelor Court Martial.

57. Wilburn Watson testimony, Sept. 13, 1954, Batchelor Court Martial.

58. Claude J. Batchelor Statement, Continuation A, 29–30, Batchelor Court Martial.

59. Claude J. Batchelor Statement, Continuation A, 31–33, Batchelor Court Martial; and FBI Report Form, Apr. 12, 1957, FBI-Corden. The fact that some of the men knew Wilburn Watson as "Clew" or "Clue" suggests that he was much more familiar to the Progressives than was revealed by the U.S. government at the time.

60. Report Form FD-263, Apr. 20, 1956, 3, FBI-Tenneson.

61. Wilburn Watson testimony, Sept. 13, 1954, Batchelor Court Martial; and Federal Bureau of Investigation Report Form, Apr. 12, 1957, 6, FBI-Clarence C. Adams. Interestingly, in Interview of Unidentified Former PW (name classified), Oct. 5, 1956, 4, FBI-Pate, Dickenson alleges that the group also charged him with "creating disunity among the non repatriates" and for "being a CID agent for the U.S. Army," resulting in his being tried in similar proceedings as had Watson, Biers, and DeGraw.

62. Wilburn Watson testimony, Sept. 13, 1954, Batchelor Court Martial; and Report Form, Oct. 24, 1956, 163–64, handwritten, upper right corner, FBI-Skinner. The form has been vetted of identifying information by the FBI; however, it is clear that Wilburn Watson was the interviewee.

63. Wesley Biers epitomized the opportunity afforded to informants against the nonrepatriates. A handwritten note in the margin of an FBI memorandum dated May 13, 1958 noted that Biers's condition of military separation had been changed from undesirable (under other than honorable conditions) to honorable. The change was made shortly before Biers provided statements against nearly all of the men.

64. Claude J. Batchelor Statement, Continuation A, 36, Batchelor Court Martial.

65. Claude J. Batchelor Statement, Continuation A, 36, Batchelor Court Martial.

66. *New York Times,* May 2, 1953; June 30, 1953; and "Without Honor," *Newsweek,* July 13, 1953, 30.

67. Claude J. Batchelor Statement, Continuation A, 36, Batchelor Court Martial.

68. Claude J. Batchelor Statement, Continuation A, 36–37, Batchelor Court Martial; and Wills, *Turncoat,* 72–73.

69. Claude J. Batchelor Statement, Continuation A, 37–38, Batchelor Court Martial.

70. Claude J. Batchelor Statement, Continuation A, 44–45, Batchelor Court Martial.

71. Claude J. Batchelor Statement, Continuation A, 40, Batchelor Court Martial; and Pasley, *21 Stayed,* 100.

72. Claude J. Batchelor Statement, Continuation A, 40, Batchelor Court Martial.

73. Claude J. Batchelor Statement, Continuation A, 40, Batchelor Court Martial.

74. Claude J. Batchelor Statement, Continuation A, 40, Batchelor Court Martial.

75. Claude J. Batchelor Statement, Continuation A, 44–45, Batchelor Court Martial.

76. Claude J. Batchelor Statement, Jan. 28, 1954, 7 of 11, Batchelor Court Martial; and Claude J. Batchelor Statement, Continuation A, 45, Batchelor Court Martial; and Prosecution Exhibit No. 17, 78, Dickenson Court Martial.

77. Claude J. Batchelor Statement, Continuation A, 41–42, Batchelor Court Martial. There were many violent and near-violent confrontations shipboard between former Progressives and Reactionaries. See Lifton, "Home By Ship," 735.

78. Wills, *Turncoat,* 71–72.

79. Claude J. Batchelor Statement, Continuation A, 43, Batchelor Court Martial; and Claude J. Batchelor Statement, 7 of 11, Batchelor Court Martial.

80. Wills, *Turncoat,* 71–72.

81. Claude J. Batchelor Statement, Continuation A, 46–47, Batchelor Court Martial.

82. Claude J. Batchelor Statement, Continuation A, 48, Batchelor Court Martial.

83. Claude J. Batchelor Statement, Continuation A, 50–51, Batchelor Court Martial.

84. Claude J. Batchelor Statement, Continuation A, 48–50, Batchelor Court Martial; and Prosecution Exhibit No. 17, 79, Dickenson Court Martial.

85. Claude J. Batchelor Statement, Continuation A, 48–50, Batchelor Court Martial.

86. *Kingsport Times-News* (Tenn.), Sept. 24, 1953; and *The Post* (Big Stone Gap, Va.), Sept. 24, 1953.

87. *Kingsport Times-News* (Tenn.), Sept. 24, 1953.

88. *Southern Illinoisan* (Carbondale), Sept. 24, 1953.

89. *Dallas Morning News* (Tex.), Sept. 25, 1953.

90. *San Angelo Standard-Times* (Tex.), Sept. 25, 1953.

91. *Southern Illinoisan* (Carbondale), Oct. 2, 1953; and "We Got Everything You Wanted," *Life,* Oct. 19, 1953, 44–45.

92. *Southern Illinoisan* (Carbondale), Oct. 2, 1953; and "We Got Everything You Wanted," *Life,* Oct. 19, 1953, 44–45.

93. Pasley, *21 Stayed,* 164–65.

94. *Southern Illinoisan* (Carbondale), Oct. 3, 1953.

95. *Kingsport Times-News* (Tenn.), Sept. 25, 1953; Mrs. Mary S. Ferrell letter, Sept. 26, 1953; Mrs. W. J. Brown letter, Sept. 25, 1953; and other letters and telegrams; folder, Prisoner & Prisoners, (only), (2); box 2504, Alpha File, White House Central Files; Dwight D. Eisenhower Presidential Library, Abilene, Kansas; and Mrs. Henry B. Wilson (Aaron Wilson's mother) letter, Dec. 27, 1953; Mrs. Albert Griggs (Lewie Griggs's mother) letter, Jan. 3, 1954; Mrs. Anna Mae Merrill (Arlie Pate's sister) letter, Jan. 9, 1954; Mrs. Carley Jones (Samuel Hawkins's mother) letter, Feb. 1, 1954; Mrs. John W. Jensen (Richard Tenneson's grandmother) letter, Aug. 16, 1954; folder, 125-U 1954; box 937, GF 125-T, General File, White House Central Files; Dwight D. Eisenhower Presidential Library, Abilene, Kansas; Mr. and Mrs. George Veneris telegram to the President, Sept. 26, 1953; White House Memorandum for Record, Sept. 30, 1953; folder, 125-U Prisoners of War 1952–1953; box 937, GF 125-T, General File, White House Central Files; Dwight D. Eisenhower Presidential Library, Abilene, Kansas; and Mrs. J. H. Adams to Dear Sir, Nov. 16, 1953, Senate Files, Box 1366, file, 1958 Case Files, Batchelor, Claude J., Oct. 1954–1958 (Korean War Defector), Lyndon Baines Johnson Presidential Library and Museum, Austin, Texas.

96. Pasley, *21 Stayed,* 187, 192.

97. *Dallas Morning News* (Tex.), Jan. 1, 1954.

7. The Returns . . .

1. Edward Swanson Dickenson Statement, Nov. 6, 1953, 8–9 of 9, Dickenson Court Martial; and Prosecution Exhibit No. 17, 79, Dickenson Court Martial.

2. *New York Times,* Oct. 21, 1953; and Prosecution Exhibit No. 17, 79, Dickenson Court Martial.

3. Edward Swanson Dickenson Statement, Nov. 6, 1953, 9 of 9, Dickenson Court Martial; and Prosecution Exhibit No. 17, 79–80, Dickenson Court Martial.

4. *New York Times,* Oct. 21, 1953.

5. *Kingsport Times-News* (Tenn.), Oct. 21, 1953; *Bristol Herald-Courier* (Va.), Oct. 21, 1953; and *Roanoke Times* (Va.), Oct. 22, 1953.

6. *Kingsport Times-News* (Tenn.), Oct. 22, 1953.

7. *Bristol Herald-Courier* (Va.), Sept. 27, 1953.

8. *Kingsport Times-News* (Tenn.), Oct. 22, 1953; *Bristol Herald-Courier* (Va.), Oct. 23, 1953; and *The Post* (Big Stone Gap, Va.), Oct. 22, 1953.

9. *Bristol Herald-Courier* (Va.), Oct. 22, 1953.
10. Oshinsky, *A Conspiracy So Immense,* 330–31.
11. Oshinsky, *A Conspiracy So Immense,* 372–73.
12. Oshinsky, *A Conspiracy So Immense,* 372–83
13. *Bristol Herald-Courier* (Va.), Oct. 22, 1953.
14. *The Post* (Big Stone Gap, Va.), Oct. 1, 1953.
15. Lech, *Broken Soldiers,* 210.
16. Edward Swanson Dickenson Statement, Nov. 6, 1953, 1 of 9, Dickenson Court Martial.
17. *Kingsport Times-News* (Tenn.), Oct. 22, 1953.
18. S. N. Prasad, *History of the Custodian Force (India) in Korea, 1953–54* (Delhi, India: Historical Section, Ministry of Defence, Government of India, 1976), 45
19. Claude J. Batchelor Statement, Continuation A, 52–53, Batchelor Court Martial.
20. Claude J. Batchelor Statement, Continuation A, 53–54, Batchelor Court Martial.
21. Claude J. Batchelor Statement, Continuation A, 54–55, Batchelor Court Martial.
22. Claude J. Batchelor Statement, Continuation A, 55–56, Batchelor Court Martial; and Prasad, *History of the Custodian Force,* 45–46.
23. Claude J. Batchelor Statement, Continuation A, 56–57, Batchelor Court Martial.
24. Alexander Luther testimony, Apr. 22, 1954, Dickenson Court Martial.
25. Alexander Luther testimony, Apr. 22, 1954, Dickenson Court Martial.
26. Alexander Luther testimony, Apr. 22, 1954, Dickenson Court Martial.
27. Federal Bureau of Investigation report form, July 31, 1953, Edward S. Dickenson FBI File, United States Department of Justice, Washington, D.C., hereinafter cited as FBI-Dickenson.
28. *Washington Post* (D.C.), Oct. 22, 1953; "Corporal Dickenson Tells Why Some GI's Stay With Reds," *U.S. News and World Report,* Nov. 13, 1953, 38–43; *Kingsport Times-News* (Tenn.), Nov. 19, 1953; and *Washington Post,* Nov. 20, 1953.
29. *Kingsport Times-News* (Tenn.), Oct. 23, 1953; Oct. 26, 1953; *New York Times,* Oct. 26, 1953; and *Kingsport Times-News* (Tenn.), Nov. 19, 1953.
30. *Kingsport Times-News* (Tenn.), Oct. 25, 1953; and *Washington Post,* Oct. 25, 1953.
31. *The Post* (Big Stone Gap, Va.), Oct. 29, 1953.
32. "One Changed His Mind," *Time,* Nov. 2, 1953; and "A Prodigal Son and His Kin," *Life,* Nov. 2, 1953, 45.
33. *Bristol Herald Courier* (Va.), Nov. 20, 1953.
34. *New York Times,* Nov. 22, 1953; and *Kingsport Times-News* (Tenn.), Nov. 22, 1953.
35. *Bristol Herald Courier* (Va.), Nov. 22, 1953; and *New York Times,* Nov. 22, 1953.
36. *The Post* (Big Stone Gap, Va.), Nov. 5, 1953.
37. *Kingsport Times-News* (Tenn.), Nov. 23, 1953.
38. *Bristol Herald Courier* (Va.), Nov. 24, 1953; and *Roanoke Times* (Va.), Nov. 24, 1953.
39. *The Post* (Big Stone Gap, Va.), Nov. 26, 1953.
40. Thelma Marrs interview, May 21, 2004, by Brian D. McKnight and Sara Roop.
41. *The Post* (Big Stone Gap, Va.), Nov. 26, 1953.
42. *The Post* (Big Stone Gap, Va.), Dec. 3, 1953.
43. *The Post* (Big Stone Gap, Va.), Dec. 10, 1953.
44. *Kingsport Times-News* (Tenn.), Oct. 22, 1953; *Roanoke Times* (Va.), Oct. 22, 1953; *Washington Post,* Oct. 22, 1953; *Bristol Herald Courier* (Va.), Oct. 23, 1953; and "A Prodigal Son and His Kin," *Life,* Nov. 2, 1953, 45.
45. Pasley, *21 Stayed,* 86.
46. Claude J. Batchelor Statement, Continuation A, 57–58, Batchelor Court Martial.
47. Claude J. Batchelor Statement, Continuation A, 58–59, Batchelor Court Martial.

48. Claude J. Batchelor Statement, Continuation A, 61–65, Batchelor Court Martial.

49. Claude J. Batchelor Statement, Continuation A, 67–68, Batchelor Court Martial.

50. Claude J. Batchelor Statement, Continuation A, 68–69, Batchelor Court Martial. See also chapter 19 of Humphrey Evans, *Thimayya of India: A Soldier's Life* (New York, N.Y.: Harcourt, Brace, 1960).

51. Claude J. Batchelor Statement, Continuation A, 68–70, Batchelor Court Martial.

52. Claude J. Batchelor Statement, Continuation A, 70–71, Batchelor Court Martial.

53. Claude J. Batchelor Statement, Continuation A, 72–73, Batchelor Court Martial.

54. Claude J. Batchelor Statement, Continuation A, 73–74, Batchelor Court Martial.

55. Pasley, *21 Stayed,* 188.

56. Hillman, *Defending America,* 51–52.

57. Claude J. Batchelor Statement, Continuation A, 74–76, Batchelor Court Martial.

58. Claude J. Batchelor Statement, Continuation A, 77–79, Batchelor Court Martial.

59. Claude J. Batchelor Statement, Continuation A, 80, Batchelor Court Martial.

60. Claude J. Batchelor Statement, Continuation A, 80–81, Batchelor Court Martial.

61. Hunter, *Brainwashing,* 284–85.

62. Claude J. Batchelor Statement, Continuation A, 80–82, Batchelor Court Martial. Indian Lieutenant General K. S. Thimmaya, chairman of the Neutral Nations Repatriation Commission, noted an important point when he asked "Why did these . . . men come out by night; logically, they should have more difficulty then. . . . But darkness helps when one feels ashamed of leaving friends surreptitiously." Paris AFP Radioteletype in English to the Americas 1748 1/3; folder, OCB 383.6 [Prisoners of War–Korean War] (file #1) (5) [Oct. 1953–Jan. 1954]; box 117, OCB Central Files Series; White House Office, National Security Council Staff: Papers, 1948–61; Dwight D. Eisenhower Presidential Library, Abilene, Kansas.

63. *Dallas Morning News* (Tex.), Jan. 1, 1954; and *San Angelo Standard-Times* (Tex.), Jan. 2, 1954.

64. *San Angelo Standard-Times* (Tex.), Jan. 2, 1954.

65. *San Angelo Standard-Times* (Tex.), Jan. 1, 1954; *Dallas Morning News* (Tex.), Jan. 2, 1954; and Prasad, *History of the Custodian Force,* 38–39.

66. *Dallas Morning News* (Tex.), Jan. 3, 1954.

67. *Dallas Morning News* (Tex.), Jan. 4, 1954.

68. Pasley, *21 Stayed,* 86–87; and Claude J. Batchelor Statement, Continuation A, 57–58, Batchelor Court Martial. The January 21, 1954 letter from Batchelor to Jewell Bell does not survive, but is quoted in Pasley.

69. Cpl. Claude J. Batchelor to Dear Sir, undated, Batchelor Court Martial.

70. Some of the newspapers carrying Batchelor's autobiography include *The Hartford Courant* (Conn.), Jan. 11, 1954; *San Angelo Standard-Times* (Tex.), Jan. 10, 1954; and the *Dallas Morning News* (Tex.), Jan. 10, 1954.

71. Claude J. Batchelor Statement, Batchelor Court Martial; and Hunter, *Brainwashing,* 242.

72. *San Angelo Standard-Times* (Tex.), Jan. 5, 1954; and *Dallas Morning News* (Tex.), Jan. 7, 1954.

8. Dickenson's Reckoning

1. Hillman, *Defending America,* 55–56.

2. Press Release from United Nations Command Repatriation Group, Dec. 23, 1953, Dickenson Court Martial.

3. Summary of Information (Corden, Richard Guy Joseph), NARAII-153-Summary. The Summary of Information sheets were apparently compiled and written during the last weeks of the repatriation process as several of them note Batchelor's return (January 1, 1954) and the possibility of enticing the other men back by the January 22, 1954 deadline.
4. Summary of Information (Douglas, Rufus E.), NARAII-153-Summary.
5. Summary of Information (Fortuna, Andrew), NARAII-153-Summary.
6. Summary of Information (Hawkins, Samuel D.), NARAII-153-Summary.
7. Summary of Information (Rush, Scot Leonard), NARAII-153-Summary.
8. Summary of Information (Griggs, Lewie Wayne), NARAII-153-Summary.
9. Summary of Information (Bell, Otho G.), NARAII-153-Summary.
10. *New York Times,* Jan. 22, 1954.
11. *New York Times,* Jan. 23, 1954.
12. Wills, *Turncoat,* 75.
13. *New York Times,* Jan. 23, 1954.
14. *New York Times,* Jan. 23, 1954.
15. *Bristol Herald Courier* (Va.), Jan. 23, 1954.
16. *Bristol Herald Courier* (Va.), Jan. 25, 1954.
17. *Bristol Herald Courier* (Va.), Jan. 24, 1954.
18. *Kingsport Times News* (Tenn.), Jan. 24, 1954.
19. *The Post* (Big Stone Gap, Va.), Jan. 28, 1954; and *Bristol Herald Courier* (Va.), Jan. 27, 1954.
20. *New York Times,* Jan. 24, 1954.
21. *New York Times,* Jan. 25, 1954.
22. *Kingsport Times-News* (Tenn.), Jan. 25, 1954.
23. *New York Times,* Jan. 26, 1954; and *Kingsport Times-News* (Tenn.), Jan. 26, 1954.
24. *Bristol Herald Courier* (Va.), Jan. 26, 1954.
25. *Bristol Herald Courier* (Va.), Jan. 28, 1954.
26. United Press release, Jan. 27, 1954, unknown newspaper; folder, 3-M Court Martial Cases (3) D; box 84, OF 3-M Court Martial Cases, A; White House Central Files, Official File, 1953–1961; Dwight D. Eisenhower Presidential Library, Abilene, Kansas.
27. Curt Sherry to Dear Mr. and Mrs. Dickenson, Jan. 23, 1954; folder, 3-M Court Martial Cases (3) D; box 84, OF 3-M Court Martial Cases, A; White House Central Files, Official File, 1953–1961; Dwight D. Eisenhower Presidential Library, Abilene, Kansas.
28. "Snafu and Showdown," *Newsweek,* Feb. 1, 1954, 18.
29. *Bristol Herald Courier* (Va.), Jan. 29, 1954.
30. *New York Times,* Feb. 19, 1954.
31. *The Post* (Big Stone Gap, Va.), Apr. 8, 1954; and *Hattiesburg American* (Miss.), Apr. 3, 1954.
32. *Bristol Herald Courier* (Va.), Apr. 20, 1954.
33. Lech, *Broken Soldiers,* 238.
34. *Bristol Herald Courier* (Va.), Apr. 21, 1954.
35. *Roanoke Times* (Va.), Apr. 28, 1954.
36. *Bristol Herald Courier* (Va.), Apr. 21, 1954.
37. James Thompson, *True Colors: 1004 Days as a Prisoner of War* (Port Washington, N.Y.: Ashley Books, 1989), 51–52.
38. *Bristol Herald Courier* (Va.), Apr. 21, 1954.

39. Dominic J. Cantillo Sworn Statement, Sept. 24, 1953, Dickenson Court Martial.

40. *New York Times,* Apr. 22, 1954.

41. *New York Times,* Apr. 22, 1954. See also John A. Davis Sworn Statement, Jan. 18, 1954, Dickenson Court Martial.

42. *Bristol Herald Courier* (Va.), Apr. 23, 1954.

43. Edward S. Dickenson to Dear Sir, Feb. 23, 1953, Dickenson Court Martial.

44. *Bristol Herald Courier* (Va.), Apr. 23, 1954.

45. Martin Christensen Sworn Statement, Jan. 7, 1954, Dickenson Court Martial.

46. Fred Obroff Sworn Statement, Jan. 21, 1954, Dickenson Court Martial.

47. Edward M. Gaither Sworn Statement, Jan. 13, 1954, Dickenson Court Martial.

48. *Bristol Herald Courier* (Va.), Apr. 24, 1954.

49. *Roanoke Times* (Va.), Apr. 27, 1954.

50. *Roanoke Times* (Va.), Apr. 28, 1954.

51. Philip Bloemsma testimony, Apr. 27, 1954, Dickenson Court Martial.

52. Philip Bloemsma testimony, Apr. 27, 1954, Dickenson Court Martial. Bloemsma identified the "fence complex" as fully manifesting itself in between three to twelve months of captivity. The speed of a prisoner's acculturation was largely dependent on the severity of his treatment. The more difficult the existence, the quicker this total survival mode was enacted. In cases of lesser coercion, the time could be more extended. In the case of those men captured very early in the war and held during the difficult winter of 1950–1951, it is reasonable to expect that the complex afflicted these men very quickly.

53. Donald L. Manes Jr., "Barbed Wire Command: The Legal Nature of the Command Responsibilities of the Senior Prisoner in a Prisoner of War Camp," *Military Law Review* (Oct. 1960), 23; *Roanoke Times* (Va.), Apr. 28, 1954; and Philip Bloemsma testimony, Apr. 27, 1954, Dickenson Court Martial.

54. *Roanoke Times* (Va.), Apr. 29, 1954.

55. *Roanoke Times* (Va.), Apr. 29, 1954.

56. *Bristol Herald Courier* (Va.), Apr. 30, 1954.

57. *Bristol Herald Courier* (Va.), May 1, 1954; *New York Times,* May 1, 1954; and *Roanoke Times* (Va.), May 1, 1954.

58. *Washington Post and Times Herald,* May 4, 1954; and *Roanoke Times* (Va.), May 4, 1954.

59. *Washington Post and Times Herald,* May 5, 1954; and *New York Times,* May 5, 1954.

60. Hillman, *Defending America,* 49.

61. *Washington Post and Times Herald,* May 5, 1954.

62. "Collaborator's Reward," Time, July 11, 1955; Lech, *Broken Soldiers,* 221; and *New York Times,* Aug. 21, 1955.

63. *Olympics, 1952.*

64. *Olympics, 1952.*

65. *Olympics, 1952.*

66. Appendix B, Counterintelligence Report, box 24, Record Group 319, Records of the Army Staff, Counterintelligence Files, 1950–1958, Textual Records, National Archives and Records Administration II, College Park, Maryland.

67. *New York Times,* Nov. 24, 1957.

68. Lech, *Broken Soldiers,* 239.

69. Memorandum from John Edgar Hoover to Assistant Chief of Staff, G-2, Aug. 5, 1955; Dickenson Defense Fund Committee to [censored], Federal Bureau of Investigation, Detroit, Michigan, Feb. 23, 1955, FBI-Dickenson; Memorandum from SAC, New York to Director, FBI, May 4, 1955, FBI-Dickenson; Memorandum from Director,

FBI to SAC, New York, Mar. 16, 1955, FBI-Dickenson; and Memorandum from SAC, New York to Director, FBI, July 26, 1955, FBI-Dickenson.

70. Oshinsky, *A Conspiracy so Immense,* 405–7.

71. Oshinsky, *A Conspiracy so Immense,* 467–71.

9. Batchelor's Reckoning

1. Joel W. Westbrook to Dear Lyndon, Apr. 13, 1954, and Lyndon B. Johnson to Dear Joel, Apr. 20, 1954, Senate Files, box 1366, file 1958 Case Files, Batchelor, Claude J., Oct. 1954–1958 (Korean War Defector), Lyndon Baines Johnson Presidential Library and Museum, Austin, Texas.

2. *Odessa* (Tex.) *American,* May 5, 1954.

3. *Hartford* (Conn.) *Courant,* June 22, 1954.

4. *Odessa* (Tex.) *American,* Aug. 3, 1954.

5. *Odessa* (Tex.) *American,* Aug. 6, 1954.

6. *Odessa* (Tex.) *American,* Aug. 10, 1954.

7. *Odessa* (Tex.) *American,* Aug. 30, 1954.

8. *Odessa* (Tex.) *American,* Oct. 1, 1954.

9. Bohus J. Janda testimony, Sept. 1, 1954, Batchelor Court Martial.

10. Harold M. Dunn testimony, Sept. 1, 1954, Batchelor Court Martial.

11. *Odessa* (Tex.) *American,* Sept. 2, 1954.

12. *Odessa* (Tex.) *American,* Sept. 6, 1954.

13. John Megyesi testimony, Sept. 8, 1954, Batchelor Court Martial.

14. Walter Lloyd Mayo Jr., testimony, Sept. 8, 1954, Batchelor Court Martial. In addition to testifying against Batchelor, Mayo also testified against Maj. Ronald Alley and may have played a role in other prosecutions.

15. "Statement of Expected Testimony," Sgt. Bernard Buli, Fort Devens, Mass., Exhibit 8, Batchelor Court Martial; and *New York Times,* Sept. 9, 1954.

16. John W. Fields testimony, Sept. 9, 1954, Batchelor Court Martial.

17. Billy E. Clark statement, June 12, 1954, Batchelor Court Martial.

18. Billy E. Clark statement, June 12, 1954, Batchelor Court Martial.

19. Robert Leo McGreevey testimony, Sept. 9, 1954, Batchelor Court Martial.

20. Robert H. Ghyers testimony, Sept. 9, 1954, Batchelor Court Martial.

21. *New York Times,* Sept. 10, 1954.

22. *Odessa* (Tex.) *American,* Sept. 10, 1954.

23. Shirley Grimmette testimony, Sept. 10, 1954, Batchelor Court Martial.

24. *Odessa* (Tex.) *American,* Sept. 13, 1954.

25. Wilburn Watson testimony, Sept. 13, 1954, Batchelor Court Martial.

26. *Odessa American* (Tex.), Sept. 15, 1954.

27. *Odessa American* (Tex.), Sept. 15, 1954.

28. *Odessa American* (Tex.), Sept. 16, 1954.

29. *New York Times,* Sept. 16, 1954.

30. Robert E. Vincent testimony, Sept. 14, 1954, Batchelor Court Martial.

31. John Edward Owens testimony, Sept. 14, 1954, Batchelor Court Martial.

32. *Odessa American* (Tex.), Sept. 16, 1954.

33. Mrs. O. L. Batchelor testimony, Sept. 17, 1954, Batchelor Court Martial.

34. *Odessa American* (Tex.), Sept. 16, 1954.

35. Sgt. William J. Skinner testimony, Sept. 17, 1954, Batchelor Court Martial.

36. *New York Times,* Dec. 17, 1954; and Claude J. Batchelor statement, Jan. 28, 1954, 5 of 11, Batchelor Court Martial.

37. Claude J. Batchelor statement, Jan. 28, 1954, 5 of 11, Batchelor Court Martial. Batchelor named Harry Copeland, Donald Disney, Howard J. Beadleson, Richard Grinier, Roscoe Perry, Leroy Carter Jr., and George R. Atkins as the appointed operatives.

38. *New York Times,* Sept. 18, 1954.

39. *Odessa American* (Tex.), Sept. 19, 1954.

40. *Odessa American* (Tex.), Sept. 19, 1954; and *Odessa American* (Tex.), Sept. 21, 1954.

41. *Odessa American* (Tex.), Sept. 21, 1954.

42. Synopsis of the Frank Noel Story, NARA-Noel.

43. Francis E. Noel testimony, Sept. 21, 1954, Batchelor Court Martial; and *Odessa American* (Tex.), Sept. 22, 1954.

44. Francis E. Noel testimony, Sept. 21, 1954, Batchelor Court Martial.

45. Francis E. Noel testimony, Sept. 21, 1954, Batchelor Court Martial.

46. *Odessa American* (Tex.), Sept. 24, 1954.

47. *Odessa American* (Tex.), Sept. 24, 1954.

48. *Odessa American* (Tex.), Sept. 24, 1954.

49. Lech, *Broken Soldiers,* 243.

50. *Odessa American* (Tex.), Sept. 24, 1954. Dr. Freedom's theories are more fully explained in Chapter 9 of Edward Hunter, *Brainwashing: The Story of Men Who Defied It* (New York, N.Y.: Farrar, Straus and Cuhady, 1956), 243–63.

51. *Odessa American* (Tex.), Sept. 24, 1954; and Lech, *Broken Soldiers,* 155.

52. *Odessa American* (Tex.), Sept. 28, 1954.

53. *Odessa American* (Tex.), Sept. 30, 1954; Edward S. Dickenson testimony, Sept. 30, 1954, Batchelor Court Martial.

54. Appendix B, Counterintelligence Report, Box 24, Record Group 319, Records of the Army Staff, Counterintelligence Files, 1950–1958, Textual Records, National Archives and Records Administration II, College Park, Maryland.

55. *New York Times,* Sept. 30, 1954.

56. *Odessa American* (Tex.), Oct. 1, 1954.

57. Lech, *Broken Soldiers,* 242.

58. *Odessa American* (Tex.), Oct. 1, 1954; *New York Times,* Oct. 2, 1954; and *Odessa American* (Tex.), Oct. 4, 1954.

59. Kinkead, *In Every War But One,* 80–81.

60. SAC, Kansas City to Director, FBI, Feb. 9, 1956, FBI-Bell; and W. W. Cardwell to Dear Senator, Oct. 1, 1954, Senate Files, Box 1366, file, 1958 Case Files, Batchelor, Claude J., Oct. 1954–1958 (Korean War Defector), Lyndon Baines Johnson Presidential Library and Museum, Austin, Texas.

61. Wm. F. Graham to Dear Senator Johnson, Oct. 6, 1954, Senate Files, Box 1366, file, 1958 Case Files, Batchelor, Claude J., Oct. 1954–1958 (Korean War Defector), Lyndon Baines Johnson Presidential Library and Museum, Austin, Texas.

62. *Fort Worth Star Telegram* (Tex.), Oct. 6, 1954.

63. Statement of Former POW Richard G. Corden in Defense of Cpl. Claude J. Batchelor, Nov. 6, 1954, Audio Recordings of Monitored Broadcasts from Asia, 1949–1960, Record Group 263, Records of the Central Intelligence Agency, 1894–2002, Textual Records, National Archives and Records Administration II, College Park, Maryland, hereinafter cited as NARAII-263-Broadcasts.

64. *Odessa American* (Tex.), Oct. 28, 1954; Oct. 29, 1954; *New York Times,* Oct. 29, 1954; Nov. 12, 1954; Dec. 3, 1954.

65. Mr. and Mrs. O. L. Batchelor to Dear Mr. President, Dec. 8, 1954; folder, 3-M Court Martial Cases, B; Box 84, OF 3-M Court Martial Cases, A; White House Central Files, Official File, 1953–1961; Dwight D. Eisenhower Presidential Library, Abilene, Kansas.

10. Men Jailed . . . and Walking Free, 1954–1957

1. Wills, *Turncoat,* 75.

2. *Kingsport Times-News* (Tenn.), Jan. 26, 1954.

3. Operations Coordinating Board Memorandum for Record, Feb. 5, 1954; folder, OCB 383.6 (File #1) (8) [Jan.–June 1954]; box 118, OCB Central File Series, White House Office, National Security Council Staff: Papers, 1948–61, Dwight D. Eisenhower Presidential Library, Abilene, Kansas.

4. Wills, *Turncoat,* 75–76.

5. Wills, *Turncoat,* 78.

6. Adams, *An American Dream,* 73.

7. Wills, *Turncoat,* 79.

8. Wills, *Turncoat,* 80; Anonymous interview #1, Nov. 15, 2007, recording and transcript in possession of the author; and *San Angelo* (Tex.) *Standard-Times,* June 16, 1954.

9. Adams, *An American Dream,* 73.

10. Wills, *Turncoat,* 80–81; and Adams, *An American Dream,* 80.

11. Wills, *Turncoat,* 81–85; and *New York Times,* July 11, 1955.

12. Federal Bureau of Investigation report form, June 5, 1958, 3, FBI-Bell.

13. It is difficult to determine which men were assigned to which positions, but Wills, Sullivan, Corden, Belhomme, Hawkins, Rush, Fortuna, Webb, Clarence Adams, and William White went to the university. Cowart, Griggs, and Bell were sent to the farm. The factory group consisted of Veneris, Skinner, Tenneson, Wilson, and Pate.

14. Wills, *Turncoat,* 88–89.

15. Rick to Dear Mother, Feb. 6, 1954, transcript included in memo from John Edgar Hoover to Assistant Chief of Staff, G-2, Apr. 18, 1955, FBI-Tenneson.

16. Akron (Ohio) *Beacon-Journal,* July 31, 1955.

17. *New York Times,* June 12, 1956; and Lowell Skinner to Dear Mom and Dad, Oct. 18, 1956, FBI-Skinner.

18. *New York Times,* Feb. 27, 1957; and Feb. 28, 1957.

19. Wills, *Turncoat,* 98; and *Washington Post and Times Herald,* Dec. 17, 1958. Richard Corden studied Chinese literature and politics at Wuhan University.

20. Adam J. Zweiback, "The 21 'Turncoat G.I.s': The Political Culture of the Korean War," *The Historian* 60 (Winter 1998), 359.

21. *New York Times,* July 11, 1955; and Federal Bureau of Investigation report form, June 5, 1958, 3, FBI-Bell.

22. Zweiback, "The 21 'Turncoat G.I.s'," 359; *New York Times,* June 19, 1955; and Federal Bureau of Investigation report form, June 5, 1958, page 3, FBI-Bell.

23. Wills, *Turncoat,* 96.

24. Zweiback, "The 21 'Turncoat G.I.s,'" 359.

25. "UN Soldiers in China," July 1, 1955, FBI-Griggs.

26. Lewie W. Griggs to Dear President Eisenhower, May 16, 1955; folder, STATE, Department of, (July 1955); box 70, Subject Series, Records as President, White House Central Files, (Confidential File), 1953–61; Dwight D. Eisenhower Presidential Library, Abilene, Kansas. Griggs also wrote General Mark Clark with a similar request.

27. *New York Times,* June 19, 1955.

28. *New York Times,* July 11, 1955.

29. *New York Times,* July 12, 1955.

30. *New York Times,* July 25, 1955.

31. *New York Times,* July 26, 1955; Article 3A had been incorporated into the U.C.M.J. after it was revealed in 1950 that Lt. Aldo Icardi had killed his superior,

Maj. William Holohan while behind enemy lines in northern Italy in 1944. See *New York Times,* Aug. 18, 1951; Oct. 21, 1953; Oct. 23, 1953; Nov. 6, 1953; and Aug. 30, 1955.

32. *New York Times,* July 27, 1955.

33. *New York Times,* July 30, 1955; and *Dallas Morning News,* July 30, 1955.

34. *New York Times,* Sept. 16, 1955; Davis and Brown telegram to President Eisenhower, Sept. 14, 1955; and White House telegram to Harold C. Brown, Esq., Sept. 15, 1955; folder, 125-U 1955; Box 937, GF 125-T, General File, White House Central Files; Dwight D. Eisenhower Presidential Library, Abilene, Kansas.

35. Mr. A. H. Belmont to Mr. L. V. Boardman, Nov. 9, 1955, FBI-Griggs; and *Washington Star,* Nov. 8, 1954.

36. *Los Angeles Times,* June 19, 1955; and *New York Times,* Nov. 9, 1955.

37. Federal Bureau of Investigation Airtel, May 23, 1956, FBI-Bell.

38. Federal Bureau of Investigation Form No. 1, May 31, 1956, 7, FBI-Bell.

39. *New York Times,* Sept. 14, 1955.

40. *New York Times,* Dec. 1, 1955.

41. *New York Times,* Dec. 4, 1955.

42. *Minneapolis Star* (Minn.), Dec. 8, 1955.

43. *Minneapolis Star* (Minn.), Dec. 13, 1955; and *New York Times,* Dec. 14, 1955.

44. FBI-Minneapolis to Director, FBI, Sept. 15, 1955, FBI-Tenneson.

45. *Minneapolis Star* (Minn.), Dec. 13, 1955.

46. *New York Times,* Dec. 14, 1955.

47. *Minneapolis Star* (Minn.), Dec. 16, 1955.

48. *Minneapolis Star* (Minn.), Dec. 13, 1955.

49. *Minneapolis Star* (Minn.), Dec. 16, 1955.

50. *Southern Illinoisan* (Carbondale, Ill.), Dec. 23, 1955.

51. *Southern Illinoisan* (Carbondale, Ill.), Dec. 23, 1955.

52. *Southern Illinoisan* (Carbondale, Ill.), Dec. 23, 1955.

53. Wills, *Turncoat,* 98.

54. Wills, *Turncoat,* 98; *New York Times,* Mar. 31, 1958; and *Los Angeles Times,* June 16, 1957.

55. Wills, *Turncoat,* 98–99.

56. Wills, *Turncoat,* 99.

57. Wills, *Turncoat,* 103.

58. William F. Tompkins, Assistant Attorney General Internal Security Division, to Director, Federal Bureau of Investigation, June 27, 1956, 20–24, handwritten, upper right corner, FBI-Skinner.

59. SAC, Springfield to Director, FBI, Sept. 17, 1956, FBI-Pate; and Interview of Unidentified Former PW (name classified), Oct. 5, 1956, 5, FBI-Pate.

60. *New York Times,* Nov. 22, 1956.

61. *New York Times,* Nov. 26, 1956; and SAC, Springfield to Director, FBI, Sept. 17, 1956, FBI-Pate.

62. *New York Times,* Dec. 2, 1956.

63. *New York Times,* Dec. 3, 1956.

64. *Southern Illinoisan* (Carbondale, Ill.), Dec. 6, 1956.

65. *Southern Illinoisan* (Carbondale, Ill.), Dec. 7, 1956.

66. *Southern Illinoisan* (Carbondale, Ill.), Dec. 7, 1956; and Dec. 9, 1956.

67. *Globe Democrat* (St. Louis, Mo.), Dec. 9, 1956.

68. *Southern Illinoisan* (Carbondale, Ill.), Dec. 12, 1956; and Dec. 14, 1956.

69. *Post Dispatch* (St. Louis, Mo.), Dec. 9, 1956.

70. *Post Dispatch* (St. Louis, Mo.), Dec. 9, 1956.
71. *Southern Illinoisan* (Carbondale, Ill.), Dec. 13, 1956.
72. *Southern Illinoisan* (Carbondale, Ill.), Dec. 24, 1956.
73. *Southern Illinoisan* (Carbondale, Ill.), Jan. 23, 1957.
74. *Southern Illinoisan* (Carbondale, Ill.), Jan. 24, 1957.
75. *Southern Illinoisan* (Carbondale, Ill.), Apr. 22, 1957; and SAC, Springfield, to Director, FBI, Apr. 26, 1957, FBI-Pate.
76. *Southern Illinoisan* (Carbondale, Ill.), Apr. 25, 1957.
77. *Southern Illinoisan* (Carbondale, Ill.), May 13, 1957.
78. *Southern Illinoisan* (Carbondale, Ill.), July 7, 1957.
79. *Alexandria Daily Town Talk* (La.), Dec. 21, 1956.
80. *Alexandria Daily Town Talk* (La.), Dec. 6, 1956.
81. *Alexandria Daily Town Talk* (La.), Dec. 7, 1956.
82. *Alexandria Daily Town Talk* (La.), Dec. 7, 1956.
83. *Alexandria Daily Town Talk* (La.), Dec. 8, 1956.
84. *Alexandria Daily Town Talk* (La.), Dec. 18, 1956; and Dec. 21, 1956.
85. *Alexandria Daily Town Talk* (La.), Dec. 18, 1956.
86. *Alexandria Daily Town Talk* (La.), Dec. 21, 1956.
87. *New York Times,* Dec. 22, 1956.
88. CHECK LIST ON RECAP-K CASES, Wilson, Aaron P., NARAII-153-CHECK LIST.
89. Prugh obituary, *San Francisco Chronicle* (Calif.), July 13, 2006. Prugh would later serve as Judge Advocate General for the U.S. Army from July 1, 1971 to June 30, 1975 and famously refused to accede to President Richard Nixon's claim that he, as president, should be able to decide Lieutenant William Calley's appeal.
90. SAC, New Orleans to Director, FBI, Aug. 6, 1956, FBI-Bell.
91. Gentlemen [Ethel Knight to FBI], Aug. 21, 1956, FBI-Bell.
92. SAC, New Orleans to Director, FBI, Sept. 12, 1956, FBI-Bell; and SAC, Seattle to Director, FBI, Sept. 12, 1956.
93. *New York Times,* Jan. 17, 1957.
94. *New York Times,* Feb. 27, 1957. Hawkins reiterated the process of his departure from China during an appearance on *The Mike Wallace Interview,* June 23, 1957.
95. *New York Times,* Feb. 28, 1957.
96. *New York Times,* Feb. 28, 1957.
97. *New York Times,* Dec. 23, 1955; Feb. 28, 1957; and June 14, 1957.
98. *New York Times,* Mar. 4, 1957; and *Dallas Morning News* (Tex.), Mar. 4, 1957.
99. Samuel David Hawkins interview on *The Mike Wallace Interview,* June 23, 1957.
100. *Ashland Daily Independent* (Ky.), June 16, 1957.
101. *New York Times,* June 15, 1957.
102. *Ashland Daily Independent* (Ky.), June 16, 1957.
103. Memorandum, SAC, Butte, to Director, FBI, Sept. 26, 1957, 1, FBI-Fortuna.
104. Mary Wills to Sir, Jan. 4, 1958, FBI-Fortuna; and Memorandum, SAC, Springfield, to Director, FBI, Feb. 26, 1958, FBI-Fortuna.
105. Memorandum, SAC, San Francisco, to Director, FBI, Apr. 8, 1958, FBI-Fortuna.
106. Memorandum, SAC, San Francisco, to Director, FBI, Apr. 8, 1958, 2, FBI-Fortuna.
107. Telegram, Detroit, to Director, July 16, 1964, FBI-Fortuna; Memo, Re: Andrew Fortuna, Aug. 28, 1964, FBI-Fortuna; and United States Department of Justice report, bureau file 100–414435, FBI-Fortuna.
108. John King Fairbank, *China: A New History* (Cambridge, Mass.: Belknap Press of the Harvard Univ. Press, 1992), 364; Wills, *Turncoat,* 105–6; Philip Short, *Mao: A*

Life (New York, N.Y.: Owl Books, 1999), 457–71; Jonathan D. Spence, *The Gate of Heavenly Peace: The Chinese and Their Revolution, 1895–1980* (New York, N.Y.: Penguin, 1981), 378–79.

109. Fairbank, *China,* 364; Wills, *Turncoat,* 106–7; Short, *Mao,* 457–71; Spence, *The Gate of Heavenly Peace,* 378–79.

110. Wills, *Turncoat,* 131.

111. Wills, *Turncoat,* 132.

112. Wills, *Turncoat,* 132–33.

113. *Washington Post and Times Herald,* Sept. 12, 1957.

114. Wills, *Turncoat,* 91; and Sidney Rittenberg interview, Oct. 17, 2008.

115. *Washington Post and Times Herald,* Nov. 17, 1957.

116. Adams, *An American Dream,* 84–88.

117. *Los Angeles Times,* Aug. 5, 1976; Nov. 22, 1981; Dec. 30, 1984; and *Washington Post,* July 15, 1976.

118. Ted Morgan, *Reds: McCarthyism in Twentieth-Century America* (New York, N.Y.: Random House, 2004), 510.

119. *New York Times,* Apr. 17, 1957.

120. *New York Times,* Nov. 24, 1957.

121. Hillman, *Defending America,* 51, 109.

122. Memorandum from SAC, Memphis to Director, FBI, Jan. 29, 1958, FBI-Dickenson; *Washington Post and Times Herald,* Nov. 24, 1957; Washington City News Service teletype, Nov. 23, 1957, FBI-Dickenson; *New York Times,* Nov. 24, 1957; and *Knoxville* (Tenn.) *News Sentinel,* Nov. 26, 1957; Nov. 27, 1957.

123. *The Post* (Big Stone Gap, Va.), Nov. 28, 1957.

124. *Bristol* (Tenn.) *Herald Courier,* Nov. 29, 1957, and *Knoxville* (Tenn.) *News Sentinel,* Nov. 29, 1957. The newspapers and radios quoted a member of the local or county police force named John Willis. Later, it was revealed that no one of that name worked for either force in any capacity.

125. *The Post* (Big Stone Gap, Va.), Dec. 5, 1957; and Dec. 12, 1957.

126. Report Form, Feb. 24, 1958, FBI-Dickenson; and Memorandum to SAC, Richmond, Feb. 24, 1958, FBI-Dickenson.

11. Outcasts in Life and Death since 1958

1. *Los Angeles Times,* Mar. 30, 1958; and *New York Times,* Mar. 30, 1958.

2. Department of State incoming telegram, from Hong Kong to Secretary of State, Mar. 31, 1958, Miscellaneous State Department telegrams re. Larance V. Sullivan, Department of State, Washington, D.C., hereinafter cited as State-Misc.

3. *New York Times,* Mar. 30, 1958; and Mar. 31, 1958.

4. *Washington Star,* Dec. 3, 1958.

5. *Washington Star,* Dec. 20, 1958.

6. SAC, San Francisco, to Director, FBI, Jan. 5, 1959, FBI-Corden.

7. *Honolulu Star-Bulletin,* Jan. 14, 1959.

8. *Honolulu Advertiser,* Jan. 15, 1959.

9. Internal Security Division memo, Jan. 23, 1959, FBI-Corden.

10. SAC, Los Angeles, to Director, FBI, Mar. 12, 1959, FBI-Corden.

11. FBI Report Form, Apr. 7, 1959, FBI-Corden.

12. Special Agent Report, Apr. 7, 1959, FBI-Corden.

13. FBI Report, Feb. 6, 1961, 2, FBI-Corden.

14. FBI Report, Feb. 6, 1961, 10, FBI-Corden.

15. SAC, Milwaukee, to Director, FBI, Dec. 21, 1960, FBI-Corden.

16. Fairbank, *China,* 368–71; and Spence, *The Gate of Heavenly Peace,* 382–83.

17. Jonathan D. Spence, *The Search for Modern China* (New York, N.Y.: W. W. Norton, 1990), 583.

18. Wills, *Turncoat,* 110–11.

19. *Christian Science Monitor,* Sept. 3, 1963; and *Los Angeles Times,* Sept. 1, 1963. The *Washington Post and Times Herald,* Sept. 1, 1963, ran a similar story, but placed the strike in 1961 and explained that it had been an overall success for Belhomme. However, no corroborating quotes from Belhomme are noted.

20. "Where Are They Now?: A Roster of American Defectors from the Korean War," Associated Press, Mar. 25, 2002.

21. United States Department of Justice, Federal Bureau of Investigation, June 18, 1964, 4, FBI-Bell.

22. United States Department of Justice, Federal Bureau of Investigation, June 18, 1964, 5, FBI-Bell.

23. *Independent Journal* (San Rafael, Calif.), Dec. 17, 1959.

24. *San Francisco* (Calif.) *Chronicle,* Dec. 29, 1959.

25. SAC, San Francisco to Director, FBI, Jan. 22, 1963, 1–2, FBI-Sullivan; Federal Bureau of Investigation Report, May 25, 1964, FBI-Sullivan; SAC, San Francisco to Director, FBI, Apr. 30, 1965, FBI-Sullivan; and Federal Bureau of Investigation Report, Mar. 30, 1967, BFI-Sullivan.

26. Taylor, *Brainwashing,* 230.

27. Director, FBI, to Assistant Attorney General William F. Tompkins, Apr. 26, 1956, FBI-Bell.

28. Sgt. Robert I. Banks statement, Dec. 9, 1953, 2–3, Dickenson Court Martial.

29. Wills, *Turncoat,* 114–24, and Information Report, Feb. 29, 1960, FBI-Skinner. In Feb. 1960, the Central Intelligence Agency, keeping tabs on the nonrepatriates in the event of future prosecution, noted that Wills was studying Chinese language at Beijing University. The CIA misidentified former Cpl. Morris Wills as Captain Morris.

30. *Southern Illinoisan* (Carbondale, Ill.), Aug. 4, 1963.

31. The case was filed as *Bell* v. *United States,* 366 U.S. 393 (1961). Washington Capital News Service, UPI-139, May 24, 1961, FBI-Bell.

32. Adams, *An American Dream,* 102.

33. Wills, *Turncoat,* 133; and *Los Angeles Times,* Aug. 22, 1963. Ralph McGill's article in the *Los Angeles Times* identified the illness as "a tubercular brain infection."

34. *New York Times,* Aug. 1, 1963; and *Pacific Stars and Stripes* (Tokyo, Japan), Aug. 3, 1963.

35. *New York Times,* Aug. 2, 1963. See also Unknown (classified Secret Service agent) to Mr. Harry Morgan, July 9, 1968, FBI-Skinner.

36. *New York Times,* Aug. 3, 1963; *Los Angeles Times,* Aug. 22, 1963; *Pacific Stars and Stripes* (Tokyo, Japan), Aug. 4, 1963; Czech and Slovak Foreign Magazine, Number 269, June 2004.

37. *Akron Beacon Journal* (Ohio), Aug. 7, 1963.

38. *Akron Beacon Journal* (Ohio), Aug. 8, 1963; and Aug. 9, 1963.

39. *Akron Beacon Journal* (Ohio), Aug. 19, 1963.

40. *Akron Beacon Journal* (Ohio), Aug. 15, 1963.

41. *Akron Beacon Journal* (Ohio), Aug. 30, 1963.

42. *Cincinnati Enquirer* (Ohio), Nov. 20, 1963.

43. *Cincinnati Enquirer* (Ohio), Feb. 9, 1964.

44. *Cleveland Press* (Ohio), Oct. 29, 1964.

45. *Akron Beacon Journal* (Ohio), Nov. 19, 1964.

46. *Akron Beacon Journal* (Ohio), Dec. 3, 1964; and *Cleveland Plain Dealer* (Ohio), Dec. 4, 1964.

47. *Akron Beacon Journal* (Ohio), Dec. 10, 1964.

48. *Akron Beacon Journal* (Ohio), Dec. 10, 1964.

49. *Akron Beacon Journal* (Ohio), Feb. 23, 1965.

50. *Akron Beacon Journal* (Ohio), May 19, 1965.

51. Special Agent Report, June 8, 1965, 10–11, FBI-Skinner.

52. *New York Times,* Aug. 31, 1963.

53. *New York Times,* Nov. 3, 1963.

54. *New York Times,* Nov. 6, 1963.

55. *New York Times,* Sept. 15, 1963.

56. *Akron Beacon Journal* (Ohio), Sept. 9, 1963.

57. *Los Angeles Times,* Sept. 25, 1963.

58. Wills, *Turncoat,* 112–13.

59. *New York Times,* Sept. 8, 1963.

60. Wills, *Turncoat,* 113.

61. *New York Times,* Sept. 8, 1963.

62. *Washington Post,* July 15, 1976; and *Los Angeles Times,* Aug. 5, 1976; Nov. 22, 1981; Dec. 30, 1984.

63. Federal Bureau of Investigation Report Form, Oct. 3, 1966, 9–10, FBI-Clarence C. Adams.

64. Federal Bureau of Investigation, Report Form, Oct. 3, 1966, 15, FBI-Clarence C. Adams. White left China nearly broke while Adams left with $9,000 (Hong Kong) and Wills took over $3,000 (Hong Kong).

65. HQ 100–407913, Dec. 29, 1965, Morris R. Wills documents, Department of the Army, United States Army Intelligence and Security Command, Fort George G. Meade, Maryland.

66. Debriefing of Morris R. Wills, Nov. 19, 1965, Department of State Airgram, 22–23, FBI-Wills.

67. Undated and untitled document pertaining to William C. White's repatriation debriefing, FBI-Wills.

68. Memorandum, Legat, Tokyo, to Director, FBI, Oct. 11, 1963, FBI-Wills.

69. Debriefing of Morris R. Wills, Nov. 19, 1965, Department of State Airgram, 23–24, FBI-Wills.

70. *Log Cabin Democrat* (Conway, AR), Aug. 17, 1965; and *New York Times,* Aug. 18, 1965.

71. *Time,* Aug. 27, 1965; *New York Times,* Aug. 20, 1965; Aug. 29, 1965; Sept. 19, 1965, supplement; and Richard B. Russell to Dear Mr. President, Aug. 18, 1965, White House Central Files, Box 7, Folder ND 9 Military Personnel, 11/22/63–8/23/65, Lyndon Baines Johnson Presidential Library and Museum, Austin, Texas.

72. Unidentified newspaper article, Sept. 20, 1965, Folder A.3800, Manuscript Collection, Center for the Study of the Korean War, Graceland University, Independence, Missouri.

73. Wills, *Turncoat,* 167.

74. *They Chose China,* produced by Claude Bonin, directed by Shui-Bo Wang, 52 min., National Film Board of Canada, 2005. DVD.

75. Wills, *Turncoat,* 168.

76. Wills, *Turncoat,* 168–71.

77. Wills, *Turncoat,* 172–78.

78. *New York Times,* Aug. 15, 1965.
79. Incoming telegram, Department of State, Oct. 23, 1965, FBI-Wills.
80. *New York Times,* May 26, 1966.
81. *New York Times,* May 27, 1966.
82. *New York Times,* June 23, 1966.
83. *New York Times,* July 5, 1966.
84. *New York Times,* July 5, 1966.
85. *New York Times,* July 10, 1966.
86. *New York Times,* Nov. 26, 1966.
87. Federal Bureau of Investigation Report Form, May 3, 1967, 2, FBI-Clarence C. Adams.
88. SAC, San Francisco to Director, FBI, Nov. 16, 1970, FBI-Griggs; and Assistant Attorney General William F. Tompkins to Director, FBI, Jan. 16, 1956, FBI-Griggs.
89. Federal Bureau of Investigation Report Form, July 31, 1967, 5, FBI-Clarence C. Adams. For more on Williams, see Timothy B. Tyson, *"Radio Free Dixie": Robert F. Williams and the Roots of Black Power* (Chapel Hill: Univ. of North Carolina Press, 1999).
90. SAC, Albany to Director, FBI, Jan. 10, 1966, FBI-Wills; and SAC, Albany to Director, FBI, Feb. 16, 1966, FBI-Wills.
91. SAC, Albany to Director, FBI, Mar. 28, 1966, 1–2, FBI-Wills; and SAC, Albany to Director, FBI, Apr. 1, 1966, FBI-Wills.
92. Mr. R. D. Cotten to Mr. W. C. Sullivan, Jan. 14, 1966, FBI-Wills; and SAC, Albany to Director, FBI, Dec. 3, 1965, FBI-Wills.
93. SAC, New York to Director, FBI, Feb. 26, 1966, FBI-Wills.
94. SAC, Albany to Director, FBI, Nov. 19, 1965, FBI-Wills.
95. SAC, Albany to Director, FBI, Feb. 16, 1966, FBI-Wills.
96. SAC, Albany to Director, FBI, Mar. 17, 1966, SAC, Albany to Director, FBI, Apr. 1, 1966, FBI-Wills; Wills, *Turncoat;* and SAC, Albany to Director, FBI, Feb. 16, 1966, FBI-Wills.
97. Transcript of *Paul Harvey News,* "The Defective Hero," Dec. 7, 1965, FBI-Wills. Recently, Paul Harvey's longtime friendship and cooperation with FBI Director J. Edgar Hoover has been discovered and investigated. For more information, see *The Washington Post,* Jan. 22, 2010.
98. "Why I Chose China," *Look,* Feb. 8, 1966, 72–84.
99. The group mentioned by Wills included:

- Israel Epstein—Born in Warsaw, Poland, during World War I, Epstein's father was working in Japan when the German army invaded. He and his mother escaped and joined Israel's father and the family moved to Tiensin, China, in 1920. Working as a journalist by the age of fifteen, Epstein moved to England, and later to the United States, but returned to China in 1951 as the editor of a nationalistic magazine. Although one of the most devoted and respected non-Chinese residents, he was arrested and jailed for five years during the Cultural Revolution and later became one of the few white men allowed to join the Chinese Communist Party. He remained in China until his death in 2005.
- Anna Louise Strong—A native of Nebraska, Strong was educated at Bryn Mawr and Oberlin, and received a Ph.D. in Philosophy from the University of Chicago. Initially devoted to the interests of children, she became involved in the labor movement during the second decade of the twentieth century. By 1921, she was traveling into the newly communist nations of Poland and Russia. She spent the next three decades traveling and writing. In 1959, she returned to China and remained there until her death in 1970.

- George Hatem—Born in Buffalo, New York, Hatem was educated at the University of North Carolina, the American University in Beirut, and the University of Geneva. By the time he left Switzerland, he held his medical degree. He moved to Shanghai and focused on treating venereal diseases in 1933, but shut down his practice and followed Mao Zedong's army treating the sick and wounded. When the communists won in 1949, Ma Haide, as he was then known, transitioned into public health. He became one of the most trusted physicians in China and is credited with many important medical developments. He died in China in 1988.
- Sidney Rittenberg—A native of Charleston, South Carolina, Rittenberg attended a military preparatory school and later, the University of North Carolina, where he became an active member of the U.S. Communist Party. After renouncing the party, he joined the army in 1942, and was trained in Chinese, and was in China by 1944. He remained there as part of a UN famine relief effort after World War II ended. Over the years, he would become associated with Mao Zedong and Zhou Enlai, but his political zeal sometimes harmed him. In 1949, he was imprisoned in solitary confinement for six years. After his release he attempted to live quietly, but was again targeted during the Cultural Revolution and arrested in 1968. He served nine years and was released in 1977. In 1980, he and his Chinese wife left China and settled in the Pacific Northwest. They operate a consulting firm that works with companies interested in doing business in China and he is on the faculty of Pacific Lutheran University.
- Sidney Shapiro—Born in Brooklyn, New York, Shapiro, like Rittenberg, joined the army and was taught Chinese language skills during the early 1940s. After the war ended, he returned to the United States, where he received his law degree. In 1947, he went back to China, where he has remained. He worked at the Foreign Language Press for nearly fifty years and is now retired.
- Michael Shapiro—Unrelated to Sidney, he was born in England to a family sympathetic to the cause of communism. Shapiro went to China in the 1940s with Allan Winnington by way of the Trans-Siberian Railway. Writing mainly for the British *Daily Worker* for the next several years, he chose to stay in China after returned PsW alleged mistreatment by him. He remained in China until his death in 1986.

100. "Why I Quit China," *Look,* Feb. 22, 1966, 91–92; and Debriefing of Morris R. Wills, Nov. 19, 1965, Department of State Airgram, 25–26, FBI-Wills. In the debriefing, Wills provided additional information about westerners in China.

- Dorothy R. Adler—The wife of Richard Adler, an English economic advisor to the Chinese government, Dorothy worked in conjunction with Michael Shapiro as the conduit between the Anglo-American community and the Chinese government.
- Betty Chandler Chang—Chandler went to China as the wife of a renowned Chinese heart surgeon. She had divorced her husband by the mid-1960s. A past employee at the Foreign Language Press and a language teacher, Chandler was described by Wills as "politically on the make."
- Joan Hinton—A nuclear physicist who was one of the few women working on the Manhattan Project. In 1949, she and her husband emigrated to China, where she reportedly lived an isolated existence on a small farm in inner Mongolia. Wills thought that much of her time in China had been spent helping China achieve its nuclear ambitions.
- Robert Winter—A literature professor who taught at University of Beijing. An early supporter of the Chinese regime, he had been suspected of spying during the early 1960s.

101. R. E. Wick to Mr. DeLoach, Feb. 15, 1966, FBI-Wills.

102. "Wills Lies!" *Orange County Evening News,* undated, FBI-Wills.

103. SAC, San Francisco to Director, FBI, Apr. 16, 1958, FBI-Wills; and Morris Robert Wills memo, Nov. 12, 1964, 2, FBI-Wills.

104. SAC, Albany to Director, FBI, Dec. 3, 1965, FBI-Wills.

105. SAC, Albany to Director, FBI, July 20, 1965, FBI-Wills.

106. Morris Wills to Dear Mr. President, July 31, 1966, Senate Files, Box 369, file, M. Wills, Lyndon Baines Johnson Presidential Library and Museum, Austin, Texas; and Ezra Vogel to Brian McKnight, Aug. 5, 2008, email correspondence, in possession of the author.

107. Morris Wills to Dear Mr. President, July 31, 1966, Senate Files, Box 369, file, M. Wills, Lyndon Baines Johnson Presidential Library and Museum, Austin, Texas.

108. Federal Bureau of Investigation FD 302, Aug. 31, 1966, 2, FBI-Clarence C. Adams.

109. SAC, Milwaukee, to Director, FBI, May 12, 1964, 1–2, FBI-Corden.

110. FBI Report, May 17, 1965, 3, FBI-Corden.

111. FBI Report, May 16, 1966, 3, FBI-Corden.

112. SAC, Chicago, and Director, FBI, Jan. 30, 1967, FBI-Corden.

113. FBI Report, May 15, 1968, 2, FBI-Corden.

114. SAC, Chicago, and Director, FBI, Feb. 6, 1970, FBI-Corden.

115. SAC, Chicago, and Director, FBI, May 8, 1970, 1–2, FBI-Corden.

116. Richard G. Corden to Mr. Clarence Kelley, Nov. 21, 1975, FBI-Corden.

117. *Washington Post,* July 15, 1976; and *Los Angeles Times,* Aug. 5, 1976; Nov. 22, 1981; Dec. 30, 1984.

118. Sidney Rittenberg interview, Oct. 17, 2008.

119. Federal Bureau of Investigation, Report Form 1, Aug. 17, 1956, 4, FBI-Clarence C. Adams.

120. Interview of Unidentified Former PW (name classified), Aug. 2, 1956, 4, FBI-Wills.

121. J. Walter Yeagley to Director, Federal Bureau of Investigation, Dec. 8, 1965, FBI-Wills.

122. Federal Bureau of Investigation Report Form, Oct. 3, 1966, 20, 38, FBI-Clarence C. Adams.

123. Federal Bureau of Investigation Report Form, Oct. 3, 1966, 20, FBI-Clarence C. Adams.

124. *Washington Post,* July 15, 1976; July 11, 1982; and *Los Angeles Times,* June 30, 1976; Aug. 5, 1976; Dec. 30, 1984. A *Washington Post* article dated July 11, 1982, credits Veneris's divorce from his second wife to the political turmoil of the Cultural Revolution, but he was still married to her well into the late 1970s.

125. *Washington Post,* June 30, 1976; July 15, 1976; and *Los Angeles Times,* Aug. 5, 1976.

126. *Los Angeles Times,* Nov. 22, 1981; Dec. 30, 1984; *Houston Chronicle* (Tex.), June 2, 1985; and *Washington Post,* July 11, 1982.

127. "'Turncoats' of the '50s," 11; and *The Free-Lance Star* (Fredericksburg, Va.), Nov. 4, 1986.

128. Information on Howard Gayle Adams taken from his personal website at: http://www.xanga.com/Gayle_Adams.

129. "'Turncoats' of the '50s"; *The Graybeards,* vol. 16, July–Aug. 2002, 10; and *They Chose China,* DVD.

130. "'Turncoats' of the '50s," 11.

131. *Ocala Star-Banner* (Fla.), Feb. 26, 1959.

132. "'Turncoats' of the '50s," 11; and *They Chose China,* DVD.

133. *Chicago American,* Dec. 22, 1965.

134. "'Turncoats' of the '50s," 10.

135. *Ocala Star-Banner* (Fla.), Feb. 26, 1959.

136. *The Post* (Big Stone Gap, Va.), Feb. 24, 1993; and unattributed and undated article, "Dickenson says he wants case reopened, instead of a pardon," by Mike Still.

137. *The Post* (Big Stone Gap, Va.), Mar. 13, 2002.

138. *Chicago American,* Dec. 22, 1965; SAC, Seattle, to Director, FBI, Jan. 6, 1959, FBI-Bell; and SAC, Seattle, to Director, FBI, July 9, 1975, FBI-Bell.

139. "'Turncoats' of the '50s," 11.

140. *The Daily Citizen-News* (Dalton, Ga.), July 5, 1984.

141. *Ocala Star-Banner* (Fla.), Feb. 26, 1959; FD-204, June 3, 1964, FBI-Griggs; and FD-204, July 17, 1964, FBI-Griggs.

142. Federal Bureau of Investigation form, Apr. 14, 1958, 1, FBI-Pate.

143. Federal Bureau of Investigation special agent report, June 25, 1964, 6, FBI-Pate.

144. Federal Bureau of Investigation form, Apr. 14, 1958, 10, FBI-Pate.

145. Federal Bureau of Investigation form, July 15, 1958, 1, FBI-Pate.

146. Federal Bureau of Investigation special agent report, June 14, 1965, 3, FBI-Pate.

147. Federal Bureau of Investigation special agent report, May 23, 1966, 1, FBI-Pate; and SAC, St. Louis, to Director, FBI, July 27, 1966, 1, FBI-Pate.

148. Social Security Death Index; Nevada Marriage Index, 1956–2005; "'Turncoats' of the '50s," 11; and *Southern Illinoisan* (Carbondale, Ill.), Aug. 4, 1963.

149. Special Agent Report, Jan. 27, 1967; Jan. 25, 1968; May 22, 1968, FBI-Skinner.

150. Interview Report, Mar. 21, 1958, (interview Mar. 12, 1958, in Alden, Minn.), FBI-Tenneson.

151. Interview Report, Mar. 21, 1958, (interview Feb. 18, 1958, in Hopkins, Minn.), FBI-Tenneson.

152. Report Form, Mar. 21, 1958, 2, FBI-Tenneson.

153. Memorandum, SAC, Minneapolis, to Director, FBI, Jan. 10, 1957, FBI-Tenneson.

154. Memorandum, SAC, New York, to Director, FBI, Aug. 6, 1969, FBI-Tenneson; and Memorandum, SAC, Boston, to Director, FBI, June 12, 1969, FBI-Tenneson.

155. Ebenezer Howe Jr., interview, Apr. 12, 2006, by Brian D. McKnight.

156. "'Turncoats' of the '50s," 11; and *The Observer-Dispatch* (Utica, N.Y.), Jan. 7, 1999.

157. Adams, *An American Dream,* 138–39.

158. Wills, *Turncoat,* 80.

159. "'Turncoats' of the '50s," 11; and *Reading Eagle* (Pa.), June 16, 1966.

12. Lessons, Learned and Ignored

1. *New York Times,* June 26, 1955; Oct. 16, 1955. Although little information is available about the total number of Germans imprisoned in the Soviet Union after World War II, a German source estimated that 9,000 prisoners of war and more than 129,000 German civilians, some of whom had been initially captured in 1941, were still being held as late as 1955. Beginning in 1953, the USSR began releasing some of the former German soldiers.

2. Judith M. Gansberg, *Stalag: U.S.A.: The Remarkable Story of German POWs in America* (New York, N.Y.: Thomas Y. Crowell, 1977), 1, 96–97.

3. Code of Conduct poster, GTA-21, 1 Oct. 1955, Box 317, Folder HD:383.6 (Code of Conduct) 1955, Record Group 112, Office of the Surgeon General (Army), Historical Division, U.S. Medical Department (AMEDD) Records, 1947–61, Textual Records,

National Archives and Records Administration II, College Park, Maryland, hereinafter cited as NARAII-112-AMEDD; and *U.S. Fighting Man's Code.* DOD Pam 8–1/DOD Pam 21–71/AF Pam 34/10/1. Washington, D.C.: Department of Defense, Office of Armed Forces Information and Education, 1955. See also *U.S. Prisoners of War in the Korean Operation: A Study of Their Treatment and Handling by the North Korean Army and the Chinese Communist Forces* (Fort George G. Meade, Md.: Army Security Center, 1954).

4. Ben Shephard, *A War of Nerves: Soldiers and Psychiatrists in the Twentieth Century* (Cambridge, Mass.: Harvard Univ. Press, 2001), 341.

5. Wm. Geo. Richards to Dear Lyndon, Oct. 1, 1954, Senate Files, Box 1366, file, 1958 Case Files, Batchelor, Claude J., Oct. 1954–1958 (Korean War Defector), Lyndon Baines Johnson Presidential Library and Museum, Austin, Texas.

6. Lech, *Broken Soldiers,* 266–67.

7. Lech, *Broken Soldiers,* 178–81, 234.

8. Harrison, "Why Did Some GIs Turn Communist?" 25–27.

9. Homer Parks to Dear Senator, Mar. 10, 1954, Senate Files, Box 1366, file, 1958 Case Files, Batchelor, Claude J., Oct. 1954–1958 (Korean War Defector), Lyndon Baines Johnson Presidential Library and Museum, Austin, Texas.

10. V. J. Holmes to Dear Sir, Nov. 1, 1954, Senate Files, Box 1366, file, 1958 Case Files, Batchelor, Claude J., Oct. 1954–1958 (Korean War Defector), Lyndon Baines Johnson Presidential Library and Museum, Austin, Texas.

11. Lech, *Broken Soldiers,* 222.

12. Russell Blair to Dear Sir, Oct. 1, 1954, Senate Files, Box 1366, file, 1958 Case Files, Batchelor, Claude J., Oct. 1954–1958 (Korean War Defector), Lyndon Baines Johnson Presidential Library and Museum, Austin, Texas.

13. LaFeren Ray Thorne to Dear Sir, undated, Senate Files, Box 1366, file, 1958 Case Files, Batchelor, Claude J., Oct. 1954–1958 (Korean War Defector), Lyndon Baines Johnson Presidential Library and Museum, Austin, Texas.

14. Taken from Lech, *Broken Soldiers,* 238.

15. "Quality of Mercy is Strained by Rank," *The Christian Century* LXXI (May 19, 1954): 603–4.

16. Lech, *Broken Soldiers,* 222–23.

17. Kinkead, *In Every War But One,* 68–69; and Don J. Snyder, *A Soldier's Disgrace* (Dublin, N.H.: Yankee Books, 1987), 133–34; 152; 159; 222.

18. Claude J. Batchelor Statement (voluntary, typewritten, double-spaced), 2 of 11, Batchelor Court Martial.

19. Robert E. Vincent testimony, Sept. 14, 1954, Batchelor Court Martial.

20. John Edward Owens testimony, Sept. 14, 1954, Batchelor Court Martial.

21. Lech, *Broken Soldiers,* 47–48.

22. Lech, *Broken Soldiers,* 268–69; and Hillman, *Defending America,* 112.

23. Rodney R. LeMay, "Collaboration or Self-Preservation: The Military Code of Conduct," M.A. thesis, Louisiana State University and Agricultural and Mechanical College, 2002, 39.

24. Carlson, *Remembered Prisoners,* 205.

25. Federal Bureau of Investigation Report Form, Oct. 3, 1966, 31, FBI-Clarence C. Adams.

26. CHECK LIST ON RECAP-K CASES, Cpl Albert C. Belhomme, continuation sheet (Price, Sfc Bob E. statement), NARAII-153-CHECK LIST.

27. Report Form, Sept. 18, 1956, 109–10, handwritten, upper right corner, FBI-Skinner.

28. James Sidbury, *Ploughshares into Swords: Race, Rebellion, and Identity in Gabriel's Virginia, 1730–1810* (Cambridge, UK: Cambridge Univ. Press, 1997), 95.

29. Sidbury, *Ploughshares into Swords,* 111.

30. Eugene D. Genovese, *From Rebellion to Revolution: Afro-American Slave Revolts in the Making of the Modern World,* The Walter Lynwood Fleming Lectures in Southern History (Baton Rouge: Louisiana State Univ. Press, 1979), 11; and Herbert Aptheker, *American Negro Slave Revolts* (New York, N.Y.: International Publishers, 1963), 61–63.

31. Edgar H. Schein, "The Chinese Indoctrination Program for Prisoners of War: A Study of Attempted Brainwashing," *Psychiatry* 19 (May 1956): 149–72; Edgar H. Schein, *Coercive Persuasion: A Socio-Psychological Analysis of the "Brainwashing" of American Civilian Prisoners by the Chinese Communists* (New York: W. W. Norton, 1971); Edgar H. Schein, *The Chinese Indoctrination Program for Prisoners of War: A Study of Attempted "Brainwashing"* (New York, N.Y.: Bobbs-Merrill, 1956); Edgar H. Schein, "Brainwashing and Totalitarianization in Modern Society," book review, *World Politics* 11:3 (Apr. 1959): 430–41.

32. *The Korean Republic,* Nov. 4, 1953, Box 2, Folder 2, USAMHI-Lawton.

33. Mrs. Edward Frazier to Dear Sir, Oct. 8, 1954, Senate Files, Box 1366, file, 1958 Case Files, Batchelor, Claude J., Oct. 1954–1958 (Korean War Defector), Lyndon Baines Johnson Presidential Library and Museum, Austin, Texas.

34. Mrs. W. S. Benton to Dear Senator, Oct. 29, 1954, Senate Files, Box 1366, file, 1958 Case Files, Batchelor, Claude J., Oct. 1954–1958 (Korean War Defector), Lyndon Baines Johnson Presidential Library and Museum, Austin, Texas.

35. Major Edward Moorer's broadcast script, Box 1, Folder 3, Ralph E. Pearson Papers, USAMHI-Pearson.

36. Unfortunately for researchers, McCarthy's thoughts on the repatriation controversy cannot yet be known. Although the senator's papers are housed at Marquette University, McCarthy's widow's second husband, who was left with the responsibility for the remaining privately held papers, refused to give them to the university unless a guarantee was made that they would be sealed until 2050. Of the papers donated, he allowed the opening of official files, but remained steadfast in his protection of the personal files. These personal files will remain sealed until the death of Tierney Minetti, the little girl Joe and Jean McCarthy were in the process of adopting when he died.

37. Oshinsky, *A Conspiracy So Immense,* 255–56, 400.

38. Oshinsky, *A Conspiracy So Immense,* 401.

39. Oshinsky, *A Conspiracy So Immense,* 417; and Snyder, *A Soldier's Disgrace,* 154.

40. "Collaborator's Reward," Time, July 11, 1955; Lech, *Broken Soldiers,* 221; and *New York Times,* Aug. 21, 1955.

41. Snyder, *A Soldier's Disgrace,* 222.

42. "Stockholm Syndrome," *Time,* Sept. 14, 2009, 19.

Bibliography

Primary Sources

MANUSCRIPT COLLECTIONS

Abilene, Kansas. Dwight D. Eisenhower Presidential Library.
National Security Council Staff: Papers, 1953–61
White House Central Files
Austin, Texas. Lyndon B. Johnson Presidential Library.
Senate Files
White House Central Files
Bowling Green, Kentucky. Western Kentucky University, Special Collections.
Pearl (Carter) Pace Papers
Carlisle, Pennsylvania. United States Army Military History Institute, Archives.
Korean War POWs—Repatriation United Nations Command—Korea
Pamphlet Collection
Ralph E. Pearson Papers
William S. Lawton Papers
College Park, Maryland. National Archives II.
Record Group 112: Office of the Surgeon General (Army)
U.S. Medical Department (AMEDD) Records, 1947–1961.
Record Group 263: Records of the Central Intelligence Agency, 1894–2002.
Audio Recordings of Monitored Broadcasts from Asia, 1949–1960;
Audio Recordings of Monitored Broadcasts from Vietnam, Korea, and China, 1968–1969.
Record Group 319: Records of the Army Staff.
Records of the Assistant Chief of Staff for Intelligence (G-2), G-2 Decimal File.
Army Intelligence Document Files, 1950–1955.
Counterintelligence Files, 1950–1958.
Record Group 330: Records of the Office of the Secretary of Defense.
Records of the Defense Prisoner of War/Missing in Action Office, Copies of Records Relating to POW/MIAs, 1951–1958.
Record Group 335: Office of the Secretary of the Army
General Correspondence, 1954.
Record Group 407: Records of the Adjutant General's Office, 1905–1981.
Classified Central General Correspondence, 1955–1962.

Independence, Missouri. Graceland University, Center for the Study of the Korean War.
Manuscript Collection

New York City, New York. United Nations. UN Archives and Records Management Section.
Korean Prisoners of War, 1952–1955
Subject Files of the Secretary General: Dag Hammarskjold

Stanford, California. Stanford University. Hoover Institution.
Firing Line television program collection

GOVERNMENT DOCUMENTS

Claude J. Batchelor Court Martial Records. Copy in the possession of Sheila Miyoshi Jager, Oberlin, Ohio.

Communist Interrogation, Indoctrination, and Exploitation of Prisoners of War. Department of the Army Pamphlet, No. 30–101. Washington, D.C.: Department of the Army, 1956.

Congressional Record. 83rd Congress. Washington, D.C.: United States Government Printing Office, 1953–54.

Department of the Army. United States Army Intelligence and Security Command. Fort George G. Meade, Maryland.
Lewie W. Griggs documents.
Morris R. Wills documents.

Development, Training Applications, and Assessment of the Code of Conduct for US PWS. Headquarters USAF Analysis Program. September 1974.

Edward S. Dickenson Court Martial Record. Copy in the possession of Sheila Miyoshi Jager, Oberlin, Ohio.

Federal Bureau of Investigation Files. United States Department of Justice. Washington, D.C.
Andrew Fortuna, FBI File.
Arlie Howard Pate, FBI File.
Clarence C. Adams, FBI File.
Edward S. Dickenson, FBI File.
Larance V. Sullivan, FBI File.
Lewie W. Griggs, FBI File.
Lowell Skinner, FBI File.
Morris R. Wills, FBI File.
Otho G. Bell, FBI File.
Richard Guy Corden, FBI File.
Richard R. Tenneson, FBI File.

U.S. Department of State. Washington, D.C.
Miscellaneous State Department telegrams re: Larance V. Sullivan

U.S. Fighting Man's Code. DOD Pam 8–1/DOD Pam 21–71/AF Pam 34/10/1. Washington, D.C.: Department of Defense, Office of Armed Forces Information and Education, 1955.

U.S. Prisoners of War in the Korean Operation: A Study of Their Treatment and Handling by the North Korean Army and the Chinese Communist Forces. Fort George G. Meade, Md.: Army Security Center, 1954.

Welcome Back! United Nations Pamphlet. 1953.

PUBLISHED WORKS

Adams, Clarence. *An American Dream: The Life of an African American Soldier and POW Who Spent Twelve Years in Communist China.* Amherst: Univ. of Massachusetts Press, 2007.

———. *Clarence Adams and the American Dream: The Story of an African American Korean War Combat Soldier and POW Who Spent Twelve Years in Communist China* (original, unedited, manuscript version).

American POW's Calling From Korea. Beijing, China: Foreign Languages Press, 1951.

Bassett, Richard M., and Lewis H. Carlson. *And the Wind Blew Cold: The Story of an American POW in North Korea.* Kent, Ohio: Kent State Univ. Press, 2002.

Berens, Robert J. *Limbo on the Yalu . . . and Beyond.* St. Petersburg, Fla.: Southern Heritage Press, 2000.

Burchett, George, and Nick Shimmin, eds. *Memoirs of a Rebel Journalist: The Autobiography of Wilfred Burchett.* Sydney, AU: Univ. of New South Wales Press, 2005.

Carlson, Lewis H. *Remembered Prisoners of a Forgotten War: An Oral History of Korean War POWs.* New York, N.Y.: St. Martin's Press, 2002.

Deane, Philip. *I Should Have Died: A Terrifying Indictment of the Methods Employed by the Russian Secret Service in Korea and the American CIA in Greece.* New York, N.Y.: Atheneum, 1977.

———. *I Was a Captive in Korea.* New York, N.Y.: W. W. Norton and Company, 1953.

Inman, Cecil Mark. *A Celebration of Life: A Prisoner of War's 54-year Journey Since the Korean War.* Xulon Press, 2006.

Jenkins, Charles Robert. *The Reluctant Communist: My Desertion, Court-Martial, and Forty-Year Imprisonment in North Korea.* Berkeley: Univ. of California Press, 2008.

Olympics: Inter Camp Olympics, 1952. Pyuktong, D.P.R.K., 1953.

Pate, Lloyd W. *Reactionary.* New York, N.Y.: Vantage Press, reprint 2001.

Peters, Richard, and Xiaobing Li. *Voices from the Korean War: Personal Stories of American, Korean, and Chinese Soldiers.* Lexington: Univ. Press of Kentucky, 2004.

Rittenberg, Sidney, and Amanda Bennett. *The Man Who Stayed Behind.* New York, N.Y.: Simon and Schuster, 1993.

Shadish, William, and Lewis H. Carlson. *When Hell Froze Over: The Memoir of a Korean War Combat Physician Who Spent 1010 Days in a Communist Prison Camp.* New York, N.Y.: iUniverse, 2007.

Shall Brothers Be. . . . Beijing, China: Chinese People's Committee for World Peace and Against American Aggression, 1952.

Shapiro, Sidney. *I Chose China: The Metamorphosis of a Country and a Man.* New York, N.Y.: Hippocrene Books, 2000.

Snyder, Don J. *A Soldier's Disgrace.* Dublin, N.H.: Yankee Books, 1987.

Spiller, Harry, ed. *American POWs in Korea: Sixteen Personal Accounts.* Jefferson, N.C.: McFarland & Company, 1998.

Strait, Sandy. *What Happened to American Prisoners of War in Korea.* Unionville, N.Y.: Royal Fireworks Press, 1997.

Thompson, James. *True Colors: 1004 Days as a Prisoner of War.* Port Washington, N.Y.: Ashley Books, 1989.

United Nations' POWs in Korea. Beijing, China: Chinese People's Committee for World Peace, 1953.

Wills, Morris R., and J. Robert Moskin. *Turncoat: An American's 12 Years in Communist China.* New York, N.Y.: Prentice-Hall, 1968.

Winnington, Alan. *Breakfast With Mao: Memoirs of a Foreign Correspondent.* London, UK: Lawrence and Wishart, 1986.

INTERVIEWS

Anonymous Subject #1 telephone interview by author, Nov. 15, 2007. Recording in possession of author.

Ebenezer Howe telephone interview by author, Apr. 12, 2006. Recording in possession of author.

Ezra Vogel to author, email correspondence, Aug. 5, 2008. Message in possession of author.

Sidney Rittenberg telephone interview by author, Oct. 17, 2008. Recording in possession of author.

Thelma Marrs interview by author and Sara Roop, May 21, 2004. Recording in possession of author.

NEWSPAPERS

Akron (Ohio) *Beacon Journal*
Alexandria (La.) *Daily Town Talk*
Ashland (Ky.) *Daily Independent*
Baltimore (Md.) *Evening Sun*
Baltimore (Md.) *Sun*
Bristol (Va.) *Herald Courier*
Christian Science Monitor
Clarion-Ledger (Jackson, Miss.)
Daily Citizen-News (Dalton, Ga.)
Dalton (Ga.) *Citizen*
Dalton (Ga.) *News*
Dallas (Tex.) *Morning News*
Detroit (Mich.) *News*
Fort Worth (Tex.) *Star Telegram*
Globe Democrat (St. Louis, Mo.)
Hartford (Conn.) *Courant*
Hattiesburg (Miss.) *American*
Houston (Tex.) *Chronicle*
Kingsport (Tenn.) *Times-News*
Knoxville (Tenn.) *News Sentinel*
Korean (Seoul, South Korea) *Republic*
Log Cabin Democrat (Conway, Ark.)
Los Angeles (Calif.) *Times*
Minneapolis (Minn.) *Star*
New York Times
Observer-Dispatch (Utica, N.Y.)
Ocala (Fla.) *Star-Banner*
Odessa (Tex.) *American*
Orange County (Calif.) *Evening News*
Pittsburgh (Pa.) *Courier*
Portsmouth (N.H.) *Herald*
Post Dispatch (St. Louis, Mo.)
Roanoke (Va.) *Times*
San Angelo (Tex.) *Standard-Times*
Southern Illinoisan (Carbondale)
The Free-Lance Star (Fredericksburg, Va.)
The Post (Big Stone Gap, Va.)

The Spokesman-Review (Spokane, Wash.)
Washington Post
Washington Post and Times-Herald
Washington (D.C.) *Star*

MEDIA

Austin, Texas. University of Texas, Harry Ransom Center.
Film Archive
The Mike Wallace Interview
Stanford, California. Stanford University, Hoover Institution.
Firing Line television program collection

Secondary Sources

BOOKS

Abner, Alan K. *Psywarriors: Psychological Warfare During the Korean War.* Shippensburg, Pa.: Burd Street Press, 2001.

Aptheker, Herbert. *American Negro Slave Revolts.* New York, N.Y.: International Publishers, 1963.

Batvinis, Raymond J. *The Origins of FBI Counterintelligence.* Modern War Studies. Lawrence: Univ. Press of Kansas, 2007.

Biderman, Albert D. *March to Calumny: The Story of American POWs in the Korean War.* New York, N.Y.: The Macmillan Company, 1963.

Blair, Clay. *The Forgotten War: America in Korea.* Annapolis, Md.: Naval Institute Press, 1987.

Bogle, Lori Lyn. *The Cold War,* vol. 5: *Cold War Culture and Society.* New York, N.Y.: Routledge, 2001.

Bornet, Vaughn Davis. *The Presidency of Lyndon B. Johnson.* American Presidency. Lawrence: Univ. Press of Kansas, 1983.

Brady, Anne-Marie. *Making the Foreign Serve China: Managing Foreigners in the People's Republic.* Asia/Pacific/Perspectives. Lanham, Md.: Rowman and Littlefield Publishers, 2003.

Brown, J. A. C. *Techniques of Persuasion: From Propaganda to Brainwashing.* Baltimore, Md.: Penguin Books, 1963.

Carlson, Lewis H. *Remembered Prisoners of a Forgotten War: An Oral History of Korean War POWs.* New York, N.Y.: St. Martin's Press, 2002.

Cary, M., and H. H. Scullard. *A History of Rome.* 3rd ed. New York, N.Y.: Palgrave, 1975.

Ch'en, Jerome. *Mao and the Chinese Revolution.* London, UK: Oxford Univ. Press, 1965.

Chinnery, Philip D. *Korean Atrocity! Forgotten War Crimes, 1950–1953.* Annapolis, Md.: Naval Institute Press, 2000.

Cimbala, Stephen J. *The Politics of Warfare: The Great Powers in the Twentieth Century.* College Station: Pennsylvania State Univ. Press, 1996.

Dallek, Robert. *Flawed Giant: Lyndon Johnson and His Times, 1961–1973.* New York, N.Y.: Oxford Univ. Press, 1998.

Edwards, Jerome E. *Pat McCarran: Political Boss of Nevada.* Nevada Studies in History and Political Science 17. Reno: Univ. of Nevada Press, 1982.

Evans, Humphrey. *Thimayya of India: A Soldier's Life.* New York, N.Y.: Harcourt, Brace, 1960.

Faber, John. *Great News Photos and the Stories Behind Them.* New York, N.Y.: Dover, 1978.

Fairbank, John King. *China: A New History.* Cambridge, Mass.: The Belknap Press of the Harvard Univ. Press, 1992.

Fehrenbach, T. R. *This Kind of War.* Washington, D.C.: Brassey's, 1963.

Gansberg, Judith M. *Stalag: U.S.A: The Remarkable Story of German POWs in America.* New York, N.Y.: Thomas Y. Crowell, 1977.

Genovese, Eugene D. *From Rebellion to Revolution: Afro-American Slave Revolts in the Making of the Modern World.* The Walter Lynwood Fleming Lectures in Southern History. Baton Rouge: Louisiana State Univ. Press, 1979.

Greenstein, Fred I. *The Hidden-Hand Presidency: Eisenhower as Leader.* Baltimore, Md.: Johns Hopkins Univ. Press, 1982.

Griffith, Robert. *The Politics of Fear: Joseph R. McCarthy and the Senate.* 2nd ed. Amherst: Univ. of Massachusetts Press, 1987.

Halberstam, David. *The Coldest Winter: America and the Korean War.* New York, N.Y.: Hyperion, 2007.

Hanley, Charles J., Sang-Hun Choe, and Martha Mendoza. *The Bridge at No Gun Ri.* New York, N.Y.: Henry Holt, 2001.

Hansen, Kenneth K. *Heroes Behind Barbed Wire.* Princeton, N.J.: D. Van Nostrand, Inc., 1957.

Hastings, Max. *The Korean War.* New York, N.Y.: Simon and Schuster, 1987.

Hillman, Elizabeth Lutes. *Defending America: Military Culture and the Cold War Court-Martial.* Politics and Society in Twentieth-Century America. Princeton, N.J.: Princeton Univ. Press, 2005.

Hunter, Edward. *Brainwashing: The Story of Men Who Defied It.* New York, N.Y.: Farrar, Straus, and Cuhady, 1956.

———. *Brain-Washing in Red China: The Calculated Destruction of Men's Mind.* New York, N.Y.: Vanguard Press, 1951.

Kinkead, Eugene. *In Every War But One.* New York, N.Y.: W. W. Norton, 1959.

Knox, Donald. *The Korean War: Uncertain Victory.* 2 vols. San Diego, Calif.: Harcourt Brace Jovanovich, 1985–88.

Lech, Raymond B. *Broken Soldiers.* Urbana: Univ. of Illinois Press, 2000.

Loken, John. *Oswald's Trigger Films: The Manchurian Candidate, We Were Strangers, Suddenly?* Ann Arbor, Mich.: Falcon Books, 2000.

Marks, John. *The Search for the "Manchurian Candidate": The CIA and Mind Control.* New York, N.Y.: Times Books, 1979.

Marshall, S. L. A. *The River and the Gauntlet: Defeat of the Eighth Army by the Chinese Communist Forces, November, 1950, in the Battle of Chongchon River, Korea.* Westport, Conn.: Greenwood Press, 1953.

Meerloo, Joost A. M. *The Rape of the Mind: The Psychology of Thought Control—Menticide and Brainwashing.* Cleveland, Ohio: World Publishing, 1956.

Mills, Nicolaus, ed. *Culture in an Age of Money: The Legacy of the 1980s in America.* Chicago, Ill.: Ivan R. Dee, 1990.

Morgan, Ted. *Reds: McCarthyism in Twentieth-Century America.* New York, N.Y.: Random House, 2004.

Murphy, Edward F. *Korean War Heroes.* Novato, Calif.: Presidio Press, 1992.

O'Brien, Michael. *McCarthy and McCarthyism in Wisconsin.* Columbia: Univ. of Missouri Press, 1980.

Oshinsky, David M. *A Conspiracy So Immense: The World of Joe McCarthy.* New York, N.Y.: The Free Press, 1983.

Pasley, Virginia. *21 Stayed: The Story of the American GI's Who Chose Communist China—Who They Were and Why They Stayed.* New York, N.Y.: Farrar, Straus, and Cuhady, 1955.

Perret, Geoffrey. *Eisenhower.* Holbrook, Mass.: Adams Media, 1999.

Polk, David. *Korean War Ex-Prisoners of War.* Paducah, Ky.: Turner, 1993.

POW: The Fight Continues After the Battle. Washington, D.C.: Secretary of Defense's Advisory Committee on Prisoners of War, 1955.

Powers, Richard Gid. *Not Without Honor: The History of American Anticommunism.* New York, N.Y.: The Free Press, 1995.

Prasad, S. N. *History of the Custodian Force (India) in Korea, 1953–54.* Dehli, India: Historical Section, Ministry of Defense, Government of India, 1976.

Redding, Arthur. *Turncoats, Traitors, and Fellow Travelers: Culture and Politics of the Early Cold War.* Jackson: Univ. Press of Mississippi, 2008.

Rees, David. *Korea: The Limited War.* Baltimore, Md.: Penguin Books, 1964.

Robin, Ron. *The Barbed-Wire College: Reeducating German POWs in the United States During World War II.* Princeton, N.J.: Princeton Univ. Press, 1995.

Rogge, O. John. *Why Men Confess.* New York, N.Y.: Thomas Nelson & Sons, 1959.

Rovere, Richard H. *Senator Joe McCarthy.* New York, N.Y.: Harcourt, Brace, and World, 1959.

Sargant, William. *Battle for the Mind: A Psychology of Conversion and Brainwashing.* Garden City, N.Y.: Doubleday, 1957.

Schein, Edgar H. *Coercive Persuasion: A Socio-Psychological Analysis of the "Brainwashing" of American Civilian Prisoners by the Chinese Communists.* New York: W. W. Norton, 1971.

———. *The Chinese Indoctrination Program for Prisoners of War: A Study of Attempted "Brainwashing"* New York, N.Y.: Bobbs-Merrill, 1956.

Schein, Edgar H. with Inge Schneier and Curtis H. Barker. *Coercive Persuasion: A Socio-Psychological Analysis of the 'Brainwashing' of American Civilian Prisoners by Chinese Communists.* New York, N.Y.: W. W. Norton, 1971.

Schirokauer, Conrad. *A Brief History of Chinese and Japanese Civilizations.* 2nd ed. Fort Worth, Tex.: Harcourt Brace Jovanovich, 1989.

Schrecker, Ellen. *Many are the Crimes: McCarthyism in America.* Boston, Mass.: Little, Brown, 1998.

———. *No Ivory Tower: McCarthyism and the Universities.* New York, N.Y.: Oxford Univ. Press, 1986.

Shephard, Ben. *A War of Nerves: Soldiers and Psychiatrists in the Twentieth Century.* Cambridge, Mass.: Harvard Univ. Press, 2001.

Short, Philip. *Mao: A Life.* New York, N.Y.: Owl Books, 1999.

Sidbury, James. *Ploughshares into Swords: Race, Rebellion, and Identity in Gabriel's Virginia, 1730–1810.* Cambridge, UK: Cambridge Univ. Press, 1997.

Snyder, Don J. *A Soldier's Disgrace.* Dublin, N.H.: Yankee Books, 1987.

Spence, Jonathan D. *The Gate of Heavenly Peace: The Chinese and Their Revolution, 1895–1980.* New York, N.Y.: Penguin, 1981.

———. *The Search for Modern China.* New York, N.Y.: W. W. Norton, 1990.

Stokesbury, James L. *A Short History of the Korean War.* New York, N.Y.: William Morrow, 1988.

Streatfield, Dominic. *Brainwash: The Secret History of Mind Control.* New York, N.Y.: Thomas Dunne Books, 2007.

Stueck, William. *The Korean War: An International History.* Princeton, N.J.: Princeton Univ. Press, 1995.

Taylor, Kathleen. *Brainwashing: The Science of Thought Control.* Oxford, UK: Oxford Univ. Press, 2004.

Theoharis, Athan. *The FBI and American Democracy: A Brief Critical History.* Lawrence: Univ. Press of Kansas, 2004.

Toland, John. *In Mortal Combat: Korea, 1950–1953.* New York, N.Y.: Quill, 1991.

Tyson, Timothy B. *Radio Free Dixie: Robert F. Williams and the Roots of Black Power.* Chapel Hill: Univ. of North Carolina Press, 1999.

Walker, Richard L. *China Under Communism: The First Five Years.* New Haven, Conn.: Yale Univ. Press, 1955.

White, William Lindsay. *The Captives of Korea: An Unofficial White Paper on the Treatment of War Prisoners.* Westport, Conn.: Greenwood Press, 1957.

Whitfield, Stephen J. *The Culture of the Cold War.* 2nd ed. Baltimore, Md.: Johns Hopkins Univ. Press, 1996.

Winn, Denise. *The Manipulated Mind: Brainwashing, Conditioning and Indoctrination.* London, UK: Octagon Press, 1983.

Ybarra, Michael J. *Washington Gone Crazy: Senator Pat McCarran and the Great American Communist Hunt.* Hanover, N.H.: Steerforth Press, 2004.

ARTICLES

"A Prodigal Son and His Kin." *Life* (Nov. 2, 1953): 45.

Biderman, Albert D. "Dangers of Negative Patriotism," *Harvard Business Review* 40:6 (Nov.–Dec. 1962): 93–99.

Brady, Anne-Marie. "'Treat Insiders and Outsiders Differently': The Use and Control of Foreigners in the PRC," *China Quarterly* 164 (Dec. 2000): 943–64.

Brinkley, William. "Almost All Released Prisoners Come Home Happily . . . ," *Life* (Sept. 7, 1953): 26–27.

Carruthers, Susan L. "*The Manchurian Candidate* (1962) and the Cold War Brainwashing Scare," *Historical Journal of Film, Radio, and Television* 18:1 (Mar. 1998): 75–94.

"Case Histories of Those 21: What Their Lives Show." *Newsweek* (Jan. 18, 1954): 52, 54–55.

"Collaborators' Reward." *Time* 66:2 (July 11, 1955): 18.

"Corporal Dickenson Tells Why Some GIs Stay With Reds." *U.S. News and World Report* (Nov. 13, 1953): 38–43.

Gallery, D. V. "We Can Baffle the Brainwashers!" *Saturday Evening Post* (Jan. 22, 1955): 20–21, 94–95, 98.

Gibson, H. C., Henry A. Segal, and Jakub G. Schlichter. "Repartiated American POWs with Special Reference to Avitaminosis, Tuberculosis, and Intestinal Parasites," *Medical Bulletin of the U.S. Army Far East* 1:9 (Aug. 1953): 154–59.

Harrison, Thomas D. "Why Did Some GIs Turn Communist?" *Collier's* (Nov. 27, 1953): 25–28.

Hunter, Edward. "Our POWs Are Not Traitors," *Combat Forces Journal* (Oct. 1953): 36–37.

Jones, Richard L. "Bending the Spirit: Mind Control in POW Camps," *Army* (Apr. 1995): 48–54.

"Korean Puzzle: Americans Who Stay." *U.S. News and World Report* (Oct. 9, 1953): 38–40.

Lavine, Harold. "Twenty-One G.I.'s Who Chose Tyranny: Why They Left Us for Communism," *Commentary* (July 1954): 41–46.

Lifton, Robert J. "Home By Ship: Reaction Patterns of American Prisoners of War Repatriated From North Korea," *American Journal of Psychiatry* 110 (Apr. 1954): 732–39.

———. "'Thought Reform' of Western Civilians in Chinese Communist Prisons," *Psychiatry* 19 (May 1956): 173–95.

Lutz, Catherine. "The Psychological Ethic and the Spirit of Containment," *Public Culture* 9:2 (1997): 135–59.

Manes, Donald L., Jr. "Barbed Wire Command: The Legal Nature of the Command Responsibilities of the Senior Prisoner in a Prisoner of War Camp," *Military Law Review* (Oct. 1960): 1–46.

Mayda, Jaro. "The Korean Repatriation Problem and International Law," *The American Journal of International Law* (July 1953): 414–38.

"One Changed His Mind." *Time* (Nov. 2, 1953): 25–26.

"One Who Won't Return." *Time* (Oct. 26, 1953): 27.

"Prisoner Talks Stalled." *Senior Scholastic* 63 (Nov. 4, 1953): 19–20

Prugh, George S., Jr. "Justice for all RECAP-K's," *The Army Combat Forces Journal* (Nov. 1955): 15–18, 22, 24, 25.

Roskey, William. "Korea's Costliest Battle: The POW Impasse," *Parameters* 23:2 (Summer 1993): 96–106.

Schein, Edgar H. "Brainwashing and Totalitarianization in Modern Society," book review, *World Politics* 11:3 (Apr. 1959): 430–41.

———. "The Chinese Indoctrination Program for Prisoners of War: A Study of Attempted Brainwashing," *Psychiatry* 19 (May 1956): 149–72.

Segal, Henry A. "Initial Psychiatric Findings of Recently Repatriated Prisoners of War," *American Journal of Psychiatry* 111:5 (Nov. 1954): 358–63.

"Snafu and Showdown." *Newsweek* (Feb. 1, 1954): 18.

"The Prisoners." *The Commonweal* (Oct. 16, 1953): 28–29.

"The Quality of Mercy is Strained by Rank." *The Christian Century* 71:20 (May 19, 1954): 603–4.

"The Sorriest Bunch." *Newsweek* (Feb. 8, 1954): 40–41.

"They Chose Red China, And Then. . . ." *U.S. News and World Report* 42 (June 28, 1957): 58–64, 67–74.

"'Turncoats' of the '50s." *The Graybeards* 16 (July–Aug. 2002): 10–11.

"We Got Everything You Wanted." *Life* (Oct. 19, 1953): 44–45.

"Why Did Many GI Captives Cave In?" *U.S. News and World Report* 40 (Feb. 24, 1956): 56–72.

"Why I Chose China." *Look* (Feb. 8, 1966): 72–84.

"Why I Quit China." *Look* (Feb. 22, 1966): 84–94.

Williamson, Carl E. "Name, Rank, and Service Number," *Military Review* 37:5 (Aug. 1957): 25–32.

"Without Honor." *Newsweek* 62:2 (July 13, 1953): 30.

Ulman, William A. "The GI's Who Fell for the Reds," *Saturday Evening Post* (Mar. 6, 1954): 17–19, 67.

Young, Charles S. "Missing Action: POW Films, Brainwashing, and the Korean War," *Historical Journal of Film, Radio, and Television* 18:1 (Mar. 1998): 49–74.

Zweiback, Adam J. "The 21 'Turncoat G.I.s': The Political Culture of the Korean War," *The Historian* 60 (Winter 1998): 345–62.

THESES AND DISSERTATIONS

Copa, Clara Amelia. "American Prisoner of War Behavior in the Korean War." M.A. thesis, Utah State University, 1970.

Coronado, Juan David. "From Death Valley to the Rio Grande Valley: World War II and Korean War Prisoners of War." M.A. thesis, University of Texas, Pan American, 2006.

Howlett, Jonathan. "Andrew Condron: The Only British Prisoner of War to Refuse Repatriation at the End of the Korean War." B.A. thesis, University of Bristol (U.K.), 2005.

LeMay, Rodney R. "Collaboration or Self-Preservation: The Military Code of Conduct." M.A. thesis, Louisiana State University and Agricultural and Mechanical College, 2002.

Poles, Joseph H. "From Koje-Do to Panmunjom: The Problem of Repatriation of Prisoners of War During the Korean Armistice Negotiations." M.A. thesis, Florida Atlantic University, 1997.

Rice, Gary Harold. "The Lost Sheep of the Korean War." Ph.D. diss., University of Texas at Austin, 1998.

Vickers, Kenneth W. "John Rankin: Democrat and Demagogue." M.A. thesis, Mississippi State University, 1993.

OTHER MEDIA

The Manchurian Candidate. Produced by George Alexrod and John Frankenheimer, directed by John Frankenheimer. 126 mins. M. C. Productions, 1962. DVD.

The Rack. Produced by Arthur M. Loew, Jr., directed by Arnold Laven. 100 mins. Metro-Goldwyn-Mayer, 1956. DVD.

They Chose China. Produced by Claude Bonin, directed by Shui-Bo Wang. 52 min. National Film Board of Canada, 2005. DVD.

Time Limit. Produced by William Reynolds and Richard Widmark, directed by Karl Malden. 96 mins. United Artists, 1957. DVD.

Index